BEAUMARCHAIS
The man who was Figaro

Frédéric Grendel

translated from the French by

ROGER GREAVES

MACDONALD AND JANE'S · LONDON

What a strange sequence of events.
How did it all happen to me?

Copyright © 1973 by Flammarion
English translation copyright © 1977 by Macdonald and Jane's and T.Y. Crowell
First published in Great Britain in 1977 by
Macdonald and Jane's Publishers Limited
Paulton House
8 Shepherdess Walk
London N1 7LW

ISBN 0 354 04021 9

Printed in Great Britain by
Redwood Burn Ltd, Trowbridge & Esher

Contents

LIST OF ILLUSTRATIONS

TRANSLATOR'S NOTES

No translation of Beaumarchais's plays was available in English until very recently. This may seem surprising, until you realize that Beaumarchais's French text is full of features that make it, strictly speaking, untranslatable: puns, syntactic compressions, allusions to Beaumarchais's own life and times and so on – all the rhetorical devices of irony. As Frédéric Grendel says in this book, Beaumarchais's penchant for word games 'comes close to destroying normal syntax at times, and his language becomes a language of the absurd'. I can't resist adding that the written text provides an *approximate* notation of fast and free French as it was spoken in the eighteenth century, and that like French musical notation of the period (with its implications of *notes inégales*) it has to be interpreted by the 'performer'.

If only Tim Reynolds had given us a Beaumarchais along the lines of his Aristophanes! But he hasn't, so I've had to produce my own versions of the extracts quoted in this book. As someone who played Figaro at school and Almaviva at the university, and wasn't very convincing as either, I approached this task with something like dread, particularly since I was bound to stay fairly close to the French text, because the author extrapolates narrowly from the writings to the life and vice versa. All the same I've tried to give my English the kind of pace that in an 'academic' translation would be judged delinquent.

These remarks hold for Frédéric Grendel's text as well, for the author of this delightful book (if I may say so) has on this occasion cultivated a style somewhat similar to Beaumarchais's – in a modern idiom, of course. (A clever copy-editor helped me here.)

I have assumed, in preparing this English edition of *Beaumarchais, ou, la Calomnie* (Paris, Flammarion, 1973), that specialists will have consulted the original. I have therefore felt free to abridge – without (I hope) distorting the author's emphases or cutting anything essential. I owe my thanks to Frédéric Grendel for suggesting the broad lines of this abridgement. Footnotes and so on were barred from the original edition, and they are from this one. (Beaumarchais regarded footnotes as examples of poor writing.) The extensive bibliography contained in the original has been replaced by a list of books in English. Naturally enough, Bazile and Chérubin and the rest appear in this translation under their original names and not under the Italianized forms foisted on the English-speaking world by Mozart and Rossini's librettists.

Finally, I would like to point out that hours of reflexion failed to provide me with a satisfactory English term for the deceptively simple word *mémoire*. I have used 'memoir', since it has the advantage of being close to the French and is in common use. But the scrupulous reader should bear in mind that as used here 'memoir' stands for half a dozen (or more) other English words: statement, report, memorial, argument, memorandum, even (a lawyer's) brief. Essentially, it means a personal record of events (or a reasoned case) designed to sway the reader in favour of the writer.

1

Son of a Nobody

After the revocation of the Edict of Nantes in 1685, French Protestants had no legal identity. They weren't allowed to marry and their children died illegitimate. They were barred from most trades, particularly those governed by the guilds – clockmaking, for instance – and if they wanted to exist in the eyes of the law, to bring up a family and practise a trade in the normal way, they had to submit. In other words, they had to abjure their religion.

They could always leave the country, of course. And they could always go into hiding. But emigration, like the other alternative, meant financial ruin and moral death to most French Protestants. Faced with the problem of feeding their children and giving them a name, few of them hesitated. They chose the solution that gave life.

'On 7 March 1721, in the church of the Nouvelles-Catholiques in Paris, I formally abjured the Calvinist heresy. Signed, André-Charles Caron.' Armed with his certificate, Beaumarchais's father, who was twenty-three, was free to leave the army (he was a dragoon), marry a Mlle Pichon, have legitimate children and open a shop in the rue Saint-Denis in Paris. He had a trade, having been apprenticed to his father who made clocks and watches in the little town of Lizy-sur-Ourcq thirty miles east of Paris.

Nothing could seem simpler or more convenient, on paper. And yet how many of us, if forced to sign away our deepest convictions, would do so sincerely? Wouldn't we just pretend to abjure and in private continue to think what we liked? Masks worn under duress often hide faces that have remained intact.

On 7 March 1721 André-Charles Caron deliberately cheated. He knew it, and his children knew it as soon as they were old enough to understand – and to rebel. Their official legitimacy struck them as spurious and they saw the bar sinister in their very name. Why

Caron? Why not Ronac? And why not Beaumarchais? Also, how could you respect a society that compelled responsible men to live a lie? How could you take it seriously? Since you had to *pretend*, life itself became a game and a sham – something to enjoy but not to be fooled by.

Beaumarchais soon realized all of this, as we shall see. He wore a mask all his life, but the pretence never prevented him from being himself. No writer in the eighteenth century *protested* more than he did. True, he was better placed than most to do so.

I had better add right away, if only to show the reader that I'm not inventing my Beaumarchais, that a file on the rights and status of Protestants in France was constantly on Beaumarchais's desk and that throughout his life he gave unstinting support to religious and racial minorities. He never forgot that he owed what legitimacy he had to his father's ruse and that he was all but literally the son of a nobody.

He has been misunderstood, and continues to be misunderstood, because he was full of gaiety and high spirits. His critics forget that gaiety is a refuge. In this respect they are like the German soldiers of 1939 who were amazed to hear people laughing and singing in the night behind the shuttered windows of the Warsaw ghetto. Yet it is a fact that comedy and humour are almost always the appanage of permanent misfortune. Anyone who has managed to survive despite heavy odds – by slipping through the net, or by abjuring – is led to see life as ludicrous, if he thinks about it. And if we can afford to take ourselves seriously, we have probably been very lucky.

Pierre-Augustin Caron was born on 24 January 1732 (Aquarius, I think) in the liveliest house in the rue Saint-Denis in Paris. André-Charles, his father, was no run-of-the-mill clockmaker. His correspondence shows him to have been intelligent, amusing and well-read. If he had been nobly born his career would have been quite different. His gifts led him, like his son later on, to take an interest in an amazingly wide variety of subjects – dredging machines, for instance, which he once studied for his friend the governor of Madrid. (Though not one to curry favour, he had more than one friend in high places.) He was clearly no ordinary man, and his family wasn't ordinary either. Once the shutters had gone up on the shop they recited poetry together, devoured English novels, played chamber music, composed. They went in for amateur dramatics, too. If I'm right in thinking that family histories owe more to shared interests than to mere kinship, there can be no doubt that the extraordinary unity of the Caron family was forged during those evening sessions of theatricals and concerts above the shop. And we shouldn't forget that family gatherings such as these were the hotbeds of the French Revolution. More young men than we tend to realize learned how to change the world while playing the viol or reading Samuel Richardson in the kind of togetherness depicted by Greuze and Diderot. One such young man lived in the rue Saint-Denis.

There were eight Carons: the father, who was very much in control; the mother, Marie-Louise, who might be described as an intelligent bystander; five daughters; and Pierre-Augustin. (Four other children had died in infancy – a not unusual proportion in those days.) Beaumarchais's five sisters were every bit as important in his life as any of his wives and mistresses. In order of birth they were Marie-Josèphe, Marie-Louise, Madeleine-Françoise, Marie-Julie (much more than a sister, a kindred spirit) and Jeanne-Marguerite. These good Catholic names, canonically double-barrelled in honour of M. Caron's abjuration, were for official use only. The sisters' pet names were simpler – Dame Guilbert, Lisette, Fanchon, Bécasse and Tonton.

It isn't unusual for boys brought up among girls – sisters, cousins or servants – to shun the fair sex at the onset of puberty. No such aversion affected Pierre-Augustin. At thirteen he wrote with untypical seriousness: 'I fancy that a companion of the opposite sex would be a constant delight in my private life.' Chérubin met his desired companion later the same year. Unfortunately the 'fond friend' made fun of his 'lusty youth' and dropped him shortly afterwards to get married, whereupon Pierre-Augustin tried to kill himself. He still recalled this early rebuff the year he died, and there can be no doubt that it hardened him. In his subsequent relations with women he kept a firm grip on his emotions. He was always mad about them, but he never gave them his soul. In any case, the woman he seems to have loved more intensely than any other was his sister Julie. This love was returned, and lasted until death. Julie never married, though she had several excellent opportunities to do so. She did have love affairs, but it was Pierre-Augustin who gave her his name – to everyone, until the day she died, she was Mlle de Beaumarchais. But I'm moving too fast. Let's go back to the beginning.

Between the ages of six and thirteen Pierre-Augustin had learned French, history and Latin at a school in Alfort. He had also taken his first communion – against his wishes, it seems, and to conform with those of his father, who knew how important it was to keep up appearances. It has been said that he was an agnostic. He probably was, though his open-mindedness led him, even at this early age, to weigh the pros and cons of the matter. The old monk who catechized him made no mistake about this, for he fed him cakes and chocolate along with the religion. 'I ran to see him,' writes Beaumarchais, 'every day I was free.'

M. Caron was an excellent clockmaker and his business was expanding. Naturally enough, he had decided that his son should follow in the family tradition. Reckoning that Pierre-Augustin had acquired all the Latin he needed by the age of thirteen, and perhaps thinking that he would be able to keep a closer eye on him if he was at home, he made him his apprentice. Over a period of years, then, Pierre-Augustin learned to measure time – plus patience, precision and mechanics. Of this decisive phase of his life we know little, apart from a few anecdotes which tend to indicate that he was the opposite of serious-minded and hard-working. There were petty thefts, escapades, furtive love affairs, undesirable friends – and a devouring passion for music that his father was obliged to temper by draconian measures. The following contract that he drew up for his son at the age of fourteen is proof enough that Beaumarchais's youth was not spent in a round of constant dissipation, as the anecdotes tend to suggest, but under the rod of a strict moral guardian:

1. You shall not make or sell, nor cause to be made or sold, directly or indirectly, anything independently of my business, and you shall never again succumb to the temptation of taking from my house anything, absolutely anything, beyond what I give you; and you shall never take in a watch for repair or any other work on any pretext or for any friend whatsoever without telling me; you shall never touch it without my express permission; you shall not sell as much as an old watch key without accounting to me for it. This clause is of such primordial importance and I am so mindful of its full observance, that I warn you that at the slightest infringement of it I shall turn you out immediately and never see you again as long as I live.

2. You shall rise at six in summer and seven in winter; you shall work until supper willingly at whatever I give you to do; I intend you to

employ the gifts that God has given you with the sole aim of becoming famous in your profession. Remember that it is shameful and dishonourable for you to move slowly ahead in your trade and that if you do not surpass everyone you will not deserve the least consideration. Your heart and mind must be given entirely to your honourable profession.

3 You shall no longer have supper in town and shall not go out in the evenings: suppers and outings are too dangerous for you; but I shall allow you to have dinner with your friends on Sundays and holidays, providing that I always know where you are going and that you always return home scrupulously before nine o'clock. I exhort you now, once and for all, never even to ask my permission for anything contrary to this clause, and I should not advise you to dispense with my permission.

4 You shall totally abandon your wretched music; above all, you shall cease to frequent young men; I will have none of them. Music and company between them have ruined you. However, considering your weakness, I will allow you the viol and the flute, but on the express condition that you never use them except after supper on working days only, and never during the day, and providing that you never disturb the neighbours or myself.

5 I shall do my best to avoid sending you out, but should it happen that I need to do so in connection with my business, remember first and foremost that I shall no longer accept any excuses for coming back late. You are already aware how much I abhor this offence.

6 I shall give you your board and 18 *livres* per month to be used for keeping yourself and your tools, as I have done hitherto and about which I will suffer no discussion, and as regards the gradual repayment of your debts it would be bad for your character and most improper in myself if I charged you for your board and paid you for your work. If you devote yourself dutifully to the greater good of my business and if your talents procure you a little business of your own, I shall give you a quarter of the profits on everything you bring in. You know my way of thinking, you know from experience that no one surpasses me in generosity. Therefore, earn more than what I promise you; but remember that I shall give nothing to words, henceforth I heed only actions.

  If my conditions are agreeable to you, if you feel strong enough to comply with them in good faith, accept them, and sign.

Pierre-Augustin signed, and kept his word: at twenty he was the greatest clockmaker in France – indeed the greatest clockmaker anywhere.

An apprenticeship in the intricate art of clockmaking is long and gruelling. At night Pierre-Augustin wasn't leading a dissipated life, he was working off his surplus energy. For a lively adolescent twelve hours on a stool with his eyes glued to tiny pieces of metal was a long time, particularly when the street outside was visible and present – much more so than in any other kind of workshop, because clockmakers were obliged by law to work in full view of the public. The goldsmiths' guild had obtained this measure from the government to ensure that their rivals didn't use precious metals, which were their monopoly. M. Caron's shop was therefore lit by four large windows and Pierre-Augustin had only to look up to be distracted. Though I can't prove it, I'm sure he looked up less often than he is said to have done.

In 1753 it was rare for two clocks or watches to keep the same time. Every clockmaker in Europe was engaged on a frantic search for a means to ensure perfect regularity in timepiece movements. But many people believed such a thing was impossible. In Versailles, Paris or London everyone, from king to commoner, lived at best to the nearest half-hour. Beaumarchais promised himself to reduce those thirty minutes to zero, and did so. The watch you're wearing on your wrist contains Beaumarchais's escapement.

A discovery which has held good for two centuries and revolutionized a craft that had existed for five centuries before that can hardly be regarded as negligible. I stress this point because it strikes me as exemplary. Most of Beaumarchais's biographers seem to belittle his invention. In their hands a mechanic of genius becomes a mere handyman, a conjurer, a Figaro of the cuckoo clock. It appears our judgements, too, could occasionally do with an escapement to keep them from going haywire.

At least one man took Beaumarchais seriously right from the start. His name was Jean-André Lepaute and he was the royal clockmaker. The title meant something in those days. Roughly speaking, it signified that Lepaute's clocks chimed the hours in every room in Versailles and (such was snobbery) in every wealthy home in Paris. In 1753, the year he encountered Beaumarchais, he was making the final adjustments to his horizontal clock at the Luxembourg Palace – the first horizontal clock in history, no less. It caused quite a sensation.

This man of the moment had not allowed success to get the better of his curiosity, and he was fond of browsing round the workshops of his fellow-craftsmen in search of new ideas. From time to time he would stop by the shop in the rue Saint-Denis, which was beginning to attract custom from all over Paris. On one of these occasions he met Pierre-Augustin and watched him at work – a trifle condescendingly, no doubt, particularly once he had spotted what the boy was after. They talked. The big hand listened to the little hand – and in a matter of minutes Lepaute sensed that he was outclassed. I find that to his credit. He was a scoundrel, but at least he was alert and humble enough to realize that a mere youth might have more imagination than the great Lepaute himself. After that first encounter, the royal clockmaker came back to the rue Saint-Denis very often, and watched the '*fils* Caron', the Caron boy, more closely than ever.

The lad's father felt flattered by these visits, and welcomed his distinguished colleague with understandable enthusiasm. Pierre-Augustin, too, was flattered – and fooled. One by one he revealed his secrets to the illustrious Lepaute, who didn't miss a trick. Comparisons were made. Pierre-Augustin's watches and Lepaute's were placed side by side in sealed boxes that were opened two days later. When checked by the sundial, the boy's watches were right to within a minute, whereas Lepaute's were all wrong. But once again Lepaute showed more cunning than envy. Instead of pooh-poohing, he applauded – and flattered. It was Pierre-Augustin's baptism of fire. He let himself be duped, for once, and the day came when he let the master of the king's timepieces borrow one of his escapements.

Shortly afterwards the *Mercure de France*, which was the equivalent in its day of *The Times*, Hansard and *Scientific American* rolled into one, published the following news item: 'The other day M. Lepaute presented His Majesty with a watch that he made recently. Its principal merit is its escapement . . .' There was more as well. By the time he had finished reading, the *fils* Caron had become Beaumarchais.

The escapement described in the *Mercure* article was in every way identical with the one made by Pierre-Augustin. Lepaute hadn't even bothered to change a detail or two before claiming it as his own. Yet this kind of thing was standard practice, and the great man had no reason to fear the slightest reaction from an obscure tyro whose father was his protégé. His appropriation of the invention was an honour to the lad, as it would have been to one of his own workmen. Why should he feel guilty or fear a scandal? In any case the invention was virtually his, officially, since he had already filed it at the Academy of Sciences, of which he was a distinguished member: 'I have discovered a means of disposing completely with the brace and counterbrace consisting of eight separate parts by placing one of the pivots in the plate etc. Thus the escapement is exempt from tilting and jamming etc.' In a word, he went the whole hog.

Two weeks later the *Mercure* published a letter from one of its young readers that created quite a stir. It must be read attentively, because it enables us to meet the real Beaumarchais at the very start of his career:

Paris, 15 November 1753

Sir,

I was extremely surprised to read in your September number that M. Lepaute, clockmaker to the Luxembourg Palace, has announced as his own invention a new escapement for watches and clocks which he claims to have been honoured to present to the King and the Academy.

In the interests of truth and my reputation, I cannot let such an infidelity go by in silence and must claim as mine the invention of this device.

It is true that on 23 July of this year, carried away by my joy in my discovery, I was weak enough to loan this escapement to M. Lepaute for a clock that he was making for M. de Julienne. He assured me that no one would be able to examine it because the clock would be fitted with his wind-driven winding mechanism and only he would have the key.

But it never occurred to me that M. Lepaute would see fit to claim this escapement as his own, since I quite clearly entrusted it to him under the seal of secrecy.

I do not want to *surprise* the public by this sudden disclosure, nor do I hope to win support on the strength of my assertions alone. However I beg your readers not to accord further credence to M. Lepaute until such time as the Academy has decided which of us is the inventor of the escapement. M. Lepaute seems to be trying to avoid any kind of explanation by declaring that his escapement, which I haven't seen, is in no way similar to mine; from his description, however, I take it to work on exactly the same principle, and if the commissioners nominated by the Academy to hear us severally and together find any differences between the two devices, those differences will be due solely to faulty workmanship, which is in itself indicative of plagiary.

I will reveal none of my points of proof, because our commissioners must hear them unweakened by prior debate. Hence whatever M.

Lepaute may say or write against me, I shall maintain complete silence until the Academy has heard us and made its decision.

Your astute readers must be kind enough to wait until then. I dare hope that their impartiality and their interest in the arts will grant me this favour. I should be humbly flattered, Sir, if you would be kind enough to insert this letter in your next number.

Caron *fils*, clockmaker, rue Saint-Denis, by the church of Sainte-Catherine

I don't think I'm wrong to say that this letter is the first real sign of Beaumarchais's greatness. Once he had written it, he had been born. Who was he, after all? Three very different kinds of man rolled into one: a practical genius, a great stylist *and* the most dazzling polemicist in French history. (He was also a man of considerable courage, but I prefer to ignore that aspect of his character for the moment. This decisive letter of 1753 is very brave, but it is a far cry from the extraordinary courage that Beaumarchais showed later on – real courage, ripened by experience, that owed nothing to the recklessness of youth.)

The letter put the Royal Academy of Sciences on the spot. They had somehow to adjudicate between one of their most distinguished members and a cocky apprentice. Two commissioners were appointed. Their lengthy report, duly debated by the Academy, gave rise to the following decision published on 16 February 1754: 'M. Caron must be regarded as the real inventor of the new watch escapement . . . M. Lepaute merely copied this invention.'

At twenty-two Pierre-Augustin had just won his first lawsuit, and his first battle. He had also struck a blow against the system, which could never be quite the same again. Lepaute, discredited (and looking very ridiculous, which was worse), was soon forced to give up his position and title as the king's clockmaker to his young rival.

Louis XV was the first in line for a watch equipped with the new escapement. He sent in his order. A few days later the *fils* Caron made his *entrée* to Versailles and was seen by the king, who had been amused by the young man's audacity. Pierre-Augustin, who wasn't exactly shy, wasn't content merely to hand the watch to the monarch, thank him for his compliments and blush. He pointed out that he was capable of making watches that were smaller and above all flatter, than any that the king had ever seen. Fashion in watches hasn't changed, it seems – the flatter the better. So, a second order; and a second success. The king was so pleased that he invited Pierre-Augustin to his *levée* and commanded him to show his flat watch to the gentlemen-in-waiting. This honour was rarely extended to a craftsman. Pierre-Augustin saw the value of the king's gesture right away: all the gentlemen of the bedchamber would be falling over one another to follow the king's example and carry a Caron in their waistcoat pockets. But they had to wait. Mme de Pompadour had put her name down for one, and the king's clockmaker knew better than to keep her waiting.

Mme de Pompadour wanted a really tiny watch. Pierre-Augustin brought her a ring. Annoyance, followed by amazement – the watch was set in the ring! Louis XV, wanting to subject this masterpiece to closer scrutiny, borrowed *Monsieur* Caron's glass and shrieked with admiration: 'Why, it's only a third of an inch across!' It was. 'But where's the winder? Haven't you forgotten the winder?' Of course not. 'Sire, the watch will run for thirty hours on a single turn of the gold circle round the watch face.'

Presented like that, it all sounds so easy. In fact Pierre-Augustin's apparent facility was based on hours and hours of hard work. Whether he was perfecting a mechanism, serving his country or writing a play, Beaumarchais was never as debonair as he seemed. He left nothing to chance. He never improvised, and if at times he tries to make us think the opposite, he's kidding.

His charm, on the other hand, was manifestly neither acquired nor affected. Without it, his life would have been quite different. To astound Versailles with flat watches was one thing; it was another to keep your foot in the door, and before long to be able to use the front gate instead of the tradesmen's entrance. To stay put you needed a lot of talent – and relentless ambition. Beaumarchais didn't aspire to please, but to make his mark despite the accident of birth. In this kind of venture, charm helps. It's even indispensable. Gudin de la Brenellerie, who was Beaumarchais's friend and his first biographer, has left us this apparently sketchy but significant portrait: 'As soon as Beaumarchais appeared at Versailles, the women were struck by his tall stature, his slim and handsome build, his regular features, his quick and lively complexion, his steady gaze, his masterful air that seemed to raise him above his surroundings, and finally his way of lighting up with involuntary ardour the minute he set eyes on them.'

This masterful air didn't always go down so well in a masculine environment. Male courtiers who had had to fight their way to the top – lesser noblemen and mediocrities – soon took umbrage at the newcomer, who, instead of keeping his distance, intended to outdistance them all; and they swore to ruin this son of a nobody.

Pierre-Augustin accepted the challenge. To play the game, but not by the rules, he added a few bearings to his coat of arms.

2

Rank, status . . .

'Nobility, fortune, rank, status: so much to glory in,' says Figaro. For the time being, however, Pierre-Augustin was still to all appearances the clever little clockmaker. If he had any burgeoning ambitions at this stage, he kept them to himself. A second letter to the *Mercure*, in which he stated, 'This success confirms me in my profession as a clockmaker' was undoubtedly sincere. Henceforth father and son were partners. In the workshop on the rue Saint-Denis they worked non-stop to satisfy their ever-growing clientele. How could he have abandoned his family at a time when they were better off than they had ever been? All the same, Versailles wasn't far away, and it was no mirage. Mesdames, the daughters of Louis XV, wanted his watches too. Before long they wanted the watchmaker as well, because he entertained them and made them forget their royal *ennui*. Pierre-Augustin's visits to Versailles were frequent, but he never stayed longer than necessary and was soon back on his stool working ten hours at a stretch.

Destiny had knocked once at the workshop door in the form of Lepaute. It knocked again the day Madeleine-Catherine Francquet stepped in with a watch for repair. Beaumarchais looked up mechanically when she tapped at the window of the shop. Hadn't he already seen her at Versailles? He had indeed. Her eyes had met his one day, briefly but significantly. Pierre-Augustin examined the watch, even though he had sized up the situation at the first glance – the lady's visit clearly had nothing to do with watches. Over the years Chérubin had acquired experience.

In comparison with the detached libertinism of the young Pierre-Augustin, the earnestness of Madeleine-Catherine appeared almost childlike. She was thirty-four or thirty-five, but she knew next to nothing about love and life, apart from what she had learned from her husband, M. Francquet. Meanwhile she wasn't getting any younger, her husband was going to die and the sand in the hour-glass was running faster every year. If she hadn't seen Pierre-Augustin at Versailles, Mme Francquet might never have done anything other than dream of passing love affairs. Having seen him, she was prepared to take any risk, starting with the biggest risk of all, which was to throw herself at him. She knew exactly what she was doing when she took him her broken watch. When he offered to mend it immediately and deliver it personally the following day, she jumped at the offer, because she was incapable of taking the next step herself. I'm not inventing anything – the lady was respectable and religious; to go to the shop at all was sheer madness by her lights; to become his mistress was unthinkable, that is to say it was a possibility conceived, desired, but rejected. In her early letters to him we find her invoking heaven and providence quite as naturally as she breathed. A born seducer, Pierre-Augustin followed her lead with equal grace. When she wrote, 'My duty forbids me ever to think of anyone, least of all of you,' he replied in the same vein: 'When I think that he is your husband, that he is yours, I can but sigh in silence, and wait for the will of God to enable me to cause you to enjoy that state of happiness for which fate seems to have made you.' This correspondence may well strike us as comic, but we shouldn't jump to conclusions. A seducer has to submit to certain imperatives. If Pierre-Augustin had written impertinently to Mme Francquet, he would never have seen her again. Bluster never got anybody into bed. In any case, Madeleine-Catherine didn't keep the handsome clockmaker sighing in silence for too long.

So much for Mme Francquet. We must now turn to the husband, whose part in this affair was far from negligible. Indeed his behaviour, odd as it may seem, was almost certainly deliberate. Without beating about the bush, here are the facts: Pierre-Augustin Francquet, lord of the manor of Beaumarchais, was Comptroller-in-Ordinary to the royal household. Yes: Pierre-Augustin, Beaumarchais, Comptroller-in-Ordinary and so on. The same first name, the same name and the same office. Let's say the first name was merely an odd coincidence. As regards the office, we should specify that Pierre-Augustin Francquet himself couldn't rest until he had disposed of his title to Pierre-Augustin Caron. As for the name . . . But that's enough for the moment. More than enough, in my opinion.

M. Francquet, who was a dying man, had one further gesture to make, as odd as the rest. Having sold his functions at court and his sword of office to the young Caron, he had the extreme tact, if that is the word for it, to die. However, I should hate to make too much fun of M. Francquet, or belittle him, because I am convinced, though I can't prove it, that throughout the affair he behaved like a gentleman.

To go from one Pierre-Augustin, Comptroller-in-Ordinary, to another can't have demanded too much of the widowed Madeleine-Catherine. After all, life must go on.

In point of fact M. Francquet's position at court had been that of Comptroller of Victuals. This office conferred on its holder the signal honour and right to precede His Majesty's meat at official banquets. The Comptroller of Victuals came immediately after the Gentleman Bread-bearer but immediately before the roast beef. This rigmarole was invented by the royal household to exploit the vanity of the middle classes. There were hundreds of honorary positions at court; needless to say, they had to be bought, and they weren't cheap. M. Francquet had obtained the office of Comptroller of Victuals because the offices of Captain of Greyhounds or Pastry-cook to the Dogs of the Bedchamber weren't vacant. Even though some fools took pride in delivering seven biscuits daily to Her Majesty's pugs, I doubt whether Beaumarchais thought much of the letters patent (9 November 1755) that granted him precedence over a steak. All the same, another 'patent' had given him the right to bear his father's name – the right that M. Caron had acquired for him by abjuring his religion. The first step in climbing a ladder is the lowest rung. No one can say that Beaumarchais climbed the rungs four at a time.

Eleven months after M. Francquet's death Pierre-Augustin married Madeleine. The time for passion was over; it gave way to impatience. Once married, the lovers were transformed. They quarrelled constantly: he told her she was bad-tempered, she resented the fact that he was often away from home. There were probably wrongs on both sides. Pierre-Augustin made frequent visits to Versailles, leaving his wife at home, and when he came home late she would sulk and refuse to sleep with him. Having lived for years with a sick husband who had considered it his duty to give in to her, Madeleine made the mistake of thinking that she could dominate Pierre-Augustin as she had M. Francquet. She may also have made the mistake of treating him as someone younger than herself and seeing him merely as a brilliant craftsman. At Versailles, Pierre-Augustin was made to feel that he was different, that he had much more to expect from life than a shop. Mesdames had forgotten that their favourite companion was a clockmaker . . . These problems, which all couples experience sooner or later, could easily have been overcome if tenderness or sex had been there to act as counterweights; but it seems they weren't. In a letter to Madeleine, Pierre-Augustin describes the mood of their marriage: 'The Julie who tended to swoon with pleasure at a loving glance in the days of intoxication and illusion has become a woman like any other. Because of domestic disagreements, she concludes that she could live without the man whom her heart once preferred to anything on earth.' We should note, in passing, that he absentmindedly calls his wife Julie. A literary device? More likely a furtive confession – his sister Julie had ruled him since his childhood.

If M. Francquet had been more ambitious than he was, he would have styled himself Francquet de Beaumarchais. The Comptroller of Victuals had possessed a landed estate; the *bos* or *bois* ('wood') *marché*, *marchai* or *marchais* (ambiguous). Madeleine, who inherited it, gave it to her new husband along with the rest. Pierre-Augustin had no wish to get rich off women, even if they were his wives. He neglected to draw up a marriage contract – and had cause to rue his noble disinterestedness, as we shall see. But he did assume the *bos*, or rather its name, with alacrity. *Bos* or *bois marché* became Beaumarchais; and Caron became Caron *de* Beaumarchais (landed gentry), then just Beaumarchais (nobility). This process took only a few months: in September 1757 Pierre-Augustin was still signing his letters Caron; in October he specified Caron de Beaumarchais; in February 1758 he was plain Beaumarchais. The practice was common in the eighteenth century. Although few people realize it, a middle-class citizen today who wishes to obtain a title from the Vatican has to wait longer and pay more than a candidate for nobility under Louis XV. Birth, noble birth, was everything in those days; but there were short cuts – things could be arranged. To be officially born, Pierre-Augustin had to be born a Catholic; to be officially born noble, he acquired a title. He himself was never taken in by this cheating nonsense, as his life and works testify. In 1773 he responded to attacks on his name as follows:

I reserve the right to take advice as to whether I should be offended by
your rummaging in my family archives and reminding me of my ancient
origins, which people had almost forgotten. Take note that I can show
proof of nigh on twenty years of nobility to date; that this nobility is truly
mine – in good parchment, it is, sealed with the great seal in yellow wax;
that it is not, like that of many people, uncertain and merely asserted;
and that no one would dare to claim it from me, because I've got the
receipt!

Such insolent mockery of one's contemporaries would be hard to
surpass.

Only ten months after the wedding Madeleine fell ill. The four
doctors summoned to her bedside by Beaumarchais – Bouvard,
Bourdelin, Pousse and Renard, the best in Paris – diagnosed 'putrid
fever' (which I take to be typhoid) complicated by a chest infection,
probably tuberculosis. The doctors could do little but observe the
rapid decline of their patient and issue a certificate of death from
natural causes. Years later, when Beaumarchais was in serious
trouble, Madeleine's parents, the Aubertins, accused him of having
poisoned his wife and of having attempted to misappropriate her
inheritance. This was a joke in bad taste, because Madeleine's death
was a catastrophe for him: 'She left me naked in the full sense of the
term, riddled with debts.' The Aubertins got all her property, while
the young widower had to pay all the creditors. Fifteen years later,
however, Beaumarchais was rich. His most famous opponents, La
Blache and Goëzman, appeared to be on the point of bleeding him of
his every penny; whereupon, up popped the Aubertins again to
claim a slice of the cake. They were finally brought to court, and they
admitted that their claim was false. Having failed to strangle
Beaumarchais, they turned to wheedling him; he made them a
charitable allowance. His lack of resentment is one of his most
remarkable characteristics. And his extreme generosity was universally known – friends, enemies and famous names alike never
knocked on his door in vain. He didn't lend, he gave – to private
citizens and to governments.

On 29 September 1757 Beaumarchais was none the less 'naked in the
full sense of the term'. All that he had left was his grief and his
borrowed name – and his genius. That was quite sufficient for him to
make his way back to Versailles.

It took real genius to please the pernickety royal family and go round the course at Versailles. Pierre-Augustin had had his moment of glory with his escapement and his tiny watches, but that moment couldn't last for ever. There were hundreds of young men like himself at the palace. The clockmaker soon realized that his wheels and springs wouldn't take him much farther, that to be successful, to draw attention to himself a second time, he would have to be creative. As luck would have it, he was musical. He played several instruments well and occasionally composed. In addition he invented a harp pedal, which has become a standard feature of the instrument. Mesdames, who were dying of boredom in the enforced seclusion of their private apartments, expressed the wish to try out his miraculous harp. Beaumarchais brought it along to the apartment of Mme Adélaïde, and when he left, it stayed. Since he also played the viol, the flute, the Jew's harp and even the tambourine, and was charming, he became *subito* and *prestissimo* the favourite teacher, the sole musical director and the preferred companion of Loque, Coche, Graille and Chiffe. (The Bourbons and the Carons shared a fondness for ridiculous nicknames.) The four old maids, who were not nearly as stupid as people say, but quite as ugly, never lost the ear of the king, their father. Since their influence was great, they were besieged by courtiers attempting to enter their good graces – usually without success. When they took a fancy to Pierre-Augustin the antechambers hummed with jealousy and envy. It was said that during an improvised concert the king had given his chair to 'that Caron' and had remained standing for twenty minutes while 'that wretch' had stayed seated. It was also rumoured that after these sessions of music-making Mesdames, who were always fond of 'stuffing themselves with meat and wine', unlocked their cupboards and invited their protégé to share their bologna, their ham and their fine champagne. In the courtiers' apartments beneath the roofs of the palace the wine turned to vinegar. It wasn't long before these sour grapes produced the first anti-Beaumarchais plot, which seems ridiculous to us but which might well have worked in the absurd and crazy microcosm of Versailles.

Gudin relates how one day each of the sisters received a fan depicting one of their concerts. The paintings were accurate down to the smallest detail, with the sole exception that Beaumarchais wasn't included in the scene. Indignant at this affront to their favourite, Mesdames showed the fans to Pierre-Augustin, who merely smiled. Whereupon the fans were returned to their senders because the 'maestro' wasn't depicted on them. This rebuff – and this 'maestro' – stopped the attic intriguers in their tracks for a while, but it wasn't long before they launched a new onslaught with more subtle means.

The striking thing about Pierre-Augustine's conduct during this period is his *sang-froid* and his sense of proportion. Anyone else would have let all this go to their heads: from his father's workshop to the royal apartments was no mean achievement for a young man of twenty-five. But Pierre-Augustin kept his head. He knew how precarious his position was. He scratched his name on a window, like any day-tripper, and added: 'I was here.' This modesty, this sense of reality might have led him to grovel; in fact he preferred to play the game straight, without pretence. 'He is the only person who speaks the truth to me,' the dauphin once said of him. The loneliness of kings in their courts is a terrible thing. At a carnival, a man without a mask stands out at once. Before Louis XV or the revolutionary tribunals Beaumarchais remained himself and was heard, esteemed and occasionally liked. But in the antechambers of power he was universally hated. All his life he had to contend with masked faces.

Once the fan gambit had failed, the masks attempted to drive a rift between him and Mesdames by inventing the story that he was ashamed of his father. It was common for minor aristocrats or men recently ennobled to hide their ancestry under a bushel, so Pierre-Augustin's enemies had to take the slander a step further. They insinuated that he treated his father badly. Mesdames had a highly developed sense of family loyalty and they couldn't fail to be outraged if they discovered that their protégé was a low-born hypocrite. But Beaumarchais got wind of the plot. He brought M. Caron to Versailles and presented him to the princesses, who discovered many similarities between him and his son and showered him with kindnesses. The plot had misfired again, to Beaumarchais's advantage.

At about this time, too, the celebrated incident of the broken watch took place. La Harpe and Gudin tell the story in virtually identical terms. Meeting Beaumarchais in one of the galleries at Versailles, a courtier addressed him sufficiently loudly to attract the attention of a large number of potential witnesses.

'*Monsieur*, I believe you know a thing or two about watches. Kindly tell me what you think of this one.'

'*Monsieur*,' Beaumarchais replied, eyeing the staring crowd of courtiers, 'since I ceased to practise that art I have become extremely clumsy.'

'Ah, *Monsieur*, will you say no?'

'Very well. But I've warned you.'

Taking the watch, he opened it, raised it as if to examine it, and dropped it from a great height. Bowing deeply, he said:

'I warned you, *monsieur*, that I was extremely clumsy.'

And he walked off, leaving the courtier, who had intended to humiliate him, quite at a loss.

La Harpe adds that this series of incidents 'soon formed a hotbed of furious and secret hatred directed against him, the aim of which was none other than to cause his utter ruin'.

In 1760 his opponents were miles off target. The king, the dauphin and above all Mesdames found Beaumarchais a pleasant fellow, an agreeable companion, at times a friend. The four sisters awaited his daily arrival at Versailles with impatience. They gave him absurd errands to run for them and would trust no one else. Their wayward-ness is legendary: Louis XV once had Choiseul woken up in the middle of the night to send a courier to the Bishop of Orléans because Mme Victoire couldn't sleep until she had tasted the bishop's quince candy which she had heard about that afternoon. Pierre-Augustin's 'chamber pot' (as the little carriages running between Versailles and Paris were called) was always crammed with parcels for the princes-ses – who cost him a lot of money, because they would conveniently forget to pay him back. Mme Sophie even borrowed the odd *louis* from her handsome music master. Ultimately Beaumarchais was obliged to send in an expense sheet to Mme de Hoppen, the princes-ses' steward, because he had barely any time left over for his work and his tailor was threatening to sue him.

'In times of poverty, the smallest crumbs are welcome,' says his letter to Mme de Hoppen. The times of poverty were about to come to a sudden end. Pâris-Duverney entered his life. From that moment on, things moved fast, amazingly so. All the same he remained, as always, on his guard: 'To tell the truth, I laugh into my pillow when I think how things are linked together in this life of ours and how very strange the paths of fortune are.'

3

Pâris-Duverney

Crabbed age and youth *can* live together, witness the passionate friendship that united until death a cocksure young man of twenty-eight and the most formidable old man of his day.

When Pâris-Duverney encountered Beaumarchais, he was over seventy-six. Even though he was no longer at the height of his power, his wealth remained colossal. What drew the two men together? The mystery is as great today as it ever was. But it is clear that there was a kind of love between them, in which complicity and esteem played equal parts. Twenty years after the banker's death, which as we shall see caused him the greatest difficulties (lawsuits, imprisonment, dishonour, ruin), Pierre-Augustin hadn't forgotten his old friend: in the garden of his mansion he placed a bust of Pâris-Duverney with the inscription, 'His deeds were my lessons; what little worth I have is his.'

Two months after their first meeting Pâris-Duverney was treating Pierre-Augustin as his own child, and calling him 'my son' in front of witnesses. But that was nothing compared with the trust that he placed from the start in the young, unknown amateur musician. From one day to the next, Pâris-Duverney opened his files, his coffers and his heart to Beaumarchais. Why?

The partnership is generally explained in terms of an intrigue concerning the Ecole Militaire, the splendid military academy that Pâris-Duverney built with his own funds as a gift for Louis xv. Cadets were already in training at the academy under the command of Colonel Meyzieu, the founder's nephew. But the king was irritated by Pâris-Duverney's continued support for Mme de Pompadour after her disgrace, and refused to open the academy. At a time when Beaumarchais's position at court was to say the least, tenuous, Pâris-Duverney had the good sense to send for the little clockmaker.

Beaumarchais succeeded in obtaining what no minister had dared to promise Pâris-Duverney – after taking Mesdames and the dauphin to visit the academy, he brought along the king.

Louis XV inspected the buildings, in which five hundred boys of noble birth were taught fencing, dancing, riding and the arts of war. After attending a tattoo and a firework display put on in his honour, the king consented to take refreshments with Pâris-Duverney.

Does this service rendered explain everything? It probably does, if we accept Beaumarchais's version, written in later life: 'In 1760, M. du Verney . . . sought to make my acquaintance and offered me his affection, his assistance and his credit if I could succeed in achieving what everyone had tried in vain to achieve for nine years.' The businesslike tone makes it all sound very much like a gentlemen's agreement. Pâris-Duverney did in fact indulge in occasional patronage: he was partly responsible for making Voltaire's fortune, although he never considered making him his business partner. No. Beaumarchais and Pâris-Duverney reached an immediate understanding, because they belonged to the same race.

The four Pâris brothers worked in their father's inn at Moirans in the Dauphiné, serving during the day and studying at night, until one evening in 1710 the Duchesse de Bourgogne stopped her coach in their yard. By the time she had finished her dinner she had made her decision: those four boys weren't cut out for trussing capons. She would make bankers of the turnspits. And off went her recommendation to the governor of the Dauphiné. The four needed no pushing. Ten years later they were immensely rich and ministers acted at their bidding. Occasionally they would encounter opposition from a man like Cardinal de Fleury and would be ruined or sent into exile. But no Fleury was ever around for long, and the Pâris brothers would soon return, richer than ever.

The most intelligent, and the most politically minded, of the four, Pâris-Duverney, was a disciple of the great financier Samuel Bernard. During the reign of Louis XV Pâris-Duverney had considerable power. Lurking behind the royal mistresses – Mme de Prix, the Duchesse de Châteauroux and especially the Marquise de Pompadour – he exerted influence over the king, the government and the army. The Maréchal de Noailles nicknamed him General Rations, because he had sole control over all military supplies. After the Seven Years' War and the disgrace of Mme de Pompadour, Pâris-

Duverney was thrown into the Opposition, or rather on to the sidelines of power. This didn't prevent him from reacting forcefully to events, from preparing his comeback and from serving his country in his own way. He belonged to the anti-Britain faction, having realized that in 1763 the greatness of France depended on the defeat of Great Britain. As we shall see, Beaumarchais defended his master's policy all his life, even when it ran counter to his interests.

In the minds of both men the position of France in the world could be equated with their own position within France – it was as unthinkable that France should abandon Canada and Louisiana for good as that they themselves should slide back to their obscure origins. At the same time, they shared a keen awareness of social realities. In as much as the system existed, they had to use it to achieve their ends. In this respect, rank and fortune were necessary incidentals, not ends in themselves; they were admission tickets, not licences to perform.

Did Pâris-Duverney see Beaumarchais merely as a kind of ambassador at court, a source of influence and information, as many writers have claimed? I think not. The banker's disgrace was far from absolute. It was more of a royal cold shoulder than a disgrace, since the old man still had the ear of the king's ministers. Furthermore, Beaumarchais himself had no political influence at this time; he was just a fad, an entertainer, a pleasant new face. The only valid explanation of the relationship, it seems to me, is a psychological one. They were united by feelings of love. Towards the end of his life Pâris-Duverney was on the look-out for an heir, a successor, maybe a disciple. Having met Pierre-Augustin, he devoted his final years to training him, to teaching him the ins and outs of politics. 'His deeds were my lessons; what little worth I have is his.'

To begin with, he gave him a secure position at court. Beaumarchais's ridiculous functions as Comptroller of Victuals and his less official role as royal music master didn't entitle him to postulate legitimate nobility. Pâris-Duverney therefore bought him what was known as a 'commoners' muck-remover': a patent as a royal secretary costing 55,000 francs and granting him a legal right to the name Beaumarchais.

For the metamorphosis to be complete, he still had to wipe out the past; in other words, he had to shut up shop. Hence the following letter which he sent to his father on 2 January 1761:

If I could choose the New Year's gift that I should like to receive from you, I should wish more than anything else that you might be kind enough to recall your promise, long deferred, to change the name over your door. A transaction that I am about to conclude may fail for the sole reason that you are engaged in trade, as you openly advertise. Nothing until now has led me to think that you intend to refuse me something about which you don't care one way or the other, but which makes a great difference to my destiny, owing to the stupid preconceptions that people have in this country. Since I am unable to change the prejudice, I must perforce submit to it, because that's the only avenue that I have towards the betterment that I desire for our common good and for that of the whole family.

The whole family were quick to see the point. Pierre-Augustin received his patent on 9 December the same year. M. Caron, who had once been forced to renounce his beliefs, knew as much about prejudice as his son did. Sadly, he changed his profession. His third daughter, Madeleine, known as Fanchon, who had married the clockmaker Lépine in 1756, was the only one to continue the family tradition. As for Bécasse, or rather Julie, who was already the friend and confidante of her ambitious brother, there can be no doubt that her opinion helped to sway old M. Caron. It was at this juncture, moreover, that Pierre-Augustin legitimized, if that is the word, their strange relationship by giving her his name. From 1762 the rolls of the city of Paris bore the names of two Beaumarchais, Julie and her brother. Was her obstinate refusal to marry inspired by a wish to keep her/his name? (She wasn't short of suitors or lovers, quite the reverse, in fact.) The odd situation of the shared name gave rise to the sneering remark made by Councillor Goëzman, whom we shall be meeting later: 'Caron borrowed the name Beaumarchais from one of his wives and lent it to one of his sisters.'

Under the guidance of his mentor and partner, Beaumarchais set about acquiring the elements of finance, banking and trade. Pâris-Duverney gave him a taste for business and speculation. Speculation. The word is in bad odour these days, but we should remember that in a nobler sense, without speculation there would have been no spirit of conquest, no industrial development and no social change. It was a desire for action, not for possession, that motivated Beaumarchais's speculations. The money he earned selling supplies

to the army was used to further American independence, to provide
Paris with a water supply, to publish Voltaire, to help pioneer
aviators and so on. Speculations if you like, but very often ruinous
ones. Oddly enough, Pâris-Duverney seems to have discovered the
delights of speculation at the same time as he was urging them upon
his protégé. Before 1760 his caution and cynicism had got the better
of all temptations. True, a banker has little to lose at the age of
eighty, apart from his fortune.

Beaumarchais's share in their joint transactions, about which we
know next to nothing except that to begin with they were concerned
exclusively with military supplies, was 10 per cent for the first few
months and 50 per cent thereafter. The apprentice soon equalled his
master, whose fondness for him increased proportionately. They
appear to have enjoyed working together. Soon their partnership
became a kind of game or ritual, with a code of its own: the *style
oriental* consisting of metaphors and inscrutable allusions (as in
oriental texts), which enabled them to communicate in highly
ambiguous terms. In 1770, for instance, Beaumarchais wrote without the slightest qualm: 'How is my dear little girl? Our last embrace
goes back far too long. What strange lovers we are! We don't dare see
one another because our parents disapprove; but we still love one
another. Oh yes, my little girl . . .' The dear little girl replied in the
same vein without batting an eyelid.

Having acquired the habit of taking short cuts in his life, Beaumarchais was about to experience his first failure, possibly because he
was in too much of a hurry. In fact he almost pulled it off. All the
same, if he had got what he was after too soon in life, would he have
written *Figaro*? Certainly not. As we shall see, *Figaro* was the product
of his defeats and his recoveries.

The first defeat involved the office of Grand Master of Rivers and
Forests, which had fallen vacant at the death of its previous incum-
bent. It was up for sale at 500,000 *livres*, but was guaranteed to enrich
its occupant painlessly in no time at all. The money presented no
problem – Pâris-Duverney promised to open his coffers. There were
eighteen grand masters in France, who formed a kind of exclusive
club. To become one of them required money, the royal consent, and
in theory a coat of arms. Beaumarchais's nobility amounted to little
more than a receipt, as we know; but on the matter of consent he

decided to play his royal flush: king, dauphin and Mesdames. To begin with, everything went smoothly. Royalty obliged and the Comptroller-General accepted Beaumarchais's bid. However, the news of his appointment aroused the other seventeen grand masters to fury; some of them even plucked up enough courage to threaten to resign. The Comptroller-General flapped and went back on his decision. The queen in her turn attempted to help Beaumarchais through the good offices of her equerry. Mesdames badgered the king constantly. But Louis XV was reluctant to intervene in such an unimportant matter: the grand masters' resistance, backed up by the continued hostility towards Beaumarchais at court, was an embarrassment to him. The grand masters' objection was that Beaumarchais's father was a clockmaker and that 'however famous a man may be in this art, such a station is incompatible with the honours attached to the rank of grand master'. With the battle half-lost, Beaumarchais couldn't resist the pleasure of deflating his noble adversaries in a superb letter addressed to the Comptroller-General:

My reply is to review the families and previous stations of several of the grand masters, about whom I have obtained strictly accurate information.

1   M. d'Arbonnes, Grand Master of Orléans and one of my most vehement opponents, is by name Hervé, son of Hervé, wigmaker. I can cite ten living persons to whom this Hervé sold wigs . . . Yet Hervé d'Arbonnes was appointed a grand master unopposed, even though he may have indulged the same weakness as his father in his youth.

2   M. de Marizy, who became Grand Master of Burgundy five or six years ago, is Legrand by name, son of Legrand, finisher and wool-carder in the faubourg Saint-Marceau, who subsequently opened a little shop selling blankets near the foire Saint-Laurent and became quite prosperous. His son married the daughter of Lafontaine, saddler, took the name of Marizy and was appointed a grand master unopposed.

3   M. Tellès, Grand Master of Châlons, is the son of a Jew named Tellès Dacosta, who started out as a jeweller and pawnbroker before making his fortune thanks to the brothers Pâris; he was appointed unopposed . . .

4   M. Duvaucel, Grand Master of Paris, is the son of one Duvaucel, son of a button merchant, subsequently connected with his brother's shop in the Petite rue aux Fers, first as an attendant, than as a partner, and finally as the proprietor. M. Duvaucel encountered no obstacles upon his appointment.

The grand masters were most unhappy to be reminded that they were the sons of Jews or wigmakers. They were unhappier still to discover that Beaumarchais actually admitted to having started out in clocks, like his Protestant grandfather and father before him. How vulgar could you get?

Louis XV, who had been forced to drop Beaumarchais on this occasion, soon had an opportunity to make amends. Beaumarchais put in for the office of Lieutenant-General of the Hunt in the Bailiwick and Captaincy of the Preserves of the Louvre. The king signed without delay and nipped the opposition in the bud. Thus Beaumarchais became the immediate subordinate of the Duc de La Vallière, Captain-General, peer of the realm and Grand Falconer of France. His high rank gave him jurisdiction over the Comte de Rochechouart and the Comte de Marcouville, whose coats of arms were more authentic than those of most of the grand masters.

His newly acquired office required him to mete out justice each week or thereabouts in a special courtroom in the Louvre. Sitting in the king's name, dressed in a long robe, he passed judgement in all seriousness on a succession of poachers caught on the royal preserves. In the system, as judge, a royal judge, on the side of the lords and masters, a paid-up member of the establishment, he kept a level head. Clockmaker, musician, financier or magistrate, he never changed, he never stopped being himself: a wag and a dissenter. The judge would go to prison more than once when he felt he had to defend justice proper, not just the royal preserves in Montrouge and Vanves.

All he needed to complete his entry into the establishment was a house fit for his family and friends. Pâris-Duverney helped him once again, and before long he became the owner of a fine town house in the rue de Condé. His 'tribe' moved in immediately: the two unmarried sisters and his father, who had been a widower since 1758. M. Caron didn't take much persuading to move house. His frequent kidney pains were so violent that they brought him to the brink of suicide, and solitude wasn't good for him, so he accepted his son's patronage with enthusiasm: 'What father will be happier than yours? I give tender blessings to high heaven that in my old age I have a son of such excellent character . . . My soul warms and takes wing at the touching thought that I owe my well-being to him alone after the Almighty.'

M. Caron didn't have only his son to warm his soul. Two ladies of respectable age had been making eyes at him for some time – Mme Gruel and Mme Henry. After a long engagement he finally succumbed to the latter. Bécasse and Tonton, alias Julie and Jeanne-Marguerite, moved into the new house, hotly pursued by their packs of suitors. Tonton celebrated the move, like her sister, by changing her name. She became Caron de Boisgarnier, in memory of an uncle of that name who had risen to the rank of captain in a grenadier regiment. A pretty young cousin from San Domingo, Pauline Le Breton, and her aunt, Mme Gaschet, along with Janot de Miron, a young lawyer, M. de la Châtaigneraie, an equerry of the queen, and the Chevalier de Seguirand, who was also from the colonies, were to be found frequently at the house in the rue de Condé, where everyone was in love – or pretended to be. 'The house,' Julie wrote, 'is a bear-garden of lovers, with no thought for anything but love and hope.'

To entertain this little society Pierre-Augustin was in the habit of writing what were known as *parades* based on the farces he had seen at the fair as a child. The *genre* was fashionable in the eighteenth century and the court and the aristocracy adored these little plays depicting humble folk whose French was 'imperfect and low'. As Jacques Scherer points out in *La dramaturgie de Beaumarchais* (1954), it is astonishing to find that Beaumarchais's *parades* are 'seasoned with the salt of politics'. Social comment such as that found in *Jean Bête à la Foire* or the other four *parades* known to be by Beaumarchais was not really part of the *genre*. But whether or not the *parades* contain the essential features of certain themes and characters in *The Barber* and *The Marriage*, I don't think there would be much point in spending a great deal of time on these trifles, which Beaumarchais dashed off for an evening's entertainment and never deemed worthy of publication. Often *parades* would be acted in semi-darkness so that the ladies might blush unobserved at the *double entendres*. It is true, however, that eighteenth-century audiences saw *double entendres* everywhere. Scherer gives a marvellous example of this mentality: 'A lady of quality attending a performance of *King Lear* responded to the line translated as "I need to be a father" by exclaiming, "Fie! How indecent!" '

Pâris-Duverney occasionally invited the company to Plaisance, near Nogent-sur-Marne, where he had a *château*. More frequently they all met up at the home of Charles Lenormant in Etioles. Charles Lenormant, financier and *fermier-général*, is best known as the husband, for better or worse, depending on your viewpoint, of Jeanne Poisson, alias Mme de Pompadour. Beaumarchais and Julie acted the celebrated *parades* in the presence of the marquise, who had rejoined her husband following her disgrace. Brother and sister formed a pair that soon became fashionable; they were invited everywhere. This period of high living provided Beaumarchais with a few furtive love affairs and even fewer friendships. As time went on, he became increasingly detached from the frivolity of wealth. In fact he never felt at home in that environment, in which everyone was out for what he could get. At least he could make fun of it, like his hero Jean Bête, and give the family trees of his illustrious hosts a hearty shake.

Not everyone found him amusing, however. A certain Chevalier des C–, whose full name hasn't come down to us, considered that he needed to be taught a lesson and, picking a quarrel with him, challenged him to a duel. They met outside the dauphin's gardens at Meudon, where Beaumarchais regretfully thrust his sword into his opponent's breast. Gudin relates the incident in his usual vein of heavy melodrama – the blood oozing from the chevalier's chest; Beaumarchais sorrowfully applying his handkerchief to stop the bleeding; the victim dying nobly with the sublime words: 'Leave me, *monsieur*. If you are seen, if people learn that you have taken my life, you are a doomed man.' Beaumarchais was greatly upset by this duel and didn't like talking about it, even though his part in the affair had been entirely honourable. The fateful incident was kept quiet. None the less the survivor preferred to inform first Mesdames and then the king, who pardoned him. He avoided fights in the future. To M. de Sablières, who picked a quarrel with him a few days later, he wrote: 'I hope to convince you that I am not looking for trouble; no one is more anxious than I must be at present to avoid conflict.' Beaumarchais never bragged about his victory, or about his skill with a sword.

Women found him less reluctant to enter the fray. It would be pointless, if not impossible, to list all his amorous conquests. The trouble is that failure in love leaves us more to go on than success does. No one writes much to a woman who puts up no resistance.

Beaumarchais wrote constantly to Pauline Le Breton because that determined young lady gave him a hard time. She was seventeen and owned a plantation in San Domingo. Orphaned in early childhood, she had been brought up by a series of uncles and aunts. She was no fool, and she knew her own mind – she wanted to get married. Although very fond of her handsome cousin, she wanted him all to herself; and that wasn't the way he saw things at all. Referring to this period of his life later on, he confessed: 'If I made women unhappy in those days, it was because each of them wished to be happy exclusively, when it seemed to me that in the immense garden called the world each flower was entitled to a glance from the fancier.'

All in all, he remained hesitant towards the lovely but exclusive Pauline. There was the matter of money, too. Beaumarchais was already quite wealthy, whereas the young lady's far-off fortunes were something of a mystery. Comparisons were made, accounts were prepared – initially at the request of Pauline, who asked Beaumarchais to look after her property. Her inheritance took the form of a large plantation valued at 2 million francs, but there was reason to believe that the place was deserted and mortgaged to the hilt. Since San Domingo was still a French possession, Beaumarchais wrote to the governor, M. de Clugny, requesting his assistance, and got Mesdames and two or three ministers to intervene for good measure. In the end he sent out a great deal of money and equipment to put the plantation back on its feet. He then dispatched a M. Pichon, a cousin of his mother's, to defend Pauline's interests on the spot and report back to him on the state of the plantation. In a word, he didn't do things by halves. I stress this point because it is generally believed that Beaumarchais's behaviour with regard to Pauline and her inheritance was motivated entirely by a desire to cash in. At the most, we can say that he was careful , and that before he invested money in this new venture he weighed the pros and cons, also seeking the advice of Pâris-Duverney.

They were in love, all the same, and remained in love for years. While Pichon was crossing the Atlantic and reaching San Domingo, and the engaged couple were attempting to arouse the interest of a doubtless wealthy uncle in their marriage, time passed. Some of their letters give the impression that the two young people remained rather coy – they kissed, held hands, played duets and so on. Yet these letters, most of which deal with business matters, along with a few shy tokens of affection, were probably written for the gallery. At seventeen, Pauline wasn't free to live and love as she chose. Other letters, very different in tone and sometimes ambiguous because they relate to events about which we know nothing, seem to me to indicate a great deal of intimacy and complicity. One of them appears to be fairly explicit. The shadow of Mme Gaschet, Pauline's strict guardian, falls across this page as we read:

> Cousin, I compliment you on your pleasures, with which I am acquainted and which would satisfy me perfectly if I were invited to share them. What do you lack, cousin? Haven't you got your Julie with you? Are you prevented from saying or thinking nasty things about your cousin? Doesn't the sly lawyer make you say often, 'Bad dog!' Cousin, pray for yourself. Since when have you been in charge of a parish? Has Julie already slept with you? Now there's something to be proud of, I must say. But who is this son-in-law my aunt mentions? Well, well. Julie is sleeping with you. If I weren't Beaumarchais, I should like to be Julie. Be patient, however.

Odd, to say the least. Mme Gaschet, who tended to fly into violent rages and would threaten to send Pauline to a convent at the slightest provocation, wouldn't, I think, have been very pleased to read such a letter.

Like Louis Latzarus, whose life of Beaumarchais was published in 1930, I think that the two cousins did more than hold hands. I agree that the letter he quotes is extremely compromising: 'Dear friend, I'm returning the shirt of yours I had. The parcel contains a handkerchief of mine which I ask you to use so that you can send back the one I forgot at your house yesterday. You can't doubt the sorrow I should feel if it were seen by your sisters . . . Sweet, cruel friend, when will you stop tormenting me and making me as unhappy as you do? My soul is vexed with you for it.'

Beaumarchais's destiny couldn't put up with this colonial languor for long. With help from a man called Clavijo, he was about to make a new mark for himself that would set tongues wagging throughout Europe.

4

Capa y Sombrero

Beaumarchais's eldest sister, Marie-Josèphe, was married to an architect by the name of Guilbert and lived in Madrid. Guilbert was slightly mad, so shortly after her marriage Marie-Josèphe asked her younger sister, Marie-Louise, known as Lisette, to join her in Madrid. The two women opened a dress shop as a sideline to life with the architect. Their life in Madrid was apparently uneventful and the family in Paris rarely heard from them. One day, however, M. Caron received the following letter from Marie-Josèphe: 'Lisette has been outrageously insulted by a man whose credit is as great as his perfidy. He has twice gone back on his word, when he was on the point of marrying her, without so much as an apology . . . The dishonour cast upon her by this event has forced us to abandon all social intercourse . . . All Madrid knows that Lisette is blameless. If only my brother . . .'

'If only my brother . . .' The SOS came through loud and clear at the end of February 1763. Yet Beaumarchais delayed his departure for two months and didn't arrive in the Spanish capital until 18 May. Why the delay? He had a highly developed sense of family honour and wasn't one to abandon a sister in trouble. At the same time he would never miss a chance to kill two or three birds with the same stone. When he left for Spain he carried with him recommendations from the highest authorities and, so it would seem, commissions in the sphere of politics and economics. This man who was received time and again by Charles III and the prime minister, Grimaldi, was no ordinary citizen. Furthermore, the trip was planned in detail at the Ecole Militaire by the two business partners.

Pâris-Duverney gave Beaumarchais 200,000 francs to cover his initial expenses, essentially for representation. The Treaty of Paris had just deprived France of most of India and Senegal, Canada and the left bank of the Mississippi. The right bank, Louisiana, had been hastily disposed of to Spain, but Choiseul and the king intended to recover the province in the near future by exploiting the links between the royal houses of France and Spain. The Treaty of Paris was signed on 10 February 1763. A few months later Beaumarchais was in Madrid. But before he did anything else he had to champion the cause of the wronged Lisette.

His account of his dealings with her infamous seducer, Don José Clavijo, is included in the fourth *Memoir* written ten years later, where it is undeniably written up, or rather dramatized, to obtain the maximum literary effect. All the same the account is essentially true, as is borne out by all the surviving documents, principally by those signed by Clavijo himself, which amount to as many confessions. There can be no doubt, however, that Lisette wasn't as pure, and Clavijo as villainous, as Beaumarchais makes out. Lisette, the 'innocent victim', was over thirty-three in 1764, while her seducer was the very opposite of a Don Juan. (The news that Clavijo was a man of letters won't surprise anyone – only a writer would have been foolish enough to stir up that particular hornet's nest and come back for more.) He was the editor of a very proper journal entitled *El Pensador* and earned his living as the king's archivist. In other circumstances he and Beaumarchais would undoubtedly have become the best of friends.

How did Clavijo, a man of some standing, come to fall for a penniless old maid, who may not even have been desirable? All we know is that he did, for he had already proposed to her *twice*.

Beaumarchais arrived in Madrid on 18 May. The very next day he knocked on Clavijo's door. The pretext for his visit was literature. Delighted, the *pensador* had his fellow-writer from France shown in, not knowing who he was. Beaumarchais immediately launched into a tale of misbegotten love which, in spite of the disguised names and situations, was really the story of Clavijo's affair with Lisette. The seducer's interest in his guest's narrative soon turned to anxiety as detail after detail fitted in with what he already knew. Before long he was in a terrible state: 'He was so surprised, so stupefied by my harangue that his jaw dropped and the words froze on his lips. His expression, at first radiant with my praise, gradually clouded over, his face fell and his complexion turned to lead.' But Beaumarchais wasn't through with him yet. After the *banderillas* and the *capa*, there came the moment of truth, the death. Beaumarchais writes:

'At the height of their sorrow, the eldest sister wrote a letter to France telling of the public outrage they had endured. This tale moved the heart of their brother to such a point that, having requested leave in order to attend to so complex a matter, he travelled post-haste from Paris to Madrid. I am that brother and I have abandoned everything – country, duty, family, work and pleasure – to come to Spain to avenge my innocent and unhappy sister. I come, bearing the arms of righteousness and determination, to unmask a traitor and engrave his soul on his face in streaks of blood. That traitor is you.'

After this *coup de théâtre*, executed with consummate artistry and narrated with the greatest skill, Clavijo had little choice. He fell on his knees and asked this sublime brother ('Ah, had I known she had a brother like you' and so on) for Lisette's hand in marriage for the third time. Beaumarchais refused. 'The time for that is past. My sister no longer loves you.' (Lisette had told him the day before that she was about to marry a newcomer to Madrid by the name of Durand.) Very self-assured, having rung for a lackey and ordered a cup of chocolate, the avenger forced the seducer to write a declaration which he, Beaumarchais, dictated.

This document, which Beaumarchais claimed to have kept, has disappeared. Are we, then, to doubt its authenticity, as most people do? I think not. If Beaumarchais, in 1774, in the middle of a lawsuit, chose to refer to this document and print its contents in the fourth *Memoir*, he really did possess it. Also, it seems that the old clockmaker saw the declaration. As Loménie points out in *Beaumarchais et son temps* (1856), he referred to it in his letter of 5 June: 'My dear Beaumarchais, how happy I am to be the father of such a son . . . Clavijo's declaration is a fine wedding present for her.' Yet it was far from certain, by the time M. Caron wrote his letter, that Lisette was going to marry Durand after all. Ten days after signing his confession the unpredictable Clavijo asked Beaumarchais, very officially, for his sister's hand in marriage. For the fourth time. The tragedy was turning into a farce.

Beaumarchais and, it would seem, the Comte d'Ossun, the French ambassador, put pressure on Lisette, who soon jilted poor Durand. Two days later, in fact, the star-crossed lovers fell into one another's arms and, to celebrate their reconciliation, signed a new contract expressing their intention to 'sanctify these promises by the sacrament of marriage as soon as possible'.

Curtain? Not a bit of it. Clavijo disappears. On 7 June, after a week of suspense, a panic-stricken attaché from the embassy arrives with a letter from the Comte d'Ossun: Clavijo has taken refuge in the military hospital and is afraid for his life, 'since a few days ago you forced him at pistol point, in his own house, to sign a paper in which he promised to marry your sister'. Beaumarchais is still reading the letter when an officer in the Walloon Guards enters and says: 'M. de Beaumarchais, you haven't a minute to lose. Leave Madrid or you will be arrested in your bed tomorrow morning.' Beaumarchais rushes off to the embassy, where Ossun in his turn urges him to cross the border as soon as he can.

The ambassador was talking to the wrong man. Beaumarchais, with what he called his 'old stout will', was not the kind to give in so easily. As Figaro says, 'the harder it is to succeed, the more you need to try'. By the following day, after winning the approval of two ministers, one of whom was Grimaldi, Beaumarchais was ushered into the presence of the king. Charles III listened, and made his decision: 'Whereupon the king . . . ordered that Clavijo should be dismissed from his post and banned from office for ever.'

There was still more to come, however. Shortly afterwards Beaumarchais received a letter from Clavijo asking him for the fifth time for Lisette's hand in marriage. ('Oh, *monsieur*, what have you done? Will you not have reason to reproach yourself eternally for having, on a whim, sacrificed a man who was in your power, just as he was about to become your brother?') In the margin Beaumarchais merely scribbled: 'You, my brother? I'd kill her first.'

That was his final answer to Clavijo, whose 'dishonour' didn't prevent him from continuing his honourable career in literature. He died in 1806. For Lisette there was always Durand, but her brother 'persuaded her to remain unmarried'. Unmarried she presumably remained. As a matter of fact no one knows what became of her. The convent? America? All that can be said with certainty is that she died before 1775, since her name doesn't appear on the list of relations who attended old M. Caron's funeral that year. Loménie, to whom I owe this piece of information, expresses his astonishment that 'the most famous of Beaumarchais's sisters is the one who has left the least trace'. Indeed the heroes of this incredible story were soon to become famous throughout Europe, when Goethe wrote a tragedy about them entitled *Clavigo*. And Marsollier, a fashionable author, came up with a comedy called *Norac et Javolci*. When Beaumarchais himself published the fourth *Memoir* containing the Clavijo saga – several thousand copies were printed – the Spanish court, the ministries concerned and the diplomats referred to raised no protest whatsoever, because the whole crazy story was true.

Let there be no mistake, however. Lisette's reputation was only the noble pretext for Beaumarchais's trip to Spain. Rather like a conjurer who draws attention to his right hand while his left hand is doing the real work, he deliberately emphasized his family activities in order to enjoy more freedom of movement in other spheres. He wrote to his father: 'I am working, writing, conferring, representing, fighting: that is my life.' His favourite spheres of action in 1764 appear to have been business and politics, the former in preference to the latter. That's how it seems anyway, though nothing relating to the eighteenth century is ever clear because everything was kept secret, particularly in the spheres haunted by Choiseul and Pâris-Duverney. Politics and business tended to overlap considerably in those days and I for one am convinced that Charles III and Grimaldi would not have given frequent audiences to an unknown young man of thirty-two if he had been concerned *solely* with business.

His principal mission was the most delicate one too, since it involved the negotiation of a twenty-year concession of Louisiana. The issue for France was to maintain some kind of presence in America pending a return to a more favourable situation. The plan that Beaumarchais submitted to the Spanish government provided for the founding of a Louisiana company similar to the Compagnie des Indes or the East India Company. In addition, Beaumarchais was supposed to negotiate a contract for the supply of Negro slaves throughout the Spanish colonies. Even though he accepted this distasteful commission, which was an intrinsic part of his mandate, there is no proof that he went through with it; indeed there is every reason to believe that he conveniently forgot it. As expected, Charles III refused to grant the concession. Louisiana was his finest colony, and to have leased it out to a foreign power would have dishonoured Spain. The French government knew this. In politics, however, it is often useful to sacrifice a pawn – and in 1764 Beaumarchais was that pawn. Later on he developed a taste for personal initiative in the service of his country; for the moment, however, he was condemned to play the role of go-between.

He was luckier in his bid for a slice of the Sierra Morena, an arid mountain region bordering on Andalusia. The Spanish Finance Minister agreed to consider his proposals for a joint venture in this region. Leaving nothing to chance, Beaumarchais commissioned an economic survey of the Sierra Morena. The points covered by his questionnaire read like a site survey for a modern factory: climate, resources, communications, local politics and so on. But he had reckoned without the lethargic indecisiveness of the Spaniards. The matter dragged on interminably. Beaumarchais therefore put forward a further proposal, again on behalf of the consortium that we might call Pâris-Duverney, Beaumarchais Inc. This was a bid for the supply of rations to the Spanish army throughout Spain, Majorca and Africa. Documents were signed, and the deal seemed to have gone through. All the same, Beaumarchais, as always, kept his head:

> I have just signed the agreement, entitling me to deal directly and personally with the Minister of War and Finance. The deal is the talk of Madrid; people are congratulating me as if it had gone through. I myself am perfectly aware that I haven't finished yet. For the moment I am saying nothing.
>
> Goodnight, dear father. Believe me, there is no reason for you to worry, one way or the other . . . I shall soon be thirty-three. At twenty-four, I was still in the shop. I am absolutely adamant that the next twenty years up to the age of fifty-five will result, after a long period of hard work, in the peace of mind that I had then, which in my opinion is not nearly as pleasant as when it is seen as a reward for the labours of youth . . .
>
> Goodnight, dear father. It is half-past eleven; I am going to drink some fern syrup, because for the past three days I have had a dreadful cold in the head. However, I am keeping myself well wrapped up in my Spanish cloak and I wear a good broad-brimmed hat. The Spanish call this attire *capa y sombrero*. When a man draws his cloak over his shoulder to hide part of his face, he is said to be *embossado*. I add this to my other precautions, and go about my business behind drawn blinds . . .

Beaumarchais's caution was well founded. The supplies deal, which was worth 20 million francs a year, fell through like the rest, thanks to Spanish indolence. If we were to rate this trip on the strength of these successive failures, we might be led to doubt Beaumarchais's skill as a negotiator. Once again, however, we should avoid jumping to conclusions. As we shall see, his credit with both Pâris-Duverney and the French government was higher after his trip than before. He must therefore have been entrusted with commissions about which both sides remained silent and which he fulfilled successfully.

In the space of a few months Beaumarchais had become the darling of Madrid society. Buturlin and Lord Rochford at the Russian and British embassies invited him to all their festivities. Festivities? Gambling for high stakes at faro, amateur dramatics (with Buturlin's wife cooing the role of Annette to Beaumarchais's Lubin in *Le Devin du Village*), and of course diplomatic representation. Lord Rochford remained a friend of Beaumarchais's and we shall be meeting him again later on.

There was also the Marquesa de Croix, who was Beaumarchais's accredited mistress throughout his stay in Madrid. This lady considered it her duty to second his cause at the highest level: for instance, she followed Charles III to bed without batting an eyelid. Her husband was a general and spent his time visiting garrisons, thereby enabling his wife to give full expression to her patriotic sentiments. I have neglected to mention that the marquesa, *née* Jarente, was a niece of the Bishop of Orleans, from whom Louis XV ordered his quince candy. She had remained French to the hilt. Interestingly, every time she received the royal favours Beaumarchais wrote off immediately to Choiseul to keep him informed. Needless to say, she was much more effective as an ambassador then the ambassador himself. The Comte d'Ossun was very proper.

The Marquesa de Croix was young, pretty and apparently very witty. Loménie discovered a medallion bearing her portrait in one of Beaumarchais's trunks years after his death. She adored Beaumarchais, in whom she had immediately recognized a kindred spirit. But the year was almost at an end. Beaumarchais was in a hurry to return to Paris, where his family, Pâris-Duverney and of course his boss, the Duc de La Vallière, were expecting him. It was to La Vallière that he dispatched the only serious letter he wrote while in Spain. It contained references to the Spanish legal system which must have made La Vallière blink with surprise, because they implied a natural inclination for protest and freedom of thought that no chief justice of France had probably ever encountered in one of his subordinates:

> Civil lawsuits in this country are encumbered by procedures even more complicated than ours, with the result that justice is so hard to come by that people resort to the courts with extreme reluctance. The manner in which cases are heard is literally the abomination and desolation predicted by Daniel. In civil actions, witnesses are sent to prison to be heard. Any honest man who happens to know that so-and-so is really a debtor or a legatee or a signatory or whatever is arrested and imprisoned at the start of the case, merely to declare what he knows or has heard . . . The rest follows the same pattern.

So it was to be home to his family, Pauline and Julie in particular. We mustn't forget Julie. The only love letter he received while he was in Spain begins: 'I feel such a need to love you today that I can only assuage it by writing you a long letter.' It is signed Julie. His bags contained several boxes of cocoa as a gift for his sister. She was mad about cocoa and mixed it with coffee to make a drink similar to the Italian *cappuccino*. Besides the cocoa, he brought home the characters of *The Barber of Seville*.

5

The Serious Sort

In 1765, having lived for a year *poco a poco*, Beaumarchais rediscovered *la vivacidad francesa*. And with it the hectic life of Paris. He felt 'such an agitation of soul, heart and mind' that he had to hold on to himself with both hands so as not to get lost in the labyrinth. While continuing to run his companies in Spain, or what was left of them, by mail, he had to push ahead with his personal and official business in Paris. He was no longer expected to process with the king's meat, having sold his comptrollership, but he remained a royal secretary – and he was still the indispensable companion of Mesdames. From Versailles he had to rush to the Ecole Militaire, where Pâris-Duverney found him equally indispensable. And thence to the Louvre to mete out justice to his poachers. (The days of the 'chamber pot' were over; he now had his own coach.)

   At the Louvre his inability to do things by halves and his passion for justice led him to issue in the space of a few months a series of directives designed to protect the peasantry against his over-zealous gamekeepers. In order to make his position clear to the tenants, he asked the parish priests under his jurisdiction to explain it to them: 'The inhabitants of the country must be convinced that the same court that punishes them when they are at fault . . . is at the same time concerned with protecting them from harassment, and punishes its keepers in their turn for stepping out of line.' Finally, to ensure that his directives were being complied with, he held public hearings in each parish. There was nothing extraordinary about any of this in itself, but I find it very revealing that Beaumarchais took so much trouble at a time when he was worked off his feet elsewhere. It is as if he was deliberately making things difficult for himself, leading five or six lives simultaneously. Figaro here, Figaro there? More of that later.

His family affairs and his love life were getting serious too. To begin with, he had to persuade his father to marry Mme Henry, which was no easy matter – not because the lady wasn't enthusiastic, but because M. Caron was playing hard to get. Mme Henry was sixty, even if she was still sprightly. M. Caron, who was eight years her senior, saw no reason why their understanding should be subjected to the test of wedlock. From Madrid, his son had tried to persuade him to take the plunge, but without sucess. The widow and widower had continued their eternal courtship, swapping aches and pains and weather reports along with sweet nothings. As soon as he got back to Paris, Beaumarchais set about jolting them out of their caution, their shyness, or rather their'fear of ridicule. Mme Henry became Mme Caron on 15 January 1766 – just in time, because two years later she was gone. M. Caron made less fuss about marrying for the third time, as we shall see later.

Tonton, alias Mlle de Boisgarnier, had different reasons for resisting the affections and desires of the unfortunate Miron. He was no fool, and his position as bursar of the convent of Saint-Cyr gave him a comfortable living; but he tended to be dogmatic and jesuitical in conversation and was rather irritating. Beaumarchais wrote: 'Yes, he plays the hurdy-gurdy, undeniably. His heels are half an inch too high. He sings out of tune. He eats raw apples in the evening and takes equally raw enemas in the morning. He is cold and didactic when he talks – or rather yelps.' All the same, having apparently had other hopes for his sister, Beaumarchais reluctantly sided with Miron.

So Tonton wed a year after her father's remarriage. Only two members of the family remained single: M. and Mlle de Beaumarchais. In Spain, Beaumarchais had not forgotten Pauline, despite the Marquesa de Croix, and he was probably prepared to marry her on his return. His interest in her had nothing to do with money, because Mlle Le Breton was now known to be broke. Cousin Pichon had found nothing but creditors and lawyers in San Domingo; the plantation was a dream, or at best a memory. Poor Pichon never made it back to France, as he succumbed to tropical fever. The money and merchandise sent out with him were lost. Beaumarchais still tried to see Pauline immediately upon his return from Spain, but she refused, giving him to understand that her feelings for him were no longer what they had been. In fact, as he soon discovered, Mlle Le Breton was virtually engaged to the Chevalier de Seguirand.

I hope you remember this young man from the colonies who was a constant visitor at the rue de Condé and a suitor of Julie's. According to Hervé Bromberger, the dedicatee of this book and one of Julie de Beaumarchais's fervent admirers, Bécasse played a highly ambiguous role in this affair. He claims that Julie, in order to hold on to her brother, encouraged Pauline to see Seguirand while he was away. I tend to agree. There can be no doubt that Julie didn't want Pierre-Augustin to marry Pauline. He would have gone off to San Domingo and she would never have seen him again. She had Seguirand to hand, ready to obey her every wish. She may even have seduced him to copy her brother. With Beaumarchais in Madrid, Julie had the cards stacked in her favour. She had all the trumps – and Seguirand. There is no proof, no letter to support this hypothesis, but Julie's exclusive love for her brother is not conjectural, it is a fact. And Pauline, even if she loved Pierre-Augustin, was no fool.

She sent him a farewell letter signed 'Le Breton'. There was no more to be said. All that remained for her to do was to marry Seguirand, which she did. A year later, she was a widow. When she later fell upon hard times, she wrote to him in a different tone, and he helped her, naturally. So this adventure, too, ended on a serious note.

To take his mind off this rebuff, Beaumarchais invented a new profession for himself – he became a forester. No backwoods for him, of course; he had to have a real forest or nothing. The Archbishop of Tours, who was short of money, decided to auction part of his forest of Chinon, totalling 2370 acres. With the assistance of his usual crony, Pâris-Duverney, Beaumarchais bought the forest for a very large sum of money. It is said that his first instalment amounted to 50,000 *écus*. He came back from Touraine in a pastoral mood, highly excited by the pleasant prospects offered by his acquisition. Unfortunately he remembered rather late in the day that the forestry code specifically barred royal hunt officials from taking part in such transactions. He therefore had to borrow someone else's name – and he made the terrible mistake of choosing his valet. This knave, Le Sueur by name, saw what his master's cheating could be worth to him and played for the jackpot. Before long the servant was the apparent master of Chinon, busily engaged in blackmailing

Beaumarchais for all he was worth. Seriously embarrassed, Beaumarchais confessed all to the Duc de La Vallière. The Grand Captain of the Hunt wasn't in the least shocked. He sided with his second-in-command and wrote to the chancellor, Maupeou. As usually happened in such cases, Maupeou sided with the master, and Le Sueur left Chinon for destinations unknown. If this affair strikes us as nasty, and it is, we shouldn't be too hard on Beaumarchais – after all, Le Sueur had deliberately robbed him. The nastiness was in the age, in its double-standard morality.

At any rate, Beaumarchais found peace and quiet and natural beauty in Touraine. When he writes from his house, Rivarennes, Rousseau is a near neighbour:

> I live at the office, which is a fine tough old farmhouse with hens on one side and cabbages on the other, and a quick-set hedge round it. My chamber, whose tapestries are four whitewashed walls, is furnished with an uncomfortable bed, upon which I sleep like a log, four straw chairs, an oak table, and a big fireplace with no mantel or any kind of decoration. But from my window I can see as I write all the copses and meadows of the valley in which I live, full of sturdy, brown-skinned men who are cutting fodder and carting it home with teams of oxen. A host of women and girls with rakes over their shoulders or in their hands are singing shrilly as they work, and their song reaches my table . . . This picture is not without charm. My meals consist of good country bread, very simple food and execrable wine.

As regards the wine he was romancing, because we know from other letters how much he enjoyed the local Vouvray. As always, this venture absorbed all his interest: he built roads, erected locks to make the River Indre navigable all the year round, set up a system of carts and barges to transport his wares to Tours, Saumur, Angers and Nantes. He was never still when he was in his forest. And if the shutters were closed at Rivarennes, they were closed because he was in Paris, at the Louvre, at the Ecole Militaire, at the house in the rue de Condé or at Versailles. A devil of a man; yet, compared with what his life was shortly to become, in 1766 he was living in slow motion.

Needing a new valet to replace Le Sueur, Beaumarchais engaged what the eighteenth century called a blackamoor. He called him by his name, which was Ambroise Lucas. But before Ambroise had had time to settle down in his new job he was removed from the rue de

Condé under the pretext that he belonged to a M. Chaillon, and was thrown into prison. Whereupon Beaumarchais grabbed a pen and wrote the following letter to the head of the Colonial Office. The Figaro of the monologue, who protests, who fights back, and who is soon shaking the very foundations of his age, is just around the corner.

> A poor boy by the name of Ambroise Lucas, whose only crime is to have almost as dark a skin as most of the free men of Andalusia and naturally curly hair, large black eyes and very handsome teeth – all of which is perfectly excusable – has been put in prison at the request of a man a little whiter than he going by the name of M. Chaillon, whose right of ownership over the darker man was approximately the same as that acquired by the Israelite merchants over the young Joseph once they had bought him from those who had no right to sell him. But our religion has sublime principles that fit in admirably with the colonial policy. All men with brown, fair or sandy hair are brothers throughout the Christian world. In Paris, London and Madrid, no one is put in harness; but in the Antilles and throughout the western world, as soon as you have the honour of being white you may harness your dark brother to a plough to instruct him in the Christian religion, all to the greater glory of God. If all is good in the universe, to my mind it is so only for the white man, since he has the whip hand.

Beaumarchais was not one to be content with writing letters or signing petitions. Ambroise Lucas's predicament upset him greatly, so he acted. It was an easy matter to buy off Chaillon, but it wasn't so easy to halt the legal proceedings. To get Lucas out of prison, he didn't hesitate to draw upon his credit with La Vallière, Choiseul and the princesses. Who ever made such a fuss about an impoverished Negro valet?

Most people were amazed by his determined stand on this apparently unimportant issue. But it won him the respect and friendship of several great men – the Prince de Conti, for instance, who as we shall see stood by Beaumarchais later on in his darkest hour. The two men had met in rather similar circumstances some time before the Lucas kerfuffle. Louis-François de Bourbon, Prince de Conti, the king's cousin, had ordered the demolition of a wall which, in Gudin's words, 'impeded him in his pleasures'. The peasant who had *dared* to build the wall *dared* to complain when it was demolished and brought a suit against Conti that was to be heard by Beaumarchais. A few days before the case was due to come before the court, Beaumarchais was 'advised' politely but firmly that a yokel's chicken run was not worth the anger of Conti. The judge saw red, rushed to see Conti and blurted out that justice would be done – he was in the wrong and he would have to pay. Conti listened to what his visitor had to say, and took him in his arms.

Beaumarchais, who felt nothing but scorn for his *parades*, had been dreaming for some time of writing a real play. *Eugénie*, which he probably began in 1759, wasn't completed until eight years later. Why so long? He *worked* at it. In *Beaumarchais et ses œuvres* (1887) Linthilac lists 'seven different manuscripts, each heavily corrected'. In other words, bursts of enthusiasm alternated with phases of discouragement and anxiety. The point is that the author of *Jean Bête* found it extremely hard to write 'straight'. In the early versions of *Eugénie*, drama sometimes alternates with farce. Beaumarchais couldn't help being funny, and had to force himself to keep a straight face. Yet incredibly enough, it was the serious style he was after. Before we smile, however, we should note that his tussles with straight drama taught him a thing or two; and I believe in all sincerity that this retrograde step wasn't entirely fruitless, in that it took him away from his usual self. The sublime monologue in *The Marriage of Figaro* is perhaps the most serious tirade in all French drama, if only we know how to read it.

But back to *Eugénie*. Beaumarchais would probably have shelved it uncompleted if the productions of Diderot's *Fils naturel* and *Père de Famille* and the success of Sedaine's *Philosophe sans le savoir* hadn't encouraged him to persist in this vein. The theme of *Eugénie* is not original – a girl seduced by a libertine aristocrat, a false marriage and so on – but Beaumarchais may be regarded as an innovator in so far as he took a certain kind of realism further than any of his predecessors. For example, Eugénie is pregnant by Clarendon; in the closing scene Beaumarchais makes her say: 'Go, you deserve to vanquish, your pardon is in my womb', and she accompanies her daring phrase with an even more daring gesture – a stage direction in one of the manuscripts reads, 'Beware of this gesture.'

A few months before the play opened at the Comédie Française, Beaumarchais had to revise his text yet again to satisfy the whims of the censor, a man named Marin. (We shall be meeting M. Marin again shortly – the eighteenth century was a small world.) As submitted to the censor, the play was set in Brittany, in a manor house. Marin ruled that so scandalous an affair was unthinkable in France, so Beaumarchais had to transfer his setting to Great Britain, where such things were apparently thinkable. At the same time he invited opinions and criticisms and gave many readings. His preferred critics were dukes, because dukes could fill a theatre for you and because he was on the best of terms with several of them. The advice he was given was sensible, as can be judged from the remarks of the Duc de Nivernais, king's minister, peer of the realm and member of the Académie Française. He produced several pages of highly pertinent suggestions, and Beaumarchais immediately took them into account a week before the play was due to open. But despite all these rewrites and revises, the first night of *Eugénie* was a flop.

In the weeks preceding 29 January, the date fixed for the play's opening, Beaumarchais was all over the Comédie Française, from the flies to the orchestra pit. He had a hand in everything – front of house, sets, lights, production, publicity. He even found time to invent improvements to the stage machinery. Those who knew Jean Cocteau at rehearsals will imagine what Beaumarchais was like when he was let loose in a theatre. Cocteau, too, was alleged by fools to be a jack-of-all-trades; but Cocteau was a sluggard compared with Beaumarchais. For instance, he wasn't, as well as all the rest, a clockmaker, musician, banker, judge, diplomat, or even a forester. And in 1767 Beaumarchais was only just beginning.

The cast was a good one. Eugénie was played by Mlle Doligny, La Clairon's rival. Later on, Beaumarchais would choose Doligny for the role of Rosine. The celebrated Préville, the great seducer of the stage (and elsewhere), was Clarendon. Préville was a friend of Beaumarchais's; in *The Barber* he would play Figaro and in *The Marriage* Brid'oison.

As I have pointed out, the audience didn't like the play. The last two acts were greeted with what is euphemistically called 'displeasure'. Baron Grimm, the unbearable Baron Grimm, a powdered, rouged, evil-minded dwarf, whose opinions could make or break a budding author, destroyed *Eugénie* utterly and dismissed Beaumarchais with a sneer: 'This man will never achieve anything, not even mediocrity. There is only one good line in his play . . . It is so good, and sounds so unlike the rest, that I wager it is not by the author of the play.'

Booed on the twenty-ninth, *Eugénie* was cheered on the thirty-first.
Between times, Beaumarchais, who wasn't the sort of man to go
under for long, entirely rewrote the last two acts, as he did with *The
Barber* later on. The respected critic Fréron wrote in *L'Année littéraire*:
'*Eugénie*, which opened on January 29, was rather poorly received and
gave all the signs of being a failure. Since then, the play has recovered brilliantly, thanks to cuts and corrections; it has been very
successful and its success is an honour to our actors.' *Eugénie* was
performed initially on seven consecutive nights – which was
remarkable in those days – and has been performed two hundred
times since, not at all bad going in the annals of the Comédie
Française. Beaumarchais's first play was soon translated and produced in most of the cities of Europe, where it went down even better
than in Paris. It was published at home and abroad in innumerable
editions. So it is quite wrong to state that *Eugénie* was a semi-failure.

True, Beaumarchais did everything he could to keep Eugénie's
head above water and have her talked about. A few days after the
first night he published an *Essay on the Drama*, which caused quite a
stir. It purports to make out a reasoned case for the drama as against
classical tragedy, but it was in fact a defence of his own play – and
good publicity into the bargain. The *Essay* was apparently written at
a single sitting. It owes much to Diderot and is very uneven, but it is
held together by a quite remarkable liveliness of style. People will
read anything if the writer has talent.

Some commentators have seen the plot of *Eugénie* as being based on the
Clavijo affair. I can't agree. Apart from the fact that the early versions of
Eugénie antedate the trip to Spain, the considerable psychological differences between Eugénie and Lisette seem to me to exclude any notion of
transposition. Furthermore, Lisette was no longer young; and she had
Durand. This is not to deny the odd fleeting resemblance between actual
and imagined experience; but that happens in any book and with any
author. With a little trouble, you could discover in your dictionary traces
of the private lives of our great lexicographers, if only in their choice of
quotations, which are sometimes confessions. Similarly, I don't think
there is much point in discussing the word *drame* and carping over
whether Beaumarchais was, or wasn't, the first person to use the term in
reference to a play and what he meant by it. Games like that seem pretty
sterile when you're passionately involved in every hour of the life of a man
who wasn't at his best when he was philosophizing.

A Mme Buffault, who was born in a kitchen and who died of smallpox in rooms at the opera house (having married the man who ran it), was a frequent visitor at the Beaumarchais home in the rue de Condé. The memorialist Bachaumont wrote of her (1777): 'She took great trouble with her looks, and sought to appear striking. She wanted to rise in the world, so she formed a kind of society of artists, wits and writers and she attempted to cover up her origins by affecting foppishness.' According to Gudin, Mme Buffault had sworn to find Beaumarchais a second wife, and she arranged a meeting with an 'amiable widow' on the Champs-Elysées. Beaumarchais appeared at the appointed hour mounted on a superb chestnut, with his man a few paces behind on a more modest mount: the beauty of the steed, the grace of the horseman and so on. A few months later, on 11 April 1768, Beaumarchais married the amiable widow. Fiddlesticks! I don't believe a word of Gudin's romance. Only the date of the marriage is correct; for the rest, here are the facts.

Geneviève-Madeleine Watebled, born in 1731, had married in 1754 a M. Lévêque, who was Master of the Wardrobe at the Revels Office. Her first husband had died on 21 December 1767. December to April is four months – so Gudin would have us believe that Mme Lévêque was out hunting for a new husband with the old one barely two months in his grave. Why the hurry? Why should a woman well known in society, whom we also know to have been respectable and reserved, behave so scandalously? And why should Beaumarchais have lent himself to such a ridiculous scheme? Why didn't he leave a decent interval between the funeral and the wedding – nine months, say? Gudin answers none of these questions and clearly doesn't want them to be asked. Manifestly, there was a reason behind this hasty marriage. The reason was this: eight months later, the couple had a child.

Gudin doesn't mention the birth, out of discretion. Instead he invented the romantic meeting on the Champs-Elysées (or Beaumarchais did) to protect the reputation and memory of Geneviève, an honest woman. She was clearly Beaumarchais's mistress during her husband's lifetime. The ceremony held on 11 April 1768 was just for the record. Yet they were genuinely in love, and the birth of their son, Augustin, added to their pleasure. Fatherhood had been an *idée fixe* with Beaumarchais for a long while, and family life seemed a happy prospect when viewed in the light of his memories of the rue Saint-Denis. Yet the women he desired, and he desired and had many, were not always fit to be mothers, whereas the women he married – decent women whom he respected – he didn't always desire. But his longing for fatherhood was quite extraordinary. He wrote: 'Become fathers; you must; nature makes this a law sweet to obey . . . Become fathers; you must. This cherished, sublime truth cannot be repeated too often to us men.' I for one find this exhortation from the lecher surprising, to say the least. But was he really a lecher? In dissipation as in virtue, Beaumarchais is never a clearcut case.

Geneviève was thirty-seven when she became the first Mme de Beaumarchais. (Poor Madeleine Francquet had had to make do with Caron at her wedding.) It would be true to say that Geneviève was socially a cut above Madeleine: her father was a carpenter and an alderman of the city of Paris, a man of some civic importance; and her first husband had been extremely wealthy. (Geneviève inherited most of his fortune in the form of an annuity.)

After their marriage M. and Mme de Beaumarchais set up house on an estate they acquired in the neighbourhood of Pantin, just outside Paris, keeping on the house in the rue de Condé (in which they occupied the whole of the first floor) as their town residence. Geneviève's health was poor, and she was pregnant. So it was decided that she should spend as much time as possible in the country – and Pantin in those days was the back of beyond. Pierre-Augustin came home every evening after an exhausting day's work in Paris. He was a model husband at this point. Gudin claims that never, on any pretext whatsoever (except for his trips to Chinon), did he spend a night away from home; not once did he sleep in a separate room from his wife, not once in a separate bed. The serious sort, I tell you.

Was it because his family life led him to neglect his connections at court that he fell out with Louis XV? I think not. The quarrel seems unimportant and inconsequential; but Beaumarchais thought it worth writing about, and referred to its cause as *A Joke that poisoned ten Years of my Life*, which is the title of his piece describing the incident. La Vallière, who was down for Good Friday supper with the king and Mme du Barry in the private rooms at Versailles, asked

Beaumarchais to slip him a few witty remarks to jolly along the proceedings. The Lieutenant-General of the Hunt expressed doubts as to his ability to be witty to order, but the duke, his captain, insisted. The lieutenant came up with two jokes. La Vallière greedily demanded a third. In the end Beaumarchais, who was generally more inspired, came up with a feeble and complicated joke proving that Louis XV owed more *livres* than there were minutes since the first Good Friday.

That same evening, La Vallière duly joked. But he was so preoccupied with remembering the punch line that he neglected to watch the king's reactions so that he could, if necessary, tone the joke down. Told by Beaumarchais, who knew exactly how to go too far, it would certainly have passed, but the duke was nowhere near as gifted a *raconteur*. Louis XV, who didn't care to be reminded of his debts on a Good Friday, and who must have been feeling particularly morose, said flatly: 'This pleasantry reminds us of the skeleton that was allegedly served among the fruit and flowers at banquets in ancient Egypt to temper the guests' exuberance. Did you think it up yourself, La Vallière?' The duke, horrified by the royal reaction to his borrowed fable, promptly named its real author. Louis XV took a long time to forget 'that clockmaker's arithmetic'.

In point of fact, this rather ludicrous incident resulted in Beaumarchais's losing the friendship of the royal family, but it didn't affect his social position. If the dauphin had still been alive (he had died after a long illness), Beaumarchais would probably have been able to make up the ground that he had lost in the affections of the king and Mesdames, because the 'saint' appreciated the frankness and insolence of the former clockmaker. In fact the more I think of it, the more I believe that Beaumarchais's true protector at Versailles was the dauphin. After his death, the attitude of Mesdames suddenly changed.

With the death of Mme de Pompadour in 1764 he had lost another valuable ally, even though her 'exile' had diminished her influence. But the time for excessive protection as a result of his youth and charm was over, and the moment had come for him to prove his personal worth. It was to his intelligence alone that he owed the friendship of the powerful head of the police, Sartines, and to his genius in politics that of Vergennes.

For the moment his only thought was for his son Augustin, born on 14 December 1768. During a stay at his farm, he ended a letter to his wife, written before going to bed ('Without you, unfortunately'), in the following terms: 'And my son, my son! How is he? I laugh when I think that I am working for him.' Augustin was all of six months: there was no time to lose!

It may well have been for Augustin's sake that Beaumarchais finally bethought himself of settling up with Pâris-Duverney. The banker was eighty-six and though still very alert, he was by no means in the pink of health. The most disinterested bystander could have seen that he was slowly sinking. As so often in partnerships governed more by emotion than by anything else, there was nothing between Beaumarchais and Pâris-Duverney – no agreement, no contract, no IOU. Yet the two men dealt in millions, and they had sunk money into countless ventures. Only they knew where they stood in this confused and complex situation. Negligence? Not a bit of it: deliberate mystification. We shall never know the whole truth about their activities, because their secrets followed them into the grave. All the same, I feel sure that politics was just as important a factor in their dealings as economics or trade. Beaumarchais in fact admits as much indirectly in a letter to the Duc de Noailles written before the opening of *Eugénie*:

> Another of my follies, which I have been forced to abandon, is the study of politics . . . I was mad about it: I read, wrote, travelled, observed, made every sacrifice for politics . . . No one, perhaps, has fretted as much as I have at not being able to see small, when I am the smallest of men. At times, indeed, I have gone so far as to grumble, in a moment of injustice, because fate hadn't placed me in a better position to accomplish the things for which I felt I was destined, especially when I considered how the mission given to their agents by kings and ministers cannot be expected to endow them with the grace of the ancient apostles, that grace which at once turned the utterest dullard into a man of sublime wisdom.

What *does* he mean by all this persiflage? What activities is he referring to? 'I made every sacrifice for politics,' he writes, at a time when to all appearances he hadn't even started his political career, and he says so to the Duc de Noailles, who must have been aware of the fact. Beaumarchais knew what he was up to. Ministers and kings agreed to see him; soon they would listen to him as well, as they had seen and listened to Pâris-Duverney before him. But what the banker had taken as fun and games became Beaumarchais's *raison d'être*, his main ambition and a decisive way of making his mark in a system that had excluded him at the outset. It is this broader view that illuminates the political activities that Beaumarchais embarked on with Pâris-Duverney before beginning his solo run, rather than the intriguing enigmas of their 'oriental' correspondence, which in itself proves nothing.

Business and politics have their secrets, but so has friendship. If Pâris-Duverney and Beaumarchais were forced to hide their professional thoughts behind a puerile code, they needed to watch out as well for the Comte de La Blache – a character of stature who must be introduced here with deference. If it hadn't been for La Blache, the whole course of Beaumarchais's life (and perhaps his fame) would have been different. La Blache was evil: formidable and yet fascinating. Of all Beaumarchais's opponents, he was probably the only one who was a match for him. Theirs was a strange battle; their relationship was stranger still. The count said of Beaumarchais, 'I hate that man as a lover loves his mistress.' And Beaumarchais said, later: 'He was the father of all my sorrows.' For once his prefacer and critic La Harpe is right: the strangeness, the madness of La Blache cannot be explained rationally. But slowly does it: the smallest detail in this fantastic ten-year quarrel is important, and counts as much as the basic facts.

Pâris-Duverney had no children, merely a nephew, Jean-Baptiste Pâris du Meyzieu, and a grand-niece, born Michel de Roissy, who was the wife of Alexandre-Joseph Falcoz, Comte de La Blache.

In 1765 the banker drew up his will, disinheriting Meyzieu and leaving everything to his grand-niece, of whom he was fond. This measure was very unfair to Meyzieu, who at that time held the rank of colonel and who had helped his uncle considerably with the building of the Ecole Militaire. A distinguished scholar, he had written several laudatory articles about the banker's activities. But Meyzieu was old and rich; Pâris-Duverney no doubt felt that his immense fortune would be more useful to his niece, hence to La Blache. Beaumarchais also mentions a quarrel between uncle and nephew that he tried to patch up, though we don't know what it was about.

Early in 1770 Pâris-Duverney and Beaumarchais settled their

accounts by means of a private agreement signed by both parties in duplicate. The agreement recapitulated the position of each partner, item by item, and set out the terms of the settlement. Beaumarchais refunded the banker to the tune of 160,000 *livres* and allowed him to withdraw from their partnership in the forestry development at Chinon. In his turn, Pâris-Duverney discharged Beaumarchais of all debts towards him, acknowledged a debt of 15,000 francs upon which Beaumarchais might draw at will, and promised a loan of 75,000 francs for a period of eight years. This private agreement was intended to protect both parties from any actions that might be brought by their respective heirs. In fact the person that it was meant to nail was La Blache. He was the one they distrusted, and with reason: he pointedly ignored Beaumarchais whenever he met him – and their paths crossed daily, at the Ecole Militaire, at court and in town. Pâris-Duverney was mightily worried by such behaviour, but he thought that the private agreement was sufficiently clear to protect his 'son' against the hatred of his grand-nephew. He couldn't have been more wrong. In life people are less virtuous than they tend to be in Beaumarchais's early writings.

At this same moment in time his drama *The Two Friends* was on at the Comédie Française. It had opened on 13 January 1770, exactly three years after the first night of *Eugénie*. Encouraged by the success of his first play, Beaumarchais had almost immediately set to work on a second; as with *Eugénie*, however, he had to go through many rewrites before he was satisfied. Six manuscripts of *The Two Friends* are known to exist, under different titles. This time round, he was after the perfect plot. Towards the end of his life he said that the structure of *The Two Friends* was better than that of any of his other works. I almost agree with him.

It is impossible to summarize *The Two Friends*, with its inextricable network of thwarted love affairs and business upheavals. The action, grouped around five main characters, takes place on several different levels at the same time. It is a play about bankers, virtuous bankers. Their nobleness, their generosity and their spirit of sacrifice overwhelm us lesser mortals. Yet the audience never loses the thread in this monstrous maze. Having jumbled up the pieces of his jigsaw puzzle, the author puts them back together again without forgetting a single one. It's all very clever. All the same, despite its clockwork precision and numerous passages in which the writing is remarkable (much more self-assured than in *Eugénie*), *The Two Friends* is an outright failure, because the characters are mere puppets and because their tribulations with drafts, bills and certificates are, to say the least, unbeguiling.

The play had a bad press. Baron Grimm signed Beaumarchais's death warrant for a second time: 'It was preferable to make good watches than to buy an office at court, play the bully and write bad plays.' Fréron was just as severe, but at least he held out hope for the future: 'As long as M. de Beaumarchais restricts himself to this narrow style . . . I advise him not to court the honours of the stage.'

His latest play may have flopped, but the drama that was about to open in his life ran for several years. Death made its comeback, and struck twice before curtain up.

Pâris-Duverney died on 17 July, without having had time to meet the two clauses of the private agreement that were in Beaumarchais's favour. La Blache, his sole heir, inherited 1,500,000 francs and a considerable amount of property. Beaumarchais must have been very upset, but he wasn't one to make a show of grief, except behind the footlights. For the time being his thoughts were far from La Blache and his machinations. In the wings, death was already rehearsing its second entrance.

Geneviève, weakened by a miscarriage, fell suddenly ill. Her doctors soon diagnosed 'a long and fatal illness' that was probably tuberculosis. Their treatment was what treatment was in those days: virtually non-existent. To make the patient sleep and stop her coughing, they gave her poppy. Beaumarchais was in despair and stayed at his wife's side constantly. At night he would lie beside her, listening anxiously to her breathing. M. Caron and Julie took fright, imagining that he might contract Geneviève's illness and follow her to the grave. They appealed to Dr Tronchin, who hit upon the idea of visiting his patient very early in the morning. Finding Beaumarchais lying next to Geneviève, he pretended to fly into a rage and 'reproached him violently for his lack of consideration for a poor woman who dared neither cough nor complain and was in agony for fear of waking him'. Pierre-Augustin saw through the conspiracy, but he did agree to have a camp bed made up in the room. Despite Julie's entreaties and the warnings from the doctors, who feared he might inhale the 'diseased miasmas', he remained at Geneviève's bedside. She died on 14 December 1770, leaving him totally distraught.

His wife's death, coming straight after that of Pâris-Duverney, left him in the direst of straits. Geneviève's fortune, as we have seen, was tied up in the form of a life annuity. Beaumarchais therefore had to work night and day to straighten out his finances rapidly. Don't forget he had his son to think of. And he'd sworn to make the boy rich.

In his grief, he met two men who soon became his friends and did their best to help him out. One was Gudin de la Brenellerie, whom we've already met, who came to the rue de Condé to read *La Napliade*, his epic poem in rhyming couplets, and who stayed on ever after, a Boswell to the un-Johnsonlike Beaumarchais; and the other was the extraordinary Duc de Chaulnes, whom we shall be meeting again a few pages hence.

For the moment we must return to La Blache, who was positively exulting over Beaumarchais's misfortunes. The thought of attacking his enemy at a time when he was on his knees made him quite beside himself. Hatred – and love? – sent him rushing into action.

6

The Devil

LA BLACHE

The outbreak of hostilities between La Blache and Beaumarchais coincided with the end of a momentous war that had lasted for three hundred years. Louis XV had dissolved parliament. This is no place to examine the whys and wherefores of the king's decision. But as Beaumarchais was seriously affected by the dismissal of the old parliament and the installation of the Maupeou parliament in its stead, we must rapidly review the facts.

In the face of systematic parliamentary opposition, Louis XV had angrily issued an edict setting forth his prerogative: 'We receive our crown from God alone. The right to make laws to lead and govern our subjects appertains to us alone, without dependency and without participation' (3 December 1770).

Since the king could always overrule the Paris parliament or the provincial parliaments, the edict undermined the principle of parliamentary control via 'remonstration'. In fact the king's decree amounted to telling the members of parliament that he meant to have the first and last word in all their debates. His proclamation also put an end to the speculations of those who felt that the time had come for the absolute monarchy to be mitigated by reforms – Choiseul, for instance, who was dismissed from his post as prime minister on 24 December 1770, three weeks after the edict, the terms of which he disapproved of. Though his dismissal deprived parliament of its main supporter, the assembly persisted in its opposition to the king, refusing to endorse a measure that implied the loss of honour, liberty, property rights, and perhaps life, for the people with no opportunity to defend themselves. Louis XV broke this deadlock on 3 January 1771 by ordering each member of parliament individually to sign the decree. When they refused, parliament was dissolved and Chancellor Maupeou was appointed to form another one that

would be more obedient, which he promptly did. Louis XV had
strengthened his authority, but he had lost Choiseul.

The Choiseul faction was also the Beaumarchais faction. Nivernais, Orléans, Conti and Lenormant d'Etioles wore the colours of
the exiled minister and the dissolved parliament. In the pitched
battle that Beaumarchais waged against La Blache, they remained
loyal to their friend. Politically the Comte de La Blache, who had
been promoted to the rank of brigadier-general, was on the other side
of the fence – which may explain why his quarrel with Beaumarchais developed into an affair of State and shook the kingdom to its
very foundations. We shall see later on how Beaumarchais, virtually
single-handed, put M. Maupeou's parliament down for the count.

La Blache dispensed with the preliminaries and came out of his
corner fighting. Having been presented by Beaumarchais's lawyer
with the deed under private seal, the count replied that he didn't
recognize the deceased person's signature.

It sounds easy, but whoever thought of it was no fool. La Blache
was no fool. If the agreement was a fake, Beaumarchais wasn't a
minor creditor of the estate, but a major debtor. La Blache was
delivered of this clever little brainchild by a specialist in crooked
causes, the lawyer Caillard.

It is hard to imagine Beaumarchais, who was far from broke,
risking his reputation for a mere 15,000 francs when he still had his
house in the rue de Condé and his forest at Chinon, and forging the
signature of a man he had loved passionately. It is easy, on the other
hand, to imagine the immensely rich La Blache inheriting a million
and haggling over a paltry sum due to his late great-uncle's partner.
But the money was only a secondary motive in this affair. The major
motivation was blind hatred, as La Blache himself freely admitted.
It was hatred, together with a kind of genius for evil and a diabolical
gift for trickery, that led La Blache to surpass himself.

There was nothing Beaumarchais could do but sue. From the
correspondence it is clear that he hesitated before reluctantly deciding to go to court – not for the money, but for his honour. As he was a
magistrate, he was able to summon La Blache before a special court
which sat in a room next to his own at the Louvre. The preliminary
hearings were dragged out by a series of legal manoeuvres invented
by La Blache and his bent lawyer – a summons for forgery and every

injunction in the book. The count made no attempt to hide what he was up to: 'Ten years, it will take him ten years to get his money – and I'll have spent those ten years blackening his name in every way I can.'

The Prince de Conti, who canvassed the *salons* for his friend, invented a slogan: 'Beaumarchais will be paid or hanged.' Sophie Arnould, the famous opera singer, who had finally fallen for Beaumarchais after holding back for a while, added, 'If he's hanged, the rope will break.' And the man himself pointedly remarked: 'If I win, don't you think my opponent should pay on the gallows?' The situation hadn't yet come to a head and his friends still saw his lawsuit as a subject they could joke about.

They were underestimating La Blache. The dashing brigadier-general was by no means wasting his time. At Versailles and in Paris, aided and abetted by the legions of those who had been offended by Beaumarchais's success and glamour, he was busily spreading rumours about his opponent. Hadn't he been caught stealing from his father as a boy? Mightn't he have poisoned his wives for the inheritance? Hadn't he been accused of cheating at the tables while in Spain? The count was careful to do no more than insinuate, and Beaumarchais couldn't catch Bazile red-handed or find witnesses because the two of them didn't frequent the same *salons*. Unfortunately the only time he got a chance to prove that La Blache was a liar and a slanderer, he slipped up.

Adding chapter after chapter to his daily fictions, the count had just invented the story that Mesdames had 'banned Beaumarchais from their presence', and that his informant had been given to understand by Mme Victoire that the reason for the ban was 'a host of dishonourable peculiarities'. Beaumarchais got wind of this latest slander. Feeling sure he could demonstrate that it was untrue, he jumped at the chance to stop La Blache in his tracks and alerted Mesdames.

Mme Victoire immediately gave him the answer he was expecting, via a lady-in-waiting called the Comtesse de Périgord:

> I have informed Mme Victoire of your letter and have received her assurance that she has never said anything to anyone that might harm your reputation, for she knows nothing about you that might have placed her in a position to do so. She has authorized me to tell you so. The Princess added that she was aware that you were involved in a

lawsuit, but that her references to you could never harm you in any way, especially in a lawsuit, and that you should have no anxiety on this score.

With the hearing only a few days away, this testimonial was very important to Beaumarchais, as it proved La Blache's extreme bad faith and exposed him as a slanderer. But how could he use it? There was no time to show the letter round, so instead he wrote a pamphlet containing the princess's reply. Before printing it, he thought it just as well to inform the Comtesse de Périgord of his intentions: 'I have the honour to enclose a pamphlet in which I have used, as permitted by Mme Victoire, the justice she has deigned to render me and the letter with which you have honoured me.' This was a momentous blunder. Beaumarchais, who was new to airs and graces and always played etiquette by ear (usually without striking a wrong note), failed to appreciate the impropriety of involving the princesses in his lawsuit. Mesdames put their displeasure in writing: 'We declare that we take no interest in M. Caron de Beaumarchais and his affair; and we did not permit him to insert in a printed and public pamphlet any assurances of our protection.'

With only five days to go before the court pronounced its verdict, La Blache realized what a godsend the princesses' declaration could be. Before Beaumarchais had even collected his pamphlet from the printer's, the count had the royal rebuff printed up by the ream. It was all over Paris within hours. With only the short, blunt denial to go on, many people began to wonder. If he could deceive the princesses, he might well have forged a signature. It was child's play for La Blache to exploit this new situation, particularly as his opponent, aghast, didn't even dare produce Mme de Périgord's letter proving him right as to the essentials. Fortunately for him, he had had the wit to show the countess's missive to the bench before La Blache published the denial: they, at least, knew what was what in the matter, and that was the main thing.

Since the hearing had begun in the autumn of 1771, Caillard had proved himself to be a virtuoso performer on the wind bag. He had argued successively that the signature was a fake; that the signature was genuine but anterior to the deed; that the deed was a fake; that the deed was genuine, as was the signature, but that the two were unconnected; that Pâris-Duverney was of unsound mind when he signed; that the absence of a duplicate proved that the original was a fake (the duplicate was attached to the will, so it must have been filched by La Blache); and so on. Beaumarchais had answered all of this in a tone of outraged virtue, like one of the characters in *The Two Friends*, not having learned yet that to beat Bazile you have to be a Figaro. None the less, he had managed to demolish each of La Blache's arguments one after the other.

In February, when the case had dragged on for six months and after the publication of Mesdames's disavowal of their protégé, La Blache and Caillard decided to pull out all the stops. The evidence included a letter from Beaumarchais to Pâris-Duverney dated 5 April 1770, which summarized the agreement into which they were about to enter. On the back of the letter Pâris-Duverney had written: 'Now we are quits.' This laconic phrase, together with the date of the letter, proved the authenticity of the deed signed a few days later. Caillard and La Blache hit upon the idea proving that the 'Now we are quits' referred to another matter and that Beaumarchais had used the sheet of paper *after* the event to support his claim: the recto had become the verso and vice versa. To prove that the side bearing the words 'Now we are quits' was originally the recto, Caillard drew attention to the words 'M. de Beaumarchais' written underneath Pâris-Duverney's phrase. The words were in Pâris-Duverney's hand, he claimed, and were partly torn and partly obscured by wax. *Ergo*, Pâris-Duverney had written a short note to Beaumarchais to accompany another document, had folded the note, addressed it and sealed it; later Beaumarchais had used the blank side of the paper for his nefarious purposes and so on.

It was a clever move. Unfortunately for Caillard, who had probably done a fine job on the tearing and sealing, a lawyer named Jonquière stood up and said, 'I wrote that. I wrote the name on the document for filing purposes.' And to prove it he promptly wrote the name Beaumarchais a large number of times. Needless to say, it was the same writing. For once, Caillard had nothing to say, and neither had La Blache. The court didn't have much difficulty in distinguishing fact from fiction. The next day, 22 February 1772, the judges pronounced in favour of Beaumarchais, dismissed La Blache's summons for forgery, and on 14 March of the same year ordered him to implement the settlement.

The Comte de La Blache didn't let the matter rest. He appealed to parliament, where he had nothing but friends. He could afford to take his time: this initial defeat was a mere setback, considering how effective his campaign had been. He felt that all the muck he had slung couldn't fail to have left some stains. And he was quite right, of course. 'No smoke without fire' should be the French national motto, as La Blache well knew. When it comes to smoke and fire, the devil is in his element.

What can the devil do, though, that hurts us as much as true misfortune? On 17 October of the same year, Augustin, the son Beaumarchais adored and for whom he was fighting, suddenly died. 'I don't know why it has never been claimed that he poisoned his son as well,' writes La Harpe, 'for it is the only crime that he was not accused of. Slander has its oversights.' We know nothing of the details of this tragedy. Beaumarchais, who revealed himself in other respects with a sincerity and an openness that might strike us as 'modern', always remained silent about his sufferings. Those who wish to see this as a sign of his lack of sensitivity may do so; but those of us who wish to see it as the opposite may also do so. Of all his love for Augustin, all that remains is a laugh: 'And my son, my son! How is he? I laugh when I think that I am working for him.' That is the way it should be.

CHAULNES

Of all the strange characters in Beaumarchais's life, the strangest was without a doubt Marie-Louis-Joseph d'Albert d'Ailly, Vidame d'Amiens, Duc de Pecquigny, Duc de Chaulnes. Chaulnes's complexity defies description. He was a mass of contradictions and excesses. 'Antiperistatic' (roused by opposition) would probably be the best epithet to describe him succinctly; less pedantically, we might say that he worked like an internal combustion engine, by means of a series of explosions. Oddly enough, this system actually got him places, via highly honourable routes, but like any automobile he sometimes caused accidents. By a quirk of fate, Beaumarchais crossed his path at a time when the duke was already out of control.

When he met Beaumarchais, Chaulnes was about thirty. He adopted him on the spot, with passion. When the two of them came into a *salon* together, the difference in their physiques made everyone laugh: whereas Beaumarchais was of average height and of slim build, the duke was a giant of some corpulence. I should add that the laughter was also caused by the presence of a large ape, which Chaulnes took everywhere and treated with great respect. The animal was the only living creature to be thus honoured with the duke's civilities – he beat his women and spent most of his spare time looking for quarrels. Since fewer people enjoy being beaten than is generally supposed, he frequently had to do without his ration of violence, and that made his rages even more formidable. Gudin, who, as we shall see, encountered Chaulnes on the rampage and who was not the sort to overstate his case, writes that in his fits of anger 'he was like a drunken savage, nay, a wild beast'. Interestingly enough, this drunken savage of a duke was a distinguished scholar. When Louis xv banished him from the kingdom to protect the Gudins of this world from his ravagings, he went to Egypt and became an Egyptologist. Upon his return from exile, he embarked with great success on a study of carbonic acid. Loménie tells us that the duke also conducted a series of experiments on asphyxiation: 'In order to test a preparation that he invented to counter the effects of asphyxiation, the duke shut himself up in a glass cabinet and asphyxiated himself, having ordered his valet to rescue him in time and apply the remedy. Fortunately, he had a punctual servant.'

It would be pleasant to ramble on about Chaulnes for several pages, but the reader might legitimately object that we had less to say about La Blache. The fact is that some characters write themselves, whereas others remain secretive. La Blache was locked up in himself and emerged from his prison only to shriek his hatred; Chaulnes, as I have already stated, was permanently out of control.

A final word about Chaulnes, or rather about his family. His father came from ancient aristocratic stock and had been in his time a respected scholar – in the natural sciences, I believe. His mother, whose maiden name was Bonnier, was the daughter of an extremely rich tradesman; she was a very scandalous lady, and half mad. Speaking of her and her money, the dowager duchess was in the custom of saying: 'Good land needs manure,' which was true but not very nice. Chaulnes, who took after his mother when it came to extravagance, didn't get along with her and even sued her several times. His relationships with women were always somewhat shaky, and usually violent, as we have seen. He didn't understand women at all; flying into a rage, he would attempt to smash them rather as a child punishes an overcomplicated toy by breaking it.

Mlle Ménard was not in the least mysterious or ambiguous, but she was not made the same way as himself and that annoyed him. He probably loved her in his way. According to Gudin, who knew them both, the duke gave her a child at the outset of their affair. Abbé Dugué, who was La Ménard's confessor, says that the child was a girl.

Where did she and Chaulnes meet? On the boulevards, where she began her career as a flower girl? At the Comédie Italienne, where she later acted and sang? Or in a *salon*? Marmontel, Sedaine and Chamfort, who were mad about her, followed her to every reception that she honoured with her entirely physical presence. Or even at Versailles in the company of the Duc de Richelieu? I don't know where they met, but I do know that she must have loved him too, because she preferred him to men who were much more brilliant, wealthy and civilized than he was. Despite what Grimm says about her (he earned his living selling spiteful stories), she must have been extremely attractive. At any rate, Beaumarchais says she was.

Like many other men, he spent a lot of time hanging around Mlle Ménard, whom he had met at the Comédie Italienne. (He had submitted a comic opera based on one of his *parades* and called *The Barber of Seville*. The title is not unknown, but the opera was rejected.) La Ménard invited him to visit her while Chaulnes was out of town. To his great surprise, he found Gudin skulking in her boudoir, looking lovesick and thwarted. Beaumarchais didn't let the grass grow under his feet. He was charming, he had a good reputation as a lover, and he was used to getting down to brass tacks without shilly-shallying. But Chaulnes, who had been sulking for a short while, returned to the love nest, presumably having had his fill of one-night stands, and all hell was let loose. Beaumarchais spaced out his visits, while the duke soothed himself by beating his mistress like a pancake batter. But La Ménard, who was still gone on Beaumarchais, was less willing to take her punishment than she had been, and she ran away to a convent. The duke, thrown out of his stride, calmed down and sent her some money to say he was sorry. Reassured, and probably bored with convent life, she went back home and sent for Beaumarchais – who did the gentlemanly thing and sent a note to Chaulnes, who was still his friend.

The duke, who wasn't the sharing sort, didn't take kindly to Beaumarchais's missive. As he had no taste and no talent for literary joustings, he emulated his military ancestors and called for his sword. But I should hate to mar your enjoyment of the least crotchet in the memorable impromptu of 11 February 1773 by adopting too fast a tempo. We possess the full score, complete with dialogue. From the top, then.

On the morning of the eleventh, Chaulnes enters Mlle Ménard's boudoir, sword in hand, and comes upon the amiable Gudin sitting on the edge of the bed.

The duke, disappointed: 'Oh, it's you.'

Gudin stands conciliatingly: 'Take my place, your grace, for it is yours.'

The duke, looking under the bed, opening the wardrobe: 'Where is he? I'll kill him.'

'But who are you looking for?'

'Beaumarchais. I must kill him within the hour.'

Mlle Ménard bursts into tears. Seeing this, and guessing why, Chaulnes rises to a paroxysm of rage and exits, uttering loud and dreadful oaths.

Good old Gudin, all loyalty, in his turn leaves poor Mlle Ménard's house. Her maid rushes for smelling salts, while Gudin races towards the rue de Condé to warn Beaumarchais. By a great stroke of luck, he meets his friend's carriage on the way, whereupon he intrepidly dives at the horses' heads and leaps on to the running-board:

'Come home with me at once, I have a serious matter to discuss with you.'

'I can't. I'm on my way to the Louvre, where I've got a case to hear. I'll call on you when it's over.'

'It will be too late!'

'Why, pray?'

'Chaulnes is after you, spoiling for a fight. He wants to kill you.'

'He'll kill nothing but my fleas.'

With this, Beaumarchais summons his coachman to drive on with a rap of his cane. Gudin, at a loss, watches the coach drive off and then walks towards his home in the place Dauphine.

On the steps of the Pont-Neuf he comes face to face with Chaulnes, who, 'employing his giant's strength, snatches him up like some bird

of prey' and tosses him into a waiting cab, the curtains of which are
drawn.

The duke to his driver: 'Rue de Condé!'

To Gudin: 'You shan't leave me until I've found that knave.'

'By what right, your grace, do you dare to hold me prisoner?'

Chaulnes, grandly: 'The right of might! Find Beaumarchais for
me or . . .'

'Your grace, I am unarmed. I trust you'll not murder me?'

'No. That Beaumarchais is the only man I'll kill. And when I've
run him through with my sword and torn his heart out with my teeth,
that Ménard woman can go to blazes.'

Gudin, with dignity: 'Even if I knew where Beaumarchais was, I
shouldn't tell you while you're in such a rage.'

'If you resist me, I'll box your ears.'

'And I'll box yours straight back.'

'Box my ears? Me? A duke and a peer of the realm?'

Gudin's insolence seems so great to Chaulnes that he decides to
punish him by pulling his hair, but he merely pulls off his wig.
Recovering from his surprise, the duke hands the poet back his
peruke and sets to 'scratching his neck, ears and chin'. Gudin cries
out that he's being murdered. His torment ends when the cab comes
to a halt in the rue de Condé. The duke jumps from the carriage to
knock at his enemy's door, while the innocent victim, frightened out
of his wits, seizes his chance and slips away.

Meanwhile, at the Louvre, Beaumarchais, in magisterial pomp, is
trying some poacher or illicit prowler.

Chaulnes has obtained the information he was after – the servants
at the rue de Condé residence panicked the minute they set eyes on
him. A quarter of an hour later he bursts into the courtroom and,
ignoring the solemnity of the proceedings, interrupts the hearing to
address Beaumarchais:

'*Monsieur*, you must come outside immediately, I have something
urgent to impart to you.'

'I cannot, your grace. The public service requires me to conclude
in due fashion the task I have begun. Guard, give his grace the Duc
de Chaulnes a chair.'

The duke sits down, but jumps up immediately: '*Monsieur*, I
cannot wait, I'm thirsty . . .'

'Guard, bring his grace a glass of water.'

'I'm thirsty for your blood! I must kill you at once and tear out your heart.'

'Oh, is that all? If it pleases your grace, let business come before pleasure.'

'I'll tear your eyes out here and now if you don't come outside with me.'

'That would be your ruin, *monsieur*. Don't forget where you are, and whom I serve here.'

Momentarily silenced, the duke sits down. The hearing continues. Before long, however, the duke gets up and strides around, calling upon the witnesses to be brief. He is led back to his chair.

Beaumarchais, hoping that his temper will cool, spins out the hearing. Chaulnes, who can't hold his tongue for more than a minute at a time, apostrophizes the Comte de Marcouville, the clerk of the court, in the following terms: 'I shall cut his throat.'

At a sign from Marcouville the guards move in, but Beaumarchais motions them to remain in their places. Eventually it is time for the last case, which concerns the failure of one Ragondet, farmer, to conform with the royal decree of 1669, clause 24 etc. The duke jumps up and plants himself in front of the lawyer: 'How much longer are you going to be?'

A quarter of an hour. Ragondet is sentenced to a fine of 100 *livres*. The hearing is over. Beaumarchais swaps his gown for a coat and joins the duke, who is mounting guard by his coach and has already attracted a little crowd of onlookers by shouting imprecations. Beaumarchais questions him. The duke replies: 'No explanations! Come and fight me this minute or I'll create a scandal here and now.'

'You must at least allow me to go home for a sword. I've only got a vile mourning sword in my carriage, and you can't expect me to defend myself with that.'

'We'll call in on the Comte de Turpin on the way. He'll lend you one. And I want him as my second.'

Whereupon the duke gets into Beaumarchais's carriage and orders the coachman to drive to the Comte de Turpin's residence. Beaumarchais follows him in, and the coach moves off, with the duke's cab in tow. During the drive Chaulnes seems highly agitated and proffers innumerable threats. In the end, totally unnerved by his opponent's silence, he shakes his fist at him and shouts: 'You won't give me the slip, let me tell you.'

Beaumarchais remains imperturbable, answering quietly: 'Since
I'm going to fetch a sword, you can't expect me to brawl like a street
bully on the way.'

The force of this argument leads Chaulnes to control himself,
though his face is contorted with rage and he growls inwardly.

They reach Turpin's house just as he is coming out of the door.
Recognizing the coach, Turpin climbs on to the running board to
greet Beaumarchais.

The latter immediately puts him in the picture: 'His grace is
abducting me, for some reason. He wants to cross swords with me.
He gives me to hope, *monsieur*, that you will be good enough to bear
witness on the conduct of the two opponents in this strange adventure.'

Seeing at a glance what a state Chaulnes is in (seething with rage,
he hasn't managed to get a word out), the count, who as a general
officer is barred from getting mixed up in disputes of this nature, has
the wit to reply that he is expected at the palace on urgent business
and won't be free until four in the afternoon (by which time
Chaulnes will hopefully have cooled off somewhat).

Turpin leaves. The duke, finding his tongue again, says: 'We'll go
to my house and wait for our second to return at four. Home,
coachman!'

'No, your grace. Just as I shouldn't care to encounter you without
seconds, in case you accused me of having attacked you, so I shan't
enter any house of yours, because you'd be sure to play some trick on
me. Coachman, rue de Condé!'

'If you get out of the coach I'll stab you at your own front door.'

'So you shall, then, for I won't go anywhere else to await the
moment that will reveal your true intentions.'

Many oaths from Chaulnes as the carriage drives towards the rue
de Condé.

Beaumarchais, conciliatingly: 'Your grace, no one who intends to
fight goes prattling on so. Come into my house and I'll give you
dinner. If I haven't managed to bring you to your senses between
now and four o'clock and you persist in forcing me to choose between
fighting or having my face scratched to bits, arms must decide
between us.'

The carriage arrives in the rue de Condé. Beaumarchais alights,
followed by Chaulnes who seems agreeable to the idea of a meal.

Inside, Beaumarchais gives instructions to the servants and reas-
sures his father, who is highly disturbed by Chaulnes's appearance.
A messenger arrives with a letter for Beaumarchais. The duke grabs
it and tears it up, uttering unimaginable oaths. Meanwhile Pierre-
Augustin soothes his father, who is on the verge of panic, telling him
that it's all a joke. M. Caron stares at his son disbelievingly.
Beaumarchais, taking advantage of a short respite, asks his valet to
bring the dinner to his study and invites Chaulnes to accompany him
to the first floor. On the stairs, he asks the lackey where his sword is.

'Out for polishing,' the fellow answers, in a voice like death.

'Go and get it. If it's not ready, bring me another one.'

Chaulnes to the dumbfounded lackey: 'I forbid you to leave the
house or I'll knock your brains out.'

Beaumarchais turns, still on the stairs, and says with a smile:
'Have you changed your mind, then? Thank heavens, for I couldn't
fight without a sword.'

None the less he gestures to his servant, who is only too happy to
withdraw and run to the cutler's to fetch the sword.

Beaumarchais places his mourning sword on a table in the study
and goes to sit behind his desk.

'Forgive me, Chaulnes. I have an urgent letter to write.'

Without a word, the duke snatches his quill and throws it out of
the window.

'Your grace, my house is a sanctuary and I shall not violate it,
unless you force me to do so by such behaviour.'

The duke's reply is indistinct. Beaumarchais tries to reason with
him. Chaulnes merely grabs the mourning sword and advances on
Beaumarchais, grinding his teeth. He now has two swords, and
informs his opponent that he is going to murder him. Beaumarchais
has no choice but to seize him round the waist in order to place
himself out of range of the swordpoint. While the giant whirls the
mourning sword like a windmill above Beaumarchais's head, the
latter attempts to push him towards the bell-pull near the fireplace.
The duke resists and scratches his enemy's eyes and face with his free
hand, making the blood run. Beaumarchais manages to reach the
bell and his servants rush in to lend a helping hand.

'Disarm this madman,' he orders.

At which the servants hurl themselves on Chaulnes's coat-tails
like the Lilliputians tackling Gulliver. Seeing them tossed aside, the

cook, who was (says Beaumarchais) as strong and as brutal as the duke, seizes a log from the fireplace and prepares to smash his grace's head in. Beaumarchais stops him with a shout:

'Disarm him, but don't harm him. He would only say that he was set upon in my house.'

The mourning sword is torn from the duke's hand, but no one thinks of removing the sword hanging at his side. (Questioned on this point later on, the servants replied that they thought it would have shown a lack of respect that might have had serious consequences for them. Strange times, weird taboos! The cook could hit the duke on the head with a log, but couldn't touch his sword.)

A creature of habit, Chaulnes grabs Beaumarchais's wig, pulling out a handful of hair in the process. The pain makes the victim punch him full in the face, and for the second time Chaulnes delivers the sublime line: 'Wretch! You have struck a peer of the realm.' (Beaumarchais writes: 'I allow that this exclamation, so extravagant under the circumstances, would have made me laugh at any other time. But as he is stronger than I am, and had seized me by the throat, I could only try to defend myself.')

The fight continues, terrifying and majestic. Before long Beaumarchais's coat and shirt are in shreds and his face is covered in blood. Enter M. Caron, who bravely attempts to 'throw himself betwixt', thereby earning his share of the 'pugilistic fury of the peer of the realm'. A fresh onslaught from the servants forces Chaulnes back towards the stairs, which he has forgotten about. Inevitably, he tumbles down the stairs, dragging the servants and Beaumarchais along with him. They all end up in a heap at the bottom. Chaulnes is the first on his feet, and the sight of the horrible mess brings him to his senses somewhat.

There is a ring at the door. Chaulnes goes to see who it is. Perceiving Gudin, whom he seizes and tosses among the servants, he rises to new heights of rage: 'No one will leave or enter without my permission until I have made mincemeat of M. de Beaumarchais.'

The noise has become so great that a crowd has begun to gather outside the house. A chambermaid opens the window and shouts that a madman is trying to murder her master. Which is true, or almost: the duke has just drawn the sword that the servants left him with and is bearing down on Beaumarchais to run him through. Eight people grab hold of him and manage to disarm him. This onslaught swells the ranks of the wounded: the footman has a gash on his forehead, the coachman receives a cut on the nose and the burly cook is stabbed through the hand by the duke's sword – a great honour.

Totally disarmed, Chaulnes runs to the kitchen to fetch a knife. The servants, close behind him, make haste to hide all the knives and choppers. Meanwhile Beaumarchais is going round the house in search of a defensive weapon, but all he can find is a pair of firetongs in his study. Thus equipped, he makes to go downstairs. And then, to his stupefaction (I again quote Beaumarchais): 'I discovered something that proved to me forthwith that the man had gone completely mad. As soon as he had lost sight of me, the duke had gone into the dining-room, sat down at the table, eaten a large dish of soup and some chops and drunk two flasks of water.'

There's a knock at the door. Napkin in hand, Chaulnes runs to open it and comes face to face with Superintendent Chenu of the police, summoned by passers-by.

The superintendent, surprised by the general chaos, and especially by Beaumarchais's bloody face, asks the master of the house what all this is about.

'A cowardly madman entered this house, *monsieur*, with the intention of dining with me. No sooner had he set foot in my study than he attempted to kill me with my own sword, then with his own. As you can see, *monsieur*, from the household that I keep, I could easily have had him torn apart, but that would have been too good for him. His parents, though delighted to be rid of him, might have made things awkward for me. I controlled myself, and apart from a great many punches to ward off his violent attacks on my face and scalp, I gave orders that he was not to be harmed in any way.'

The duke speaks up in his turn: '*Monsieur* and I were due to fight at four in the presence of the Comte de Turpin. I couldn't wait till the appointed hour.'

M. Chenu, stupefied and speechless, stares at the duke. Beaumarchais seizes his chance: 'What think you, *monsieur*, of this man, who, after creating havoc in my house, divulges in the presence of a public official his unlawful intent, compromises a general officer by naming him as a designated second, and destroys with a single utterance any chance of going through with his plan, which, as this cowardly act proves, he never seriously intended to go through with?'

At these words the duke explodes anew and rushes at Beaumarchais. The two of them are separated before it is too late. The superintendent asks Beaumarchais to remain where he is and leads Chaulnes into another room. On the way the duke threatens to break a few mirrors. At this juncture, alas, the valet returns from the cutler's with a brand-new sword. Beaumarchais has to explain: '*Monsieur*, I never intended to fight a duel and never will. However, even though I didn't accept this man's challenge, I shall go about town wearing this sword constantly, and if he insults me, since the fuss he is creating around this horrible incident proves that he is the aggressor, I swear that I shall deliver society, if I can, of a coward who dishonours it.'

Though intimidated by the duke, M. Chenu asks Beaumarchais if he wants to lodge a complaint against him.

'I didn't have him arrested this morning in court, and I shan't have him arrested in my house. Between gentlemen there is another method of redress and I shall employ none other.'

Reassured, the superintendent crosses the hall. He is surprised to find Chaulnes in the process of punching his own face and pulling out his hair in handfuls. Chenu begs him to stop: 'You are being too hard on yourself, your grace.'

'You don't know what you're talking about, *monsieur*. It isn't contrition that makes me do it, but rage – rage at having failed to kill him.'

Respectfully, the superintendent persuades Chaulnes to go home. Before leaving, however, the duke throws a few last sparks of pride and madness.

Calling for the valet he had wounded on the forehead, he orders him to comb his hair and brush his clothes. Once he has been spruced up, he exits.

So much for the main event of this day of madness, which, as I have already hinted, was to have nasty consequences. Once he had returned to his desk Superintendent Chenu had the unenviable task of reporting on the events to Sartines, the chief of police. In a long, carefully worded letter, Chenu recounted what he had seen and heard. It is obvious, however, that he took great pains to spare the high-ranking madman, from whom he feared reprisals. For instance his report concludes with the following words: 'I have nothing but praise for the way his grace behaved. He didn't even say anything unpleasant to me.' That 'even' is eloquent, for my money.

The duke told the story after his own fashion, laying great stress on the fact that he had been Beaumarchais's guest. At his headquarters in the rue Neuve-Saint-Augustin, Sartines didn't have much difficulty in unravelling the affair and in knowing who was guilty – he was a friend of both men. In any case, Sartines always knew everything. In a letter to Catherine the Great, Diderot wrote of Sartines: 'If I were to spend an evening in low company, M. de Sartines would know about it before going to bed. If a foreigner arrives in the capital, within twenty-four hours the rue Neuve-Saint-Augustin knows who he is, where he comes from, why he is here, where he lives, with whom he is in correspondence, whom he lives with.' Unfortunately for Beaumarchais, Sartines was not alone at the helm of state.

That same evening Beaumarchais was expected at the house of a M. Lopes, or Lopès, a *fermier général*, to give a reading of an early version of *The Barber of Seville*. The *fermier-général* had invited all the fashionables to his party. When by seven, eight, then nine o'clock the star attraction of the evening hadn't made his appearance, the tongues started to wag. At this point Beaumarchais showed up – bandaged, wigged and sprightlier than ever. When questioned he recounted his adventure as casually as if it had happened to someone else. Then he read the five acts of his draft of *The Barber*. The reading was a great success. After supper he played the harp and then sang *seguidillas* half the night. 'Thus it was,' writes Gudin, 'that in every circumstance throughout his life he was entirely absorbed in the thing at hand, without worrying about what had gone before or what would follow, so sure was he of his faculties and his presence of mind. He never needed to rehearse. His mind was never diminished in any way, and his principles were so sound that they never failed him.'

When long after midnight he arrived back at the rue de Condé, he found a letter waiting for him in his room. It was from Mlle Ménard, the cause of all the rumpus. She had decided to take refuge from Chaulnes by entering a convent. Her confessor, Abbé Dugué, had already found a place for her daughter at the Convent of the Presentation. She put her trust in God, and immediately after God in Beaumarchais, for the protection of her daughter and herself. And she was his very humble and very obedient servant.

La Ménard was rather prone to entering convents. But was it her

idea this time, or Sartines's? The role played by Abbé Dugué in this
affair seems rather mysterious. This worthy cleric appears to have
been perfectly willing to work for the police, providing he stayed out
of trouble. The letter he wrote to Sartines four days after the
momentous events of 11 February shows that in those days there
were many short cuts between the spiritual and the temporal.
Dugué, amusingly enough, addresses the lieutenant of police with
the same style as his bishop – *Monseigneur*.

> *Monseigneur*,
> Upon leaving you I went to the Convent of the Presentation to see, in
> accordance with your orders, whether it might be possible to find refuge
> there for the mother and the child. I speak of Mlle Ménard and her
> daughter, whom I took to the convent on Thursday evening, as I had the
> honour of informing you last Saturday . . . If what concerns her in the
> present circumstances interests you sufficiently to authorize me hence-
> forth to speak to you about her, deign to assign a moment. While obeying
> your orders, I shall be answering the singular trust which she has placed
> in me. May my humble services alleviate her difficulties without my
> being compromised. I am, with respect, *monseigneur*, your very humble
> and most obedient servant.

Meanwhile Chaulnes was still intent on killing Beaumarchais.
Gudin was in the green room at the Comédie Française when the
duke burst in, expecting to find his man there. (The theatre had
begun billing *The Barber*, so his assumption wasn't unreasonable.)
Seizing Gudin by the wrists, Chaulnes informed him of his latest
intentions: 'Tell your friend, wherever he is, that I mean to brain
him.'

Gudin hid in the wings and wrote a message to Beaumarchais
sounding the alarm. But Beaumarchais was already in trouble elsewhere. The Duc de La Vrillière, minister of the king's household,
had summoned him to his office to suggest that he should go off to the
country for a few days. Beaumarchais refused, because the order
dishonoured him – he couldn't leave town after Chaulnes's threats
without losing face. La Vrillière saw the point and suggested he
place himself under house arrest until he had given an account of
himself to the king.

However, the scandal created by Chaulnes's murderous outburst
at the Comédie Française brought the affair within the jurisdiction of
the Marshals of France, who were traditionally responsible for main-

taining law and order at the Comédie Française, and in particular for settling disputes between noblemen. The marshals heard Chaulnes on both counts, and Beaumarchais on the dispute. Their findings exonerated Beaumarchais, whose house arrest was immediately lifted, whereas Chaulnes was dispatched under royal warrant of imprisonment to the castle of Vincennes on 19 February.

All the same, Beaumarchais sensed that his tribulations weren't yet over. To sound out the situation he went to see La Vrillière, who was out, and then Sartines, who assured him that he could go freely about his business.

When he reached home he found a young man waiting for him. He was the son of one of the twelve marshals of France. His sister had sent him 'to ask for the return of her letters and her portrait'. Fishy! '*Monsieur*,' Beaumarchais replied sharply, 'in the uncertainty in which I find myself these days I cannot accept all the invitations I receive. I shall give you back your dear sister's portrait and her letters, nicely wrapped up and properly sealed. Here, take them.' The sister's name, and her liaison with Beaumarchais, have remained a mystery. The editor of Gudin's memoirs, Maurice Tourneux, states that the girl was either a Broglie or a Richelieu, but for our purposes it matters little whether she was one or the other. The point is that Beaumarchais had realized that if she wanted her letters back she knew that he was in danger and was afraid that his house might be searched. That does matter.

On 26 February Gudin received the following letter from Beaumarchais written at the For-Lévêque, a relatively comfortable prison in the rue Saint-Germain-l'Auxerrois, on the banks of the Seine:

> By virtue of an unsealed letter, known as a sealed letter, signed Louis, contersigned Phélypeaux, counter-countersigned Sartines, enacted Buchot and collected Beaumarchais, I am lodged, my friend, and have been since this morning, in a room without hangings, at a rent of 2160 *livres*, where I have reason to hope that I shall want for nothing, save what is necessary. Was it the family of the duke, whom I saved from trial, whose life and freedom I saved? Was it the minister, whose orders I have constantly obeyed or anticipated? Was it the peers of the realm, with whom I can never have any unpleasant dealings? I know not. But the sacred name of the king is so fine a thing that it must for ever be propagated and put to good use. And so it is that in every well-policed

country those who cannot justly be found guilty are unjustly tormented. Where's the remedy? Wherever men exist, odious things happen; and the great wrong of being right is always a crime in the eyes of a government that will ever punish and never judge.

Although there is no need to specify who 'Louis' was it is probably necessary to point out that 'Phélypeaux' stood for La Vrillière. Quick changes of station were fairly common in those days. The duke had been born a Phélypeaux, just as Beaumarchais had been born a Caron, *fils* Caron. (Incidentally, final consonants and nasal vowels were not pronounced in the same way as they are in modern French. *Fils* was pronounced *fi* and Caron sounded more like 'Caro'.)

'*Fi(ls)* Caro(n)', then, without further comment for the moment. *The Barber*, and hence Figaro (get it?), were out of the picture for the time being. Marin, the first of many censors, had passed the play, Sartines had signed the performing licence on 12 February, but the play was banned because its author was in prison. ('At once I saw, from the depths of my carriage, the drawbridge of a castle being lowered for me. At its gate I left behind hope and liberty.')

The devil had three tricks up his sleeve. Chaulnes was only the second.

THE GOËZMANS

The Goëzmans made Beaumarchais. His encounter with this evil and ridiculous couple changed the entire course of his life. By overwhelming him with the most terrible misfortune they endowed him with genius.

Had it not been for them, he wouldn't have written either Figaro's monologue or the four great *Memoirs*. I say 'great' even though these extraordinary texts, which made Beaumarchais famous throughout Europe and which Sainte-Beuve regarded as equal to the best of Pascal's *Provinciales*, have only their fame to keep them alive today – they have been out of print for several decades. The Goëzmans gave him, albeit unwittingly, the intellectual maturity he still lacked. With the Goëzmans everything changed – his tone, his style, his ambitions, his morals. At forty Beaumarchais discovered that life is more than cheating, pretending, abjuring. Society tolerates masks on condition that they respect the rules of the carnival: easy come, easy go. At Versailles and in Paris and Madrid, Beaumarchais was in disguise: he lived in disguise, he wrote in disguise. Had it not been for this terrible ordeal he might well have died in disguise.

The last paragraph of his letter to Gudin contains the following essential statement: 'And so it is that in every well-policed country those who cannot justly be found guilty are unjustly tormented. Where's the remedy? Wherever men exist, odious things happen; and the great wrong of being right is always a crime in the eyes of a government that will ever punish and never judge.' *Where's the remedy?* On 23 February Beaumarchais is at a loss and seems prepared to accept his fate, to yield, to bow down, to scheme or, like his father, to abjure. Yet as we have seen, his natural tendency was to face up to things. Even so, his confrontations with Lepaute, Clavijo and La Blache had occurred within the system, respecting its customs, hierarchy and authority. *Where's the remedy?* Why not resist? Resist right down the line? As we shall see, Beaumarchais's refusal to accept the *status quo*, his great battle with Parliament and hence with the man or men who had invented it was a model of its kind. At the close of this fantastic year-long battle his judges, pressured by the executive, might reprimand him as much as they liked, but the victory was his. All Europe knew this at the time. Since then the historians have diligently played down his political importance. Figaro? Come, come, let's be serious! The French in particular, like Molière's M. Jourdan, always have a high regard for philosophy tutors. With that, let's return to the For-Lévêque.

This little castle was a four-star prison, but Beaumarchais spent his first few nights there in an uncomfortable attic. Sartines intervened, however, and the prison governor, Jean-Hubert Dinant du Verger, gave him a more pleasant room, the one that had been occupied several years earlier by Mlle Clairon of the Comédie Française, following an actors' quarrel that had created quite a stir at the time. Brian Morton, in his edition of Beaumarchais's correspondence, notes that Verger, the governer of For-Lévêque, had an idealistic view of his mission. In a report to parliament concerning the organization of his prison he wrote: 'Nothing is more sacred than the liberty of each citizen.' M. Verger presumably subscribed to the belief that anything sacred is best kept under lock and key.

There were no grounds for holding Beaumarchais at the For-

Lévêque. In fact La Vrillière had used him to demonstrate to the marshals of France that he was their superior: since they had ventured to lift the house arrest he had imposed, he had doubled the stakes – all in the name of the king, of course. There may be other explanations besides. One duke deciding to side with another, for example, as Loménie suggests. Or this one, which has occurred to me: La Blache. With his enemy in prison, the count was free to act. Did La Vrillière do him this favour? Why not? The two men were acquainted, and they obviously belonged to the same faction. Anyway Beaumarchais's internment helped the count considerably. He seized his chance – if chance had anything to do with it – and obtained permission from parliament to bring forward the date of the appeal hearing to 6 April. La Vrillière released Beaumarchais on 8 May, after La Blache had won his appeal. Sheer coincidence?

When Beaumarchais heard how his chief enemy was turning his imprisonment to his advantage, he alerted his friends. Sartines, in particular. The chief of police, seeing his point (and the rather special points of Mlle Ménard, who as usual had left the convent after a couple of weeks), got permission for him to leave the For-Lévêque for a short period each day, guarded by a police officer, so that he could prepare his case and visit his judges, in accordance with custom. Permission was hard to get. It had to be signed by La Vrillière, who, for no apparent reason, rejected the request twice, stating that it would be 'improper' to grant this favour to Beaumarchais. What was improper on 1 March and 10 March became proper, however, on 22 March.

On 23 March Beaumarchais was at last in a position to organize his defence. He had just two weeks to turn the tables on La Blache, who for the last month had been going the rounds of the parliamentary councillors, repeating his allegations, lies and slanders, and stating that any man banished under a royal warrant signed by Louis XV was obviously guilty, guilty by definition. The fresh batch of councillors who had replaced those who had refused to grovel listened complacently to this brigadier-general, who appeared to be well placed at court. A fight against the odds never discouraged Beaumarchais. 'Difficulties of all kinds have never checked me in anything.' But to visit your judges accompanied by a police officer doesn't always create the best of impressions, and being compelled to return to your cell at fixed times, twelve and six, doesn't exactly make it easy to arrange appointments. No matter, Beaumarchais dragged the unfortunate Santerre from one end of Paris to the other. The policeman, who was soon won over by his prisoner, didn't have an easy time of it, because after traipsing round with Beaumarchais all day he had to write a detailed report to Sartines every evening. After a week of this exhausting hiking, Santerre still writes: 'We walk round for most of the day without managing to find more than three or four of the gentlemen at home.'

There was no making up for lost time. Beaumarchais saw that the climate had turned against him. He was hated for his insolence, his success, his carriages, his money. And his crimes. La Blache had returned to his embroidery, talking in the *salons*, buying journalists, financing pamphlets and flattering the Parisians' taste for insinuation and scandal. Apart from Sartines, Beaumarchais's friends could do nothing for him except sympathize and stand up for him, which was sometimes dangerous. If it's true that a man's character can be told from his friendships, there can be no doubting the nobility of the man La Blache called 'the consummate monster' and 'the poisonous beast that society must be purged of'. Quite apart from his family, whose behaviour was extraordinary, as we shall see, the constant loyalty, affection and admiration of people like the Contis, Gudin and Lenormant d'Etioles made up for the foulness, the villainy and the treachery of high society. At the For-Lévêque, Beaumarchais received a letter from a little boy of six: 'I am sending you my purse, because people are unhappy in prison. I am very sorry that you are in prison. Every morning and evening I say an Ave Maria for you.' The letter was signed 'Constant'. Constant was the son of Lenormant d'Etioles, who had remarried after Mme de Pompadour's death. Beaumarchais wrote to Mme d'Etioles that the letter and purse had made him 'childishly happy'. 'You are fortunate in having a son who is capable of an action like this at the age of six. I, too, had a son, but he is dead.' The same day he wrote to Constant: 'My little friend Constant, I am very grateful for your letter and the purse you enclosed. I have distributed their contents fairly according to the different needs of my fellow-prisoners and myself, keeping for your friend Beaumarchais the best share of all, I mean the prayers, the Ave Marias, which I am in great need of, and giving to poor people in distress all the money that was in your purse.'

The letter to Constant is dated 4 March 1773. Before long

Beaumarchais was in sore need of those Ave Marias. On 1 April the court, having reserved its judgment, nominated an assessor, upon whom the outcome of the case now depended. It was customary for the judges to merely endorse the assessor's opinion. As the assessor's report had to be tabled before parliament on 5 April, Beaumarchais had only four days in which to plead his case before the man whose decision could make or break him. His name was Louis-Valentin Goëzman de Thurne.

The councillor was a walking image of the new parliament – obscure, servile, but riddled with secret ambitions. Maupeou's men had discovered him in Alsace, where he was a member of the Sovereign Council, and the chancellor had appointed him a councillor of the Grand Chamber in Parliament in 1770. Goëzman was reputed to be a sound jurist with a somewhat retiring personality. Like most of his colleagues, he had felt obliged to write a learned work for his fame to rest on: his *Common Law of Fiefs* had been published by Lejay. Physically, Goëzman cannot have been very attractive, yet his position and the mysteries of the female heart had enabled him to marry twice. His second wife, younger and prettier than he was, had plenty of character and not many scruples. The morality of the new parliament was equal to that of the old – it was venal. Illicit commissions had been banned by Maupeou, but the new men increased their incomes by accepting, even soliciting, bribes. To keep his hands clean and to maintain his dignity, a councillor would recruit a third party, usually his wife, to collect on his behalf. Mme Goëzman, *née* Gabrielle Jamar, had acquired considerable skill in this ancient art. She didn't hide her light under a bushel, either – publicity was bound to bring in new clients. 'When my husband is nominated as an assessor,' she had announced, 'I'll pluck the pigeons so nicely they won't even squeal.'
The councillor lived on quai Saint-Paul, but it was one thing to know his address and another to get through his front door. Still followed by Santerre, who noted down his every movement, Beaumarchais called on his judge three times on 1 April. Goëzman, who must already have been in league with La Blache, replied via his maid that he was out. The next morning, same thing, and in the afternoon as well. Goëzman, doubtless amused by the sufferings of his pigeons, appeared at his study window and mocked his visitor.

Beaumarchais soon realized what Goëzman was up to, but with so little time left he didn't know how to go about sweetening his judge's temper. Before returning to the For-Lévêque on the evening of 2 April, he called at the house of Mme Lépine, his sister, whose at-home day it was. Those present included the family, of course, plus many friends, and a young man called Bertrand Dairolles (or d'Airolles) who lodged with the Lépines and who may have been Fanchon's lover. In response to their questions, Beaumarchais told them of his difficulties. Dairolles promptly announced that he knew of 'a way'. Ways and means were his business, it seems. To cut a long story short, Dairolles was well connected with Lejay, Goëzman's publisher. According to Fanchon's protégé, Lejay was the appointed go-between, so the only way to reach Mme Goëzman was through him. In fact the pigeon plucker had told Lejay, 'If a generous client with a just cause and honest intentions should happen along, I shouldn't feel that I was offending my sense of propriety by receiving a little gift.'

Certain, as always, that he was in the right, Beaumarchais had no desire to bribe Goëzman. He simply wanted to speak to him, and that seemed to be all but impossible. He made Dairolles and his sister promise that any bribery of the scrupulous Mme Goëzman would go no further than a request for an interview. It was essential that he should keep his hands clean in his conflict with La Blache. Dairolles and Fanchon promised. While they went to see Lejay, Beaumarchais returned to his prison.

Mme Goëzman asked for 100 *louis*. It was a high price for merely opening a door. Beaumarchais got angry when told of the pigeon plucker's pretentions the following morning. To begin with he refused to pay, but his entourage urged him to reconsider. What was 100 *louis* compared with the 50,000 *écus* he would lose through having failed to instruct his assessor? To settle the matter, a friend, La Châtaigneraie perhaps, gave Fanchon two rouleaux of 50 *louis* apiece.

Fanchon returned to see Lejay and thriftily tried to haggle over the price. Lejay went to see Mme Goëzman, who would have none of it. Back at his shop, the bookseller told Mme Lépine what she had said: 'When someone makes a sacrifice, it must be an honest one, or it loses its value; and your brother would be most displeased if he knew that at least four hours had been wasted in order to save a little money.'

There was no arguing with that, so Fanchon gave Lejay the 100 *louis*. The bookseller swore to alert Dairolles as soon as Mme Goëzman informed him of her latest intentions. The plucker had a gift for prolonging the agony, and she knew how to cover her tracks by using a number of go-betweens.

Dairolles was duly alerted in the middle of the afternoon of the third. He contacted Beaumarchais and told him what he had to do: 'Present yourself at M. Goëzman's door this evening. You will again be told that he is out. Insist that you must see him. Ask for Madame's lackey and give him this letter, which is merely a polite request to the lady to procure an interview for you, in accordance with the agreement between her and Lejay. You're bound to be let in.'

At first sight the Goëzmans' behaviour may seem ridiculous, or puerile. But a moment's thought reveals how clever it all was: the councillor closes his door, and remains blameless, while his wife opens it, and earns the housekeeping money.

That same evening Beaumarchais, 'meekly obeying', went to the quai Saint-Paul for the sixth time. His lawyer, Falconnet, and the inevitable Santerre were with him. The comedy was acted out exactly as Mme Goëzman had directed. To begin with the maid refused to admit the visitors, on the pretext that her master wasn't at home. Whereupon Beaumarchais, following his instructions to the letter, asked for Madame's lackey, who eventually showed up, after a long delay. Beaumarchais handed him Lejay's note, as instructed, and asked for it to be delivered immediately. Madame's lackey answered that this was out of the question, because Madame was with Monsieur at the moment. Obviously the poor fellow was used to dealing with the plucker's lovers and had got it wrong for once – these visitors had something else in mind.

'If Madame is with Monsieur,' Beaumarchais replied, 'all the more reason to hand her my letter immediately. Your masters will not hold it against you, mark my words.'

His mission accomplished, the lackey asked the three visitors to follow him to Monsieur's study, pointing out several times that his master was going there directly 'by the inner stairs'. The Goëzmans could do nothing openly or straightforwardly. Santerre, who was no fool, watched the behaviour of the magistrate and his wife in amazement, taking mental notes for his report.

At last the door was open and the invisible Goëzman was about to materialize. It was nine at night – a most inconvenient hour for a man out on parole. The councillor had obviously delayed his stealthy encounter with the formidable Beaumarchais until his wife had received the all-clear from Lejay.

Goëzman, who was wearing a dressing-gown (no honourable magistrate expects to be disturbed at nine in the evening!), asked his (paying) guests to sit down. The lawyer questioned him about the file. Had he examined it carefully? What impression did he get from it? Did he have any questions to ask? Goëzman, who seemed to be dropping off to sleep, avoided answering. In the end, forced into an answer, he consented to give an opinion. It was short and to the point:

'It's a cut-and-dried case.'

The lawyer and his client looked at one another in amazement. Santerre, who was used to judges and their tricky ways, could hardly believe his ears.

'Come, *monsieur*! Have you even opened the file?' Beaumarchais exclaimed, controlling himself with the greatest difficulty.

Goëzman, narrowing his eyes, gave him a look of gentle mockery, then sighed: 'Yes, I've looked at it. The statement of account between M. Duverney and yourself cannot be regarded as binding.'

'Why not?'

Goëzman, suddenly turning nasty: 'Because all the amounts are written in figures!'

Shaken, Falconnet asked to see the statement. Goëzman handed it to him. The lawyer looked, and found that all the amounts were indeed written in figures. Falconnet flushed with consternation. How could his client, in full knowledge of the law, have made such a blunder? Goëzman was looking bland again.

Beaumarchais leant towards Falconnet: 'Turn over. You'll see that the amounts are written out in full to comply with the law. The councillor gave you the statement back to front. On the back, as permitted by law, the amounts are recapitulated in figures.'

Utterly amazed, Falconnet stared at Goëzman accusingly. Why had he tried to trick him? Since the councillor appeared to be deep in a brown study, Beaumarchais spoke up in his stead: 'One of two things. The first explanation is honourable: the councillor hasn't had time to study the file. The second explanation is not honourable: the councillor has made up his mind without looking at the file at all.'

'You are completely wrong there, *monsieur*. I know your case intimately. It is, I repeat, crystal clear, and I hope to give a correct account of it to the court the day after tomorrow.'

'But which aspect of the case makes you think so?'

Goëzman, slyer than ever, if that were possible: 'Since you insist, Monsieur de Beaumarchais, I can point out to you, as your friend, that these documents are highly illegal, for example, under the terms of the declaration of 1733.'

This time it was the lawyer who got angry: 'But as you well know the two parties to the deed were covered by an exception in the law! It is current practice, you can't pretend to . . .'

A wave from Goëzman, intending to be reassuring: 'Written out in full or written in figures, what difference does it make? Laws and exceptions! Why get angry, since justice will be done?'

The councillor stood up. The interview was at an end. Before leaving, Beaumarchais noticed 'a twitch of laughter' in Goëzman's face that alarmed him considerably.

In the cab taking him back to the For-Lévêque, Beaumarchais appeared to be extremely anxious. If Councillor Goëzman, who knew his job, had said the first thing that came into his head, it was because he was not a judge in this case, but a party to it. Or else he had kept back a more decisive argument than the ones he had produced in their presence. Having nothing further to lose with Goëzman, Beaumarchais decided to see him again, determined to force him into a serious discussion even if it turned him into an enemy. Before returning to 'the cool lodging with good shutters and an excellent door, completely safe from robbers and not crammed with superfluous ornaments, at the heart of a castle in a pleasant situation in Paris on the banks of the Seine', he asked Falconnet to take his decision to the 'happy band', those whom Goëzman would later call 'the infamous clique' – his family and friends.

The 'happy band' went into action early the following morning, which was a Sunday. Twenty-four hours were left before Goëzman tabled his conclusions. Fanchon and Dairolles went once more to see Lejay, the pigeon plucker's go-between. Approval soon came through for a further interview at the same price. Since they couldn't get hold of 100 *louis* on a Sunday, Lépine offered a diamond watch worth far more, with which the expert plucker declared herself well pleased. Suddenly yielding to greed, however, or perhaps because she was short of cash on a Sunday, she demanded 15 *louis* extra, allegedly to cover her secretary's expenses. This was a lie, of course, as the secretary in question was perfectly honest. Falconnet, who knew him well, was positive that he had always refused any gifts and rewards, even when they were offered legitimately. But the councillor's wife wouldn't back down – she wanted her 15 *louis* or there would be no deal.

The surcharge was remitted to Lejay with bad grace. The bookseller took the money straight to Mme Goëzman, who in exchange promised an interview at seven o'clock. But that evening the Goëzmans' door remained mysteriously closed. As soon as they heard what had happened, Mme Lépine and Dairolles rushed to see Lejay, who was visibly embarrassed by the news. The bookseller promised to intervene very early the next morning and swore to obtain a fresh appointment. But he looked worried. This turn of events only a few hours before the assessor was due to report on his findings was a bad sign. Guessing that he wouldn't see Goëzman again before the case came before the court, Beaumarchais asked a notary and his friends to get together all the documents concerning his affair and spent all night in his room at the For-Lévêque drawing up answers to an imaginary series of questions likely to be asked by the most finicky and formidable of judges intent on tripping him up.

At breakfast time the next morning Lejay told the three friends: 'It's not the lady's fault if you didn't get in. You can go back and ask to see her husband this morning. She is so honest that in the event of your being unable to arrange an interview before the hearing, she gives her assurance that everything she has received will be faithfully returned.'

A seventh visit was made to the quai Saint-Paul. It was Beaumarchais's last chance. Not unexpectedly, the maid refused to let them in. Yes, Monsieur was at home, and so was Madame, but neither of them wished to see Monsieur de Beaumarchais. It took a great deal of insistence, a few threats and 6 francs slipped to a lackey to extract an assurance that the documents prepared by the notary and by Beaumarchais would be taken straight to the councillor.

At midday Goëzman tabled his conclusions before parliament. On his way out he appeared very pleased. When Falconnet questioned him he didn't hide the fact that his opinion had been 'greeted with nods of approval'. The smile on the face of La Blache was a further sign – Beaumarchais had lost.

The following morning the court published its findings. The statement of account between Pâris-Duverney and his partner was ruled to be null and void. Beaumarchais was no longer accused of wilful misrepresentation, but of forgery. The court's decision dishonoured him – and ruined him, since it forced him to pay 56,000 *livres* to La Blache, plus the enormous costs of the court case.

That same evening Lejay sent Fanchon the two rouleaux of 50 *louis* and the diamond watch. With regard to the 15 *louis*, Mme Goëzman felt that they should still go 'to the secretary'. When Falconnet questioned him the secretary indignantly replied that he was mortally insulted that anyone should have thought him capable of such an improper act.

Why did Mme Goëzman give back the 100 *louis* and the watch and keep the 15 *louis*? It seems odd, but a moment's thought makes it easy to find an explanation. Goëzman, who used the plucker to boost his income, knew very well that she had received the 100 *louis* and the watch. Having decided in the meantime to table the harshest of conclusions, the councillor thought it wise to return Beaumarchais's presents. Without libelling the memory of this sinister parliamentarian, we can easily imagine that he had received presents from the Comte de La Blache that he felt were more appropriate to his status. The 15 *louis*, I think I am right in saying, were paid on the side, so Goëzman knew nothing about them. His fine pigeon-plucker of a wife had kept them for herself. And she probably made the mistake of not returning them because she has spent them.

On the evening of 6 April Beaumarchais's situation was far from brilliant. He was confined to the For-Lévêque and no longer had any grounds for visiting his judges, so he could do nothing to prevent the total ruin of his reputation and his finances. The findings of the court had implicitly accused him of forgery. Paris, which hates wealth and success, was preparing to drag his name in the mud with evil glee. Slander, every slander imaginable, was about to 'rear up, hiss, swell and grow before your very eyes'. Again he was about to be branded a poisoner and a murderer. In April 1773, writes Grimm, 'he was the horror of all Paris. Everyone, taking his neighbour's word for it, believed him to be capable of the most heinous crimes.' True, Paris is the most fickle city in the world, and the man she hates in the evening she will adore the next morning.

For the moment, it was Beaumarchais's evening – his afternoon, even. La Blache was out on the prowl. Not content with having destroyed his enemy's reputation, he was intent on bleeding him of everything he possessed. It was all over in a few days. Unable to straighten out his affairs because he was still in prison, Beaumarchais remained powerless while La Blache ransacked his finances. It was the end of everything. The furniture at the rue de Condé was seized and the seals were put on the house in Pantin. The bailiffs descended in hordes, cheered on by the count, who had obtained a fistful of court orders and costs running to 500 francs per day. The Aubertins, Beaumarchais's exparents-in-law, emerged from their hole at the head of a pack of so-called creditors hoping to make a profit out of his misfortunes. If the statement of account was false, so was everything else. Sue him! The envious, the pusillanimous, the distant relatives (by marriage), the tailors, the wine merchants, every Tom, Dick and Harry began to produce drafts, invoices, bills, letters and claim that the signature was false. The hounds had smelt blood. His forest in Touraine was seized in the king's name because he couldn't pay his dues to the crown, as he was in prison. His beloved father and sister Julie found themselves penniless overnight. They were forced to leave the rue de Condé, which La Blache had completely emptied. For the first time in his life M. Caron went to stay with friends, while Julie had to take a room in a convent.

As I have pointed out again and again, Beaumarchais eventually fought back with incredible tenacity and intelligence. But for a few days he faltered. It was too much, even for him. On the ninth, three days after the court ruling, he dashed off the following despairing letter to Sartines:

> I am at the end of my tether. Rumour has it that I'm totally ruined. My credit has fallen, my business is wasting away, my family are in distress without me to support them. *Monsieur*, I have done good all my life unostentatiously, and I have always been torn to shreds by the wicked. If my hearth and family were known to you, you would see that as a good son, a good brother, a good husband and a useful citizen I have reaped nothing but blessings at home while being brazenly calumnied abroad. Whatever the source and nature of this revenge for the wretched affair with Chaulnes, will there be no end to it? It has been shown beyond all doubt that my imprisonment has cost me 100,000 francs. This iniquitous court ruling – substance, form and all – makes my blood boil, yet I can

do nothing to remedy matters so long as I am detained in a horrible prison. I have strength against my own woes; I have none against the tears of my estimable father, aged seventy-five, who is dying of grief at the abjection into which I have fallen; nor have I any against the sorrow of my sisters and nieces, who have already felt the horror of dire necessity to come, owing to the disordered state into which my detention has thrown both myself and my affairs. All my thoughts are directed against myself, my situation is killing me, I am struggling against an acute illness, the first symptoms of which are insomnia and loss of appetite. The air in my prison is rank and is destroying my poor health . . .

Having touched bottom, however, he soon surged back to the surface like a high diver at the end of his dive. The first to realize it was the Duc de La Vallière, who had decided, with some reason, to place restrictions on the rights and privileges of his lieutenant-general. In his cell M. de Beaumarchais recovered health, insolence and true nobility as if by magic. His letter to the duke is too long to quote, and is apparently concerned with minute details of etiquette, but it bursts with pride from start to finish. It is in misfortune that Beaumarchais *emerges*. From now on he will never again lower his voice. We shall see him speaking louder and louder to dukes, ministers and sovereigns.

He had realized that, for essentials, he could rely only on himself. After much thought, he would launch from his cell an apparently formidable onslaught against the Goëzmans. But an attack on the Goëzmans was an attack on parliament as a whole, hence on the government, hence on Louis XV. No conflict was possible between the new assembly and the executive, for one was the mirror image of the other. In 1773 anyone calling check on the king by taking a knight was playing a very dangerous gambit indeed – single-handed, too, because nobody would be crazy enough to risk his freedom by joining him. Yet Beaumarchais didn't hesitate. To recover his honour, he took every risk in the book. And on 21 April, when he advanced his opening pawn by writing to the councillor's wife, he was fully aware of the danger he was exposing himself to. *Omnia citra mortem*, everything short of death – that would be his punishment if he failed. *Omnia citra mortem* – the penitentiary, the galleys, the pillory. The stakes were truly enormous, particularly since the extent of the potential winnings was unknown. Twenty years earlier Pierre-Augustin had won his first battle against

Lepaute by taking the king as his arbiter; but in 1773 he had to do battle against both Goëzman and the king. The only possible arbiter in this fight against the system was the people, or more specifically public opinion. In April 1773 public opinion was against him, to put it mildly. He could always have backed down, and would probably have recovered the favours of the king and the friendship of the royal family if he had; but at forty he no longer wished to compromise. 'You were the only one who dared to laugh in their faces,' he was told after *The Marriage*. To laugh in someone's face you have to be well and truly on your feet.

On 21 April, then, Beaumarchais sent Mme Goëzman the following letter:

> I do not have the honour, *madame*, of being known personally to you, and I would refrain from importuning you if, after the loss of my lawsuit, when you were good enough to send back my two rouleaux of *louis* and the diamond watch, I had also been repossessed on your behalf of the fifteen gold *louis* which our mutual friend who acted as negotiator also left with you.
>
> I have been treated so horribly in your husband's report, and my arguments in my defence have been so crushed by a man who might have been expected, according to you, to consider them with due respect, that it is unjust to add to the enormous losses that this report has cost me the further loss of fifteen gold *louis*, which cannot have gone astray in your hands. If injustice must be paid for, no retribution can be expected from a man who suffers so cruelly on its account.

Beaumarchais was presenting Mme Goëzman with the following alternative: either return the 15 *louis*, or deny having received them. In the first instance she would be obliged to acknowledge that she had withheld a sum of money destined to be paid to her secretary. In the second instance the risk of dishonour was greater still, since a number of witnesses could prove that she was lying. In either instance, the councillor's dignity and integrity were likely to be jeopardized.

The minute she received the letter Mme Goëzman went to see the bookseller. We shall never know what plot was laid between the all-powerful pigeon plucker and poor Lejay, nor how she managed to get round him – though we might hazard a guess. At all events, two hours later the bookseller, greatly embarrassed, was round at Fanchon's blurting out what he had been told to say: 'Mme Goëzman is outraged and fails to understand how anyone has dared to ask for the 100 *louis* and the watch, which she has already returned. She wishes to inform M. de Beaumarchais, should he insist, she will speak to the ministers who are in her husband's pocket.' This announcement was greeted with stunned silence by Mme Lépine and those of her friends who were present. Had Lejay gone mad? Had they heard him properly? He repeated his lines without changing a word. Where-upon Fanchon sternly reminded him that it was a matter of 15 *louis*, as he well knew. Unable to deny the obvious, the bookseller looked wan and held his tongue. They fired questions at him, but to no avail. Before leaving, however, he recovered his wits sufficiently to announce to those present that he would deny 'having had any part in this affair, should it take a turn for the worse'.

Beaumarchais had just lost his principal witness. Shortly after-wards, however, he retrieved his main advantage: freedom. The Comte de La Blache had got what he wanted, so La Vrillière had no further reason for keeping Beaumarchais in prison. On 6 May he signed the order for his release – a political blunder if ever there was one, for the man he had unjustly sent to the For-Lévêque to oblige a friend was more of a threat to the régime than he could ever have imagined.

On the morning of 8 May Beaumarchais was set free. His first thought was to save his last sticks of furniture and to make some money. M. Caron, Julie (who was fretting in the abbey of Saint-Antoine), and the two sisters who had returned penniless from Madrid all depended on him for their livelihood. In the space of a few days, using his wits and what credit he could find, he went back into business and managed to recover his forest at Chinon. This semi-security gave him a narrow margin which would allow him to spend the greater part of his time in fighting the Goëzmans.

At night, in the cafés and *salons*, Beaumarchais talked about his adventure with the plucker and her husband. Within a few weeks the story of the 15 *louis* had gone the rounds of Paris. The innumerable enemies of parliament discovered to their delight that Maupeou's councillors were no better than their predecessors when it came to bribes. Someone came up with the dictum: 'Louis XV toppled the old parliament, 15 *louis* will topple the new one.' Guy Target, a renowned barrister, who had constantly and scrupulously refused to plead before parliament, organized a let's-be-friends-again supper for Chaulnes and Beaumarchais. From then on the two men were inseparable until the end of the battle for which their quarrel had been the absurd pretext.

Goëzman had much more to his name than the 15 *louis*. He was no fool, particularly when it came to points of procedure. With his dignity threatened, a laughing stock and almost compromised, he decided to defend himself vigorously in the classic manner – by attacking.

After obtaining two signed declarations from Lejay, in which the bookseller admitted 'having received 100 *louis* and a diamond watch from a friend of M. de Beaumarchais, having had the weakness to offer them to Mme Goëzman to corrupt the justice of her husband, and having been repulsed by her with *hauteur* and indignation', the councillor, complacently assuming that he had the whip hand, requested a further warrant of imprisonment for his infamous opponent. This time La Vrillière turned a deaf ear. Sartines, whose influence was on the up and up, did nothing to help the councillor. Goëzman knocked at other doors, too – doubtless at that of the important personage of whom Beaumarchais writes: 'He enjoyed everyone's esteem and trust.' We cannot put a name to him – perhaps Aiguillon, the Foreign Minister – but we do know that Beaumarchais had had the sense to write to him and forestall Goëzman. Here is the letter:

Monsieur,
Concerning the complaints allegedly lodged against me by M. Goëzman, who claims that I attempted to bribe him by offering money to Mme Goëzman which she rejected, I declare that this account is false, whatever its origin. I declare that I did not attempt to bribe M. Goëzman with a view to winning a lawsuit which I have always believed I could not be made to lose, except by error or injustice.

With respect to the money offered by me and supposedly rejected by Mme Goëzman: if it is a mere rumour, M. Goëzman cannot know whether I subscribe to the rumour or not; as a judge, he ought not to incriminate me so lightly . . . If he thinks he has grounds for complaint, he should attack me in court. I have nothing to hide. I declare that I respect all judges appointed by the king; today, however, M. Goëzman is not my judge. He is said to be lodging a complaint against me. In so doing he becomes a citizen like any other, and I hope that the government will kindly remain neutral in the affair. I shall not attack anyone;

but I declare that I shall defend myself openly if provoked, within the bounds of moderation, modesty and the consideration that I vouchsafe to everyone.

At this point a moment's reflection is called for. I have quoted this letter because it seems to me to reveal Beaumarchais's state of mind. Obviously he wants Goëzman to sue; he wants to be brought to court for attempted bribery. Why? To all appearances he had everything to lose in this affair. It was customary for parliament to try cases of attempted bribery in secret session, and the court was not obliged to give any grounds for its judgment. The councillors were behind Goëzman to a man, whereas they were hostile to Beaumarchais at the outset, since his preference for the old parliament was well known. They would not hesitate for a moment between a distinguished member of their own conclave and the disreputable Beaumarchais. And yet, knowing that his cause was already lost, Beaumarchais still flung himself into the fray. Why? Trials for bribery carried horrific sentences: everything short of death. How could a man straight out of prison with every chance of recovery take such a risk? To my knowledge, no one hitherto has tried to solve this riddle. Since Beaumarchais won in the end, his biographers have contented themselves with describing the battle and celebrating his victory, without explaining why he took on parliament in the first place.

As I have already pointed out, the fight was unnecessary. In 1773 the process of government was hopelessly warped by the traditions of personal rule, arbitrary imprisonment, privilege, corruption and injustice. People just accepted these things, or put up with them. So many people had been in prison in 1773. So many had been sentenced unjustly. All you had to do was to bow your head, let the storm pass and wait for things to get better. It was never long before things did get better – the king and his ministers and his judges had ready pardons. In this paternalistic society *par excellence*, all the king's men were his children. In the last resort, he could always pat them on the head and let them off. But Beaumarchais wanted, at the age of forty (this is the true explanation, I think), to become an adult at last. At Versailles with Mesdames, at the Ecole Militaire with Pâris-Duverney, in Madrid, at the Louvre, he had been playing in the kindergergarten – brilliantly, but without breaking bounds. When the king had caught him misbehaving, and had sent him into the corner, he had meekly obeyed. But at forty he was tired of the playground. The pretence had lasted long enough. Who was he in 1773? I repeat: a carnival mask. Did he realize that in deciding to become himself and stop pretending he was embarking on a battle that went way beyond him? Without the slightest doubt. Did he realize as well that in the long run he was helping to pave the way for the collapse of the system? I think so. And did he realize that the logical consequence of his revolt was patricide? Certainly not.

Strangely enough, Goëzman entered the lists with rather less enthusiasm. True, everyone who mattered was eating out of his hand and he was sure of victory; but at the same time he felt instinctively shy at the idea of entering the public arena. Judges prefer to live in the shadows – mystery enhances their respectability. But Goëzman, having failed to obtain a warrant of imprisonment, was forced into the limelight. On 21 June he formally lodged an accusation of bribery; four days later the assessor, Doe de Combault, opened the file. Mankind having acquired a taste for liberty, it has remained open ever since.

HIS OLD STOUT WILL

Revolutions begin the moment a consensus questions or impugns institutions, customs or judicial processes. However, if one man is to bring down a régime or an institution, help is needed from the only source available to him – public opinion. Providing it exists, that is. In 1773 it virtually had to be invented. True, the eighteenth century was a century of polemics: Beaumarchais wasn't the first to take up his pen to attack or to defend. Before him, however, pamphlets, broadsheets and tracts weren't intended to be read by the man in the street. They were printed in mere hundreds for a select public. Frequently they were destroyed before they even left the printers, or remained largely undistributed. At best, as with Voltaire's pamphlets, they circulated among the *cognoscenti*, who were perfectly capable of merriment, astonishment and even indignation for an evening or so, but were hardly given to revolt. To attack his judges, Beaumarchais memoed the world. That was something new. His *Memoirs* were immediately translated into a number of languages. In

North America, for instance, they met with considerable interest, and Beaumarchais was known as a defender of liberty long before he played a decisive role in the War of Independence. Public opinion in France and elsewhere, such as it was, knew what it was about: Beaumarchais's fight against Goëzman was a fight against oppression, injustice and tyranny in all their forms.

The most remarkable thing in this respect is that the *Memoirs* never stray from the matter in hand. Beaumarchais takes care not to generalize or philosophize. At first sight they are mere statements of what happened, but it is their extraordinary power of reasoning, their humour, their brisk style and above all their verve that make them qualify as masterpieces.

Yet these qualities in themselves (and the ingredients of what is known as a 'good plot': a sincere and passionate defendant, great risks, a villainous parliament) do not fully explain the memorials' tremendous popularity. The secret of Beaumarchais's extraordinary success lies in a single word – comedy. It is because he was clever enough to treat his enemies as characters, to write scenes in which they move and speak, and to stage himself as himself that Beaumarchais found an audience and reached the people. Unlike a reader, who keeps his impressions to himself, an audience participates (by laughing, exclaiming, applauding and so on) in the way a play turns out: the play cannot end without its audience, and it cannot end *against* it. As we shall see, Paris took to the streets the day the trial ended to acclaim Beaumarchais and boo his adversaries. But the people took no notice of the real outcome of the trial: they cheered Beaumarchais as if he really had beaten parliament, because a comedy has to end with the triumph of the hero and the defeat of his enemies. Now when an entire city thinks it is at the theatre, it is not far short of revolution: the final curtain fell on the Maupeou parliament on 26 February 1774.

Avoiding caricature, Beaumarchais turns the palest and most insignificant of individuals into a corrosively funny and rounded character. In his hands the interminable confrontations with the councillor and his wife become brilliant comedy; yet he hasn't invented a single word of dialogue – the effect is achieved by the liveliness of the writing.

Gabrielle Goëzman cleverly avoids answering questions directly by quibbling over absurd details. When asked to keep to the point, she jibs: 'Let me be, *monsieur*. If I were to be expected to answer such impertinence, we should still be cavilling over this silly letter tomorrow morning.' When Beaumarchais or the commissioner point out that she has contradicted herself from one day to the next, she replies without batting an eyelid: 'I didn't know what I was saying. I wasn't myself at all, I was in a critical state.' Asked what this singular affliction might involve, she says: 'In truth, there are times when I don't know what I'm saying and don't remember a thing.' At times, however, the plucker's pirouettes throw her off balance. This is Beaumarchais talking:

> Then I asked her to be so kind as to tell us clearly and unambiguously whether or not she had asked Lejay for fifteen *louis* for the secretary, and whether or not she had placed them in her bureau when the bookseller brought them to her.
>
> 'I shall answer, clearly and unambiguously, that Lejay never mentioned any fifteen *louis*, or presented them to me.'
>
> 'Mark you, *madame*, it would be more worthy to say, "I refused them" than to maintain that you never knew anything about them.'
>
> 'I maintain, *monsieur*, that they were never mentioned. What would be the point in offering fifteen *louis* to someone of my quality, particularly when I had refused a hundred the day before?'
>
> 'Which day before do you mean, *madame*?'
>
> 'Why, the day before . . .'
>
> She stopped short, biting her lip.
>
> 'The day before the day the fifteen *louis* were never mentioned?' I said, 'Is that it?'
>
> 'Stop,' she said, rising in a rage, 'or I shall box your ears. You're just trying to muddle me and catch me out with all your nasty insinuations, but I swear in truth that I shall not answer another word.'

Any judge worth his salt wouldn't have allowed Mme Goëzman to get bogged down in her absurd lies for more time than it took to say truth. But for months on end the commissioners continued these insane cross-examinations, waiting for a mistake, a slip, on the part of Beaumarchais, since he was the one they were supposed to find guilty. Of course Goëzman, their co-dignitary, colleague and standard-bearer, couldn't be anything but innocent.

But these honest judges had reckoned without the success of the *Memoirs*. The first of them, and its supplement, ran into tens of thousands of copies in the space of a few days. The scenes with Mme

Goëzman became *parades* overnight. They were acted in the streets, in the cafés, in the *salons*, and finally at Versailles. Mme du Barry adored hearing Préville as Beaumarchais and La Dugazon as Mme Goëzman. And it seems the royal family eventually took to acting the *parades* themselves. What could Chancellor Maupeou hope to do against the most subtle of all forms of subversion, the sort that made people laugh?

To deal with Goëzman himself, who was lurking in the wings of this strange theatre where a man was playing for his liberty with a laugh, another tone was needed. Sure of himself and his parliament, the councillor was awaiting Beaumarchais's punishment without much anxiety. *He* was on the side of law and order. *He* had his wife and two or three wags (the Baculards and Marins of this world, whom we shall discuss later) to make mud for him and plaster it shamelessly over a defendant who had the nerve to claim he was innocent. What were the risks for Goëzman, if the worst came to the worst? If he was held responsible for his wife's lapses, he could always send her to a convent! He would do anything to save his reputation, except descend into the arena in person. I said he was in the wings. In fact, he was in the flies, along with the *papier-mâché* gods and the sun and the thunder machine. Beaumarchais's tactic was to force him down and demonstrate that he was crooked. Goëzman had made only one mistake, but it was a big one – he had banked on Lejay. It was typical of a judge to imagine that publishers exist only for their authors; unfortunately for him, Lejay, who had signed two false statements, had cracked under Beaumarchais's questioning, and his confession had been taken down in writing by the clerk of the court. He told, for example, of his final encounter with the councillor in the rue de l'Etoile near the lawcourts:
'My dear Lejay,' the honourable author of *Common Law of Fiefs* had said to him. 'I sent for you to tell you not to worry. I have arranged that you will be heard as a witness and not as a defendant.' Coming from a judge, the phrase was a strange one, as Beaumarchais hastened to point out: 'You have *arranged, monsieur*! You, the bailee of the scales and the sword, have thus for the one two weights and two measures, and you thrust with the other or hold back at will, so that a man is a witness if he agrees with you, a defendant if he demurs!' Goëzman did not so much as blink at this reproach: he was immune

to irony. In the course of this same encounter Lejay had tried to
explain to his accomplice that he had signed the statements under
pressure and wouldn't sustain the lie before a court of justice;
whereupon Goëzman, the honourable Goëzman, had answered:
'I'm sorry for you, Lejay, but it is too late: you have made two
statements and my wife will stick by them to the end. If you change
your tune, so much the worse for you.' (This 'it is too late' inspired a
fine tirade in which Figaro admonishes Brid'oison: 'It is too late!
What, sir, is there ever a time when it is too late to tell the truth? Out
of weakness for you a man signed a false declaration than can ruin
several honest people for ever, and because his repudiation of it would
hurt your feelings, it is too late to repent! . . . Too late! And you a
magistrate! Great gods in heaven, what next!')

As regards changes of tune, Goëzman was sure that it was he who
was calling the piper. To throw Beaumarchais on to the wrong foot
and force him to quadrille instead of rigadooning, he had several
dances played at once. No musician himself, and intent on remaining the master of ceremonies, he adopted La Blache's solution and
hired the minstrels of calumny. Goëzman's fiddlers three were called
Marin, Bertrand and Baculard d'Arnaud.

Marin, Bertrand and Baculard would have sunk into oblivion today
if Beaumarchais hadn't had cause to immortalize them, rendering
good for evil so to speak. Marin, Bertrand and Baculard, chosen by
Goëzman (and by La Blache no doubt) and hired for a fat fee, set to
work. Since Beaumarchais had dragged the debate into the market
square, Goëzman was obliged to follow him – not in person, of
course (too demanding), but by delegating his three factotums.
Thus, Marin, Bertrand and Baculard each wrote, or put his name
to, a pamphlet. Goëzman knew enough about human nature to
choose acquaintances of Beaumarchais's who were also writers:
experience proves that a man's friends really are his worst enemies at
times, and as we all know, jealousy and envy are facile muses.

Baculard d'Arnaud was quite well known as a writer of novels in
the funereal vein. According to Loménie, he was proud of his 'senti-
mental rotundity'. He was also a diplomatic attaché, like many a
writer before and since, except that in 1773 the job meant more than
it does today. Baculard was expected to undertake missions that
were not always diplomatic – stopping that bounder Beaumarchais,

for instance. He had a further reason for helping Goëzman and serving his government – the councillor had just done him a favour over a lawsuit he had had with La Tournelle. In short, poor Baculard was on the spot. Was it his lack of conviction that led him to pad out his pamphlet with rotundities? I don't know, but no writer of novels, however bad, can be functioning normally when he writes: 'There are hearts into which I read with a shudder, finding within all the dark depths of hell. At which I cry, "Are you sleeping, Jupiter? Will you not loose your bolts?" ' From one end of the wretched Baculard's pensum to the other, there is only one phrase written naturally and without rotundity: 'I was on foot and in the rue de Condé I met M. Caron in a coach, in his coach!' Baculard could be himself once he was able to express himself sincerely – and what could be more sincere than this expression of self-pity and hatred! Beaumarchais seized his opportunity to take the envious Baculard for a ride:

> *In his coach*! you repeat with a big admiration mark! Who could fail to think, from that 'I was on foot' and that big admiration mark that chases after my coach, that you are envy personified? But I, who know you for the kind fellow you are, am well aware that this phrase 'in his coach!' doesn't mean that you were annoyed to see me 'in my coach' but merely that you would have liked me to see you in yours. It is because you never say what you mean that you are always misunderstood.
>
> But take comfort: the coach I was driving in was no longer mine when you saw me in it. The Comte de La Blache had had it seized, along with all my belongings. It was being guarded at my house by men in blue coats who came with cartridge belts and rifles and drank my wine; and to cause you, unwittingly, the distress of perceiving me 'in my coach' I had been obliged, that very morning, to experience the equal distress of calling on these bailiff's journeymen and asking them, cap in hand and a big tip to the fore, for permission to use it – as I did, save your displeasure, every morning. And while I am speaking to you so calmly, the same affliction still exists in my house.

Thus Beaumarchais turned a clumsy attack into a murderous defence. Baculard was held up to ridicule; above all, his pamphlet was completely demolished by this 'you are always misunderstood because you never say what you mean'. And it was a fine stroke to take La Blache and his bailiffs for a ride in that coach as well. A lot of good work was done in those few lines of text! With Baculard reeling. Beaumarchais closed in for the knock-out blow:

> Forgive me, *monsieur*, if I have not answered your many insults with a work written expressly for you. Forgive me if . . . seeing you discover within my heart 'all the dark depths of hell' and exclaim 'Are you sleeping, Jupiter? Will you not loose your bolts?' I have replied irreverently to so much puff. Forgive me. You were once a schoolboy, no doubt, and must know that even the most carefully inflated of balloons cannot withstand a pinprick.

The sword was too good for Baculard – a pin would do for him. As I have already pointed out, and will have further cause to repeat, the most astonishing aspect of Beaumarchais's character is that he was incapable of bearing a grudge. When years later Baculard, like so many of his former enemies, appealed to his generosity, Beaumarchais opened his purse without hesitation and 'lent' close on 4000 *livres* to the man who had seen him in the 'dark depths of hell'. While we are on this subject, I can't resist pointing out as well that when Mme Goëzman fell upon hard times it was of course Beaumarchais who stepped in to help her.

Of the three hacks employed by Goëzman, Marin seems to have been the most remarkable. Certainly not for his writing: if Baculard's style is inflated, Marin's is shrivelled. (I mean it smacks of the scribe – copyist or teacher. Marin was both.) No, for the range of his gifts. Tired of teaching, he turned his hand to journalism. He more or less ran the *Gazette de France*, which had government connections and published no news but good news. Full of zeal, he occasionally twisted the truth in the right direction; for instance he wouldn't hesitate to double any figures that favoured the government and halve them when they did the opposite. A further outlet for his zeal was censorship. As we have seen, he and Beaumarchais met when the latter was seeking clearance for *Eugénie*. In addition, Marin officiated at the Librairie de France, working round the clock to ensure that writers who had been censored could have their works, which he himself had banned, smuggled into France from printers in Holland and Switzerland. It is said that Voltaire was an appreciative beneficiary of Marin's conscientious importations. From time to time, with a view to deceiving the authorities (i.e. himself), Marin

sent one of his own pedlars to the galleys. It goes without saying that
anyone who could get away with this kind of game just had to belong
to the police. Marin undoubtedly did, as one of Maupeou's hench-
men. Voltaire, who saw him merely as a devoted and mediocre
fellow writer, had considered supporting his bid for election to the
Académie Française in 1770. Having read Beaumarchais's memoirs
at Ferney, however, Voltaire broke with the villainous Marin. The
writer Bernardin de Saint-Pierre, who had crossed swords with the
man, wrote to Beaumarchais at the height of his trial: 'I pity you for
having come across such a dangerous, such a deeply treacherous
man . . .' Is my nasty piece of work complete? No, just one more
touch – before taking on these jobs, Marin had written books, in
particular a *History of the Sultan Saladin*.

At the start of the trial Marin had offered to help Beaumarchais.
He was a friend, as his favourable opinion of the *Barber* showed, and
had influence. If Beaumarchais would take his advice, he would
forget all about those wretched 15 *louis*, in his own interests, and then
he, Marin, would 'make things easier' for him. When Beaumarchais
didn't appear to be receptive, Marin dropped his pretence and
changed sides. The journalist seized his quill and perpetrated a
poisonous pamphlet that begins with a quotation from the Persian:
'Do not give your rice to a snake, because the snake will bite you.'
Marin never calls a spade a spade. It is all done with insinuations,
and is extremely effective. While assuring the reader that it is not his
custom to 'harm my own enemies', he piles on the denunciations:
Beaumarchais is an opponent of the parliament; in private, he
attacks ministers and officials with reprehensible boldness; and he
says dreadful things about the magistrature and religion. Obeying
his own logic, Marin ends by urging the Bench to punish Beaumarchais pitilessly, and even writes: 'When calumny spread by libellous
means destroys the reputation of an honest citizen, its authors must
be sentenced to penal servitude, transportation or even, in many
cases, death.'

In this charming character Beaumarchais met his ideal adversary.
The wicked, ridiculous and servile journalist was highly unpopular,
making him a perfect target for Beaumarchais's darting wit. For
instance, here is what he made of Marin's habit, dating from his
childhood at La Ciotat, of using the Provençal word *quesaco* ('what
does that mean?'):

Ah, M. Marin! You have come a long way since those happy times when with shaven head and in long linen robes, the symbol of your innocence, you delighted La Ciotat with your little tunes on the organ and your pipings in the choir!·. . . He's not the same man, is Marin! Look how evil can grow and spread when it isn't nipped in the bud. This Marin, whose only vice at first was to

> Present the vicar at the altar
> With the offering or the psalter,

discards his surplice and galoshes and jumps from the organ to teaching, to censoring, to secretarying, and finally to the *Gazette*. And there's my Marin with his sleeves rolled up to his elbows fishing for evil in troubled waters . . . At last, slithering, climbing, jumping and leaping, ever flat out, he has done so well by his journeywork that he has been seen, the pirate, driving to Versailles in a coach and four emblazoned with his coat of arms. In the escutcheon shaped like an organ case, his bearings are gules a Fame with clipped wings, inverted, scraping the string of a trumpet *marine*, supported by a sickened figure representing Europe, the whole draped in a cassock lined with gazettes surmounted by a doctor's cap whose tuft bears the following inscription: *Ques-à-co? Marin.*

Thus Beaumarchais executed his would-be executioner. The tirade still seems amusing today and we can still admire the composure and verve of a man who can laugh off a formidable opponent only a few days before the fearsome sentence. Yet we cannot imagine the effect that this *quesaco* produced on the whole of Europe. It would be an understatement to say that the word was soon all the rage. For a month or more, everything was *quesaco*. Even the ladies' head-dresses. Marie-Antoinette in person launched the *quesaco*, a tuft of feathers worn on the crown of your wig.

Councillor Goëzman's third quill-pusher is not unknown to us. He's called Bertrand, Bertrand Dairolles. We saw him at the Lépine's, where he had feathered his own nest, and as the main negotiator with Lejay. A 'man of affairs', in more senses than one, Bertrand Dairolles was well in with everyone. He was for hire, and espoused the cause of the highest bidder. Fanchon, who probably had a weakness for him, mistook him for a hotspur. Out of bed, he was a poltroon. Marin, who could tell a poltroon when he saw one, had already sized him up. Both of them came from Provence, so they spoke the same language. Marin had no difficulty in putting the wind up Bertrand. When it was pointed out to him that his support for Beaumarchais might have irritated the all-powerful parliament, he quickly saw the point and turned his coat. Throwing himself heart and soul into the cause of the pigeon plucker, he changed his evidence in its entirety. To give his new assertions more weight, the little banker saw fit to make published prose of them, partly in Latin. He was undoubtedly helped with his homework, for he was something of a dunce; but he did sign it, proving that at least he knew how to hold a quill. His unreadable pamphlet, 'sprinkled all over with opium and ossa fœtida' as it was, duly received an answer from Beaumarchais: 'I have only scanned it, because it smacks of something nasty and brackish and *marinated*, making it wholly distasteful. But since it appeared under your name, I shall answer it as if it were by you. It is not always easy, *messieurs*, to tell which of your Provençal wares is genuine or counterfeit.'

All these quotations should not lead us to conclude that the memoirs were merely brilliantly entertaining rhetoric. La Harpe writes: 'What is particularly striking, and what I have found nowhere else, is his alternation, and sometimes his juxtaposition, of indignation and gaiety, which he communicates to the reader either in turn or simultaneously. He makes you angry and he makes you laugh, which is rarer and more difficult in art than in nature.'

Beaumarchais realized, however, that it wasn't enough to plead his own cause and mock his opponents'. As a judge, Goëzman had one great advantage: his word couldn't be questioned. The man in the street is always powerless when he is trapped in this situation. In fact, he is only making things worse for himself if he obstinately contradicts the policeman: even today defendants are told that it is better to confess and apologize than to stand up to the word of a representative of the law. But that wasn't Beaumarchais's style at all. To beat Goëzman, he had to desanctify the word of the law; in other words, he had to prove that the councillor was an ordinary liar, and had perjured himself. Beaumarchais had a hunch that Goëzman wasn't as clean as he pretended to be, and began to scout round for proof. By a stroke of luck he was able to establish on 15 December 1773 that Goëzman was guilty of committing and uttering a forgery.

He had discovered from a poor couple, Antoine-Pierre Dubillon and his wife Marie-Magdeleine, that for the last five months their daughter's godfather had failed to fulfil his promise to send them an allowance for the child's upkeep. This dutiless godfather was Goëzman. Naturally, Beaumarchais wanted to know more. Mme Dufour, the midwife who had delivered Mme Dubillon's daughter, Sophie, gladly gave him the information he needed, and before long he was in a position to enlighten the public, and hence the court, about the use to which Goëzman put his word and his signature:

> I wanted to determine whether it was true that this magistrate, who was refusing to aid these poor folk, had valid reasons for helping them. I went to the parish of Saint-Jacques de la Boucherie and consulted the certificate of baptism . . . I was surprised to find that it read: 'Louis Dugravier, bourgeois of Paris, dwelling in the rue des Lyons, parish of Saint-Paul, godfather of Marie Sophie.' Could it be that M. Goëzman, who parades so much virtue, had mocked the house of God, and religion, and the most serious of documents . . . by signing *Louis Dugravier* instead of *Louis Goëzman*, and giving a *false address* as well as a false name?

Unmasking the honest, the incorruptible, the virtuous Goëzman was fair play under the circumstances, but Beaumarchais didn't like doing it, and felt that he had to justify himself: 'I have myself been denounced unjustly, and the most brazen insults have been heaped upon me, together with reproaches that were as untrue as they were irrelevant to the case in hand. I am using every means I have to defend myself.' There were some weapons that Beaumarchais didn't like using. His reluctance strikes me as another point in his favour.

It has often been said that the four *Memoirs* were the joint work of the 'infamous clique'. It is true that they were read over and over again, and occasionally corrected, by the family. At Fanchon's house, where Beaumarchais had taken refuge, there was the same cultural climate as in the rue Saint-Denis. Old M. Caron had a lively pen, Tonton and her husband were avid readers, Lépine and Fanchon were far from ignorant, but it was Julie who was especially gifted. At the same time, it is clear from her voluminous correspondence and from the little book she published in 1788 (*The Reflective Existence, or, A Moral Glance at the Value of Life*) that her style and thought were very different from her brother's. Both in her more licentious moments and in her moments of piety, Julie's style is always refined. It is obvious that elegance and polish are prime considerations with her, as they often are in writings by women. This, for instance, is how she writes to Tonton: 'I must scratch at the door of your heart, and dance attendance on your mind; I must awaken your footmen *kind words*, pay your maid *memory* and rouse your butler *good relations*.' And so on. At her best, Julie still whimpers and keeps an eye on herself in the glass. Now I for one find the memorials remarkable because they are natural and free to the point of being vulgar. Like all great writers, Beaumarchais doesn't recoil from crude language or looseness of expression. Only the fops among writers shun vulgarity like the plague, writing the way they walk – on tiptoe. And to my mind the four memorials, like it or not, are similar in their liveliness and their unmistakable pace, which is Beaumarchais's own pace – quick, light, crisp. Julie didn't have this gift for ellipsis, this genius for compression, and nor did any of the others. True, it can be shown that Julie often helped in drafting the memorials, but in my opinion that is no reason to conclude that they were written collectively. The corrections, cuts and interpolations in the manuscripts are far less numerous than they are made out to be. And few writers ignore the opinions of their entourage, especially when, as with Beaumarchais, their lives depend on what they write.

In fact the family would have preferred him to stick to the Goëz-mans and their accomplices. They viewed with alarm his increasing tendency to make the debate political. Instead of compromising, he seemed intent on taking on the system single-handed. I am deliber-ately stressing this aspect of Beaumarchais's revolt, his sudden and solitary rejection of the regime, because this attitude doesn't fit in with the image that most people have of him. What about you, reader? Have I convinced you, or are you still hesitating, like Bailly, who opens his book with this statement: 'He leaves us with an anxiety, a doubt'? If so, read the next few lines carefully. They were published a few days before the court pronounced its decision. What kind of man would dare to put the Bench on public trial before they sentenced him?

> If arbitrary limits were placed on everything, extending or restricting each man's rights to suit particular circumstances, what certainty would remain? The courts would no longer know the extent of their jurisdiction, and the citizens would not know the extent of their liberty. If disorder and confusion were to serve as a basis for everything, oriental-style disorder would be less dangerous than such anarchy. If, instead of being

impartial in disputes, like the law they serve, the magistrates were more attentive to the spirit of their order than to the spirit of justice that they owe us, and stamped on the citizens' rights, either the system of such legislation would be bad, or we should need a still higher court than the supreme courts to which each citizen might justly appeal.

To give some idea of the climate during the last few days of the trial, and to see how 'serenely' parliament was taking it all, I might mention a minor incident that was of the greatest significance. On his way to give evidence, Beaumarchais met Judge de Nicolaï, a former cavalry colonel, marching at the head of a column of magistrates. Without reason or motive, Nicolaï pointed at Beaumarchais and cried, 'Guard, throw that man, Beaumarchais, out! He is only here to defy me!' The guards laid hands on him. Pushing them away, Beaumarchais called to the large crowd of onlookers, 'I call on the nation to bear witness to the public outrage that is being done to me.' 'The citizens', 'the nation': strange terms to use in 1773. Stranger still, Nicolaï was forced to back down, 'the nation', i.e. the witnesses of the altercation, having leapt to the 'citizen's' defence and rescued him from his guards. To explain this outburst, Nicolaï claimed that Beaumarchais had stuck out his tongue at him. All the same when a senior judge of the sacrosanct parliament (and an ex-colonel into the bargain) felt he had to justify himself, anything he might say was tantamount to retreat. Beaumarchais, really defying Nicolaï this time, recklessly published this story in his fourth memoir, thus whipping the wrath of the Bench to sheer fury.

We have seen 'the nation' in action. From December 1773 to February 1774 popular unrest grew from day to day. In the cafés, in the streets, people began to demonstrate for Beaumarchais and above all against parliament. The demonstrations were spontaneous, of course. But one man's fight against arbitrary authority had suddenly become almost everyone's fight. True, no protests were as yet being levelled against the king, whom Beaumarchais himself had exonerated. For a time, he would remain above the fray. In 1773 the protests didn't go beyond the puppet parliament. But this break with the past, this first growl of anger, anticipated the great revolution of 1789, still fifteen years away. As Beaumarchais wrote in his fourth memoir: 'This whole affair has become too serious to be kept within individual bounds.'

Voltaire, who had been in favour of the Maupeou parliament, soon changed his mind once he had read the memoirs: 'I'm afraid this brilliant scatterbrain may be fundamentally right and everyone else wrong. What knavery! Heavens, what horrors! What vileness in the nation! What a setback to parliament!' In a letter to d'Alembert he went further: 'What a man! He can achieve anything – jests, seriousness, reasoning, gaiety, firmness, pathos – every form of eloquence, yet he seeks none of them, and confounds all his adversaries, and lays down the law to the Bench. His naivety is a delight, and I forgive him his moments of rashness and petulance.'

Most of the great writers of the age, avoiding jealousy for once, stepped forward to salute these four texts and their author. Rousseau answered those who accused Beaumarchais of not having written them himself: 'I don't know whether he writes them himself, but I do know that no one writes pamphlets like that for someone else.' Bernardin de Saint-Pierre was prophetic: 'You will soon be as famous as Molière.' Goethe organized public readings of the fourth memoir in Frankfurt. Horace Walpole wrote to Mme du Deffand: 'I have received Beaumarchais's memoirs. I have reached the third, and find them very amusing . . . Considering the party spirit in France at the moment, I can see that this affair must be causing a great sensation. I was forgetting to tell you how horrified I was by the judicial processes in France. Is there a country in the world that would not have punished this Mme Goëzman severely?'

But Beaumarchais's success, however flattering, did not blind him. The dice were still rolling. Everything depended on the executive in the long run, and the signs were contradictory. The government had permitted a run of *Eugénie* in January (ovations), but banned *The Barber of Seville* in February, a day before the opening. The ministers' hesitations are understandable: to give in to public opinion was tantamount to limiting absolute monarchy; to condemn Beaumarchais could only make the monarchy more unpopular. Experience shows that governments generally choose the middle way when confronted with an alternative. But that is *our* experience, whereas in the eighteenth century political life was only just beginning. The nation existed only in books, unaware as yet of its strength. Facing the king, his ministers and his parliament there was nothing but a void – a dizzying prospect for everyone.

Then came 25 February, the day before the court was due to

pronounce. The news was bad. Dining in town, honourable parliamentarians had made it known that a decision had been reached. On the morow, according to them, Beaumarchais would get the maximum sentence, but not the death penalty. He knew every detail of what Chancellor Maupeou's judges had in store for him. It began almost nicely: *kneeling with a large yellow candle in his hands to make honourable amends*. It went on rather more cruelly: *pilloried, with boards on his chest and back bearing the words 'briber' and 'slanderer'*. It continued with skilful tortures, a show put on for an audience of connoisseurs: *stripped naked with a rope at his neck, whipped, thrashed with rods, branded with a hot iron*. And it ended in horror: *sent to the galleys for life*. Conti, Gudin, the few friends he had left, and above all his family, urged Beaumarchais to make his escape while he was still free. The guards watching from a distance would certainly have turned a blind eye. His escape would save his life and cause rejoicings in parliament. The temptation to flee was strong: a few hours away from the pillory and the galleys, freedom might still be his. Everything could be saved – except his honour. But as we know, Beaumarchais had taken his decision, the only decision he could take. To the Prince de Conti, who told him for the last time, 'If the hangman gets hold of you, I shall be powerless thereafter,' he replied magnificently: 'Rest assured that the hand of infamy shall not sully a man whom you have honoured with your esteem.' Figaro was no valet, even in livery.

Naturally enough, he wanted to remain alone, so his friends left him. He spent the night calmly putting his affairs in order, then, around five in the morning, walked to the parliament house.

> Alone and on foot, crossing in the darkness the noisy bridge that leads to the House, struck by the silence and all-pervading calm that enabled me to make out the sound of the river, I told myself as I walked through the fog: 'How strange my fate is. All my friends, all my fellow-citizens are at rest, and I am perhaps walking towards infamy and death. Everything is asleep in this great city, and perhaps I shall never lie in a bed again.'

On Saturday, 26 February, the chambers went into session at six in the morning. Why so early? No doubt because parliament imagined that at that hour Paris would be asleep. But at six in the morning, Paris was awake and present: a considerable crowd, silent, maybe slightly intimidated by the majesty of the setting, a little scared by the number of guards, above all new to it all, not yet daring to appreciate their strength. Time passed. Behind locked doors, the judges were deliberating. The scales tilted back and forth all day. Around midday, Beaumarchais sent a note to the Prince of Monaco, who had invited him to supper to show whose side he was on: 'Beaumarchais . . . begs the Prince of Monaco to be so gracious as to favour him with his bounties another day.'

Twelve o'clock, two o'clock: the councillors are still in session. A little information leaks out: the assembly is split and hasn't yet reached a majority decision. The dice are still rolling. At two o'clock Beaumarchais knows that he has half the assembly against him; at two o'clock it is the pillory, the penitentiary, or worse. Then, since an early outcome seemed unlikely, he did an extraordinary thing – he rose from his seat, left the parliament house and went to bed at Fanchon's. No one stopped him leaving. He had been followed. They knew where to fetch him.

The crowd wasn't as calm as he was, however. As the hours went by their impatience changed to anger. Paris growled, booed the guards and clerks. The councillors no longer dared to leave the session hall for fear of being given a rough handling. It was dark by five. Parliament was probably waiting for the people of Paris to grow weary, to feel hungry and cold, to go home. But Parliament had miscalculated. The people settled down to wait, eating and drinking where they sat. Street traders were somehow alerted and arrived with their carts, baskets and barrows, selling coffee, chocolate, chestnuts and 'ladies' pleasures' (which Kunstler informs us in all seriousness was a very hard biscuit). Eventually, at nine at night, the doors opened, and the presiding judge read the sentence: Mme Goëzman and Beaumarchais were both sentenced to public reprimand before parliament; the four memoirs were condemned to be burnt by the hangman for containing 'foolhardy, scandalous and insulting expressions and imputations against the magistrature'; and Beaumarchais was enjoined to refrain from composing 'any such memorials in future on pain of corporal punishment'.

There was more as well, but the remainder of the sentence was lost in the uproar. The crowd was furious. The guards had to be called in to protect the judge while he finished reading the sentence. But no one was listening to him. It wasn't until later that people learned that Goëzman had been struck off the rolls, and that Lejay and Dairolles had been sentenced to admonishment. Baculard and

Marin alone, already condemned by ridicule, were left out of the prizegiving. True, they had both been acting on the orders of Maupeou.

As soon as the sentence had been announced Gudin, much relieved, went to Fanchon's to wake Beaumarchais. The worst hadn't happened. Beaumarchais made no comment on the inept sentence, but soon the cheers of all Paris showed him that he had won a kind of victory over injustice. The councillors had been forced to leave the parliament house by the back doors, followed, booed and jostled by the crowd. They had clearly lost, even if Beaumarchais hadn't won.

Throughout the night 'the whole city signed in at his house.' The splendid Prince de Conti was the first to arrive. Taking Beaumarchais in his arms, he said: 'I want you to come to my house tomorrow. I am of good enough stock to set France an example of how she should treat a great citizen such as you.' The Duc de Chartres was next, and until the early hours there was a constant procession of princes, dukes, writers, actors and friends – the number of his friends on this Saturday, 26 February, had magically increased – while in the streets the other victors of the day, the crowd of working people who had played a significant part in the astonishing sequence of events, chanted their hero's name tirelessly. After midnight Sartines in his turn came to congratulate his friend, but also to warn him not to expect too much. The chief of police knew from experience that Paris is a fickle city. He knew, too, that only Louis xv could restore Beaumarchais's civil rights. That is why, after embracing him, he murmured in his ear: 'A reprimand is one thing, modesty is another.'

7

M. de Ronac

The outcome of his trial left Beaumarchais in a situation that struck him as highly incongruous. On the one hand he was a public hero: 'The nation, outraged, received me with open arms; rich men offered me their purses, barristers sent me the address of their chambers, and hotheads used their pens to perpetrate bad verse defending me and terrible placards attacking parliament.' On the other hand the reprimand deprived him of all his civil rights (the right to have a name, to marry, to make a will, to enter public office, to run a business, or to have a play put on at the Comédie Française); furthermore, it involved the disgrace of making amends before parliament on his knees. He was dead as a citizen, shameful in the eyes of the law, but he still had his renown and the admiration of the public. It was a great deal, and it was nothing. He had been put on a pedestal, but he couldn't climb off it lest he be arrested.

As a result he urgently needed to obtain his rehabilitation by having the sentence quashed. It was also of supreme importance to him to take his interminable quarrel with La Blache to appeal and save himself from financial ruin. On both these issues he was entirely in the hands of the king and the king alone. At the same time he had to take steps to get out of the ridiculous ceremony of the public disgrace, 'kneeling beside that Goëzman woman before Nicolaï and co.', which was enforceable within the week. We shouldn't forget this essential feature of his predicament, which, I believe, partly explains his hasty departure for Flanders two or three days after the sentence. Sartines was probably hinting that it would be advisable to leave when he asked him 'not to appear anywhere', adding, 'If an order were to come from the king, I should have to obey it.' I imagine that he packed reluctantly, all the same – for the first time in many years he was happy.

The important visitors who came to his house on the evening of 26

February to present him with a token of their esteem included a highly attractive girl who asked to see the great man on the craziest of pretexts – she wanted to borrow his harp! This detail, recorded by Gudin, who was present at the interview, surely can't be fictitious. Its very absurdity is a guarantee of its authenticity. Her name was Marie-Thérèse Emilie Willermawlaz (or Willer Mawlaz) and she was twenty. Rather shy by nature (she was Swiss on her father's side) and of exemplary morals (all the sources agree on this point), the young Marie-Thérèse achieved in a single evening what no brazen courtesan would have dared even to attempt. Wearing a *quesaco*, which said plenty in itself, she came alone, without the least recommendation, at night, to the house of a man whose reputation with women she must have been aware of.

Beaumarchais saw at once what her visit meant. She was undeniably throwing herself at him, giving herself – but it was for life. Strangest of all is that love mattered more in their relationship than lust, even on that first evening. It was admiration, mutual esteem and a kind of affectionate complicity that brought them together; and, in the words of the prudish Gudin, 'their hearts were united from that moment on'. For Marie-Thérèse would later become the last Mme de Beaumarchais, and give him the child he longed for. However, for reasons that we shall attempt to analyse further on, he didn't marry her immediately. In fact she didn't become his wife until twelve years after this first meeting, and nine years after the birth of their daughter, Eugénie. All the same, he regarded her as his lawful wife from that first evening. We shall be returning to this point, too. For the time being we have to ask ourselves whether Marie-Thérèse wasn't also responsible for his sudden departure to Flanders. Did she go with him? There is nothing to support this hypothesis, but there's no reason why I shouldn't share my hunch with you. Marie-Thérèse had connections with Flanders on her mother's side, and she was born in Lille. I for one cannot conceive of their having separated a few hours after they had met; nor can I see Marie-Thérèse suddenly turning sensible and going back on her impulse. If they had parted that night, the chances were that they would never have seen one another again. When a girl knocks at a strange man's door and asks to borrow his harp (which he refuses to lend, *dixit* Gudin), it means that she is prepared to follow his lead in a duet for better or for worse.

Ligne and Conti organized the departure, which took place secretly and at night to hoodwink Maupeou's agents. A few days later
he/they was/were near Ghent, whence Beaumarchais dispatched a
letter to his friend Jean-Benjamin de La Borde, first gentleman-in-
waiting to Louis XV. It would seem that the letter was really intended
for the king. Beaumarchais wrote that his departure to 'no-man's-
land' was justified since he was anxious to strengthen his position by
remaining stubbornly silent. He was making for London, where he
would remain for 'five and a half months, as silent and as forgotten as
in the Bastille'. (Five and a half months represented the amount of
time he had left to appeal to the king. He had been sentenced on 26
February, so he had until 26 August of the same year to lodge his
appeal, since the law allowed a maximum of six months for this
procedure.) The letter went on to assert, with apparent artlessness,
that there was little point 'in severing from society an honest subject
whose gifts might have been put to good use in the service of the king
and the State'. Obviously, Beaumarchais wasn't offering his assistance in this way without a reason. Sartines hadn't come to see him
on the evening of the twenty-sixth to exchange pleasantries. That
night the two men had to find a way for Beaumarchais to recover his
legal identity; and that could only be achieved by a successful appeal
to the crown. Secondly, we know that Beaumarchais had dined at
the Conciergerie just before the trial, on 24 or 25 February, as the
guest of the Comte de Lauraguais, who was 'in the king's service'. (I
am trying to make my point with circumspection. It is hypothetical,
but highly probable. In Beaumarchais's life the year 1774 is a jigsaw
puzzle, and some of the pieces seem to have been lost for ever. Hence
we have to tread warily in this chapter, in which the service of the
king becomes at times the service of France. I should add that
nothing is ever simple in politics, and that Beaumarchais could offer
his services to Louis XV *without* going back on himself; for instance at
the level of the Maupeou parliament he continued to fight the king's
will in every way he could.) La Borde took Beaumarchais's letter to
the king, who read it and slipped it into his pocket, saying (or so it
would seem): 'At last! I only hope he'll keep his word.'

Beaumarchais reached England at the beginning of March,
perhaps on the fifth. 'In Paris that day the four printed memoirs were
torn up and burned at the foot of the palace steps by the public
executioner in the presence of Alexandre-Nicolas-François Le Bre-

ton, clerk of the court, and two ushers.' That day, as well, Beaumarchais received in London, via the diplomatic bag, a note from La Borde telling him that Louis XV wished to see him at Versailles on urgent business. So he didn't even have time to unpack. Figaro here, Figaro there! His travels had begun, and he would need all the tact he could muster: 'I stand prepared to serve Your Excellency anew in whatever way he may please to command me.'

Old Almaviva received Figaro with a great show of friendship. 'I remember how talented you always were. I am told that you have a gift for negotiation as well. If you could use it successfully and secretly on my behalf . . .' If you could use it successfully, I would quash your sentence. Although nothing was actually said on this subject, the king's meaning was clear – he was offering a deal. For a man whom, ten days previously, twenty king's councillors out of fifty had voted to send to the pillory and the galleys, while the other thirty had ordered the reprimand, thereby depriving him of his citizenship, it was rather an unexpected turn of events!

At first sight Beaumarchais's royal mission wasn't an attractive one. Louis XV had learned that a pamphlet by a greatly feared lampooner called Théveneau de Morande was about to be published in London. It had to be suppressed.

Barely a month went by without a virulent and sometimes scurrilous satire directed against an individual in France being published in England. It was a kind of industry. Generally the lampoons were advertised before publication to give their victims ample time to subscribe the entire print run in advance. Fear of ridicule being what it is, the lampooners did good business. Louis XV had sent police agents to England on several occasions with orders to kidnap the most troublesome members of the clique. But they had come back empty-handed, or hadn't come back at all. Officially, of course, England was the land of freedom where a man could write whatever he liked; in fact the cold rivalry that had existed between England and France since the Treaty of Paris led the British government to view the activities of the lampooners with something less than displeasure. Not all of them were scurrilous hacks. Some of them were sincere opponents of the French regime, and two or three were double agents working for both countries.

The uncrowned heads of this little group of exiles (voluntary and otherwise) were the Chevalier d'Eon, the Marquis de Pelleport, Mme de Godeville and Théveneau de Morande. It was Morande whom Beaumarchais had instructions to silence. The lampoon in question was entitled *The Memoirs of a Public Woman*, and the lady attacked in it was Mme du Barry. Morande had already given her short shrift in an obscene pamphlet (*The Gazetteer in Armour*) that the king hadn't managed to suppress. It had caused the countess much loss of face. (She was a favourite target for the London lampooners towards the end of the reign, in such productions as *The Life of a Courtesan on the Throne of France* and *How a Whore became Mistress to a King*. Needless to say, the filth was aimed at Louis XV rather than at Mme du Barry herself.)

All Beaumarchais's biographers, following the lead given by Loménie, decry the mission he undertook at the behest of the ageing monarch. It didn't *seem* very glorious, I agree, even though, as Loménie himself admits, he had the best of excuses, because 'his rehabilitation was blocked by the king, who could . . . open or close at will the road to an appeal against sentence, who could give him back his credit, his fortune, his legal identity, and who, all-powerful, was asking him for a personal favour in return for his gratitude.' But I am convinced that the mission was *in fact* more important than it seemed. And I shall tell you why.

After giving Beaumarchais his orders, Louis XV sent him to see the Duc d'Aiguillon, Maupeou's right-hand man and an acquaintance of Goëzman's! The minister received him with much consideration and discussed the details of his mission with him. The Comte de Lauraguais had been instructed to accompany Beaumarchais – or rather, M. de Ronac – to London. Ronac? Beaumarchais had decided to travel under a false name, claiming that his celebrity might be an obstacle to the success of his mission – sheer vanity, of course, and sheer insolence as well, coming from a man who'd been deprived of his legal identity and was back where he'd started, the son of a nobody, at forty-two. In any case, what could be more transparent by way of a pseudonym than this anagram of Caron?

Yes, why did Louis XV call in Beaumarchais? If the mission merely involved buying off Morande, as has been claimed, any of the king's agents could have done the job – Lauraguais, for instance, who was no fool and who knew Morande personally. Yes, why choose Beaumarchais, who had just been sentenced to reprimand and who was known to be an opponent of the regime? If Louis XV and Aiguillon took this serpent to their bosoms, they had good reason to do so; in other words, further negotiation was involved. I am convinced that the three missions that Beaumarchais undertook in 1774 and 1775 had a false bottom, so to speak, like the suitcases used by smugglers. There was the illusion, and there was the reality – M. de Ronac *and* Beaumarchais. If M. de Ronac really was under orders to deal with Morande, Beaumarchais had instructions to negotiate simultaneously with the British government. I am not advancing this hypothesis rashly. Beaumarchais had a considerable advantage over all of the king's agents, as he was a personal friend of a member of Lord North's government. In Madrid, you will remember, he had become a close friend of the British ambassador, Lord Rochford. The friendship that had developed during that convivial year of music-making, gambling and enjoyment had undoubtedly had political consequences at the time, and this political connivance had survived the passing of the years, probably because the two men had continued to correspond.

William Henry Nassau de Zuylestein, fourth Earl of Rochford, who had been at the Paris embassy after leaving his post in Madrid, played a permanent role, indirectly but by no means negligibly, in the strained relations between Britain and France. This diplomat, about whom opinions differ to a degree that prevents us from knowing whether he was stupid or clever, had a great liking for France, and manifestly tried to improve relations between the two countries. Whether he did so on his own initiative or whether he had orders to do so, I am in no position to say. Choiseul, who didn't care for him, wrote in 1768: 'The Earl of Rochford is so thoughtless, so indiscreet and so blinkered that he can hardly be judged worthy of our trust; however, since he is also incompetent, he will perhaps behave more appropriately in his present post than he did while he was in France.' His present post was secretary of state for the southern department in the British government. Aiguillon, Sartines and, later, Vergennes knew from Beaumarchais's briefs that up to a point Rochford was their man. How far did the collaboration go? I don't know, but I can draw attention to the following phrase from a letter of Beaumarchais to Sartines dated 7 July 1774: 'When I received his lordship's secret offers of assistance concerning everything that [Louis XV] might desire of me . . .' I shall quote further references to this collaboration that are rather more explicit. For the time being, however, let us follow Ronac to London, though without losing sight of Beaumarchais.

M. de Ronac duly travelled back to England accompanied by the Comte de Lauraguais, who put him in touch with Théveneau de Morande. The king's negotiator didn't beat about the bush. Morande named his price: 20,000 francs cash down and a life annuity of 4000 francs. He gave M. de Ronac a copy of the *Secret Memoirs of a Public Woman* and, as an additional incentive, the manuscript of a forthcoming pamphlet dealing with the Duc d'Aiguillon. To clinch the bargain, Ronac obtained Morande's pledge that he would turn his coat as soon as he received the money. For his part, Beaumarchais talked to Lord Rochford, who proved extremely understanding. Our double agent Ronac-Beaumarchais promptly returned post-haste to Paris and Versailles.

Beaumarchais first saw the king, who, Gudin writes, 'surprised by the promptness of his success, expressed his satisfaction'. As can be imagined, it was the result of his first interview with Rochford that most interested Louis xv. The king, who seems to have had 'preserves' of his own, asked Beaumarchais not to tell the Duc d'Aiguillon that he had been received at Versailles. Consequently, M. de Ronac's report to the minister dealt only with Morande. Delighted by the success of the operation, Aiguillon told his visitor, 'Either you are the devil, or you are M. de Beaumarchais!' In fact the duke was particularly pleased to have been able to stop the publication of the second pamphlet, which attacked him directly. He asked Beaumarchais to obtain for him the names of Morande's informers in Paris or Versailles. Beaumarchais refused point blank. The duke grew angry and threatened to alert the king. 'Go ahead,' Beaumarchais told him. 'I shall acquaint him with my reasons for not complying with your request. His Majesty will judge for himself which of us is right.' He wrote to the king forthwith, saying that he would do his utmost to prevent the publication of any present or future lampoon, whatever its nature, but 'the faithless notions or the treacherous confessions of a man as infamous as Morande' were not worth a farthing, and he would regard it as utterly dishonourable to denounce people in France who might well not have been involved in the lampoons any more than he himself had been. He therefore refused 'to play the shameful role of an informer and to be the cause of persecution that might become widespread and the torch of a war involving prison cells and dungeons'. Louis XV naturally came down against the Duc d'Aiguillon, who backed down with extremely bad grace.

Beaumarchais returned to London to conclude his dealings, accompanied on this occasion by Gudin. The three thousand copies of the *Secret Memoirs of a Public Woman* were destroyed in a limekiln, in the presence of Gudin and himself. After this *autodafé* he handed over the 20,000 francs and the annuity deed, and then, as agreed, enrolled Morande in the secret service. He immediately reported back to the king:

> I have established in London, as my political spy, the author of one of the lampoons, who has instructions to inform me about everything that is planned in this vein in London. He is a clever poacher, whom I have contrived to convert into an excellent gamekeeper . . . This man's work will also involve discovering the names of all the French who pass through London and the purpose of their visit. His connections with all the printers in London will enable him to track down any manuscripts that are brought to them.
>
> This secret correspondence may be extended to cover a wide variety of other political subjects. The king will be kept informed of these by means of secret abstracts, which I shall pass on to him.

In the same letter Beaumarchais reported on the result of his real mission. I am loath to make up the reader's mind for him, but I believe that the following passage demonstrates how useful the 'diplomatic jockey' was to France. As we shall see, Lord Rochford continued to 'collaborate' with Beaumarchais, and this 'friendship' was to be extremely valuable to him in his great American adventure. Here is the passage in question:

> Furthermore, I have agreed with Lord Rochford, minister of state, that as soon as I let him know of any sort of lampoon he will provide me, with the greatest secrecy, and with the sole aim of being agreeable to the king, with all necessary means for stifling these works at birth. He made the condition that anything he said or did in this respect should not be regarded as an affair of state, and would be known to no one but myself and His Majesty. He merely wants to be sure that only the service of the king my master inspires me to crave his good offices in this event, and then he will join in with me secretly with the best grace in the world.

In a further message he added: 'This affair has further ramifications concerning the king, and they are just as interesting for Your Majesty, but they cannot be written down. I must speak about them with Your Majesty in private.' What were these ramifications? We shall never know for certain. Disembarking from the ferry at Boulogne, Beaumarchais and Gudin learned that the king 'had been attacked by smallpox'. They reached Paris the day before he died, 9 May.

So Beaumarchais was back where he'd started. He wrote: 'I marvel at the strange fate that pursues me. If the king had lived a week longer I should have been restored to my former state, which iniquity deprived me of. I had his word as king that this would be so, and his unjust censure of me, prompted by my enemies, had changed into benevolence and even liking.'

As usual, France promptly forgot the dead king and rejoiced in his successor, who was a mere boy. Since Louis XVI was virtuous at the tender age of twenty, it became fashionable for a time to be virtuous also. We have seen worse examples of hero worship. But the euphoria of the accession couldn't hide for long the very real problems that were lurking behind the throne. Briefly, the problems were as follows. The monarchy was ailing, because it was old, set in its ways and antiquated. The unity of the State was merely apparent, since from one region to another, institutions, customs, idioms differed. France, that 'unorganised aggregate of disunited peoples' (the words are Mirabeau's), aspired to unity, but no Frenchman wanted to give up his privileges. The past gripped the present in a stranglehold. What sort of rule could hold the country together and stave off foreign aggression? Louis XV had used the strong-arm approach; Louis XVI attempted to liberalize the system. In fact both kings lagged behind their times. Their action was never the result of a considered policy. Instead they proceeded by leaps and bounds, and acted either at the wrong moment or too late. In this connection, I find their attitudes to parliament revealing. Louis XV was undoubtedly right to throw out the corrupt magistrates who defied both him and any institutional change in order to protect their prerogatives and their commissions, but he was wrong to replace them by obedient lackeys with derisory responsibilities. Similarly, Louis XVI was right to dismiss the Maupeou parliament, but he was wrong to recall the extortioners. The monarchs, paralysed by the ailing health of their State, had no real foreign policy, except an ineffectual kind of 'wait and see' (a concept all too common in French diplomacy, alas); and while France waited, Britain saw her chance, and seized it. Both Louis XV and Louis XVI had the good fortune to find ministers capable of redressing this unhappy situation and giving a new lease of life to the monarchy. But Louis XV quarrelled with Choiseul and Louis XVI lost Vergennes two years before 1789. It strikes me as altogether remarkable that the great ambitions of the crown – the modernization of the State, national unity, the abolition of privileges – were implemented by the Revolution.

After toying with the idea of recalling Choiseul, Louis XVI finally plumped for Maurepas as his chief minister. Turgot replaced Abbé Terray at the Ministry of Finance, and a short while later Vergennes succeeded Aiguillon at the Foreign Ministry. Maupeou was forced by popular outcry to relinquish the seals of justice to Miromesnil. Those were the main changes. Less important for the historians, but highly relevant to us, a further nomination was made which helped Beaumarchais considerably – M. de Sartines moved from the police and became Minister for the Navy.

I said earlier that Beaumarchais was back where he'd started. So what? He started again:

> Sire,
> When I appeared to be fleeing from injustice and persecution last March, the late king your father alone knew where I was, as he had honoured me with a very delicate special mission in England, for the purposes of which I have made the journey from London to Versailles four times in the space of less than six weeks . . .
>
> This delicate affair concerns Your Majesty in its continuation as it concerned the late king in its existence. The report that I was about to make to him is for Your Majesty's ears alone; there are some things in it which, indeed, only the king may hear. I humbly beg Your Majesty to honour with your orders in this respect the most unfortunate, but the most submissive and the most zealous of your subjects.

Louis XVI sent for the most zealous of his subjects forthwith. Beaumarchais told him that an extremely virulent pamphlet entitled *Notice to the Spanish Line concerning their Rights to the Crown of France, in the Absence of Heirs* was in the press in London and Amsterdam. Needless to say, this long-winded title promised a filthy diatribe against Marie-Antoinette – the inference was that she was barren. Rochford couldn't intervene on this occasion, since the author of the work in question was neither a British subject nor a French immigrant.

Louis XVI ordered Beaumarchais to stop the pamphlet before publication and probably gave him another mission as well. As can be
readily imagined, Beaumarchais must have raised the question of his
personal situation, or rather his lack of a personal situation, with the
king, who must have promised to think about it before 26 August,
since no appeal would be possible after that date. By an odd coincidence, which I find, to my great astonishment, has not previously
been noticed, Maupeou, Beaumarchais's political enemy, was dismissed on that very day, 26 August 1774.

Beaumarchais reached London in early July, after a bad Channel
crossing. He was never a good sailor and suffered from dreadful
seasickness at the slightest swell, but this time the sea had been so
bad, and his vomiting so violent, that he had had 'an internal
rupture in the chest', followed by a hæmorrhage. Three days after
his arrival, by his own admission, he was still unable to think
straight, so shaken was he by this experience. Rochford welcomed
him less warmly than usual, no doubt astonished at the state his
visitor was in, though he also had other reasons for being cool.
Aiguillon, who was close to the end of his period in power, had sent a
number of agents to London with a view to obtaining the information that Beaumarchais had denied him. The presence of these
agents, their clumsiness and their ambiguous status were a constant
irritation to the British government. Furthermore Rochford, understandably, couldn't commit himself with Beaumarchais without
knowing whether he was still enjoying the protection of the king, now
that Louis XV was dead. Who was acting for France, Beaumarchais
or the Duc d'Aiguillon's agents? By asking the question, Rochford
was putting Beaumarchais on the same level as a load of small-time
spies and he 'blushed like a man who had lowered himself by
accepting an unworthy commission'. An explicit order from Louis
XVI had become indispensable to forestall misunderstanding and put
an end to Rochford's hesitations. On 5 July Beaumarchais sent
Sartines from London a form of mandate for the king to sign. It read:
'M. de Beaumarchais has been entrusted with my secret instructions
and will leave for his destination as soon as possible. The discretion
and speed with which he will comply with my orders are the most
pleasing proof that he can give me of his zeal in my service.'

By return post, Louis XVI sent the document requested. Copying
the draft sent to him by Sartines, he didn't change a single word,

though he did venture to add a comma, and of course he signed it and dated it 10 July.

M. de Beaumarchais, delighted, acknowledged receipt of the missive in a highly unceremonious note that must have surprised the young Louis XVI: 'A lover wears the portrait of his mistress round his neck, a miser wears his keys, a votary his reliquary. As for myself, I have had a gold case made. It is a large, flat, lens-shaped oval; inside it I have placed Your Majesty's order and I have it hanging round my neck on a gold chain, as the most necessary thing for my work and the most precious thing for myself.' Even when he was being servile (which wasn't often), Beaumarchais couldn't help being different.

The author, publisher or owner of the *Notice* was a man called Atkinson, who also styled himself Angelucci. Beaumarchais had learned of his existence during his previous stay in London, probably from Théveneau de Morande, his gamekeeper. On his return to England, Beaumarchais – or rather M. de Ronac, even his passport bore that name – had first of all to examine the pamphlet and decide whether or not it was worth all the trouble. He did so in rather odd circumstances, as he wrote to Sartines:

> It was handed to me secretly last night in Vauxhall Gardens, on condition that I should return it before five in the morning. I came back home, read it, copied bits of it out; and at about four o'clock I opened my parlour window, which gives on to the street, and tossed out the rolled packet to the man who had lent it to me. He made himself known by giving the agreed signal – and the devil is still running. So I now know what is involved. Please read what I have to say very carefully and weigh my words, because this affair concerns you as much as myself – more so, in fact, since the slightest negligence on this occasion could cost you the consideration of the queen, make her your sworn enemy and block a career that is becoming most promising.

It is obvious that Marie-Antoinette knew nothing of the lampoon, and her royal husband must have asked his envoy to exercise the utmost discretion. Hence Sartines and Beaumarchais were engaged in a highly tricky affair. They had no choice but to succeed, because if the mission misfired it would be likely to get them into very serious trouble. As Beaumarchais wrote to Sartines: 'The first maxim in politics is "once you start, succeed". If you don't succeed, all your

efforts and services will be considered worthless.' Marie-Antoinette
was a quick-tempered woman and might turn against them if things
went wrong. 'Do you know of any woman who's capable of forgiveness once she's in a rage?' I'm stressing this aspect of the affair
because it seems to me essential to show that Beaumarchais had
nothing to gain by it. The king's friendly attitude towards him, the
ministerial reshuffle and Sartines's promotion all indicated that he
was about to be rehabilitated anyway. He had no reason to *invent* it
all and stage an incredibly complicated and dangerous hoax. He
wasn't a fool, and he was no masochist either.

Once he'd duly evaluated the nastiness of the *Notice*, M. de Ronac
decided to buy it out in both editions, in English and in Dutch. On
the road to Oxford one night he met for the first time the man
Atkinson, who was accompanied by two apprentice printers. In the
carriage that had brought the trio to the rendezvous were the four
thousand copies that made up the first edition. As agreed, Atkinson
handed over the manuscript of the pamphlet as well. Looking at it by
lantern light, however, M. de Ronac realized that it was a copy and
grew heated. Atkinson, who needed the money, raced off to London
to fetch the original. Three hours later he was back with the genuine
article and got his money. Before parting, the two men arranged to
meet again in Amsterdam for the Dutch edition. Having burned the
four thousand volumes, the 'diplomatic jockey' made for Holland,
where Angelucci (as Atkinson styled himself on the Continent) was
waiting for him. A further meeting by night, a further delivery, a
further payment and a further *autodafé*. And a further dirty trick:
Angelucci held back one copy of the pamphlet and took off for
Nuremburg!

Let us consider: on 26 and 27 July Beaumarchais was in Calais
(letter to Sartines); he didn't start chasing after Angelucci until 8 or
10 August, a mere two weeks before his reprimand became irrevocable. Now most historians maintain that Beaumarchais embarked on
his crazy trip to Germany, allegedly inventing one picaresque
episode after another as he went along, with the sole intention of
obtaining his rehabilitation! Yet this hypothesis won't hold water for
a second. On 1 August he could have returned to Paris and reported
positively to Louis XVI. After all, two editions had been burned, and
he had Angelucci's signature. At least a month would have gone by
before the rogue had managed to have a third edition printed, and

Beaumarchais would meanwhile have been rehabilitated. There can be no question about that. He left for Germany because he had to. But why? That's another question. Let's be reasonable. Either the adventures in Germany are true, or Beaumarchais made them up. In either case it seems obvious that he wasn't acting on his own behalf but on behalf of the State. So, acting for the king, *either* he got mixed up in a grim spying affair that almost cost him his life, *or* he made up the whole incredible story that follows with a view to approaching Empress Maria Theresa. No further hypothesis can be put forward, save that he had gone mad. Yet with the exception of Linthilac all the historians dismiss Beaumarchais's story with heavy sarcasm and a knowing smile. Even the solid Loménie, who adored Beaumarchais and without whom his biography would be much the poorer, feels ill at ease and merely tells the story without comment.

This is what happened. On 8 or 10 August M. de Ronac set out in pursuit of the man whom Gudin called 'the most determined of rascals'. He began his journey in Amsterdam, and travelled in a post-chaise with a German coachman named Dratz and an English valet who had been with him since his stay in London. In Cologne he fell ill with a bout of fever, but pressed on notwithstanding. Before reaching Nuremberg he caught up with Angelucci (13 or 14 August) and contrived to relieve him of a copy of the *Notice*, apparently the last copy in existence. Then he allowed Angelucci to leave, or the fellow gave him the slip once again.

One day (or a few hours) after retrieving the last copy of the lampoon, M. de Ronac alighted from his carriage in the forest of Neustadt, as he himself relates:

Yesterday, around three o'clock in the afternoon, I was travelling in a chaise with a single coachman and my English manservant on the outskirts of Neustadt, some twenty miles from Nuremberg. I alighted in a fairly sparse pine forest to answer a call of nature and my chaise drove on at a walking pace, as it had done every time I alighted. After a short pause I was about to start walking to catch up with it, when a man on horseback barred my path, jumped to the ground and approached me. He uttered a few words in German, which I do not understand, but as he had a long knife or dagger in his hand it wasn't hard to guess that he wanted my money or my life. I rummaged in my front pocket, making him think I'd understood and that my gold was already his. He was alone. Instead of my purse I drew my pistol, and aimed it at him without speaking, raising my cane in my other hand to parry a blow in case he should attempt to strike me. Then, backing to a large pine tree and rounding it nimbly, I put the tree between him and me. Once here I was no longer afraid and looked to see whether my pistol was primed. This assured countenance had indeed stopped him in his tracks. I had already backed to a second and a third tree, rounding them as I reached them, with my raised cane in one hand and the pistol in the other, aimed at him. I was manoeuvring fairly steadily, and my progress was about to point me back in the right direction, when a man's voice forced me to look round. I saw a sturdy rogue in a blue jerkin with his coat over his arm, running towards me from behind.

The growing danger caused me to collect my thoughts swiftly. I decided that as the greater peril lay in allowing myself to be taken from behind, I must reposition myself in front of the tree and rid myself of the man with the dagger, so that I could tackle the other brigand afterwards. All of this was pondered and performed in a flash. Running at the first robber to within a cane's length, I fired at him with my pistol, but the wretched thing failed to go off. I was done for. Sensing his advantage, the man advanced on me. I was still parrying with my cane while backing towards my tree and reaching for my other pistol in my left-hand pocket when the second robber, having reached me from behind, although I had my back to the pine tree, seized me by the shoulder and pulled me backwards. At this the first fellow struck me with his long knife full in the chest, using all his strength. I was undone. But to give you a proper idea of the combination of incidents to which I owe, my friend, the joy of still being able to write to you, you must know that I wear on my chest a gold case. It is oval, quite large and very flat, and lens-shaped, and hangs from my neck on a gold chain. I had it made in London, and it contains a paper so precious to me that without it I should not be travelling as I am. While passing through Frankfurt I had a silk cover made for this case, because when I was very warm if the metal suddenly touched my skin it chilled me somewhat.

Now, by chance, or rather by good fortune, which never abandons me in the midst of my greatest woes, the dagger blow levelled at my chest, though very violent, struck against this case, which is quite broad, just as I was being pulled back against the tree by the second brigand – which made me lose my balance and fall head over heels. All of this occurred simultaneously, and meant that instead of piercing my heart, the knife glanced off the metal – slitting the cover, denting the case and making a deep gash in it – and then grazed my upper chest, pierced my chin from below and emerged at the bottom of my right cheek. If I had lost my head at this moment of extreme danger, it is certain, my friend, that I should have lost my life as well. 'I'm not dead,' I told myself, jumping to my feet. I immediately saw that the man who had struck me was the only one who had a weapon, and I threw myself at him like a tiger, risking all. Gripping his wrist, I attempted to tear his long knife away from him, but he pulled it back forcefully, cutting the whole palm of my left hand to the bone, on the fleshy part of the thumb. But the effort he deployed in pulling back his arm, together with my own forward movement, threw him backwards in his turn. I stamped heavily on his wrist with the heel of my boot and made him drop the dagger. I picked the dagger up, and leapt on to his stomach, pressing down with both knees. When the second bandit, who was even more of a coward than the first, saw that I was about to kill his companion, instead of assisting him he leapt on to the horse, which was grazing a few yards away, and galloped off. When the other wretch, who was pinned down beneath me and being blinded by the blood streaming from my face, realized that he had been abandoned, he twisted himself away just as I was about to strike him, and rose to his knees, clasping his hands and crying pitifully: 'Monsieur! Mine friendt!' And many words in German that gave me to understand that he was pleading for his life. 'Infamous rogue!' I said, and continued my original movement and was about to kill him. But on second thoughts I suddenly saw that to kill a man on his knees with his hands imploringly clasped was a form of murder, an act of cowardice unworthy of a man of honour. But I still intended to teach him a lesson and at least give him a serious wound. He fell prostrate, crying: 'Mein Gott! My God!'

Try to follow these conflicting thoughts as they flashed across my mind and you will perhaps appreciate, my friend, that in the midst of the greatest danger from which I have ever had to preserve myself, I suddenly grew bold enough to hope that I might tie this man's hands behind his back and lead him thus pinioned to my chaise. All this came to me in a flash. Once I'd made my decision, I promptly cut his strong chamois leather belt at the back, with a single stroke of his knife, which I was holding in my right hand. I had no difficulty in so doing as he was lying prostrate.

But as the knife stroke was as fierce as it was swift, I wounded him badly in the small of his back. This caused him to give a great howl and he rose to his knees, clasping his hands again. Despite the violent pain I felt in my face, and particularly in my left hand, I am convinced that I would have managed to carry him off, because he offered no resistance when I took out my handkerchief, flung the knife some distance away, because it was hindering me as I had my second pistol in my left hand, and prepared to tie him up. But my hope was short-lived. I saw in the distance the other bandit, coming towards me with several rogues of his ilk. So I had to concentrate on my own safety once again.

I admit that at this juncture I saw what a fool I'd been to throw away the knife. I would have killed the man without a qualm at that moment, and that would have been one enemy the fewer. But I didn't want to fire my second pistol, which was all I had left to drive off the men who were coming for me – my cane was at best a defensive weapon. Overcome by fury, I struck the kneeling man a violent blow on the mouth with the butt of my pistol. This dented his jaw and broke a few front teeth, making him bleed like a stuck pig. He took himself for dead and fell to the ground. At that moment the coachman, worried at my long absence, walked into the wood to look for me, and sounded a little horn that all German coachmen carry slung over their shoulders. Hearing this, and seeing him, the rogues faltered. This gave me time to retreat, brandishing my cane and flourishing my pistol, without being robbed. When they realized I had reached the road, they scattered, and both my lackey and the coachman saw the rascal in the blue jerkin with his coat over his arm slipping across the road near them and my chaise. This was the fellow who had pulled me to the ground – perhaps he was hoping to ransack my carriage after failing to do the same to my pockets. My first concern, when I saw that I was safe and sound and within reach of my chaise, was to urinate. I have found from frequent experience that after a period of great excitement it is one of the best of all sedatives. I then soaked my handkerchief in urine and washed my wounds with it.

The wound on my upper chest turned out to be a mere graze, but the wound on my chin was very deep. If the blow had gone in straight it would undoubtedly have reached my brain, but as I was falling backwards when I received it the knife had glanced off my lower jawbone. The wound in my left hand is even more painful, as this part of the body is never still. It has struck deep into the fatty area inside the thumb and right down to the bone.

My lackey was appalled and asked me why I hadn't called out. But quite apart from the fact that my chaise had continued along the road and was therefore much too far off for me to make myself heard, I had deliberately refrained from shouting, knowing full well that the easiest way to use up your strength is to waste it in pointless yelling.

A few days earlier the same brigands had attacked the post chaise on the same spot and robbed the passengers of 40,000 florins. Beaumarchais's account of the incident, taken from a letter to a man called R— (presumably Roudil, his watchdog in Paris), is pretty astonishing, and its exaggerations make us smile. But we should remember various points: firstly, Beaumarchais was still suffering from the effects of the fever he contracted in Cologne; secondly, he really was wounded, quite seriously in fact; thirdly, in the eighteenth century, particularly in central Europe, robber bands were quite common. Yet Linthilac, the most favourably disposed of all Beaumarchais's biographers, writes quite firmly: 'The story of the brigands is a fiction. The news of the attack on the post chaise, which Beaumarchais heard about during his journey, gave him the idea for this little drama.' This amounts to accusing Beaumarchais of deliberate lying – and of wounding himself!

Like many others, Linthilac was probably misled by an ambiguous phrase in Gudin's treatment of this incident, which makes out that the encounters with Angelucci and the brigands occurred within a few minutes of one another on the same day, whereas they were manifestly quite distinct. (Gudin quotes Beaumarchais's report to Sartines, which says at one point, but obviously without intending to be literal: 'Just as I was rejoicing at having retrieved the remaining copy of the work, I was set upon by brigands.' It is clear from Beaumarchais's affidavit taken down in Nuremberg that he himself saw no connection between the two incidents.)

When he reached Neustadt later the same afternoon M. de Ronac, who was wounded and feverish, refused to make a statement to the police. He wanted to continue his journey and get to Nuremberg as soon as possible so that he could have his wounds attended to. The coachman was changed, and the chaise set off again at full speed. Dratz, the first coachman, made a statement to the authorities that clearly put his client in the wrong: 'I do not know whether this gentleman is of sound mind. I reckon he must have caused his wounds himself with his razor.' This statement has given rise to the most insulting theories. Yet it is obvious from the coachman's report that he was very worried that M. de Ronac might spread unfavourable rumours in Nuremberg about the Neustadt road (thereby depriving him of his livelihood). German roads and German coachmen in the eighteenth century are given an equally bad press in the writings of all the great travellers of the day. All the same, let us allow that Dratz was acting in good faith. He merely gave his opinion, but proved nothing.

In Nuremberg M. de Ronac and his valet stayed at 'The Red Cock'. The innkeeper, Conrad Grüber, thought the traveller rather daft because he 'got up very early and paced up and down the house.' By these lights, we must all be raving madmen. But we shall let Grüber have his say as Dratz did.

When M. de Ronac eventually made his first statement it was to a high-ranking civil servant, Carl von Fezer. It contains one extraordinary detail: during the skirmish the two brigands had called one another by their names, the first robber answering to the name of Angelucci, the second to that of Atkinson! At this point the historians either sigh or smile, depending on the sort of men they are. Beaumarchais, they say, was so caught up in his own lies that he was talking through his hat. Now we know from his report to Sartines that Beaumarchais gave the examining magistrate a description of the brigands, *and* of Angelucci-Atkinson. ('While giving the magistrate in Nuremberg the location and the manner in which I was attacked near Neustadt, I took great care to give him an accurate. description of my Angelucci as well.') The mysteries of translation, added to the state of fatigue and excitement that Beaumarchais was in, probably explain this confusion. In the record of the evidence the bandits are named as 'Angelussi und Adginson'. Words can change their meanings alarmingly from one language to another, and sometimes from one ear to another. There is a kind of poetry in misunderstandings.

His difficulties, which were not wholly of a linguistic nature, made M. de Ronac want to leave Nuremberg forthwith and head for civilization, i.e. Vienna, where civil servants felt honour bound to speak French. He met the mayor of Nuremberg and told him that he had to see the Empress of Austria immediately (thereby adding to the Nurembergers' notions of his oddness), then, afraid that the bumpy roads would be bad for his wounds, hired a boat and sailed down the Danube. It was in the course of this four-day river cruise that he wrote the famous letter to Gudin dated 16 August 1774 – a long, rambling, reflective epistle which unfortunately loses much of its savour if it isn't quoted in full. However, I want to quote a few lines from it which to my mind are all Beaumarchais – a man who was very much out of the ordinary, charming at times, often vain, but incapable of a mean action:

> What career is fuller than mine of good and evil? If time is measured by the events that comprise it, I have been alive for two hundred years. I am not weary of living, but I can leave the enjoyment of life to others without despairing. I have loved women passionately, and this particular sensitiveness has been a source of the greatest delight – whereas the necessity of living among men has caused me any number of woes. But if I were

asked which has prevailed in me, good or evil, I should say the former, without the least hesitation. And even though this is not the happiest of moments to raise the question of such preference, I still do not hesitate in my choice.

M. de Ronac reached Vienna on 20 August. If he thought his adventures were over he was wrong. He walked straight from *Tom Jones* into *War and Peace*.

It all began with a letter he sent to Empress Maria Theresa requesting an audience. Maria Theresa hesitated: who *was* this M. de Ronac? Her secretary, Baron Nenny, who had seen him, said that he hadn't understood a word of his adventure, but had found him 'presentable'. More and more puzzled, Maria Theresa asked Count Seillern to see the mysterious foreigner – and Ronac produced the credentials signed by Louis XVI. He was received at Schoenbrunn on the evening of 22 August, two days after his arrival. Beaumarchais made a detailed report to the king on his 'historic interview' with the empress and the untoward events that followed. It presents his version of the facts, and is dated 15 October, by which time Louis XVI had every scrap of information on his desk and could therefore judge the affair in its substance. How could Beaumarchais have been stupid enough to lie, this being so? Louis XVI, at any rate, considered that M. de Ronac had fulfilled his mission brilliantly. What had gone wrong then?

Maria Theresa's first reaction was mistrust. Was this man Ronac really Beaumarchais? She couldn't be certain. The scarred, feverish and agitated fellow who had made speeches at her all evening might well be an imposter – perhaps even the murderer of this Beaumarchais. At all events, the affair was worth looking into, so she asked Chancellor Kaunitz to investigate. Kaunitz was soon back with his findings. Ronac was indeed Beaumarchais, i.e. a rogue. He reported as much to the empress, adding that in his opinion Beaumarchais had not only invented the attack, but was also the author of the *Notice*. This grave accusation was made without any proof, except for the statements made by the coachman, the innkeeper and the examining magistrate. None the less, it was decided that Beaumarchais should be interned pending information from Versailles. In the meantime Beaumarchais furiously wrote letters to every Austrian he knew the name of. To calm him, he was sent a man called Sonnenfels, half writer and half civil servant, who attempted to make his internment less unpleasant and at the same time keep an eye on him. From prison M. de Ronac sent Maria Theresa a long letter offering to print an expurgated version of the lampoon 'to forestall very great wrongs' and to avoid causing distress to Louis XVI. This document, though admittedly disconcerting, doesn't prove that Beaumarchais was the author of the *Notice*. It merely shows how confused he was. In any case his report to Louis XVI mentions this letter, albeit in passing.

Did Beaumarchais write the *Notice*? Chancellor Kaunitz's thesis was hard to nail. Such is the force of slander, a number of authors subscribed to it readily. True, the very existence of Angelucci posed a problem for years, as no one was able to find any trace of him. Then one day Linthilac came across two letters written by Beaumarchais to a woman called Fabia, one of which is dated 12 August and was therefore written before the incidents. It establishes incontrovertibly the existence of Guillaume Angelucci. It contains the following request: 'Kindly tell the friend who will give you this letter [Roudil?] that if by any chance he receives a bill of exchange of mine worth 100 *louis* and made out to Guillaume Angelucci he is to refuse payment under any circumstances. Although I issued it, I do not owe on it, as my thieving rascal has welshed on all the promises he made to obtain it.' Now no one refuses to pay a bill of exchange made out to a person who doesn't exist! We may ask ourselves, none the less, who this Fabia was. Did she really exist, or was the name merely a *nom de guerre* given to, say, Marie-Thérèse Willermawlaz? (We have already seen how fond Beaumarchais was of giving his correspondents nicknames.)

However that may be, the style and content of the *Notice*, which was published by Alfred von Arneth in 1868, prove that Beaumarchais didn't write it. Violent and hamfisted, the pamphlet contains defamatory passages about several men Beaumarchais liked and respected. Sartines, for example, was openly accused of embezzlement – a blatant lie if ever there was one. In any case, there can be no doubt that if there had been even a grain of truth in the libel concerning the authorship of the *Notice*, Beaumarchais's real enemies would have shrieked like ghouls at a witchery. As René Pomeau writes, 'How much would the Comte de la Blache have given to be able to prove that Beaumarchais was the author of the *Notice*?'

All these intrigues, which, as we have seen, were directed against Sartines as well, may have started with the Duc d'Aiguillon. Beaumarchais had sensed that he was up to something, and wrote to the new Navy Minister: 'Some important personage is certainly working the bellows, for I have never seen such a vendetta. Might there not be something of d'Aiguillon in it all? It rather looks like his way of doing things. One thing you lacked was a scandal. Now you've got nothing left to hope for – you've got your scandal.'

Alerted by Kaunitz, the formidable Count Mercy-Argenteau (Austrian ambassador at Versailles) went to see Sartines, who defended his agent, or rather the king's agent, in such a peremptory manner that Mercy could but acquiesce. He reported back to Kaunitz and a few days later Beaumarchais was set free. 'It would seem,' Kaunitz wrote to Mercy, 'that the exceedingly slack morals of M. de Sartines go hand in hand with the personal interest he may have in avoiding the criticism that might justly be levelled at him for having given the king a fellow like M. de Beaumarchais to carry out so delicate a commission.' It is worth noting in passing that despite his bad temper the chancellor has dropped his allegations of imposture and speaks merely of 'so delicate a commission'. Kaunitz was excusable in so far as his views were based on information obtained from Mercy, who was more of a spy than a diplomat and had ferrets working for him throughout Versailles, even in Marie-Antoinette's bedchamber. The ambassador, who detested Beaumarchais, must have raged inwardly when he was forced to present him, later on, with a magnificent diamond on behalf of the empress – a nice gesture from Marie Theresa that was intended to make up for her 'hospitality' in Vienna.

After leaving prison Beaumarchais returned to France with his faithful English manservant. I suppose that it was during the return journey that he attended a performance of Goethe's *Clavigo* at a theatre in Augsburg. About ten days later, at the beginning of October, he was back in Paris. All that winter the city sang, hummed and whistled the refrain of a song he had composed *en route* to celebrate his return to the capital: 'The same, the same, he's the same as ever.'

The same as ever? Certainly not. He had changed. His tribulations had made him still tougher. And when, in his song, he called himself a clown and a jester, he did so because he still couldn't take himself seriously. Like most of us, he had two faces. But shyness or detachment made him show only the facetious one. Those who tend to simplify things believe that it was the only one he had. Did his family and the friends who feasted his return know the other Beaumarchais? I'm not sure, particularly since Pierre-Augustin, unlike the jester in his song, changed his features and his nature slowly, like a sculptor chipping away with a chisel.

Now that Maupeou had been dismissed, parliament was in chaos, and Beaumarchais was no longer in a hurry to have his sentence quashed. Misfortune had made him demanding. The king and his ministers had been politely informed that M. de Beaumarchais expected to be rehabilitated with proper ceremony. Even in an absolute monarchy, that was easier said than done. No matter, he could wait. It was now the turn of the outlaw to lay down the law. I say this in all seriousness. The king had decided to recall the old parliament. But how was the recall to be effected? And what powers would the new assembly have? The ministers dithered and disagreed. Arbitration was needed. But who, in October 1774, was best qualified for the task? Why, M. de Beaumarchais, of course! Thus the non-gentleman, the non-citizen, the *persona non grata* was officially asked to write a 'short, elementary report in which his principles, propounded without inflation or ornament, might be readily understood by the common man'.

Beaumarchais jumped at the chance to expound at the government and instruct the nation. A few days later he submitted to Maurepas and Miromesnil a report entitled *Elementary Ideas on the Recall of the Parliaments*. This highly serious text in three parts (preamble, development, conclusion) might have been written by Montesquieu. But it is one thing to air one's political theories in a work of philosophy, and quite another to embody them in a report to the king and his ministers. The least one can say is that the latter course calls for greater audacity. In the preamble, before getting down to the parliaments, Beaumarchais unabashedly set out his views on the monarchy:

> The king swears, at his coronation, to uphold the laws of the Church and the realm. If the laws of the realm were but the arbitrary wishes of each king, none of them would need to swear at his coronation to uphold any

laws whatsoever, for the oath would be absurd. No one binds himself to himself.

Hence there exists, in every monarchical state, something other than the arbitrary will of kings. Now this cannot be anything but the corpus of the laws and their authority, which is the only valid basis for the authority of kings and the well-being of their people.

Instead of leaving to the crown's authority the eternally sound and respectable foundation of the laws on which that authority rests, mankind has fallen into an error that is highly nefarious to that authority by saying that the king's right to rule comes solely from God and from his sword – a misleading and unreal phrase which represents a tissue of absurdities . . .

In a king who is just towards his subjects, the right of the sword, being the same as the right proceeding from God, which merely represents the right of might, is not a right at all, since it can pass in turn to all parties that are capable of being the strongest. This absurd right merely constrains without involving, without ever creating a bond of gratitude; and this is the exact opposite of the crown's authority, which is founded, not on force, but on justice. This authority binds and obligates all of his subjects to the prince whose covenants are just, reasonable and sacred; and these covenants in their turn bind the prince to his subjects and are rightly known on this score as the fundamental laws of the realm . . .

This text deserves to be quoted in full – not because the ideas it contains are particularly original, but to exorcise the demon of doubt in the reader's mind. Whether he is dealing with clocks or with constitutional law, Beaumarchais reveals the same sense of responsibility, and his conviction that he is right leads him to take great risks. In the event the government ignored his proposals, or at least those concerning parliamentary 'resignation' in the event of a prolonged conflict with the king, even though Beaumarchais considered this measure to be essential in that it counterbalanced the supremacy of the monarch.

The old parliament was recalled on 12 November 1774, and Maupeou's 'Goëzmans' were sent packing. Beaumarchais, who hadn't yet seen the terms of the edict, promptly expressed his enthusiasm in a letter to Sartines dated 14 November: 'Never has there been a keener, stronger, or more universal sensation. The French people have gone mad with enthusiasm, and I am not surprised by their reaction. It is extraordinary that a king of twenty, who may be supposed to have a great love for his newly acquired authority, has so loved his people that he has been moved to give them satisfaction in such an essential area.'

A day later, having read the official texts, he was heartily disillusioned – the ministers had completely emasculated his project. He wrote to one of them forthwith: 'The conservatives are going around in a rage proclaiming that there is no longer a king in France, only a parliament. And I firmly believe that there is only a king in France, and no parliament. *Messieurs les ministres*, who have restored freedom in France, I shall not give you my freedom to restore if I can help it.' His jibe was clear-sighted. The edict of 12 November 1774 was the first failure in the 'royal revolution'. It was by no means the last.

The year ended in ambiguity, but neither Louis XVI nor the people, absorbed in their respective rejoicings, were aware of the fact. For Beaumarchais 1774 had been as eventful as ten years in an ordinary life, yet the twelve months had flashed by as quickly as a single day. For the time being he had to settle M. de Ronac's accounts. Once he had totted up the bill, which was a large one, he sent it in to the appropriate ministry. A number of authors, some of them perfectly respectable ones, have expressed their surprise that he should have done so. That's the way things go in literature – when La Fontaine gripes because his pension is late, he's divine, but when Beaumarchais sends in his expense sheet, he's the very devil.

Speaking of the devil, here's the note that accompanied his bill:

I enclose a statement of my expenses and receipts under the reign of the late king and that of our present master.

Since last March I've covered close on four thousand miles. Not bad going, I think! I've put three monsters out of business by destroying two lampoons and stopping the printing of a third. To do so, I left my own affairs to run to rack and ruin; I encountered all kinds of dangerous situations; I was deceived, robbed, attacked and imprisoned, and my health is quite destroyed. But what does all that matter providing the king is happy? Ask him merely to say 'I am happy' and I shall be the happiest man in the world. I ask for no other reward. The king is surrounded by far too many avid petitioners already. I would have him know that in a corner of Paris he has at least one disinterested servant. That is my only ambition. I count on your good offices for that.

I hope too that you don't want me to remain officially censured by the villainous parliament that you have just buried under the debris of its dishonour. The whole of Europe has well and truly avenged me for that heinous and absurd sentence. But that is not enough – there must be a further decree to quash the first one. I'm going to work at it, but with the moderation of a man who no longer fears either intrigue or injustice. I am counting on your help in this important matter.

M. de Ronac had to wait for his reimbursement, and so did M. de Beaumarchais for his rehabilitation. Both processes took two years. In the meantime he became famous in another direction, as we are about to see.

8

'The Barber of Seville'

Here we go. With this devil of a man, nothing is ever signed, sealed and delivered. There is always a reason for starting all over again. As he wrote to Gudin in 1774, 'I have been alive for two hundred years.' It would take a good couple of centuries, and innumerable books, to tell his life story. At this point in his labours, the author of this biography feels his mind reel. As he discovers the errors made by others, he realizes how many he has made himself. At every step he feels the urge to go back over what he has written and start the impossible task all over again. Appearances are there to blind him; if he is to understand, he has to interpret. Beaumarchais never appears without a mask, and to throw us off the scent he is constantly changing his disguise.

The voluminous scholarly works inspired by *The Barber* alone haven't nearly exhausted the subject. Alongside the transparent, sparkling comedy whose workings are obvious, there is an obscure, ambiguous work which, albeit less mysterious than *The Marriage*, poses a number of problems. 'So what,' you may say, 'since the work is a great one and can still make audiences laugh two hundred years after it was first performed?' To this objection, I reply that perfection is conditioned by enigma. The magic of a masterpiece depends on the extent of its veiled overtones. *Dom Juan*, a very imperfect play, is still Molière's best work, because it remains undefinable.

The same applies to *The Barber of Seville*, the title page of which bears the following epigraph: 'And I was a father and I could not die! (*Zaïre*, act II)' Why? In his excellent critical edition of *The Barber*, Georges Bonneville refers to this 'enigmatic epigraph borrowed from Voltaire'. The eminent professor at least had the grace to confess he was puzzled. The difficulty isn't easy to resolve, but I shall try to throw some light on the matter in a moment.

Even before its first performance the play had already had its ups and downs. It is thought to have started out as a *parade* and it is known to have become a comic opera, which was rejected by the Comédie Italienne, before being turned into what it is today – a stage play which went through at least three successive versions. The first version, in four acts, which passed the censor (Marin, as it happened) in 1773, was due to be staged at the Comédie Française on 12 February 1774, but was banned on 11 February because Beaumarchais had created a scandal on 10 February with his fourth memoir. The second version, in five acts, opened on 23 February 1775, and was booed on its first night. Two days later, however, the play was a triumphant success in its final reworked version in four acts. The changes from one manuscript to another are considerable – a close study of them would take up a hundred pages of this book at least. The work has already been done by a cohort of experts headed, as usual, by Linthilac, so I shall not linger over such questions, since my subject is limited to our knowledge of the author.

Having flopped on the Friday, *The Barber* was back in triumph on the Sunday. 'At the first night the comedy was booed; at its second performance it was an extravagant success,' writes Mme du Deffand. Anyone who knows a little about the theatre can imagine what this *tour de force* represented. But, as Figaro tells Almaviva, 'The harder it is to succeed, the more you need to try.' Not only did the author have to rewrite his play at lightning speed, but the actors had to learn new lines and the stage manager had to rehearse the new scene changes. Beaumarchais, who only really came into his own when tackling the impossible, surpassed himself. As usual, his apparently easy triumph was in fact the result of much hard work.

In its final version *The Barber* appears to be the simplest of comedies. The author himself sketched the plot as follows: 'An old man in love intends to marry his ward tomorrow; a young suitor, more adroit than he, thwarts him, and marries the girl today under the guardian's very nose and in his house.' This plot, one of the oldest in the world, has given rise in France alone to thousands of farces, pantomimes, plays, operas and what have you. Beaumarchais knew some of them – Scarron's *The Pointless Precaution*, for example, as he acknowledged in the title of his own variation on the theme, *The Barber of Seville, or, The Pointless Precaution*. He knew Molière's *School for Wives* as well. But Scarron and Molière had their own sources,

Italian or Spanish ones. Who cares about such niceties? The thing that matters is that Beaumarchais made the theme his own. No one before him, not even Molière, had used the devices of ellipsis and punning so freely and so naturally. Beaumarchais's experience of *parades* and his penchant for word games come close to destroying normal syntax at times, and his language becomes a language of the absurd. Like Molière, though with less restraint, he makes great use of repetition. And of course the play works like clockwork. Everything is prepared and executed with incredible precision – everything but verisimilitude, that is. The play has nothing to do with reality: it is set in the spheres of *imbroglio*. Bartholo is alternately keen-sighted or short-sighted, quick of hearing or almost deaf, to suit his author. He never recognizes Almaviva, but he does notice the letter tucked into Rosine's bodice and the ink stain on her finger; in the same scene he tells Almaviva to speak louder because he's deaf and to lower his voice because he isn't deaf. Beaumarchais isn't content with justifying these contradictions, he also uses them to make us laugh. In the third act Almaviva, Rosine and Figaro try to get rid of Bartholo for a short while so that the girl can be given an essential piece of information. Their attempts to get the old man to leave last for five marvellously funny scenes, at the end of which the guardian finally exits – but Beaumarchais contrives with diabolical skill, but contrary to all logic, to avoid giving the information, thereby giving the action a fresh twist. It isn't Bartholo who is duped, but the audience, to their great delight.

What is more, Beaumarchais succeeds in rejuvenating the characters of the traditional comedy. I am not thinking here of Wakeful, who spends all his time yawning, or Youthful, who is old, but Bazile of course, and above all Bartholo. This reactionary bourgeois doesn't try to conceal the horror he feels for his own times: 'What have they produced to make them praiseworthy? All kinds of nonsense: freedom of thought, gravity, electricity, religious tolerance, inoculation, quinine, the *Encyclopedia* and new-fangled plays.' He is by no means a fool. Foxy, quick-witted and intuitive, he is a formidable opponent for Almaviva, Rosine and Figaro. His intelligence enables him to thwart all their attempts to dupe him and gives the comedy its source of tension. If Almaviva is no match for Molière's Dom Juan, though he does resemble him, Bartholo has more judgement and personality than Arnolphe has. He also accepts his defeat with great dignity, and that too strikes me as something new in the traditional vein of tiresome old men.

But enough of these trifles! They are taking us away from our subject. The quick style, the brilliant construction and Bartholo's character don't explain the magic of *The Barber*. If it weren't for Figaro would we even be discussing the play? As a character, he is undeniably necessary to the action; but oddly enough it is what he has to say *outside* the action that gives the comedy its quality, its resonance and, I repeat, its magic. If you were to entertain yourself by cutting Figaro's great speeches altogether, you would see that the structure and the dynamics of *The Barber* wouldn't suffer in the slightest. In fact you'd end up with a better play. But it wouldn't be a masterpiece. The appearance of Figaro marks a decisive turning-point in French literary history. With Figaro, the author comes on to the stage for the first time. Writers such as Montaigne or Rousseau expressed themselves directly, and in the first person, by means of reflexion or confession. Beaumarchais, in both *The Barber* and *The Marriage*, enters his work by stealth, and his unexpected presence disturbs the action and confuses the issues. From that moment on our interest as spectator or reader is diverted towards the fascinating stranger, and without our realizing what is happening, the intruder captures all our attention. On the stage there are two Figaros, the barber *and* Beaumarchais, just as in *Remembrance of Things Past* there are the narrator *and* Proust. In 1775 this irruption of the author among his characters seemed scandalous, though the age was expecting that particular scandal – the memoirs had laid the foundations for it. After the prodigious success of these four texts, Beaumarchais realized that he was at his best when writing about himself.

In the French theatre, in which servants feature prominently, three valets are really up in arms against the system: Molière's Sganarelle, Beaumarchais's Figaro and Hugo's Ruy Blas. To my mind, it is wrong to think of Sganarelle as a clown. Superstition isn't his only character trait. The judgements he passes on Dom Juan are often pertinent and at times virulent. But he never dares to attack his master to his face. Also, his morals are those of a conservative, and he doesn't speak for Molière, who if anything is on the side of Dom Juan. Ruy Blas, on the other hand, is an unrestrained and arrant rebel. But still less is he the author; at best he is a pawn on Hugo's dramatic chessboard, a nobody. We are left with Figaro between the pusillanimous Sganarelle and the nonexistent Ruy Blas. Figaro may still call his master 'Your Excellency' or 'My lord', but he does so only to conform with custom. In other respects he doesn't keep his distance, but closes in to thrust straight and hard.

> ALMAVIVA: . . . I recall that in my service you were not especially obedient.
> FIGARO: The poor have their weaknesses like everyone else, my lord.
> ALMAVIVA: Lazy, argumentative . . .
> FIGARO: To judge by the virtues demanded of a servant, does Your Excellency know many masters who are fit to be valets?

None of which is very kind to Almaviva, and it was even less kind to the Comédie Française audience, which I believe included few servants at the time.

'I have a lackey's coat but you have a lackey's soul,' Ruy Blas would say much later. When writing this line, which is very reminiscent of Figaro's, Victor Hugo was running no risk, save that of offending his maid. Hugo merely goes visiting among the poor like a charitable beadle. Nine times out of ten he deals with them in a frock coat, wearing a countenance to match. Beaumarchais laughs at misfortune, because he is used to it. He hastens to 'laugh at everything lest [he] be obliged to weep at it'. To laugh and to bite:

> ALMAVIVA: I didn't recognize you. Just look at you, with your pot belly and your double chin. . .
> FIGARO: That's poverty for you, my lord!

This line lashes like a whip, yet it is generally understood the wrong way round. The point is that Almaviva, too, has a do-gooder's preconceptions – the poor are supposed to be skinny!

In the short quotations I have just given, the person speaking is still the character. Beaumarchais hasn't yet taken Figaro's place. He doesn't really make his entry until the 'republic of letters' speech, five minutes after the curtain has gone up. Up to then there have merely been a few furtive allusions, winks to the knowing few in the audience. But then suddenly comes the big surprise – Figaro is transformed into the author:

> ALMAVIVA: . . . But you haven't told me what made you leave Madrid.
> FIGARO: My guardian angel, Excellency, seeing that I have been fortu-

nate enough to meet my old master again. Realizing that the republic of letters in Madrid was in the hands of the wolves, for ever fighting among themselves, and that all the insects – gnats, midges, critics, maringoons, journalists, booksellers, censors – and all that clings to the flesh of the unfortunate authors, driven to contempt by this ridiculous squabbling, were tearing and sucking at the little bit of substance that remained; tired of writing, bored with myself, sickened by others, riddled with debts and short of money; convinced in the end that the useful revenue of the razor is preferable to the pointless honours of the pen, I left Madrid; and, with my bags on my back, strolling philosophically through the two Castilles, La Mancha, Estramadura, Sierre Morena and Andalusia; welcomed in one town, imprisoned in another, and everywhere above the fray; praised by some, reprimanded by others, helping along good times and putting up with bad; making fun of fools, standing up to villains; laughing at my poverty, and cocking my razor at everybody; here I am with my home in Seville, and ready to serve Your Excellency anew in whatever way he may please to command me.

An odd valet, and an even odder barber, I think you'll agree. So Figaro is a writer. Hmm. But who are these insects? These maringoons? *Quesaco*? That's right! And these booksellers? Poor Lejay! 'Riddled with debts', well, well. The 1775 audience cottoned on immediately. From then on it wasn't Figaro they were listening to, but Beaumarchais. 'Welcomed in one town, imprisoned in another, and everywhere above the fray' – the audience had no difficulty in following him from London to Vienna. But for their rejoicings to be complete, he had to add this little phrase: 'Praised by some, *reprimanded* by others.' Beaumarchais added these six words a few days before the play opened. As can be imagined, the censors would have felt duty bound to 'suck' that little bit of substance! The tirade ends with the announcement that Figaro, back in Seville, i.e. Beaumarchais back in Paris, is ready to serve His Excellency anew. Which Excellency? Almaviva or Louis XVI? Almaviva *and* Louis XVI. Most extraordinary of all is the fact that a modern audience, who know nothing of all this – they have never heard of Marin and don't know that Beaumarchais had received an official reprimand – react to this speech wonderfully well, although much of it is double Dutch to them and although it slows down the action.

One further example. Were you aware that at one time Beaumarchais wanted to call Bazile by the name of Guzman? He dropped the idea shortly before the first night, probably because he thought it too obvious, but he must have felt some regrets, for Brid'oison in *The Marriage* is called Don Gusman Brid'oison. So Bazile stayed as he was. However, the day before the first night, Beaumarchais wrote in a single, hurried sitting the extraordinary 'slander' tirade, which immortalized the councillor even as his name was removed from the dramatis personae. This Goyaesque character makes the audience laugh, but a hollow laugh. Bazile is patently a character from a nightmare. In modern parlance, he is traumatic. Yet if we reread *The Barber* we find that Bazile is merely a rogue, who sells his services to the highest bidder. How then can we explain the impact of his appearance in the play? The way he is dressed? Come now, behind Bazile there are all Beaumarchais's misfortunes, i.e. Councillor Goëzman, or the devil. The audience don't know this, because they don't even know who Goëzman was, but they *guess*. The tirade itself, which is dramatically pointless, is so far removed from the subject in hand that Bartholo has to point out how absurd it is:

> BAZILE: Slander, sir! You don't know what you're pooh-poohing. I have seen the most honest of people almost overwhelmed by it. Tell yourself there's no blatant unkindness, no horror, no absurd fable that a man can't get adopted by the idle folk of a large city if he goes about it in the right way – and we have people here who are very, very clever! To begin with, a mere rustle, skimming the ground like a swallow before the storm, whispers *pianissimo* along and shoots the poisoned arrow as it goes. Some mouth or other takes it in, and *piano, piano*, slips it niftily into your ear. The evil has been done; it sprouts, it creeps, it crawls, and *rinforzando* from mouth to mouth it goes like the devil, then all of a sudden, don't ask me how, you see slander rear up, hiss, swell and grow before your very eyes. It rushes, swoops, loops, surrounds, uproots, carries off, bursts and thunders, and becomes, glory be to heaven, a general outcry, a public *crescendo*, a universal chorus of hatred and proscription. Who the devil could resist that?
>
> BARTHOLO: What in the blazes is all this drivel you're blethering, Bazile? And what has your *piano-crescendo* got to do with my situation?

Obviously, Bazile cannot reply. But Goëzman has suddenly moved across the stage, as he was intended to. Once again the purely dramatic logic of the play runs counter to the hidden logic of art.

At the end of the first act, after a rip-roaring scene with Almaviva, Figaro begins to exit, but is called back by the count, who reminds him opportunely that he keeps a barber's shop: 'But where do you live, you scatterbrain?'

FIGARO: Oh, good heavens, I've quite lost my head! My shop, only a step from here, blue front, leaded windows, three pallets for a sign, an eye in a hand, *Consilio manuque*, FIGARO.

Is he a barber (blue shop front, three pallets for a sign) or a clock-maker (an eye in a hand, leaded windows like those in the rue Saint-Denis)? *Consilio manuque*, FIGARO: signature and confession. Long before I thought of writing this book – or any book, for that matter – I felt that FIGARO must represent *fils* Caron. To my joy, I discovered much later that Jacques Scherer, a scholar of high repute, felt the same as myself. It seems that other specialists disagree with M. Scherer, but their quarrel is an academic one, and their main argument doesn't strike me as being particularly convincing. They say that in the early versions of *The Barber* the name was written with a 'u', Figuaro. Figuereau, Bigaro, Durant – what does it matter? Beaumarchais loved playing with names, as we have seen. Considering that he had already turned his own name inside out in London and Vienna, I cannot imagine him baptizing gratuitously the character whom he intends to make his spokesman. And I cannot conceive of a man who had been dogged all his childhood and youth by a name pronounced 'Ficaro' choosing a name like Figaro merely by chance.

The Barber contains a very furtive reference to a daughter of Figaro's. There was much speculation at the time about this little girl, as there has been since. In 1775 the author merely joked when asked who this child was, where and when she had been born and who her mother was. It was thought that he might explain the situation in *The Marriage*, since he was well aware of his public's curiosity, but strangely enough he chose to avoid the issue once again. *The Marriage* was completed in 1778, and it was given its first performance six years later. In 1777 Marie-Thérèse Willermawlaz had given him a daughter, so there could be no question of joking about the little girl of Figaro's who had slipped into *The Barber* by mistake, so to speak. Beaumarchais is an odd fellow, you have to admit. He adores talking about himself and turning the clock back. Then at times he smilingly turns the hands in the other direction, so that he can mention his daughter two or three years before she is born!

Let's return to our mysterious epigraph. 'And I was a father and I could not die!' There is no mystery about how writers choose the phrase or lines of verse that they quote as a motto at the beginning of their book. More often than not, it is not so much a deliberate choice as a choice made for them by a chance encounter, an immediate infatuation. The words themselves are often more important than their meaning; a writer who underlines or jots down a little phrase from *Zaïre*, for instance, doesn't always know why he has done so. The imagination frequently bypasses consciousness altogether.

So much for generalities. Now to the point. I spent a long while trying to solve this riddle, and my efforts ranged from the sublime (allusion to his dead son; two statements, a *and* b) to the ridiculous (father = author: his work makes him immortal). It was Loménie who eventually put me on to what I think is the right track. After quoting a speech of Figaro's that Beaumarchais cut between the first and the second performances ('Not to mention the fact that I have lost all my fathers and mothers; I have been an orphan of the last of them since last year'), Loménie notes: 'It is rather odd that Beaumarchais, whose excellent qualities as a son, a brother and . . . a father are now known, should have allowed himself to be led astray by his systematic intention of creating a type of universal braggart, to the point where he makes Figaro utter mocking remarks about a type of sentiment that even comedy generally respects.' Since I am, possibly, less squeamish than my illustrious predecessor, I admit that Figaro's snide remarks about his family don't shock me overmuch, in fact I quite like them. The point is that you can love your father and mother and still cast doubts on the value of blood relations *per se*. As I wrote at the very outset of this book, Beaumarchais was the son of the clockmaker Caron *and* he was the son of a nobody. Loménie's surprise urged me to take this line of reasoning a little farther.

In his famous *Moderate Letter on the Fall and the Critical Reception of The Barber of Seville*, Beaumarchais gives the plot of an absurd tragedy that he might have written instead of his comedy. Figaro, abandoned by his father, who is none other than Bartholo, is stolen from his mother (Marceline!) by a band of gipsies while he is still a child. 'By changing his condition without knowing it, the ill-starred youth changed his name without wishing it; he brought himself up under the name of Figaro; he lived.' Once he'd discovered the truth about his birth he might have turned his razor against himself and/or have achieved, thanks to Bartholo's marrying Marceline, a state of 'happiness and legitimacy'. This astonishing outline was to yield, of course, not a tragedy but a second comedy, *The Day of Madness, or, The Marriage of Figaro*. For the moment, the point I want to pursue is that Figaro's mystery is the mystery of his birth. And ('forced to travel the road that I took without knowing it') Figaro's secret is Beaumarchais's secret – a fundamental obsession, hidden, buried or, in modern parlance, repressed, an obsession that can be expressed only by the indirect means of laughter. I repeat, the magic of *The Barber* depends on its veiled overtones, its indefinability. What an extraordinary situation, when the lightest, clearest, most light-hearted playwright that France has ever had turns out to be the darkest, the most obscure and the most disconcerting man imaginable! (This doesn't of course alter the fact that his two comedies will remain what they always have been – lively and brilliant. It would be madness to upset the audience with our commentaries. In the theatre you need only enjoy yourself with Figaro. But in what is commonly known as a biography we are obliged to take a closer look at things, even if it does mean spoiling the fun at times.)

All the same, the signs are there for those who wish to see them, even in the play itself. As Beaumarchais jokingly (of course) points out in his preface, Figaro is a model son. When asked whether he knows Bartholo he replies, 'Like my mother', because, as Beaumarchais pretends to explain, 'every man draws his comparisons from whatever interests him most'. On one level this line is merely funny, but on another level it links up with what I am trying to explain: Beaumarchais, who knows, makes Figaro, who doesn't know, say that he knows Bartholo like his mother, addressing himself to an audience who don't know either that Bartholo is in fact . . . But I am labouring my point. The hands turn, and we read the hour, but who cares about escapements and springs, apart from a clockmaker?

'I was a father and I couldn't die.' I couldn't die because I loved my son; but I ought to have died, because to give life is absurd. 'What a strange sequence of events! Why these things and not others? Forced to travel the road that I took unknowingly, just as I shall leave it unwillingly.' Forced: I couldn't die. Bartholo cannot recognize Figaro, and Figaro cannot imagine that the doctor is his father. When Marceline, in *The Marriage*, asks him whether nature hasn't told him a hundred times that Bartholo is his father, he replies bluntly: 'Never.' His relationship with his mother is just as false, just as faked, but Beaumarchais knows only his obsession – as the son of a nobody, some day in his turn he too will be a nobody for his child: he will be a father and he won't be able to die. And all of this goes on simultaneously with the affection that we know he felt for old M. Caron and with his violent longing to be a father. 'Become fathers; you must,' he wrote after the birth of his daughter. Two contradictory attitudes: need and refusal. Isn't it odd that a conflict of this order, and one that was never resolved, should have produced two comedies, one at least of which is all surface, all mirrorlike polish? Glancing at it, André Gide saw nothing but glitter; he hadn't looked properly. Was it in spite of this conflict, or because of it, that Beaumarchais turned his life into one great adventure? What makes Figaro tick? If he was to survive a Protestant had to turn his coat, and a Barber had to serve the designs of his master – that was the law. But Beaumarchais-Figaro decided to break the law by rebelling, by acting, and by challenging the system. I cannot be myself except against my father and against the king, who, the one by weakness and the other by force, have decided that I shall be another. Ultimately Beaumarchais was to discover that every man is born a Protestant but promptly undergoes compulsory conversion. You are my father, and you are also Bartholo. I don't want to become Bartholo in my turn. I want to remain Figaro, a Protestant, but if I fail to do so I shan't make a tragedy of it: 'What gave you such a cheerful philosophy?' 'Being accustomed to misfortune. I hasten to laugh at everything lest I be obliged to weep at it.' We need to remember that without this laughter we should have neither Figaro nor Beaumarchais.

Old M. Caron, about whom we had a few harsh words to say a few moments ago, could not and would not die. Scandalizing his family, he impenitently insisted on marrying, at seventy-seven, for the third time. The apple of his eye was a wily spinster only a few years younger than himself called Suzanne-Léopolde Jeantot, with whom he had been triumphantly living in sin for the past few months. This Jeantot woman, who made M. Caron's old legs cut a frisky caper, followed him to the altar on 18 April 1775 with an enthusiasm that was justified by the marriage contract, which unfortunately we haven't heard the last of. To achieve her ends she had merely to fan the old man's ardour beyond his strength. As she was by no means backward in coming forward, M. Caron led her to the heights of ecstasy by dying six months after the wedding. Bartholo says of Rosine, 'I'd rather she wept at having me than that I should die from not having her.' Between old André and old Léopolde, things were rather different: she didn't weep at having him; he had her and died from it. On the day of the wedding, which his father had kept from him, and on the day of his death, the news of which reached him too late, Pierre-Augustin was in London once more, grappling with a lady who wasn't much younger than Léopolde, and who, like her, knew a bargain when she saw one. Before meeting her, however, I think it would be better to start a new chapter.

9

The Sex of the Dragoon

Consilio manuque, FIGARO. As his character had said, Beaumarchais was ready to serve anew His Excellency, the *gran corregidor* of Andalusia, in other words Louis XVI. And the king and his ministers seemed quite prepared to have further recourse to the services of a man with an eye in his hand. M. de Ronac had been more successful in London and Vienna than the best agents in the secret service. 'Intrigue and money, now you're in your element,' Suzanne tells Figaro in *The Marriage*. But the words are hers, and she is merely repeating what his reputation had to say of him. Our own opinion is different: Beaumarchais's real fascination was for politics. It was politics he was involved in on the other side of the Channel – politics at a high level, as Versailles was well aware. But the pronounced fondness for mystery that was prevelant in his day, together with the faults of the system, led the sovereign and his counsellors to adopt the most devious of approaches to diplomacy. Furthermore, there was always a certain amount of confusion between the private affairs of royalty and the affairs of the State. It is hard to appreciate how much energy and time were wasted by men like Choiseul or Vergennes on settling problems of the bedchamber or buying off imaginative journalists.

In short, Beaumarchais was expected to continue the mission he had commenced in London, which was of a political nature. At the same time the indispensable M. de Ronac was ordered to pursue his investigations into the sordid intrigues that were being plotted in the English capital. M. de Ronac's undertakings would act as a cover for Beaumarchais's and serve him as a pretext. This last point was quite important. Apart from the fact that he couldn't officially trespass on the preserves of the French ambassador, the particular nature of his policy, which was very hostile to Britain, required the utmost discretion. His contacts with Rochford, for example, were necessarily off the record. Yet this ambiguous undercover role that the government wanted him to play wasn't greatly to his liking. He said as much testily to Sartines: '*Monsieur*, kindly place at the king's feet my justifiable distaste for the sort of commission that is more difficult to carry out than the most difficult of political missions.' His irritation is understandable. All that the public saw of the two parts he was acting was their apparent duplicity. Beaumarchais the trickster, the intriguer, the spy – those who were always ready to see him as a mere adventurer clung to their prejudices all the more firmly because that is what he seemed to be. Even today, in spite of the evidence, he is still persistently judged on appearances. Figaro is legitimate, Beaumarchais isn't. And never was: he died the son of a nobody. As a result, he was constantly being blackballed. When the time comes, we shall ask ourselves whether he didn't secretly produce the black ball from his own pocket.

At any rate, he left for London on 8 April 1775. The person he was going to meet was a captain of dragoons, one Chevalier d'Eon, whom you may have heard of. On the road to Boulogne he soon noticed that he was being followed by 'a man on horseback who kept within sight of him and changed horses every time he did'. (The words are Gudin's.) For the first time in his life, the hunter had become the quarry. He managed to shake off his pursuer all the same and reached London without incident. The day after his arrival M. de Ronac found an anonymous letter on his mat suggesting that he might meet with an accident if he didn't return to France without delay. Now Beaumarchais's main virtue was courage. Unlike most men, the older he grew, the more he enjoyed taking risks. As we shall see, he became less and less cautious and grew accustomed to staking his life at double or quits. His unknown enemy or enemies had got the wrong man. Instead of going into hiding or taking on a body-guard, he put himself on display. To begin with, he dropped his pseudonym and announced that he was Beaumarchais. From then on he could be met in public places without an escort, surrounded by admirers who drew attention to him all the more. In a letter to the papers, he invited his correspondent to make himself known.

Instead of the visitor he was expecting, Beaumarchais received a visit from a Mme Campagnol and an unfrocked monk by the name of Father Vignoles. This unsavoury pair dabbled in lampoons. Their works, if that is the word for them – and if they actually wrote them themselves, which is doubtful – attacked the young King of France. Mme Campagnol accused poor Louis XVI of acts *that he alone was incapable of committing at the Palace of Versailles, whereas the phoney monk, who was craftier or more inspired than his companion, denounced another kind of impotence in the king: according to Vignoles, Louis XVI was mentally deficient, a puppet ruler at the mercy of his ministers or the Empress of Austria. Beaumarchais, probably with the aid of Rochford, had no trouble in defusing these half-cocked squiblets. Once they were out of the way he turned to politics again without delay. To make the king realize that he intended to devote himself entirely to political activities, he sent him a long memorandum beginning with the following lines, which left no room for ambiguity:

> After taking measures to destroy this nest of vipers without compromising anyone, I have devoted myself to more noble study and more satisfying research, and as my name alone has sufficed to give me access to members of different parties, I have been able to find out from the proper sources about everything connected with the government and the present situation in England. I am in a position to submit to Your Majesty instructive and very faithful reports, highly detailed or succinct, on men and events.
>
> I can give the most accurate estimate of the action of the mother country, on her colonies and the effect of colonial disorder on England; what the result may be on both sides; the extreme importance that all of these events have for the interests of France; what we can hope or fear for our possessions in the West Indies; what can bring us peace and what war etc.

Beaumarchais dispatched this letter and his first report ten days after his arrival, which shows that he hadn't been wasting his time. My reason for quoting this very formal missive is that I needed to choose a point of departure to show how far Beaumarchais's character would develop over the next few years. After offering, or rather imposing, his services with the greatest of deference, he would soon become aware of the role that he could play and begin to speak with greater authority – before long, he would be unrestrainedly lecturing the king. But before influencing the course of events and serving France and changing the face of the world in accordance with his profoundest ambitions, he had to pass yet another test and emerge

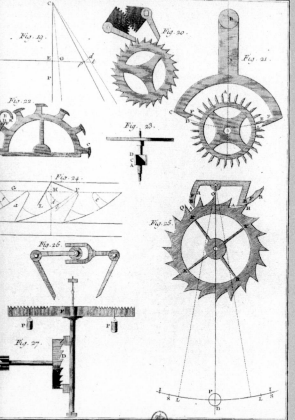

A clockmaker's shop in 18th century Paris.

Various types of escapement.

Portraits by Nattier of two of
the princesses, Adélaïde (left)
and Victoire (above).
The court portraitist has somewhat flattered them.

Beaumarchais (above left) and three of the men who influenced his career: Pâris-Duverney (below left) his friend and business partner; the Comte de La Blache, his most formidable opponent (above right) and the Earl of Rochford (below right), whom Beaumarchais befriended in Madrid in 1763.

Sartines (above), chief of police and Nav[al]
Minister, who stood by Beaumarchais in h[is]
darkest hour.

Beaumarchais's most powerful friend and al[ly]
the Prince de Conti (left).

victorious from his encounter with the dragon – I mean, the dragoon.

Among the London French, three ruled supreme: Morande, Mme de Godeville and the Chevalier d'Eon. Before Beaumarchais got mixed up with them, this formidable threesome had the French government over a barrel. We have seen how M. de Ronac turned the poacher Morande into the most diligent of gamekeepers; we shall see later on how Beaumarchais would lead Mme de Godeville back to the fold by tumbling her in the hay. Eon was a different kettle of fish. He was much more intelligent than Morande and, despite his assertions to the contrary, he was definitely not built the same way as Mme de Godeville.

Charles-Geneviève-Louis-Auguste-André-Timothée d'Eon was one of the eighteenth century's oddest figures. And he has remained controversial to this day. It must be said that this captain of dragoons did everything in his power to draw attention to himself, or rather to a specific feature of his anatomy. But it was a case of much ado about nothing. Charles-Geneviève d'Eon, despite his ambiguous name, despite his even more ambiguous fame, had all the normal attributes of a man. When he died, in 1810, a swarm of doctors descended on his corpse like misfortune on this poor world of ours and to their great disappointment had no difficulty at all in discerning that the dragoon was not a dragooness. One of them signed the following document: 'I hereby certify that I have examined and dissected the corpse of the Chevalier d'Eon in the presence of Mr Adair, Mr Wilson and Father Elysée, and have found the male genital organs to be perfectly formed in every respect. Thomas Copeland, surgeon.' Now these doctors secretly hoped to prove that Eon was androgynous, hence the careful post-mortem. If there had been the least doubt, the slightest external or internal malformation, the doctors would gleefully and dutifully have felt bound to say so in learned articles, communications to the college of surgeons, and public lectures. Disappointed, but honest, they told what they had seen, convinced that they had cleared up the mystery. They had reckoned without the fabulators who know their clients' tastes. Even today large numbers of people occupy their minds with speculations about the handsome chevalier's secret – though secret is scarcely the right word in this connection.

When Beaumarchais first met him Eon was close on fifty – an old
gentleman. As we all know, men who have kept their youthful looks
far into manhood end up worse than the rest. Their face sags and
collapses into wrinkles and suddenly loses its radiance; from one day
to the next, Dorian Gray becomes loathsome of visage. It would
seem that this is what happened to the Chevalier d'Eon. At twenty,
his grace and beauty were evident and he could be mistaken for a
girl. As he had already shown a talent for diplomacy, didn't conceal
his taste for the secret service and had plenty of courage, Louis XV
sent him to St Petersburg, where he succeeded in obtaining a post as
maid-in-waiting to the Empress Elizabeth. According to the legend,
Charles-Geneviève won the affection of the czarina and thereby
effected a valuable *rapprochement* between the Russian and French
courts. When he had reached his thirties and confusion was no
longer conceivable, Geneviève became Charles again and occupied
several posts in the diplomatic corps. For the next twenty years or so,
no one dreamed of doubting his virility. Charles 'drank, smoked and
swore like a German squire' and never said no to a fight. An
invincible swordsman, he made many widows and many enemies.
After the Treaty of Paris Louis XV appointed him to a post in
London, where he was promoted plenipotentiary under the ambas-
sadorship of Guerchy. In fact his mission was top secret. The king
had ordered him to make preliminary studies for a French landing in
England, which shows that he was trusted implicitly.

The chevalier worked hard at his mission, meeting many members of the British government and George III himself. Some authors,
following the lead given by Gaillardet, assure us that the dragoon
pursued his advantage as far as Queen Sophie-Charlotte's private
apartments and should therefore be regarded as the real father of
George IV. To save the queen's honour, they say, he put out the
rumour that he was a woman; and these 'historians' conclude that
George III's attacks of madness were caused by his saucy doubts and
fears. This imaginative interpretation of history is virtually ground-
less. Loménie, who didn't believe a word of it, tells us that the only
thing that 'adds some force to this theory' is a letter from Aiguillon to
the chevalier, but logic and the rest of the evidence more than
outweigh this slender document. The fact remains that no one
thought of taking the dragoon for a lady before the death of Louis XV.

Eon's violent quarrel with Guerchy, towards the end of the reign, really did occur. The two men were bound to fall out sooner or later, since the ambassador received his orders from his minister, whereas the plenipotentiary was an emissary of the king's and furthermore sworn to secrecy. Mystified by the king's double dealing, Guerchy jumped to conclusions and took Eon for a British spy. He had his papers searched in an attempt to back up his suspicions, and, according to the chevalier, tried to have him poisoned by a man called Treyssac de Vergy. At any rate the affair blew up into a blazing row. There was a duel. Guerchy's son swore to avenge his father. Louis XV was greatly put out and had to dismiss the chevalier officially, though he asked him in writing to pursue his mission confidentially. Whereupon the king died and, as so often happens in this kind of affair, Eon, the secret agent, found himself abandoned, isolated, and ruined – a lost soul. But he had one ace up his sleeve – his correspondence with the late king. Before long he decided to play it.

This flashback was, I feel, essential if we were to understand the kind of relationship that existed between the Chevalier d'Eon and Beaumarchais. It is generally alleged that Beaumarchais met Eon by chance, but this strikes me as unsatisfactory. The correspondence between Vergennes and his 'diplomatic jockey' suggests that the mission had been prepared in advance, and that the chevalier had already stated his claims to Vergennes in a letter written a few months previously. In a word, the dragoon intended to horsewhip the government for close on 300,000 *livres*, part of which sum was owed to him in back pay (the crown was a bad debtor, as we have seen). It was implied that he would hand over the precious documents once he had obtained satisfaction.

They met at the end of April or the beginning of May, and the negotiations began. 'Both of us probably felt drawn to one another by the kind of natural curiosity for encounter found in all extraordinary animals,' the chevalier wrote. Beaumarchais was bound to like him – he was brilliant, witty, cynical; and he knew London inside out. He was a friend of the rich and was invited everywhere for his wit and his extravagance. He had just enhanced his charisma by inventing and publicizing the fact that he was really a woman. Gudin, who had followed Beaumarchais to London, met him at the lord mayor's residence.

I first met d'Eon at a dinner party given by Wilkes and was struck by the sight of the cross of Saint-Louis glinting on his breast. I asked Mlle Wilkes who this chevalier might be and she told me his name. 'He has,' said I, 'a woman's voice and that is presumably why all these things have been said about him.' I knew nothing further at that time. I had still to learn of his relations with Beaumarchais. I soon heard about them from the lady herself. She told me, weeping (it seems this was d'Eon's wont), that she was a woman, and showed me her legs, which were covered with scars – the result of wounds she had received when her horse had been killed under her and a squadron had galloped over her body, leaving her dying in the field.

What a boon for London society to have an elderly cavalry captain going around sobbing that he was a woman, and rolling his trousers up (or down?) to exhibit his battle scars! Some, like Gudin, believed every word of what he told them; others pretended to swallow the story so as not to spoil the fun. No one ever asked him, for instance, how it was that no surgeon in a field hospital somewhere had ever discovered a slight anomaly when stitching him back together. But raising the question was the same as answering it, and no one wanted to be a wet blanket. In the much less select places to which Beaumarchais followed the chevalier (and to which he returned more often than he should have, since he eventually caught clap), bets were laid on the sex of the dragoon. Quite large amounts were wagered on 'Mr Sterling and Miss Guinea.' But the bets were not settled until much later, in 1810.

I shan't describe the deals in detail – they were long and complicated because the chevalier was reluctant to hand over the documents before he had got what he wanted (his back pay, a life annuity of 12,000 *livres* and the right to return to France). The hardest point to settle was the last one. Louis XVI agreed to allow the chevalier back into France on condition that he disguised himself as a woman. A letter from Vergennes to Beaumarchais dated 26 August seems to me to set out the problem clearly:

Whatever my desire to see, know and listen to M. d'Eon, I will not, *Monsieur*, hide the fact that I am very worried. His enemies are on the watch, and will be loath to forgive him for what he has said about them. If he comes here, however wise and circumspect his behaviour, they may attribute to him utterances that run counter to the silence that the king has imposed. Denials and justifications are always embarrassing to honest men. If M. d'Eon wished to disguise himself, that would be an end on the matter. He must decide that for himself; but for the sake of his peace of mind he would be well advised not to live in France, for a few years at least, and definitely not in Paris. You may use this observation in any way you deem appropriate.

To my mind, this letter enables us to answer a vexed question: why did the chevalier dress as a woman in France? The explanation may sound odd today, but the plain fact is that in male attire Eon would have been assassinated. Anne and Claude Manceron are quite right to say that in the eighteenth century it was unthinkable to kill a woman spy. It was just as unthinkable to challenge a woman to a duel. In fact Guerchy's son, who had sworn to avenge his father, respected 'Mlle d'Eon' from the moment she entered France. It is indeed, conceivable that the dragoon's behaviour in London was cleverly designed to prepare for his return to France, or to make it possible. But we must avoid simplifications – M. d'Eon would never have lent himself to such a pretence if he hadn't had something to gain from it in terms of personal advantage or pleasure; yet at the same time there was nothing feminine about him apart from his voice. There is absolutely no question of ascribing his odd antics to conscious homosexuality. M. d'Eon was fond of women, moderately but exclusively. On the other hand, he loved showing off and attracting attention. He delighted in being a living enigma and a flesh-and-blood hoax, and it may well be that his girlish attire at the court of St Petersburg had given him a few quirks.

This letter, together with others that are no less clear in their implications, shows that neither Vergennes nor Beaumarchais was taken in for a moment by the old dragoon. But the legend has somehow stuck. Some authors have been misled by the occasional joking references to Eon in the feminine in the correspondence between the minister and his envoy. Here's one from Beaumarchais: 'Everyone tells me this queer lady is queer about me'; or this from Vergennes: 'Do you think your amazon . . .?' The male lead played his part in the charade with glee, writing to Beaumarchais on one occasion: 'There never was any engagement between us; anything you may have said about our imminent marriage . . .' and so on. The very tone of these pleasantries strikes me as leaving no room for doubt. None the less, as I have said, a number of historians, some of them quite distinguished, maintain that Beaumarchais was duped by the ageing dragoon. If it had been true I should have enjoyed recounting such a spicy tale, but I can't go against my convictions or against the facts.

To conclude his negotiations with the chevalier, Beaumarchais had to travel back and forth between London and Paris several times. We shall soon see that he also had other reasons for talking with Vergennes and Louis XVI, but this doesn't mean that he took his first task lightly. Here, for example, is the kind of question he had to submit to Louis XVI, plus the king's reply, a few days before the final settlement, once the principle of the dragoon's 'femininity' had been agreed:

> Will the king allow Mlle d'Eon to wear the cross of Saint-Louis on her female attire?
> ANSWER: Only in the provinces.
> Does Your Majesty approve of the gratuity of 200 *écus* that I have made to the lady for her trousseau?
> ANSWER: Yes.
> If so will she be permitted to dispóse freely of all her civilian clothes?
> ANSWER: She must sell them.

In the end the bargain was struck and after attempting to throw dust in Beaumarchais's eyes as a final flourish the chevalier handed over all the documents in his possession. A kind of contract was signed with appropriate solemnity: 'We the undersigned, Pierre-Augustin Caron de Beaumarchais, special private envoy of the King of France . . . and Mlle Charles- Geneviève- Louise- Auguste- Andrée- Timothée d'Eon de Beaumont, spinster . . .' A few days earlier Beaumarchais had obtained permission in writing from the king for the former cavalry captain to keep his uniform, helmet, sabre, pistol, rifle and bayonet, 'as one preserves the cherished remains of a departed loved one.' And this was written into the contract along with the rest.

Now that he'd been stripped of his treasure, the dragon – I mean the dragoon – had lost his teeth and no one was scared of him anymore. As he kept putting off his return to France, he was forgotten. Embittered, and probably hurt by the fact that Beaumarchais dropped him as soon as he'd signed the agreement, he tried to attract attention to himself by accusing the negotiator of having witheld a large sum of money. This time, however, Beaumarchais, who was beginning to know a thing or two about calumny, had taken precautions, and the chevalier was forced to drop those particular allegations. But as he had plenty of time and wit, he invented other slanders. Dipping his pen in highly corrosive acid, he wrote to Beaumarchais, or to Vergennes about Beaumarchais, several quite amusing epistles, then related their contents about town. Of all his epigrams at Beaumarchais's expense, the one that comes closest to hitting the nail on the head is this one: 'Beaumarchais has the insolence of an apprentice clockmaker who has chanced to discover perpetual motion.'

Oddest of all in this odd story is the fact that the Chevalier d'Eon made little use of the right he had fought so hard to obtain. He didn't return to France until 1777 and left again almost immediately. With characteristic aplomb, he appeared at Versailles in full-dress dragoon regimentals. He was informed that he no longer enjoyed the privilege of wearing such attire, so he came back the next day in a different outfit. Mlle Bertin, the princesses' dressmaker, had fitted him out in the latest fashion. Grimm, who was lucky enough to see the dragoon in this disguise, was startled: 'It is hard to imagine anything more extraordinary and more indecent than Mlle d'Eon in skirts.'

10

I, Beaumarchais

Beaumarchais's trip to Spain had enabled him to taste the pleasures of politics – not the pleasures of embassy life or of rubbing shoulders with the famous, but the keener satisfaction of intervening in the course of events. Madrid was his apprenticeship. No doubt he failed there. He was too young at the time to interpret orders, and too anxious to succeed to make allowances for local circumstances. During the ten years that followed, which, as we have seen, were incredibly eventful, he had to reflect – in other words he had to work. All his feats, though they appear so effortless, so easy, were the result of hard work. He gave himself to France as he had given himself to his watches – passionately. For ten years he strove for understanding. Then when he at last felt sure that he held the keys he needed, he suddenly changed his tone. Kings and ministers who had until then listened to him with astonishment and interest treated him overnight as an equal. Now that he was sure that he was right, he stopped scheming to gain a hearing and merely raised his voice. I, Beaumarchais. But the real mainspring of his action was his love for France, a love so intense that his own destiny merged with that of his country. This state of grace lasted for only a few months. Most politicians don't aspire to anything more than staying put and dispatching the day's business. Statesmen with the urge and the ability to write history are rare. Rarer still are the amateurs (beware Figaro!) who changed the face of the world.

His origins remain the key to his greatness. Beaumarchais – son of a nobody, bearer of borrowed names, illegitimate, then reprimanded (i.e. deprived of his civil identity) – always seems to be doomed to prove that he exists in spite of the law, in spite of the system, and that he really is Beaumarchais. Yet in the space of only a few months he would emerge victorious from this seemingly endless battle. For a short while in 1776 he would be Beaumarchais, a legitimate citizen – and he would be France.

The Treaty of Paris, which had put an end to the Seven Years' War, had also put an end to the preponderance of France in Europe. Even though her economic and demographic situation was superior to that of Britain, her power was inferior. Britannia ruled. Since 1763 the Continent had been kept in leading-strings. Dunkirk, with her fortifications destroyed and occupied by the British, testified to the humbling of France. The acquisition of Lorraine (by inheritance) and Corsica (by purchase) hadn't restored the honour lost at Rossbach, Quebec and elsewhere. As has always been the case in France, moral and intellectual degradation went hand in hand with political humiliation. Even the French language itself, which had long been universal, showed signs of declining like the rest. At court, and in all right-minded circles in Paris, Anglomania was the order of the day. Moral capitulation had followed defeat in battle. At Versailles the executive dithered, beset with financial difficulties. The pro-Austrian clan led by the dreary Mercy-Argenteau added to the confusion.

Fortunately for France, that was not the whole picture. The spirit of resistance and the desire for revenge lived on in the hearts of many Frenchmen, as the demonstrations following the disgrace of Choiseul showed. It must be said right away that the young Louis XVI believed that it was his mission to restore his country's glory. That he intended to stop the advance of Britain is undeniable. Moreover, in spite of the insistent pressure put on him to join the Habsburgs in their imperial adventures, he always steered clear of a *rapprochement* with Austria. He had had the perspicacity to choose as his Foreign Minister a man who adored France and knew that her recovery was necessarily bound up with the decline of Britain. But Vergennes and Louis XVI were both peace-loving and cautious men. And the king had a predilection for virtue and morality in government. Frederick the Great summed him up as follows: 'Louis XVI is almost always in a position to talk idealistically.' But to dream of France and to long for her recovery, without really doing anything about it, was the same as doing nothing.

In London, Beaumarchais wasn't exactly doing nothing. He was continuing to lead four lives at once, taking as passionate an interest in Captain Cook's discoveries as in the current research on the pulse, negotiating the purchase of a forest on behalf of the French navy, making love right, left and centre, and beginning to jot down the first lines of *The Marriage of Figaro*. All of which was a mere trifle compared with his main preoccupation – politics. The workings of the British government no longer held any secrets for him, as Rochford had introduced him to most of the key men. Wilkes had also piloted him round the troubled waters of the Opposition. Beaumarchais discovered before anyone else that Britain, having reached the apogee of her power, desperately wanted to climb down again. In particular the lively analysis he made of the conflict between the United Kingdom and her American colonies led him very quickly to believe that, by aiding the insurgents, France, though in no position to wage war on Britain directly, might weaken the British stranglehold and at the same time recover her own supremacy. His reasoning strikes me as being all the more remarkable as it took into account the character of Louis XVI and the cautious mentality of his ministers. Maurepas, who was close on eighty, was no longer available for any kind of adventure; at the War Ministry, Saint-Germain was dissipating most of his abundant energy reforming the army; at the Ministry of Finance, Turgot and his successor Necker were chiefly preoccupied with defending the franc. Vergennes and Sartines, who were more receptive to Beaumarchais's arguments, were both peace-loving men, and their interpretation of the facts made them lean towards moderation. Vergennes had been put on his guard by what had happened to Choiseul, and greatly feared the possible consequences of a conflict; and Sartines was only too aware of the extreme weakness of his navy. The king himself, I repeat, was torn between the rigours of virtue and a desire to restore the position of France. Sure of himself, certain that he was right, and convinced that he was capable of winning, Beaumarchais applied himself single-handed, with perilous aplomb and the stubbornness of genius, to bringing Louis XVI and Vergennes round to his way of thinking. And he pulled it off.

The fact that Beaumarchais took the historic initiative of involving France in the quarrel between Britain and the nascent states of America, and that he played a decisive part in all the momentous events that led up to the Treaty of Versailles, is incontrovertible. The evidence is there and all the historians have had access to it for years.

I maintain that for a few months Beaumarchais was France – single handed and alone. But at times the truth is hard to take. If you believe that it would be improper to marry France to a man like Figaro, even for a single day, then you must load the dice of history and acclaim the Marquis de La Fayette, as people have been doing for exactly two hundred years.

If he was to have his way Beaumarchais had to convince Louis XVI and Vergennes and he applied himself to this task with growing authority. As early as September 1775 he wrote to the king to get him gradually used to the idea of French intervention:

> Sire, Britain is in such a crisis, such a turmoil both within and without, that she would be virtually ruined if her neighbours and rivals were themselves in a position to attend to her seriously. Here is a faithful report on the situation of the British in America. I obtained the information from an inhabitant of Philadelphia recently arrived from the colonies, and who had just emerged from a conference concerning them with the British government, who were greatly dismayed by his account of the situation. The Americans are determined to suffer anything rather than submit, and are filled with the same enthusiasm for freedom as has frequently made the little nation of Corsica a formidable foe for Genoa. They have an effective force of thirty-eight thousand armed and determined men beneath the walls of Boston; they have forced the British army to choose between starving in this town or seeking their winter quarters elsewhere, which is what they will shortly do. About forty thousand well-armed and equally determined men are defending the rest of the country, yet this total force of eighty thousand men has not meant that a single farmer has had to leave his land or a single workman his factory. All those who worked in the fisheries, which the British have destroyed, have become soldiers and believe that it is their duty to avenge the ruin of their families and the freedom of their country. All those who were in maritime trade, which the British have stopped, have joined the fishermen to wage war on their common persecutors; all the harbour workers have joined the ranks of this army of angry men whose every act is motivated by vengeance and rage.
>
> I say, Sire, that such a nation must be invincible, especially since they have behind them as much land as they need for retreat, even supposing the British had gained the mastery of all their coasts, which is far from being the case. Every reasonable person in Britain is therefore convinced that the colonies are lost to the crown, and that is my opinion also.
>
> The overt war being waged in America is much less fatal for England than the civil war that must shortly break out in London, where party

conflicts have reached the heights of excess since the King of England declared the Americans rebels. This ineptitude, this masterpiece of folly on the part of the government has renewed the strength of all its opponents by uniting them against it. They have resolved to break openly with the court party in the opening debates in parliament. It is thought that these debates will result in seven or eight members of the Opposition being sent to the Tower of London, and that is the moment they are waiting for to raise a hue and cry. Lord Rochford, my friend of fifteen years, told me with a sigh: 'I am very much afraid, *monsieur*, that before the winter is out a few heads may roll, either in the king's party or in the Opposition.' Also, the Lord Mayor, Mr Wilkes, in a moment of joy and relaxation at the end of a splendid dinner, said to me in public: 'The King of England has long honoured me with his hatred. I myself have always done him the justice of despising him. The time has come to decide which of us has shown better judgement and which way the wind will make the heads roll.'

With Vergennes, he was more insistent and showed his impatience:

All of this must have been discussed in council yesterday, yet this morning you send me no word. The most fatal things in any form of business are uncertainty and time wasting.

Am I to await your reply here, or must I leave without any reply at all? Was I right or wrong to sound out the people whose intentions are becoming so important to us? Shall I, in future, allow my information to abort, and reject any revelations which must have a bearing on the present revolution, instead of weclcoming them? In fact, am I an agent of some use to his country or merely a deaf and dumb tourist?

The truth of the matter was, as Brian Morton notes in his edition of the correspondence, that Vergennes, in September 1775, didn't entirely trust Figaro's judgement. To verify his statements he sent one of his agents, Achard de Bonvouloir, to America. Achard left France on 8 September.

Beaumarchais's information was correct. It came straight from Philadelphia, where the second continental congress had met in May with such men as Adams, Lee, Dickinson, Jefferson and Franklin representing the various colonies. Nails, bolts and stones had rained down on General Gáge's British soldiers at Bunker Hill on 17 June. George Washington had been chosen as the strategist and tactician of the resistance fighters. But the war hadn't really begun yet. As André Maurois writes in his *History of the United States* (1954), it was George III who forced the colonies to cross their Rubicon. In his speech from the throne in October 1775 the King of England announced that the mother country would never give up her colonies, that she would enforce her rule, but that she would receive with tenderness and mercy her deluded children if they asked for the king's pardon. Beaumarchais immediately realized what the inevitable reaction would be to this kind of speech. His American contacts were becoming more precise. During a brief visit to Paris he sent Louis XVI a long memorandum which in itself proves what I have been saying. In this altogether remarkable and extremely impudent missive Beaumarchais lectures the king, as Figaro lectured Count Almaviva. But whereas Figaro talked like a valet, Beaumarchais speaks like a master.

A few days before he embarked on his decisive battle with the king, he told Vergennes how extremely worried and concerned he was 'lest in so easy and so necessary an affair, perhaps the most important affair that the king will ever have to decide upon, His Majesty should make a negative decision.' And he insisted that the king should take no decision before hearing what he had to say, if only for a quarter of an hour. Here, then, is Beaumarchais's address to the king, and his peremptory call to action:

Sire,
When Your Majesty disapproves of a plan, it is usual for those responsible for it to defer as a matter of course.

But some projects are so surpassingly important for the well-being of your kingdom that a zealous servant may think it proper to present them to you more than once, lest at first they were not seen in their best light.

The project which I do not name here, but which Your Majesty knows of via M. de Vergennes, is one of these. All I have to get it adopted is the strength of my arguments. I beg you, Sire, to weigh them with all the attention that an affair of this kind deserves.

When you have read this address, my duty will be done. It is for us to propose; for you, Sire, to dispose. And your task is much more important than ours, for we are answerable only to you for the purity of our zeal, while you are answerable to God, Sire, to yourself and to an entire nation entrusted to your care, for the good and evil resulting from your preferred choice.

M. de Vergennes writes to me that Your Majesty believes that it is in the interests of your justice not to adopt the proposed expedient.

Hence the objection rests neither on the immense utility of the project nor on the dangers involved in its execution, but solely on Your Majesty's niceness of conscience.

Such motives for refusal are so worthy of respect that it would be right to condemn oneself to silence and desist forthwith if the extreme importance of the purpose did not make it desirable to study whether it is really in the interests of justice of the King of France not to adopt a like expedient.

Generally speaking there is no doubt that any idea or project that violates justice must be rejected by a man of integrity.

But, Sire, State policy is not the same as private morality. A private person may do no wrong to his neighbour, whatever good may result to him from it, because all men live under the rule of civil and common law, which has provided for the safety of all.

But a kingdom is a large and isolated body. It is more widely separated from its neighbours by differing interests than by the sea, the citadels and the fences that enclose it. A kingdom and its neighbours have no common law to guarantee the kingdom's safety, for relations between a kingdom and its neighbours are dictated solely by the natural law – in other words, they are enjoined on the kingdom by the need to safeguard the well-being and prosperity of every citizen. They have been modified in several ways to form the 'law of nations', the essence of which, according to Montesquieu himself, is, firstly, to look after oneself, and, secondly, in so doing to do as little harm as possible to other states.

And this maxim has been so rigorously established as a political principle that a king ruling over a destitute and starving people, since he is bound to regard himself as foreign to any other people and as the father of his own people, could not justly prevent his unfortunate subjects, if they had no other means of subsistence, from seizing what they need from neighbouring states, even by force of arms.

For the justice and protection that a king owes to his subjects is owed narrowly and absolutely, whereas the justice and protection which he can accord to neighbouring states is purely a matter of expediency. It follows that national policy, which maintains states, differs in almost every respect from the civic morality that governs private people . . .

But, Sire, has there ever been, can there ever be, a single bond between France and Britain that may give Your Majesty pause? . . .

This audacious, unbridled and brazen nation will always have to be dealt with. My plan is aimed at Britain alone. It is Britain, Sire, whom you must humiliate and weaken, if you do not wish her to weaken and humiliate you at every turn. Have her usurpations and outrages ever had any bounds other than those of her capacities? Has she not always waged war on you without prior declaration? Did she not even start the last war at a time of peace by suddenly seizing five hundred of our vessels? Was it not she who reduced you to the humiliation of destroying the finest of your seaports, forced you to put all the others out of commission, and fixed the small number of vessels that you would have to make do with thereafter? Was it not she who very recently subjected your merchant vessels to search in the northern regions, when not even the Dutch wished to inflict such a humiliation upon you, and when it was not inflicted on any other nation? Such a humiliation would have made Louis XIV eat his arms rather than not avenge it, and it makes every true Frenchman's heart bleed, especially when he sees our insolent rival attract Russian vessels into those same regions where we do not dare to land, showing them the route to our possessions in America, so that some day they may be able to help our enemies to take them from us.

If you are so scrupulous that you do not wish to favour even something that can harm our enemies, how can you, Sire, permit your subjects to vie with other Europeans for the conquest of countries belonging by right to poor Indians, savage Africans, or Caribs who have never offended you? How can you allow your vessels to seize by force and shackle black men whom nature had made free and who are wretched merely because you are powerful? How, Sire, can you suffer three rival powers to carve up the remains of Poland before your very eyes, when your mediation ought to carry great weight in Europe? How can you have a pact with Spain whereby you bind yourself, in the name of the Holy Trinity, to furnish men, vessels and money to this ally to help her to wage any war, even an offensive war, the moment she demands your aid, without having reserved so much as the right to investigate whether the war in which you are to be involved is just or whether you are not aiding a usurper? It is not Your Majesty, I know, who did or permitted all these things. They existed before you came to the throne, and they will continue to exist after your reign, for that is the way things go in politics. There are so many examples of this kind that I have simply recalled a few of them to prove to you, Sire, that the sort of politics that upholds nations is different in almost every respect from the morality that governs private people.

If men were angels, we ought no doubt to despise or even detest politics. But if men were angels, they would have no need of religion to enlighten them, or laws to govern them, or magistrates to restrain them, or soldiers to subdue them; and the earth, instead of being a living image of hell, would itself be a region of heaven. But in the end we must take them as they are, and the most just of kings cannot go farther with them than the lawgiver Solon, who was wont to say: 'I have not given the Athenians the best possible laws, but merely those most appropriate to the place, the times and the men I am working for.' It follows that politics, though based on very imperfect principles, does at least have a basis. And a king who alone wished to be absolutely just among the wicked and to remain good among the wolves would soon be devoured, along with his flock . . .

Hence I beg you, Sire, in the name of your subjects, to whom you owe your first concern; in the name of the domestic peace to which Your Majesty rightly attaches so much importance; in the name of the glory and the prosperity of a reign that began under such favourable auspices – I beg you, Sire, not to allow yourself to fall victim to the glittering fallacy of false modesty: *summum jus summa injuria* [excessive justice is excessive injustice] . . .

I have dealt summarily with the gravest of the questions lest by expanding on my reasons I should emasculate them, and above all lest I should try Your Majesty's patience.

Should there remain any doubts in your mind after having read my letter, Sire, delete my signature, have this essay copied by another hand so thay my lowly status may not lessen the effect of my arguments, then offer this study to someone who has great experience of the world and of politics, for his comments. If there is a single person, starting with M. de Vergennes, who does not agree with my basic ideas I shall say no more. I shall throw on to the fire Scaliger, Grotius, Pufendorf, Gravina, Montesquieu, all the authorities on constitutional law, and I shall admit that my whole life's study has been a waste of time, since it has not enabled me to persuade my Master on a subject which seems as clear to me as it is important to his interests . . .

. . . It is quite impossible to deal in writing with everything that concerns the substance of the affair, since absolute secrecy is necessary. Yet it would be extremely easy for me to show that no risks are involved; that the venture is simple and bound to succeed; and that an immense harvest of glory and repose would result for your reign, Sire, from the sparsest sowing at such an appropriate moment.

May the guardian angel of this State make the heart and mind of Your Majesty favourably disposed towards my plan. If he gives us this first success, all the rest will follow of itself and without difficulty. I guarantee it.

I guarantee it; I, Beaumarchais.

The British and the Americans had begun to realize that he was France. Lord Stormont, George III's ambassador to Versailles, had him followed at every turn. In London his life seemed to be threatened once again: 'The precarious and dangerous position in which I find myself, owing to the suspicions and the severe inquisition that result from my every venture, makes my zeal more ardent.' However, this time, aware of the importance of his mission and believing that he was the only person capable of fulfilling it, he forgot his usual temerity and asked for protection. His request, if that is the word for it, was sent to Vergennes: 'Yet do not neglect, Count, to press M. de Sartines on the matter of my safety. It is the least that is due to me.' The Americans had sent the sinister Arthur Lee to Beaumarchais, whom they saw as 'the right man in the right place'. 1776, January, February, March. Time was running out. George Washington was at the gates of Boston with his men and France was still doing nothing. In a few months it would be too late: America would have conquered without France, or Britain would have put down the rebellion. Beaumarchais saw red. He wrote to Vergennes, sensing that he was less undecided than he had been. He managed to find the right words to rouse a man whose patriotism was as ardent as his own, though more circumspect.

> Will you not have the courage to show the king once again how much he has to gain in this single campaign, without striking a blow? And will you not try to convince His Majesty that this paltry aid they are requesting, which we have been arguing over for a year now, must enable us to harvest all the fruits of a great victory without exposing ourselves to the dangers of battle? Tell him that this aid can restore to us, while we sleep, all that the shameful peace of 1763 deprived us of; and that an American success, by reducing his rivals to the status of a second-class power, would put us back in the first rank, and enable us to dominate the whole of Europe for many years to come.

Vergennes answered all of Beaumarchais's letters. Theirs is a model correspondence, the fiery violence of the one being matched by the serenity and caution of the other. The author's addresses were answered by the minister with philosophical reflexions that had to be read between the lines. Whereas Beaumarchais had, since the Goëzman affair, resorted to dialectic to defend his theses, Vergennes used the devices of the unspoken conclusion and rhetorical understatement with great skill. The minister can't always have approved of the behaviour of his very extraordinary envoy and the tone of his letters; but if he was stung at times to reply firmly and to lecture the 'diplomatic jockey' in his turn, it was never long before he was praising him and treating him with the utmost consideration. Witness this letter, which begins with haughty irony but ends on a note of intimate complicity. Vergennes knew what he owed to Beaumarchais, and he knew that in this instance the author was the better diplomat.

> I received on the 1st inst. the letter you did me the honour of writing on the 26th ult. It is as easy to talk well as it is difficult to act well – that is an axiom that all administrators, not excepting the British ministers, will vouch for. Those whose role is to reason look at a question from an isolated viewpoint, and loftily deduce what advantages may be gained thereby. But if they could embrace the whole they would quickly realize that the alleged advantages, though brilliant in theory, would in practice be merely a source of setbacks, each more deadly than the rest. I was in the pit for many years before I climbed on to the stage, and I rubbed shoulders with people from every class and of all temperaments. On the whole all of them were rebellious and censorious. Nothing was ever right in their view. Some of them, from being self-appointed judges, exposed themselves to being judged. I have seen almost all of them make the very mistakes they had once so severely condemned, for there is no doubt that there is an impulsive force, or a *vis inertiæ*, call it what you will, that always draws mankind back towards a common centre. This preamble is not intended to refute your foresight, which indeed I praise, and which I approve. But don't think that, because people don't appreciate it at once, it has been dismissed. It is prudent to progress by slow stages, and not all sleep is lethargic. Although the path that I am following is a safe one, I am not sufficiently confident about it not to curb my longing to tell you all my thoughts. But I count on your perspicacity to guess what they are. Think carefully about it, and you will find that I am closer to you than you imagine.

France, as she progressed slowly from 'stage' to 'stage', lost even more status than before. But in 1776 Beaumarchais, driven by a force that reason cannot explain, would have made the earth turn in the other direction if France had been likely to gain some advantage from it. In fact the virtuous Louis XVI and the foxy Vergennes expected him to undertake an exercise that was just as difficult – he was to represent France in secret and deliver the arms in their stead. He got the message. To sway the king's decision he 'offered' to act alone, he, Beaumarchais. Naturally, Bazile has concluded that that was what he had been after all along. ('Money, now you're in your element!') It seems obvious to me that in acting as an intermediary

Beaumarchais sacrificed himself. True, he found the whole adventure very exciting, and he gave himself to it wholeheartedly, for such was his nature; but as for profits, as we shall see, there was nothing doing. He had ambitions, of course. He would have liked to become a minister, for instance, and he almost did – but at the last moment someone produced a black ball from his pocket.

On 29 February 1776 M. de Vergennes handed the king a further sealed missive marked 'For the king alone'. Louis XVI had no difficulty in recognizing the writing. While he unsealed Beaumarchais's last message, on the other side of the Atlantic George Washington was forcing General Howe to beat a hasty retreat from Dorchester Heights. But matters hadn't yet reached the point of no return, either in America or in Europe. Louis XVI began reading. As he finished each page, he passed it to Vergennes, whom he had ordered to sit at his side:

> Sire,
>
> The famous quarrel between America and Britain, which will soon split the world and change the system of Europe, means that every power must examine with great care the ways in which this secession may affect it, for better or for worse . . .
>
> In an initial memorandum submitted to Your Majesty three months ago by M. de Vergennes, I attempted to make out a solid case for saying that Your Majesty's justice could not be harmed if you took sensible precautions against enemies who are never too scrupulous about the precautions they take against us.
>
> Today, when a moment of violent crisis is fast approaching, I am bound to warn Your Majesty that our ability to hold on to our possessions in America and the peace that you appear to desire so strongly depend solely on this single proposition: we must aid the Americans. I shall demonstrate the truth of this.
>
> The King of England, the cabinet, parliament, the Opposition, the nation, the British people and the political parties by which this State is torn asunder, all agree that it is no longer possible to flatter themselves that the Americans will rally to the crown, nor even that the great efforts being made today to subdue them will succeed. Hence, Sire, the violent debates between the ministry and the Opposition, the ebb and flow of agreements and disagreements, which, though not getting anyone anywhere, merely add fuel to the flames . . .
>
> On the other hand, Mr A.L. (M. de Vergennes will tell Your Majesty his name), the colonies' secret envoy in London, is so utterly depressed

because the efforts he has made via me to obtain aid in the form of powder and supplies from the French ministry have been quite futile, that he said to me today: 'One last time, is France absolutely determined to become the victim of Britain and the laughing-stock of Europe, owing to her incredible lethargy? I must give a positive answer, but I await your final answer before giving my own. We are offering France, in return for secret aid, a secret trade treaty which will transfer to her, for a specific number of years after the peace, all the profits with which we have enriched Britain for a century, plus as much protection for her possessions as our strength will allow. Don't you want this? . . .(If not), whichever way you turn, this war you are avoiding and are so afraid of will become inevitable, for either you must accept our seizures of English vessels in your ports or you must reject them; if you accept them, a break with England is bound to follow; if you reject them, Congress will promptly accept peace on the conditions laid down by the mother country. The Americans will be furious and will join forces with England to attack your islands and prove that the fine precautions you took to keep your possessions were the very ones that were to deprive you of them for ever . . .'

That, Sire, is the terrible and startling picture of our position. Your Majesty sincerely wants peace! The means of maintaining it, Sire, will be the contents of this memorandum . . .

You will maintain the peace you so desire, Sire, only if you prevent, at all costs, any peace being concluded between Britain and America, and prevent the one triumphing completely over the other. And the only means of achieving this is to give enough aid to the Americans to balance their forces with Britain's but no more. And believe me, Sire, that saving a few millions today may cost France much blood and money before long . . .

If I am told that we cannot give aid to the Americans without offending Britain and bringing upon ourselves the storm I intend to avert, I shall answer in my turn that we shall not incur this danger if we follow the plan I have put forward on so many occasions – if we help the Americans secretly without compromising ourselves, by imposing on them as our first condition that they will never send any captured ships into our ports, and that they will do nothing that is liable to disclose the fact that we have helped them, which we could cease to do at the first sign of indiscretion on the part of Congress. And if Your Majesty has no one available who is more skilful, I am willing to see to the treaty myself, without compromising anyone else . . .

He won.

Louis XVI at last gave in and accepted the broad terms of the plan. So Beaumarchais alone was involved, as Vergennes had insisted he must be: 'The operation must appear to the British government, and even to the Americans, to be essentially a private speculation, which has nothing to do with us. If it is to seem so it must also be so, up to a certain point.'

On 10 June 1776 Beaumarchais became a personal ally of the Insurgents, and began to supply them with arms. Three weeks later came the words: 'We hold these truths as evident: that all men are created equal; that they are endowed with certain unalienable rights, that among them are Life, Liberty and the pursuit of Happiness . . .'

Three weeks before that 4 July, France had climbed aboard the historical roundabout just in time; her last-minute decision led her progressively towards the Treaty of Versailles in 1783. But we shall have more to say about this war, which, before being France's war, was M. de Beaumarchais's, as we can see from the message he received from Congress, which rightly belongs in the present chapter:

> *By order of Congress, sitting in Philadelphia, to M. de Beaumarchais*
> 15 January 1779
>
> Sir:
>
> The Congress of the United States of America, recognizing the great efforts which you have made in their favor, presents to you its thanks . . . The generous sentiments and the breadth of view, which alone could dictate a conduct such as yours, are the eulogy of your actions, and the ornament of your character. While, by your rare talents, you have rendered yourself useful to your prince, you have gained the esteem of this young Republic and merited the applause of the New World.
>
> John Jay, President

This magnificent homage cannot have failed to move the statesman in Beaumarchais. And it must have consoled him for the ingratitude of some people, the dishonesty of others and the silence of his own country.

11

Figaro here, Figaro there

MARCH 1776

He writes and submits his last memoir, which we have quoted, and meets Vergennes almost daily.

After conferring with Maurepas he presents a petition to the privy council to obtain 'letters of relief temporal'. (He was still under sentence of reprimand, and he had forfeited his right of appeal eighteen months ago because the period of six months' grace had expired. As he was insisting on an outright quashing of the sentence and full rehabilitation, he had to get special proceedings opened.) Daily visits to Maurepas, to the Minister of Justice, and many conferences with his adviser, the barrister Target.

He is also preparing his new suit against La Blache, with another lawyer. (The grand council had just quashed the iniquitous judgment that had ruined and dishonoured him. The matter had been referred to the Provence parliament. The count, knowing that his enemy was busy in Britain, had been trying to hurry the proceedings through in the hope of catching him unprepared or even getting the case heard in his absence.) Beaumarchais takes steps to have the hearing postponed.

Léopolde Jeantot, his father's widow, surrounded by a bevy of lawyers, exacts her pound of flesh. (Old M. Caron, in his dotage, had made the craziest of wills, leaving her everything he owned, plus a widow's dower and more besides. Yet in fact he didn't own anything in his own right any more, as his income had been in the form of a life annuity and a large pension paid by his son. Léopolde, who had expected to inherit a fortune, claimed that she had been robbed and threatened to sue – a shrewd move on her part and her lawyers, since Beaumarchais couldn't defend himself in a court of law while he was under sentence.) Meetings, discussions, transactions. Beaumarchais gives his mother-in-law 6000 francs and she promptly becomes all sweetness and light. Closing the file, he writes on the cover: 'Infamy of my father's widow, forgiven.'

Another file: the eternal Aubertins, who keep cropping up to waste a few precious hours for 'Caron de Beaumarchais, the greatest enemy of all that is called "wasted time" '. The words are his.

Rehearsals at the Tuileries for a revival of *The Barber*.

Every evening he rejoins his family: his dear sister and Marie-Thérèse (whom Julie wryly calls 'French wit on a Swiss pedestal'). Despite his innumerable sexual adventures – Figaro here, Figaro there – or perhaps because of them, he is becoming increasingly attached to his Swiss pedestal. Affection hasn't killed lust, far from it, and Eugénie is conceived around this time, if my sums are right.

So much for one month, and I've told you only the half of it.

APRIL, MAY

At the beginning of April Beaumarchais is back in London for the tenth or twelfth time. His daily reports are those of a very exceptional ambassador. The information he gives Vergennes is always of the highest political interest. Britain can't make a decision without his knowing it immediately, and America can't take an initiative without his becoming aware of it a couple of weeks before the echo bounces back to the European chancelleries. Vergennes seems to think he's the devil incarnate, or a kind of magician. But *Consilio manuque* is the motto of a craftsman, not a cabbalist. Beaumarchais's only secret, apart from wit and hard work, is the network of high-ranking informants he can draw on. Ordinary diplomats obtain their information by talking to minor politicians or reading the papers like everyone else. This means that they learn nothing, since all the real decisions are taken behind locked doors by a few men who know the value of discretion and surprise. Since his stay in Madrid Beaumarchais had got used to going straight to the top. The doors he knocked at were the locked doors I referred to above. The only mystery is that he knocked, and it was opened unto him.

What other explanation but sheer fascination can there be for the power he exercised for years over a man like Rochford? True, the

English minister thought he was swapping confidence for confidence, and may have believed at times that he had duped Beaumarchais. In fact, he was *dominated* by Beaumarchais into becoming his agent willy-nilly – yet Beaumarchais, who had personally declared war on Britain and was fighting hard at home, had nothing to give him in return, apart from a few sallies of wit. Around 15 April Rochford came to ask Beaumarchais whether he should accept the post of viceroy of Ireland, which he had been offered by George III. The conversation drifted from one thing to another, and the minister made a number of revelations. That is how Beaumarchais discovered, that day or the next, that the British government had recruited 30,000 mercenaries in Hesse for the American campaigns. Lord Rochford's indiscretion may strike the reader as odd. It was. But whether he was dishonest or merely unwise, the British minister remained a gentleman, and the 'diplomatic jockey' respected his regard for appearances: 'I have seen in England the most foolish actions accomplished with an air of reflexion that filled ordinary men with awe, and at times in France I have seen the most reasonable acts lose all their merit because of the air of witlessness that accompanied them.'

As he could no longer give the Chevalier d'Eon as a pretext for his visit to Britain, he was ostensibly involved in purchasing Portuguese piastres on the London market by arrangement with the French government. This mission enabled him to mislead the authorities, who had him under close but discreet watch – Stormont's constant warnings to his government were beginning to have some effect. All the same, the cover operation took up a great deal of his time. He was 'for ever parleying with brokers, bankers, financiers and gold merchants'.

Yet in a day's work he collected more information than 'piastres or moyadores'. On 26 April, for example, he sent four long letters to Vergennes by secret courier and by different routes. To give an idea of the quality and the abundance of his information, here is just part of the *postscript* to the last of these letters:

> Since I closed my package I have received several items of news which I shall dictate, because I am so tired I can no longer hold my pen.
>
> We can be certain General Lee has had all suspects in New York disarmed and that he is in command of an army of 20,000 men. That vessel has arrived at Merroy in Ireland; it was carrying many letters,

which the government has intercepted. The vessel, which is called the *Polly*, Captain Montayne, had first been confiscated by the customs men, as it had on board hemp and cannabis, the seed of the hemp, which had been loaded in America. But . . . it has been released. The arrival of this vessel was known, but the name of the port of arrival and the facts concerning the intercepted letters have not yet been made public.

A large number of the convoy vessels dispatched to America have been cast upon the coasts, along with two detachments of the 45th and 56th regiments. This setback and the American seizures of ships have made it impossible to obtain wholesome provisions in Boston, and even essential commodities are very scarce. Everything is in the same parlous state in the town, and in the provincials' camp commanded by Washington, who was almost relieved of his command for not making any attack or move on Boston all winter, things are much the same.

There have been letters from Arnold (Montgomery's lieutenant), who is not a prisoner but who has been wounded by a shot through the left leg. Montgomery really has been killed, along with 60 men of his own and around 300 prisoners. General Carleton lost only 88 men in this attack. Arnold is at the head of a detachment that he has rallied; they are near Quebec, dug in in positions where they cannot be captured.

The reason why Lord Howe has refused to go to America is that he doesn't want to go unless he has a free hand to negotiate a conciliation. Apparently he was granted this freedom by the cabinet, but the king refused, insisting on unconditional surrender, as if such a thing were possible. Lord Bute is acting behind the scenes here, but is there someone else behind him or not?

In his speech to parliament Lord North gave figures comparing the present trade situation with the first campaign in Germany against the French, which was followed by the most glorious of conquests and events . . .

Lord Littleton [*sic*] and Lord Carlisle are both asking to be appointed ambassador to Spain. As Lord Grantham is about to be recalled, it is said that Lord Carlisle, son-in-law of Lord Gower, will be preferred. The Duke of Malbrough [*sic*], it is said, will replace Lord Stormont, whom Lord Mansfield very much wants to send to Ireland. You know what I wrote to you about Ireland, but it is still a secret . . .

Thus, day after day until his return to Paris (he was back on 24 May), Beaumarchais gave Vergennes Britain and America on a silver platter. He even had an opportunity to include France when he warned the Foreign Minister about plots being laid against him at Versailles, and informed him that a faction led by Turgot was plotting his dismissal. Vergennes stayed, Turgot went.

It was probably at this time that Beaumarchais's affair with Mme de Godeville began. More of that later. For the moment I need only say that this woman deprived him of sleep, but not of bed – she was indefatigable.

I am exaggerating. She left him alone for long enough (an hour?) to write a short story, or rather a 'club story', in the form of a letter to the editor of the *Morning Chronicle*, who published it on 6 May.

JUNE

Having returned to Paris on 24 May Beaumarchais saw Vergennes the next day or the day after. The minister informed him that Louis XVI had at last decided to assist the Americans, by proxy. In other words, France was asking Beaumarchais to act in her stead, and on her behalf. In the first instance, therefore, he had to found a trading company and charter a fleet to supply the Insurgents with fresh arms and ammunition. In exchange for this material, the Americans would provide France with agricultural products – tobacco and indigo, for example. But absolute secrecy was essential. Vergennes gave Beaumarchais to understand that he would be obliged to drop him, or even to condemn him publicly, if the British accused the French government of complicity.

Financially, the operation would work as follows: the French government would give Beaumarchais one million *livres* in cash, and they promised to obtain a similar amount from the Spanish government. Although the scheme was to be unofficially subsidized by France to begin with, it was essential that it should become self-supporting within a very short space of time. This was naturally impossible, because the Insurgents didn't have enough time between battles to collect their merchandise and make arrangements for exporting it. But the appearances had to be kept up. Adding to the contradiction, Vergennes told him that he would obviously be compelled to extend 'every possible facility' to the Americans. That was indeed the way Beaumarchais saw things. As he wanted to act fast, and was convinced that the French government wouldn't abandon him *en route*, he accepted all these conditions. Never was a trading company founded on such shaky principles. The plain fact was that Beaumarchais had to acquire ships, pay crews, buy arms – and reimburse himself by selling indigo! A profiteering blackguard, indeed!

As Loménie points out, Beaumarchais might have asked himself three questions: 'What will happen to my operation if my vessels are seized by the British cruisers? What will happen if the government, frightened by British threats, not only abandons me but sacrifices me? Finally, what will happen if the Americans are defeated, or if, after receiving my wares, they deem it unnecessary to send me goods in return?' He asked himself none of these questions.

Two days later he launched his firm: Roderigue, Hortales & Co. Its managing director set up his office and a private suite in the fine Hôtel des Ambassadeurs de Hollande, a magnificent mansion in the Marais quarter that all who love Paris know well. It was no easy matter to find the place, lease it, move in, buy office furniture, hire staff, train them, and get things moving overnight. But he did it. By 10 June he was ready to send his first coded message to Miss Mary Johnson, alias Arthur Lee, whom he believed was still the official and exclusive envoy of Congress. However, as we shall see in a moment, there were rivalries and intrigues on the other side of the Atlantic as well as in Europe.

Marie-Thérèse, who was four months pregnant, moved in with him. In point of fact, the Swiss pedestal didn't only manage his house, she also took on important adminstrative responsibilities on behalf of her lover. Mlle Willermawlaz, whom Beaumarchais had been calling for some time Mme de Villers, which was simpler and more amusing, had quite a head on her shoulders. Julie, who was never objective about the women her brother lived with, though she liked Marie-Thérèse more than she had the others, couldn't help underestimating her, as when she wrote of her 'vague melancholy (the sun in the clouds)' and her 'soul assailed by doubt'. But Mlle de Beaumarchais soon joined the illegitimate couple in the Marais. Speaking of illegitimacy, we shouldn't forget that Beaumarchais, who was still stripped of his civil rights, couldn't marry – though by the same token he had no right to engage in trade either!

On 16 June he left Paris for Bordeaux, accompanied by Gudin. He arrived on the twentieth. Just before his departure he had voiced his anxiety about the outcome of his petition. Maurepas had replied: 'Go ahead and leave. The council will manage to reach a decision without you.'

In Bordeaux he bought ships, arms and gunpowder. The gun-powder wasn't easy to obtain. The arsenal, at Château-Trompette near Bordeaux, at first refused to release the 150 hundredweight that Beaumarchais requested. The refusal was apparently made on orders from Saint-Germain. Letters, discussions, ten trips to and from Château-Trompette. In the space of ten days all the problems were ironed out, and on the evening of the tenth day Gudin and Beaumarchais went to the theatre. As soon as he entered the auditorium Beaumarchais was recognized. The audience rose to their feet and gave him an ovation, intoning his private anthem: 'The same, the same, he's the same as ever.'

After attending a few parties thrown in their honour, the two friends returned to their hotel late at night. But Gudin shall tell us what happened next. His style may remind you, as it does me, of Dr. Watson:

> On our return Beaumarchais found several letters from Paris waiting for him. He read them while I was undressing, for I was so tired that I was in a hurry to get to bed. I asked him whether he was satisfied by the news in his letters.
>
> 'Very much so,' he said, without the slightest emotion.
>
> I got into bed and fell asleep. My bed was quite near his. At the crack of dawn I felt someone tugging at my arm; I woke with a start, recognized him, and asked him whether he was feeling poorly.
>
> 'No,' he said. 'In half an hour we're leaving for Paris.'
>
> 'Heavens! Why? What's happened? What did your letters say?'
>
> 'The council has rejected my petition.'
>
> 'Oh, good gracious me! Why didn't you tell me last night?'
>
> 'I didn't want to spoil your beauty sleep, my friend. It was quite enough for *me* not to sleep. I've spent the night thinking over what I must do. My decision is taken, my plan is formed, and I'm leaving to put it into action. They'll see, those fellows who came out of the council saying: 'So much the better, that's the last anyone'll hear of him'. They'll see, I tell you, whether it's the last anyone'll hear of me – or of them!'

Sixty hours later they were in Paris, which was remarkably good going, especially since their carriage was involved in an accident twenty miles from the capital. Pausing only to brush down his clothes and shave, Beaumarchais drove off immediately to Versailles. The minute he arrived he burst into Maurepas's office, making the prime minister jump with surprise at seeing him back so soon, and exclaimed: 'What the deuce! While I'm chasing from one end of France to the other doing business for the king, you foul everything up for me at Versailles!'

'It was a blunder by Miromesnil,' the premier replied. 'Go and get him, tell him I want to speak to him, and come back together.'

Beaumarchais strode off to find the Minister of Justice, grabbed him by the arm without explanation and dragged him off to see Maurepas.

Miromesnil sheepishly explained that the council's decision had surprised him, too. In fact most of the councillors were former members of the Maupeou parliament and had no reason to love their sworn enemy. The two ministers gave Beaumarchais their solemn promise that the question would be examined by a different procedure, 'for there were procedures for every kind of case, foreseeable and unforeseeable'.

Beaumarchais, placated, returned to doing business for the king.

JULY

On 2 July the States of America had made a permanent break with Britain, yet the situation of their armies was worsening daily. True, Washington was still keeping the British troops at bay, but whereas the British were receiving considerable reinforcements of men and supplies, the Insurgents were running out of just about everything, except courage.

Rodrigue therefore had to hurry. Having learned of the French change of heart, Congress had immediately sent Silas Deane of Connecticut to negotiate with Paris. Deane reached France at the beginning of the month and Vergennes put him in touch with Beaumarchais, implying that, for the time being, he was France. Beaumarchais, who had genuinely believed that Arthur Lee was the official representative of Congress, decided, once he had recovered from his surprise, to ignore him and deal solely with Deane. Beaumarchais's harshness with men he disliked is a quite remarkable aspect of his character. Harshness, or indifference? At any rate he dropped Lee from one day to the next – and gained an enemy. Lee, like the Chevalier d'Eon who had received the same treatment, decided to avenge himself. Later on he informed Congress that the

arms consignments for which Beaumarchais had acted as intermediary were a gift from France, and that Beaumarchais was a
swindler. As we shall see, Congress pretended to believe Lee to get
out of paying its debts. As he was sworn to secrecy Beaumarchais
couldn't defend himself, and Lee's slander gained some currency in
America. But the American was distrusted by his own government,
even though they were prepared to use him for a time, and when he
discovered that his mythomaniac view of himself as the saviour of
America wasn't recognized back home, he lashed out in all directions, accusing Deane and Franklin of embezzlement. Most historians are hard on Arthur Lee, but I can't help thinking that he had
good reason for being angry – he'd done all the spadework in England, whereas Deane was getting all the glory in France.

In July Beaumarchais made a further enemy, who might have
become just as formidable as Lee. A man called Dr Dubourg, who
was more of a financier than a medic, and who had formerly met
Franklin in London, bethought himself of becoming the go-between
for the arms deals. When he found out that the government had
given the job to Beaumarchais, he approached Deane and Vergennes in an attempt to oust him. As virtue was still in fashion, Dubourg
wrote an outraged letter to Vergennes claiming that his rival loved
high living and kept several women. When the minister showed the
doctor's missive to Beaumarchais, he asked for a pen and paper and
scribbled the following reply:

> So what if I like gadding about town and keeping women? What has that
> got to do with the business in hand? The women I've been keeping for
> twenty years, *monsieur*, thank you kindly for your interest. There used to
> be five of them – four sisters and a niece. Over the past three years, two of
> them have died, to my great sorrow. I have only three to keep now, two
> sisters and my niece, which is still quite an extravagance for a fellow like
> myself. But what would you have said, if, knowing me better than you
> do, you had been aware that I was scandalous to the point of keeping
> men as well – two pretty young nephews and even the poor father of so
> scandalous a pimp? And my ostentation is even worse. For the past three
> years, believing lace and embroidery to be too paltry for my vanity, I
> have even been arrogant enough to adorn my wrists with the finest plain
> muslin! The most superb black serge isn't too fine for me. At times I have
> even been seen to take my foppishness to the extent of silk, when the
> weather is very hot. But I beg you, *monsieur*, not to write such things to M.

le Comte de Vergennes, or else you'll end up by utterly destroying me in his eyes.

You had your reasons for writing to him to malign me, a man you don't even know. I have my reasons for not being offended by this, though I do have the honour of knowing you. You are, *monsieur*, a gentleman so excited by the urge to perform a great good, that you have felt you could allow yourself a little wrong to achieve it.

This letter greatly amused Vergennes and vexed the doctor, who had no choice but to await the arrival of his friend Benjamin Franklin. He greeted him with horror stories about Beaumarchais. Franklin, whose puritanism was a lightning conductor against vice, immediately felt distaste for the 'ostentatious pimp', and created many difficulties for him along the way.

Silas Deane didn't share Lee's persecution mania, and he didn't judge men on the strength of gossip either, as Franklin did. Once he'd got to know Beaumarchais, he trusted him completely. Deane had fully grasped Beaumarchais's odd situation, and realized that the front of private enterprise was a necessary adjunct to this kind of official business. The envoy of Congress therefore gave his solemn promise, in writing, that America would pay off her debts towards Rodrigue, Hortales & Co. within a year at the very latest. Rodrigue agreed to extend credit to Congress in the following terms: 'As I believe I am dealing with a virtuous nation, it will be sufficient for me to keep a careful account of all the funds I advance. Congress will decide whether to pay for the merchandise at its usual value on the date of its arrival on the American continent, or to accept it on the basis of costs, delays and insurance, plus an appropriate commission, the amount of which cannot be fixed at this stage.' Once agreement had been reached on these preliminaries, the negotiations proper began.

The Insurgents' requirements were considerable. According to Deane, expenditures on plant alone represented an outlay for the firm of 3 million francs. But that was nothing compared with the fortune invested in arms and ammunition, since Deane had ordered 200 cannon pieces, a large number of mortars, 25,000 rifles and powder by the ton. All of this was decided within a few days. Over the same period, Beaumarchais continued to visit the arsenals and to organize his first fleet, which comprised ten large vessels, the *Andromède*, the *Anonyme*, the *Mercure*, the *Romain* and so on. To throw dust in the eyes of Stormont and his agents, he had to fragment his purchases and dispatch them to various different ports for lading – Le Havre, Lorient, Nantes, Rochefort, La Rochelle and Bordeaux, where his ships were waiting. This was essential if he was to avoid arousing the suspicions of the British, but it made his job more difficult. He also had to contend with the reluctance of the French War Minister, Saint-Germain, to allow him access to the arsenals. In addition, he had to handpick his captains to ensure that they were good sailors, and discreet, honest and courageous men. And he had to find the money for all this, because the million he had received from Vergennes, via an intermediary, had already been spent. How did he do it? Who today, with planes, telephones, computers and other time-saving hardware at his disposal, could get through in a single month as much as a quarter of this programme? Yet Beaumarchais managed it virtually single-handed – only just, no doubt, because at the end of this crazy month he didn't have a moment left for his correspondence, and kept in touch with Vergennes via elliptical notes in the style of this one: 'See Saint-Germain; decision on artillery; squeeze the Spanish ambassador; constant protection for your humble servant.'

AUGUST

While he was chasing round Paris from one appointment to another, Beaumarchais learned that his old friend the Prince de Conti was dying. Conti, who was only in his fifties, had burnt himself out in relentless pursuit of rare objects, politics and sex. He had been as important in Pierre-Augustin's affections as Pâris-Duverney. The innkeeper's son turned royal banker and the prince of the blood with a fondness for protest had both fallen in love with Beaumarchais, and both remained faithful to him till the end. Conti was expecting a last visit from Beaumarchais. He had two. After the first visit, the Conti family pleaded with Pierre-Augustin to persuade his friend to receive the last sacraments, for it was unthinkable that a prince should leave this world as an infidel. Beaumarchais, of whom the least I can say is that he had about as much faith as his dying friend, none the less agreed to try. He went back into the bedroom and persuaded Conti to see the Archbishop of Paris, as a result of which

Dragoon and dowager – two images of the
Chevalier d'Eon.

The young Louis XVI, whose hesitations almost caused Beaumarchais to lose his battle for the freedom of America.

Louis XV, whose patronage of Beaumarchais launched his career.

Eugénie, the daughter of Beaumarchais and Marie-Thérèse.

Marie-Thérèse Willermawlaz, who asked to borrow Beaumarchais's harp one evening and became his third wife. (She is wearing the famous head-dress known as the *Quesaco*.)

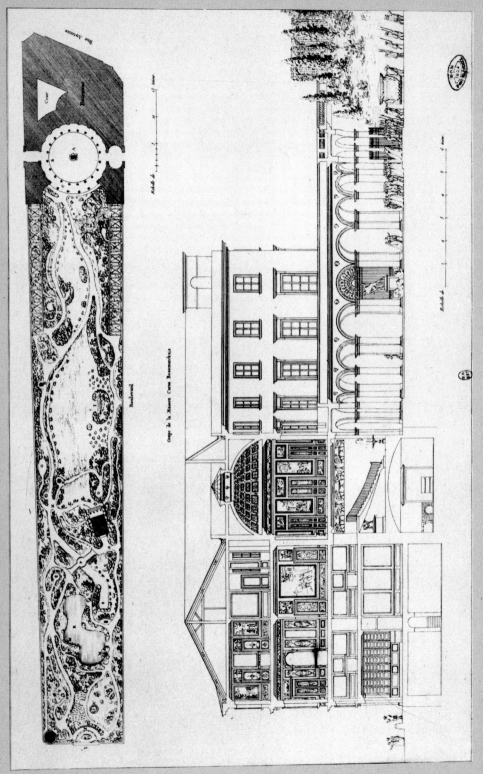

An architect's drawing of the dream palace and *jardin anglais* that Beaumarchais designed and built a year before the French Revolution.

the prince received the last rites. Why cavil at this? None of us is all of a piece. The little boy who gave up his holidays to chase off to see an old monk who talked to him about God and fed him with chocolate, was *also* Beaumarchais.

Conti died on 2 August. 'Imagine my grief; it is excessive,' Beaumarchais wrote to Vergennes the next day. But he had to return to his affairs without delay: 'They start going wrong as soon as I leave them.' He had to badger Maurepas to circularize the comptrollers general; overcome the reticence of Saint-Germain, who was refusing to deliver the bronze cannons; come to an agreement with Sartines over his crews; negotiate with the Spanish ambassador to get the second instalment paid as soon as possible (it came through on the eleventh); dodge Lord Stormont's spies who cropped up everywhere he went and who had discovered where Silas Deane was living ('Mr Deane informed me last night that he was being tailed'); and, together with Vergennes, prevent the king from being swayed by the pro-British faction.

Stormont was right to increase his vigilance, because M. de Beaumarchais was in the process of trebling the stakes. Between 10 and 15 August he took it on himself to engage what modern governments euphemistically call 'instructors', i.e. officers, mainly from the artillery, whose job was to advise and lead the Insurgents. Having obtained an assurance from Vergennes that he would turn a blind eye to two or three officers being dispatched to America, he signed on about fifty. They received their sailing orders immediately. Some of these officers, such as the Marquis de La Rouerie, distinguished themselves in America before the arrival of La Fayette, and were honoured by Washington on the field of battle. Once his first expeditionary force was ready, he wrote to Congress: 'An officer of the highest competence in artillery and engineering, accompanied by lieutenants, officers, artillerymen, gunners and so forth, will leave for Philadelphia before you have received my first convoys.'

That same week he had to set up his import firm: 'So many things have to go ahead together, not to mention the sheet and canvas works, that I am having to take on more employees. This politico-commercial venture is going to become immense, and I would soon get bogged down in the details, along with the few clerks I have employed so far, if I didn't take on a number of assistants.'

He didn't get bogged down. He thought of everything, for instance of having the royal coats of arms removed from the cannons. In all the hurry, no one had thought of obliterating this proof of origin, which the British would have been very interested in. Skilled work-men whose discretion could be counted on had to be found to do the job quickly. Like Napoleon, Beaumarchais had a gift for organizing ten different things at the same time – and like him, in this crazy month he crossed swords with the Comédie Française, about which more later.

Was that all? Not a bit of it! He still hadn't recovered his civil rights, and parliament was about to go into recess. As the slowness of judges irritated him more than anything else, he raced off to see the prime minister and dictated letters addressed to the president of the tribunal, the public prosecutor and the attorney general. Such was his credit at present that the elderly Comte de Maurepas took up his pen without showing the slightest sign of annoyance. Here is the letter received by Séguier, the attorney general:

> I am informed, *monsieur*, by M. de Beaumarchais, that if you do not have the goodness to speak for him on this matter, it is impossible for him to obtain a decision between now and 7 September. The aspect of the king's affairs with which M. de Beaumarchais is entrusted requires him to make a journey fairly soon. He is afraid to leave Paris before his citizen-ship has been restored and he has been anxious on this score for so long that his wishes in this respect are perfectly legitimate. I am not asking you for a favour regarding the substance of such an affair, but you will oblige me infinitely if you do something to make sure that it is heard before the recess.
>
> I have the honour of being very truly etc.

> Maurepas

This time the parliamentarians, who had disobeyed the Minister of Justice, set about complying with the government's wishes – they had felt the iron fist beneath the velvet glove. All that Beaumarchais now had to do was to prepare his final plea with his lawyer. Martyr Beaumarchais and Virgin Target, as they called themselves, got their defence together in a few nights' work. Guy Jean-Baptiste Target had lost his virginity since the recall of the old parliament had replaced the objectionable Maupeou assembly. When parliament met in solemn splendour on 6 September 1776, Target spoke as follows: '. . . It is in the midst of this happy concord, before the eyes

of the public, and from the hands of the law, that M. de Beaumarchais is about to recover, as his due right, the prime asset of man in
society – his honour, which, pending the return of order, he had
entrusted to public opinion'. The public, who had turned out in force
to acclaim Beaumarchais, gave Target's speech an ovation. The
presiding judge had to call for silence before Séguier in his turn
requested full restoration of Beaumarchais's civil rights. This was
immediately granted by the court. 'The public,' writes Gudin, who
was present, 'rapturously applauded the announcement of the decision. Beaumarchais was jostled, surrounded and praised by
everyone. He was borne by the crowd, amidst clapping, from the
Great Chamber to his carriage. He was seen as the saviour of justice.
Never, perhaps, was so much consideration shown to an ordinary
citizen.'

Before entering his coach, the hero of the day scribbled a note to
the man who, for the time being, was his main accomplice,
Vergennes:

Paris, Friday, 6 September 1776

Monsieur le comte,
I have just received judgment – dereprimanded to universal applause.
Never has an unfortunate citizen received more honours. I hasten to
inform you and beg you without fail to place my heart-felt gratitude at
the king's feet. I am trembling with joy, so much so that my hand can
barely write all the respectful sentiments with which I am, *Monsieur le
comte*, your most humble and obedient servant.

Please do me the favour of passing on this good news to M. de
Maurepas and M. de Sartines.

I have four hundred people round me, clapping, kissing me, and
making an unholy din that sounds splendidly harmonious to my ears.

So, as if by magic, he had recovered his honour, his identity, his civil
rights, and even his seat at the Louvre. The good fairy had defeated
the bad fairy. Yet, lucid as ever, he knew that they were the same,
and that justice of that kind weighed men on rigged scales. So the next
day he published an *Address to Parliament*, which he would actually
have made to his judges in person if his friends hadn't prevented him
from doing so. With the publication of this text, which cast a great
chill round him, Beaumarchais showed that he could serve his king
and his country without relinquishing the very least of his ideas.

I now want to leave our calendar of Beaumarchais's multifarious activities open at 7 September 1776 and, before dealing in greater detail with the great American adventure, his finest of all, I would like to upset the chronology slightly by following him to Provence, where Pâris-Duverney's estate was finally being settled.

A few months after his triumphant rehabilitation, which had restored his civil rights, M. de Beaumarchais became a happy father. His daughter Amélie-Eugénie, was born on 5 January 1777. Although the birth didn't inspire him to marry Marie-Thérèse (the couple remained illegitimate for a further eight years), it did commit him to the necessity of putting some order into his affairs. Oddly enough, fatherhood always brought him back to earthy realities – and to money. Referring to his son, you will remember, he had written in 1769: 'I laugh when I think that I am working for him.' Yet the American venture, though glorious, was not lucrative. To support his private war against Britain, and to ensure financial security for Eugénie, he simply had to recover his fortune, which was for the moment held by La Blache.

The judgement on appeal against Beaumarchais had been quashed in 1775, and the case had been referred to the Provence parliament. As we have seen, La Blache had done his utmost to push the hearing through while Beaumarchais was tied up in England and before he obtained his rehabilitation. Beaumarchais had opposed these tactics, and had managed to get the case postponed until the summer of 1778.

In June of that year Beaumarchais left for Marseilles, accompanied by Gudin, who had just been elected to the Académie Provençale. Needless to say Figaro had more than one trick up his sleeve in Marseilles: he also organized the sailing of one or two large vessels bound for America, and staged performances of his serious dramas and *The Barber*. He enjoyed himself too. Gudin, who was always mildly astonished by everything, tells us that his travelling companion 'covered his share in government affairs with the veil of his amusements.' Maybe he did. But the fact remains that Beaumarchais never had to force himself to jump into bed; in that respect, too, he was the same as ever.

Meantime his arch enemy, his anti-lover, his devil, was swanning about Aix in his general's uniform. The count hadn't changd his habits. Every man, woman, child and donkey in Aix wore his colours. In a few months he had swamped the town in brochures, placards and pamphlets, bugling up all the jealous, envious fools he could think of. The Aubertins had star billing, of course. And, scraping the bottom of the barrel, he had even hired the literary services of the Chevalier d'Eon. In short, in sleepy Aix, where Beaumarchais's feats were unknown, La Blache was fighting in conquered territory. He had approached all the judges, who felt flattered to be treated with grace and generosity by such a fine gentleman. And he tried to hire the services of every single barrister in Aix – a splendid flourish, and a crafty one. To tell the truth, two or three of them turned him down.

'Learning of these tactics,' writes Gudin, 'Beaumarchais composed in Marseilles a memoir worthy of those that made him so famous.' It was out of the question to bring it out in Aix, because the count had hired all the printers there. In any case, feeling was running so much against him in Aix that it was in his interest to prepare his attack outside his enemy's stronghold. It is generally agreed that this pamphlet, entitled *An ingenuous Reply to the insulting Opinion disseminated in Aix by Count Alexandre Falcoz de La Blache*, is inferior to its predecessors, whatever Gudin might think of it. In fact it suffers from the absence of Mme Goëzman. The pigeon-plucker dominated the four great memoirs and made a brilliant comedy of them. Beaumarchais had sketched her from life, and I think he immortalized her – she is as great as Bazile, if not greater. In addition, in the *Reply*, Beaumarchais is forced to repeat himself, because his opponent had fallen back on all his former lies and calumnies to upset the good people of Aix. In the main, however, by which I mean in its style, the *Reply* is in no wise inferior to the previous pamphlets. Indeed it frequently surpasses them in its tautness of expression and its varied vocabulary. Improvement was Beaumarchais's watchword in every sphere. A craftsman, I tell you.

The copies of the *Reply* were distributed in Aix one morning between 10 and 15 July. By midday everyone was reading them. At two, the town capitulated. Mathieu, the magistrate Beaumarchais had chosen to countersign his pamphlets, as was required by law, took his client in his arms and said, 'You've turned the whole town around – it's inconceivable!' In two hours! As Gudin remarks, 'Never was there so prompt a revolution.'

La Blache and his 'legion' of lawyers attempted to win back the ground they'd lost by printing slurs and slanders, so Beaumarchais became tougher and on 19 July published a corrosive supplement entitled *The Tartar to the Legion*, which crushed them into the ground.

On 20 July Beaumarchais presented his defence before all the judges in assembly in a speech that lasted five hours. 'His eloquence,' says Gudin, 'was a compound of energy, logic, and simplicity.' The parliamentarians, who were already disturbed by the verve of the two pamphlets and the conviction they carried, were won over by the clarity of his address. By changing his style quite naturally, Beaumarchais surprised his audience. They were expecting the Tartar, and they got Cicero.

The next morning La Blache, supported by his legion of lawyers, attempted to win the sympathy of the court in his turn. The general also spoke with great talent, but in a different style. Beaumarchais had stripped the truth naked; the count covered it, veiled it, disguised it with the skill of a couturier. But beneath its flashy costumes the judges sensed the truth as they had seen it earlier – without a stitch on. They didn't forget it.

At nightfall the Provence parliament, sitting at Aix, announced its decision after a long retirement. Beaumarchais had won his cause unanimously. The execution of the deed signed by Pâris-Duverney before his death was ordered. La Blache, nonsuited on every action, was ordered to pay damages of 12,000 *livres* in respect of his slanders, plus costs.

The whole town was waiting in the streets and as soon as the verdict became known they set about celebrating the event. Bonfires were lit at the crossroads; improvised concerts were held until dawn; and the young people danced round the fountains. The victor had to appear on his balcony time and again to answer the calls from the crowd. Beaumarchais announced that he would provide a dowry for fifteen poor girls of the town, thus adding to the excitement.

It wasn't only Beaumarchais's victory that Aix was celebrating. That evening, as the people had immediately realized, hope had been born. For the first time in the history of the Provence parliament, a nobleman had been nonsuited in an important case. It was the end of privilege, or at least that's what they hoped. But had justice really stopped having 'one law for the rich and another for the poor'?

> Soldier stealing a bracelet
> Gets hung without remission;
> But as for the contribution
> That a general puts in his pocket,
> It's thought a noble deed

– as Figaro would have sung if the censors hadn't already considered it to be an attempt to undermine the morale of the army.

After honouring two or three large dinner parties with their presence, Gudin and Beaumarchais left Aix. For once Beaumarchais made an odd psychological blunder. When Gudin referred to their return to Paris, he answered: 'My friend, we shall not return immediately. We shall probably take a little trip along the Swiss border. My noble opponent, whom the court has just declared to be a slanderer, won't forget that he owes this label to my memoirs. As he is a brigadier general, he will have recourse to his sword, and our encounter will take place beyond the confines of the realm.'

Beaumarchais was wrong. La Blache, who had a weird kind of love for him, didn't intend to kill him. They both had to remain alive. 'I hate him as a man loves his mistress,' he had once said. He clearly didn't wish to break off the affair. When Beaumarchais died, depriving him of his reason for living, he soon followed him to the grave.

At Lyons, where they spent a night, the two travellers were invited to an impromptu reception held in their honour. As Beaumarchais was crossing one of the *salons*, a handsome young man rushed forward and embraced him passionately. Dumbfounded, Gudin came over to discover the reason for this extravagant behaviour. Without letting go of Beaumarchais, the young man introduced himself. He was the Chevalier de Falcoz, the younger brother of the Comte de La Blache. Pulling himself together, Jean de Falcoz explained that, as he hated his brother Alexandre, he felt bound to love the man who had 'covered him with ridicule that can never be effaced.' What a family!

On his return to Paris, Gudin was alarmed to discover that he was under warrant of arrest. He had sent the *Courrier de l'Europe* some verse that he had written in Aix to celebrate in his own way the victor of a battle that had lasted for eight years. In this offering, the poet (if I may call him that) referred to Goëzman as follows:

> Thus has Parliament's strictest justice
> Quite confounded thy enemies' malice.
> Yet dared they hope their dark skills and lewd,
> Which a vile senator's venal balance
> In these unhappy times had skewed,
> Would bend our true magistrates' prudence.

Now that the vile senator had been dismissed, the only danger was that Gudin might rile the pigeon-plucker. But the editor of the *Courrier*, succumbing to a habit that newspaper editors still haven't lost, saw fit to alter the fourth line to 'Which a *profane senate's* venal balance.' This made it sound as if the whole senate was being accused of venality. As a number of Maupeou's judges had managed to find employment for themselves in the Grand Council, there were a few squeals at Versailles, and a warrant went out for Gudin's arrest. Beaumarchais had already left for La Rochelle, where one of his squadrons was waiting for him. Gudin therefore decided to take refuge in the Temple, which the Knights of Malta had turned into a place where well-born minor offenders might find temporary shelter from the constabulary. He was overjoyed to meet up with Mme de Godeville in the Temple. She was hiding from her creditors. 'With her,' he writes, 'I found the sweetest asylum that ever a man on the run found on this earth.'

Back in Paris, Beaumarchais saw red. He went to the Temple, collected Gudin, took him to his own house, and informed Maurepas that M. Gudin de la Brenellerie was under his protection. He now knew how to deal with 'those gentlemen'. At Versailles, the king whistled, and the judges came to heel.

The trip to Provence had a further, and odder, sequel. In December of the same year Beaumarchais received a letter from Aix. It was ten pages long, and told a love story. Its author admitted to being only seventeen years of age. It was the story of a seduction: its heroine had met her lover when she was twelve, and then he had gone away. 'Five years without seeing a man one adores, oh 'tis contrary to nature!' When she got him back after so long a separation, nature spoke, and at seventeen the girl had 'already lost [her] reputation', because her lover had left again. 'Alas, I feel I love him all the more. I cannot live without him. He must be my husband, and he will be . . .' He will be if you so wish it, M. de Beaumarchais. 'Do not abandon me, I place my fate in your hands.'

Fairytale, reality, a romantic girl trying to play a trick on him, a little tragedy of provincial life – who knows? Anyway, Beaumarchais found time to answer her with tactful advice: 'You heart is deceiving you when it advises you to make the kind of outburst that you envisage, and although your misfortune may secretly appeal to all sensitive people, it is not the kind of thing for which you can seek a remedy at the foot of the throne.'

She wrote back. A correspondence sprang up. She sent him screeds twelve pages long; he read them carefully and answered every one of them. In the end she calmed down, or rather he calmed her down. Whereupon he tied her letters into a bundle and labelled it: 'Affair of my young client, whom I never met.'

However, he had known her first name from the beginning. 'If you favour me with a reply, kindly address your letter to M. Vitalis, rue du Grand-Horloge, Aix, and head it simply: "To Mlle Ninon." '

Please don't forget that name.

12

The 'Fier Rodrigue'

In a letter to Congress dated 29 November 1776, Silas Deane wrote that he would never have been able to fulfil his mission had it not been for the indefatigable, generous and intelligent efforts of M. de Beaumarchais, to whom the United States owed more than to anyone else on that side of the Ocean. Indefatigable, generous and intelligent – Beaumarchais had managed to overcome all resistance, get round the difficulties and triumph over his many opponents.

Three of his ships, the *Amphitrite*, the *Romain* and the *Mercure*, had sailed from Le Havre and Nantes with a cargo of arms, ammunition and equipment – altogether enough material to equip twenty-five thousand men. The convoy had left in the nick of time. Britain had pulled herself together, and for the most part was forcing Washington on to the defensive. New York had fallen to Sir William Howe. A large army led by Sir John Burgoyne was moving down from Canada to meet up with Howe. The Insurgents' bravery and the audacity of their commander-in-chief couldn't make up for their lack of equipment. Unless they received aid in the very near future the Americans had lost the battle. Two men had drawn the obvious conclusions – Lord Stormont and Beaumarchais. In this instance the British ambassador showed proof of his character and his political shrewdness. Realizing that Beaumarchais was the most important and the most effective enemy of his country, he set about deploying all his energies in an attempt to thwart him. He was constantly making representations and remonstrances to the French government, with the result that orders were issued forbidding any French officer or ship to sail for America. Beaumarchais had ignored these orders. On two occasions during this period Vergennes had been obliged to drop Beaumarchais, or rather Rodrigue, Hortales. Louis XVI, Sartines and Vergennes were at times subject to what Arthur

Lee called 'trembling hesitation'. The Comte de Maurepas, for his part, was too old and too conservative to prefer the risks of any adventure to the delights of the *status quo*. To sway the decision in his favour, Beaumarchais had to rush from one to the other and argue incessantly. All the same, it would be dishonest to mock the French government, who, to put it mildly, were playing with fire. Neither the king nor his ministers were upset to learn that Beaumarchais's convoy had reached its destination without hindrance, cheered by thousands of Americans. In success, Rodrigue was no longer alone.

Nor was Silas Deane. Congress had just sent Benjamin Franklin to Paris. The arrival of the famous Dr Franklin had caused a great stir. On the other hand, that of Arthur Lee from London received less attention, except perhaps from Beaumarchais. With Lee, the devil entered his life again. As each of the three American envoys wanted to be the top man, they soon fell out among themselves. Franklin refused to choose between Deane and Lee, who were at daggers drawn, and like the crafty old cat Raminogrobis in La Fontaine's fable arbitrated in his own favour. But these domestic quarrels didn't make Beaumarchais's life any easier, because he had to negotiate with all three of them. He had candidly believed that Franklin would respect Deane's commitments. But Raminogrobis, listening with one ear to Lee's insinuations and with the other to Deane's assertions, feigned embarrassment. This policy of neutrality had at least two advantages: it placed Franklin above the fray, and it enabled Congress to economize. The cargoes of rice, dried fish, tobacco and indigo promised by Silas Deane in return for the military equipment delivered by Rodrigue, Hortales & Co. didn't leave the American ports. Had the arms been sold to the Insurgents (Deane's version of the facts) or were they really a present from the French government (Lee's version)?

At his little house in Passy, Franklin weighed the pros and cons, playing for time. Since France was supposed to know nothing about these negotiations, Raminogrobis was on velvet. Ambiguity and secrecy were *de rigueur* on both sides. But although ambiguity simplified the lives of the ministers, it made Beaumarchais's life impossible. As we have seen, his firm had been founded on a very shaky basis. It had taken a lot of enthusiasm, and nerves of steel, even to consider the venture. Let me remind you that the company received a subsidy of two million francs in 1776 (a million apiece from France and Spain). The equipment Beaumarchais supplied to America in the first six months of 1777 had cost him over five million francs. In the short term, this spelled bankruptcy. As Franklin continued to dodge all his requests, Beaumarchais sent letter after letter to Congress. 'I have exhausted my money and credit,' he wrote in December 1777. 'I was counting on receiving goods in return, as was promised on many occasions, and have greatly exceeded my funds and those of my friends. I have even exhausted other, powerful sums in aid that I had procured to begin with against my express promise to repay them shortly.' This appeal, like the rest, fell on deaf ears. The young republic was poor, we have to admit. It is known, for instance, that its three representatives in Paris were without resources – Deane lived for a year off what Beaumarchais gave him. Franklin himself soon informed the French government that a loan would be welcome. Vergennes gave him 2 million francs in cash. Thus France and America were daily aggravating the misunderstanding, the former financing, and not financing, the latter's war. Oddest of all in this situation is the fact that this subtle policy would have collapsed if Beaumarchais had gone out of business. Everything depended on him and his firm. That was no doubt why Vergennes sent him a further million francs in 1777, by which time, however, the liabilities of Rodrigue, Hortales & Co. had already topped the 10 million mark.

To make up this growing deficit, Beaumarchais was obliged to launch other business concerns alongside the first. As he was a brilliant businessman, as well as everything else, he somehow managed, by working even harder than before, to balance his budget. To help America, and France, he made money. The historians have concluded, strangely, that money was what he was after. Was he thinking of his detractors when he noted at this time a splendid witticism of La Bourdonnais's: 'A director of the Compagnie des Indes once asked the famous La Bourdonnais how it was he had done so badly for the company and so well for himself. La Bourdonnais replied with the kind of pride that I admire, "The reason is that I did for myself by my own lights, and for the company in accordance with your instructions."' Remarkable financier that he was, Beaumarchais died virtually ruined, with fantastic sums owed to him but unpaid. For the time being, I merely want to stress that the United States of America won the War of Independence with French equipment, one-tenth of which was paid for by Louis XVI's government and nine-tenths by Beaumarchais.

A leader's abilities are judged by, among other things, the quality of his lieutenants. In politics, war, industry, or commerce, the choice of collaborators is crucial. With bad backing from his assistants, a minister, a general or a managing director will be misrepresented, misunderstood and consequently disobeyed. From this point of view, Beaumarchais always saw immediately which men (and sometimes which women) he could count on, come what may. Surprisingly enough, however, he invariably chose his seconds-in-command from his immediate entourage. Their intelligence, their loyalty, and frequently their spirit of sacrifice were in proportion to the affection and admiration they felt for him personally. Unlike most leaders, Beaumarchais reasoned with his heart; and he listened to its opinions. Gudin's brother, who was his chief cashier for quite some time and who had to deal with some extremely complicated transactions, showed great loyalty to him later on, in his most difficult moments. Théveneau de Francy, younger brother of the sinister Morande, whom Beaumarchais engaged on the spot as soon as they met, was a marvellous executive – the two men understood one another perfectly, each thinking along the same lines as the other. When Beaumarchais sent Francy to America, they exchanged business letters that are astonishingly full of feeling.

Francy and the other Gudin are only two examples among many. Can anyone believe that a man is loved on the strength of appearances? He may be for a month, but most definitely not for a lifetime. Beaumarchais was given so much by his friends because he gave them everything. Some have concluded that because he was undemonstrative he was cold and calculating. Of course. A thousand years hence, when the public libraries have collapsed beneath the weight of their psychology sections, we shall still be judging one another by appearances. Beaumarchais's twenty-year-old nephew, Fanchon's son, who served in the artillery under Washington as 'Major des Epiniers' and who had sailed on one of his uncle's ships to fight his uncle's war, knew better: 'Your nephew may well be killed, but he will never do anything unworthy of someone who has the honour of belonging to your family. That is as certain as the fondness that he will always feel for the very best of uncles.'

Beaumarchais was admittedly not all of a piece. (Who is?) Even though he was the proud Rodrigue and had a number of sublime moments in his life, he always remained a man of pleasure. He was an alloy of gold and lead. In the words of Baudelaire, who knew what he was talking about: 'In every man, at every moment, there are two simultaneous postulations: one towards God, the other towards Satan.' Intriguingly, it was in the most noble moments of his life that Beaumarchais was the most prone to debauchery. He went in for it, like everything else, wholeheartedly, but as he was the sanest of men in this respect he never confused his 'housewives' and his 'sluts'. Leaving his love at home, he set out to foray for sex like a soldier on active service. (The simile may seem too simple. The hard thing to convey is the notion of simultaneity – the warrior-hero is out after vice and virtue at once, not just bed after the combat. We should distrust holy men, and not let them play with our children!) Whenever he was intensely himself, writing history and feeling that he was truly Beaumarchais, he exploded, and at such times he preferred whores to housewives. When, on 5 January 1777, Marie-Thérèse gave him the child he had always hoped for, he was already at a pinnacle. His squadron had dropped anchor off the shores of America, and thanks to him the face of the world was about to be changed. The birth of Eugénie increased his happiness still further. How he loved his housewife, Marie-Thérèse, at that moment! He owed her everything: his child, his success (she had worked very intelligently alongside him at Rodrigue, Hortales), his happiness. All these fine sentiments led him irresistibly into the arms of Mme de Godeville.

He had met her in London, where she had a terrible reputation. She would have been a godsend for an early twentieth-century novelist. She had lost her husband, her honour and her country – but she had managed to keep a lively pen. She ruled, alongside the Chevalier d'Eon, over the *demi-monde* of French *émigrés*, and undoubtedly inspired a mass of lampoons attacking the fine ladies of Versailles, probably to reassure herself. A 'lost woman' (as Galsworthy might have called her), she felt less out on a limb once she had 'lost' all the others. Beaumarchais would have no truck with her political nonsense. He asked her to be silent, and she followed him to Paris. Their affair lasted for close on a year. When he couldn't join her in her usual bed, he sent her long letters full of the lust he felt for her. 'If you ask me why people are for ever "poking their noses" into your affairs "all over the place", I answer in the oriental style that as you are eminently pokable, even "all over the place" . . .'(The ellipsis dots are his.) From 'oriental', he passed into Latin. '*Madame* reads my letters twenty times and doesn't understand a word. *Oculos habent et non videbunt.* [Eyes have they, and see not.] I shan't continue my Latin quotation, because I can't say *Manus habent et non palpabunt* [They have hands, and handle not], because *madame* has pretty hands, and *madame* shall handle.'

These extracts, chosen from among those least likely to shock, date from early 1777. Marie-Thérèse had just given birth. Eugénie was only a few weeks old, and he was writing to his 'baggage': 'How is our son? Has his mother arranged a cosy little apartment to receive him? A nice, soft movement to rock him when he enters? I am very worried about this poor little fellow who tickles my nether regions every evening and says: "Papa, I should like to go and spend eight or nine months *chez* Mama." ' This ribald literature is rather sickening, I agree. But does that mean should we ignore it? One more quotation, and I'll have done: 'I hope to be fortunate enough to come and answer the rest of your letter this evening. Alas, my dear one, as true as your cunt has been a maiden since the day it was so rebellious, I give you my sacred word of honour that my prick has been a virgin since that moment. Hello, hello, I've just heard of the safe arrival of one of my richest vessels. You can congratulate me this evening.' There are scores of letters written on this level. In his correspondence with Mme de Godeville, Beaumarchais used what he himself called *le style spermatique*. In the end, however, he had to stop seeing her, because she had grown jealous of Marie-Thérèse. She wanted to be both his mistress and his housewife. He tried to reason with her: 'Why try to change a lust relationship into a disastrous romance? Really, you are a mere child . . . I don't want to become involved because I cannot, and must not.' It was a waste of time. To get rid of her, Beaumarchais hit upon the idea of giving her to Gudin, who accepted. Now you know why the kindly fellow was so happy to be shut away in the Temple with Mme de Godeville – she was his mistress. 'With her, I found the sweetest asylum that ever a man on the run found on this earth.' As you can see, Gudin's style was hardly *spermatique*. With him, Mme de Godeville found her winter quarters.

'I don't wish to become involved because I cannot, and must not.'

When he wrote that sentence he was thinking of his work – the work he was writing single-handed across the Atlantic. That was his sole and exclusive folly at the time. His family, sex, the other matters he had to oversee in order to survive, and even *The Marriage*, which he had now begun to write, were secondary to that single, huge commitment. His soul was on the ocean with the *Fier Rodrigue*, his flagship. In this battle, which transfigured him, he found a note of sincerity and nobility that I for one find exceptional. We have proof that he was not showing off, not merely posing for the camera of history. The confidential memos he sent to Francy in America show how obsessed he was by his passionate involvement. Not to Vergennes, but to his young friend, the obscure Francy, he writes: 'Amid all these disagreements, the news from America overwhelms me with joy. Brave, brave people! Their military conduct justifies my esteem and the fine enthusiasm that the French have for them. Well, my friend, I want homeward freight only so that I shall be in a position to serve them anew, and to meet my commitments in order to be able to contract further commitments in their favour.'

Loménie dismisses these scribbled remarks, written four days before Christmas 1777, as 'fatuous and naïve'. Admittedly the 'my esteem' bit is rather surprising. But what man, knowing he is playing a historic, decisive role, isn't led to speak naturally about himself with a measure of condescension? Pride, for some great leaders, is like the north star – it guides them on their way. After the adventure, the battle or the term of office, these exceptional people climb down and turn out to be amazingly modest and humble. This remarkable change upsets ordinary mortals, but that's the way things are. Action is sometimes as good as a coronation. The War of Independence crowned Figaro. Writing to his young disciple, he could reveal his secret and say simply: I am a king.

> Do as I do: despise petty considerations, petty measures, and petty feelings. I have associated you with a magnificent cause; you are the agent of a just and generous man. Remember that success is in the hands of fate, that the money due to me is staked on a great concourse of events, but that my reputation is my own, just as you today are the artisan of yours. Let it be always good, my friend, and all will not be lost, even if all the rest is. I salute you as I esteem you and love you.

Admittedly, any noble father might have written in this manner to his son, and his nobility would in the event be without significance. But every word of Beaumarchais's corresponds to a precise reality. It is action that inspires him, and changes him. No pretence in these words. When he writes thus Beaumarchais is sure of himself, and sure that he is mad.

He was no longer content with delivering gunpowder. He mobilized officers, engaged generals – the Pole Pulawski, the Prussian von Steuben, the Irishman Conway. It was his war, his fleet, his army. He kept a friendly eye on La Fayette, whose qualities he had detected the minute he met him, and on more than one occasion he saved him from his creditors. Finally, off his own bat, he took the ultimate step – he turned his merchant vessels into warships: 'I am sending you on ahead the corsair *Zephyr* to inform you that I am ready to send to sea a fleet of twelve sail headed by the *Fier Rodrigue* . . . This fleet may comprise five to six thousand tons, and it is completely fitted out for war.'

On 17 October 1777 Beaumarchais's cannons, rifles and powder weighed heavily in the balance. Sir John Burgoyne, encircled in Saratoga, was obliged to surrender. Equipped, organized and led, the rebels were henceforth in a position to confront the British in line, and to beat them. The days of harassment, ambushes and sabotage were over. Real warfare had taken their place. Hope was about to change sides. A colonial army or a repressive force can be victorious when the resistance has not had time to get itself properly organized. Invincible Britain, by hesitating, by letting one chance after the other fizzle out, had condemned herself to failure, if not defeat.

In October 1777 Beaumarchais realized that the time had come for France to commit herself more fully. As he had forced Louis XVI to aid the Insurgents, so he urged him to enter the war, that is to say to fight against Britain. It was not an easy undertaking. The king was split between his two rival tendencies, idealism and patriotism, between the example set by Louis XIV and the teachings of Fénelon, between his love for France and his faith in treaties. Old Maurepas, his other mentor, constantly advised him to be cautious. On the verge of acting Louis XVI balked time and again. But he was no coward, and he always came back to the issue with renewed energy. It was an odd situation. On the advice of Sartines, the king, with admirable enthusiasm, was fitting out a new fighting fleet. The royal navy, like Sleeping Beauty, was waiting for a sign to emerge from its lethargy. Vergennes, for his part, was steadily preparing the king for the all-important decision. In the first instance France had to recognize the independence of the United States without delay in order to take advantage of the head start obtained with the aid of Rodrigue, Hortales & Co. At any moment the Opposition might come to power in England and sign a conciliatory peace with the American provinces, thereby putting France back where she started. Beaumarchais, who was well aware of the king's hesitations, and who knew the respective positions of his ministers, decided that the moment had come to intervene.

On 26 October, nine days after the victory at Saratoga (which he can't have known about), he drew up a *Memoir for the King's Ministers*, in which he set out the lines of his policy and answered the objections of each minister in particular. The writing of this memoir marked the summit of Beaumarchais's life. For a short while he acted like a head of government. In October 1777 he knew that he would be heard. I was going to to say obeyed. Loménie is quite right to emphasize that 'the substance of his plan is carried over into the official declaration made by the French government to the British crown' in March 1778, and to add that Louis XVI 'did some of what Beaumarchais advised him to do'. The memoir (which is extremely detailed and deals with all the pros and cons and possible consequences of the proposed action) is too long to quote in full. Here are the main lines of its arguments:

> In the state of crisis to which events have come, in the certainty we have that the British people are clamouring shamelessly for a war against us . . . what options remain open to us?
>
> We still have three to choose from. The first is worthless, the second would be the safest, the third is the most noble. But a combination of the second and the third can make the King of France the premier power in the known world once again.
>
> The first option, which is worthless, absolutely worthless, is to continue doing what we are already doing, or rather not doing . . . waiting for the event without acting . . . for the British ministry to change . . . and for the British to sign a peace with America with one hand, and with the other an express order to attack our vessels and fall upon our possessions . . .

The second option, which I regard as the safest, would be to accept publicly the treaty of alliance proposed for over a year by America, comprising the fishing franchise on the Banks, the mutual guarantee of possessions . . . the positive promise of reciprocal diversionary aid in the event of an attack or of continuing hostilities against a co-signatory, together with a secret plan for seizing the British islands [in the West Indies], and a solemn commitment between the three powers, America, Spain and France, to agree upon a meridian to be imposed upon the British in the Atlantic between Europe and America, beyond which all their vessels would be liable to seizure both in peacetime and in war . . .

It must be admitted that as soon as the British learn that they have no further hope of negotiating with a country that has negotiated with us, they will forthwith declare open war on us, alleging that we were the aggressors by the fact of signing the same treaty. But war for war, since it is inevitable today, the Americans, Spanish and French united are more than a match for this haughty nation, should they be frenzied enough to attack us thereafter. . . .

The third option, the most noble of all . . . without compromising the faith that [the king] believes he must ascribe to the existing treaties, would be to declare to the British in a good manifesto . . . that the King of France, after long remaining, out of consideration for Britain, a passive and tranquil spectator of the war between the British and the Americans, to the detriment of his country's trade . . . without wishing to declare war on Britain, and still less to wage war against her without prior declaration, as has become all too odiously common in this century, and without wishing even to enter into any treaty that might harm the interests of the British crown . . . contents herself today, as a consequence of the neutrality she has always observed, with declaring that she holds the Americans to be independent, and intends henceforth to regard them as such in relation to their trade with France and French trade with them . . .

Such is, more or less, the manifesto that I am putting forward to the king's council. It is very true that this document merely extends French rights to neutrality and places both contenders on a perfectly equal footing, and may thereby irritate the British without satisfying the Americans. To go no farther than this might well mean that Britain could yet forestall us, and offer America the same independence in return for a treaty of union that would be very damaging to us.

Now, in the present chaotic situation, where so many different interests overlap, won't the Americans prefer those who offer them independence and a treaty of union to those who content themselves with acknowledging that they have had the courage to succeed in making themselves free? I would therefore dare, concurring with the opinion of M. le Comte de Vergennes, to suggest that we should add to the third option the secret conditions of the second. That is to say, at the same time as I declared America independent, I would enter into a secret treaty of alliance with her . . .

At the same time as I declared independence . . . I would begin by garrisoning the Atlantic coasts with sixty to eighty thousand men, and I would get my navy to adopt a highly formidable air and tone, so that the British would have no doubts as to whether I meant to stand by my decision . . .

Finally, if, to keep up an appearance of respecting the treaties, I did not rebuild Dunkirk, whose present state is the eternal shame of France, I would at least begin a port on the Atlantic sufficiently impressive and close to the British for them to regard the plan to contain them as a deliberate and irrevocable measure.

I would consolidate my liaison with America in all its forms, since at present her guarantee alone can preserve our colonies for us; and since the interests of this nation can never overlap with ours, I would place as much trust in their commitments as I would distrust any forced commitment of Britain's; and I would never again let slip a single opportunity of humbling this perfidious and headstrong neighbour who, after perpetrating so many outrages against us, in her present rage vents more hatred against us than she does against the Americans, who have deprived her of three quarters of her empire.

But let us beware of spending in deliberations the single instant that remains to act, and realize that by dint of wasting time in for ever saying 'It's too early', we may be forced to exclaim sorrowfully: 'Heavens, it's too late!'

This historic document, which is normally ignored because it runs counter to the preconceived idea that people have of Beaumarchais, hit its target, as we have seen.

On 13 March 1778 the French government declared in London that it held the Americans to be independent and so on (third option).

But (second option), as early as 17 December 1777 Louis XVI had informed Franklin that he was ready to sign a treaty of trade and friendship with the United States. The secret document was drawn up and initialled on 6 February 1778 by Gérard, Louis XVI's secretary of state and Vergennes's right-hand man, on behalf of France, and by Franklin, Deane and Lee on behalf of the United States.

Shortly afterwards Louis XVI visited Cherbourg and selected it as 'a port on the Atlantic sufficiently impressive and close to the British . . .'. Dumouriez, whose ideas pleased the king, was ordered to build a naval base for forty men-of-war. Before retiring for the night, Louis XVI wrote to the queen from Cherbourg, 'I am the happiest king in the world.'

On 18 June France suddenly rose to her feet from the submissive posture into which she had been forced by the Treaty of Paris. Attacked by a British squadron off Morlaix, an isolated French frigate called the *Belle Poule* sank an enemy vessel and emerged victorious. Throughout the kingdom enthusiasm knew no bounds. What happened next belongs to history, and everyone knows the story, which for the French is the story of Grasse, Chartres, Rochambeau, and of course La Fayette. Poor Beaumarchais! Before tasting the bitter fruit of Franco-American ingratitude, he none the less experienced a moment of great joy.

In July 1779 the *Fier Rodrigue*, serving as escort to ten merchant vessels and sailing under Beaumarchais's flag took a decisive part in the battle off the island of Grenada between the squadrons commanded by Admirals d'Estaing and Biron. After the battle the Comte d'Estaing sent Beaumarchais, via Sartines, the following letter:

> On board the *Languedoc*, off St George,
> Island of Grenada 12 July 1779
>
> I have just time to tell you, *monsieur*, that the *Fier Rodrigue* held her position well and contributed to the victory won by the king's ships. You will forgive me all the more for having used her as your interests will not suffer on that score – that you may be sure of. The excellent M. de Montaut [her captain] was regrettably killed. I shall shortly be sending my declaration of prize monies to the minister, and I hope that you will help me to petition for those which your navy has most justly deserved.
>
> I have the honour of being, with all the sentiments that you inspire so well, *monsieur*, your most humble and obedient servant,
>
> Estaing

The admiral's message reached the Navy Ministry on 6 September and was immediately delivered to Beaumarchais on Sartines's instructions. The next day, bubbling with joy, Rodrigue wrote to his friend the minister:

Paris 7 September 1770

Monsieur,

I am obliged to you for sending me the letter from M. le Comte d'Estaing. It was very noble of him, in the moment of his triumph, to think that a note in his hand might be very acceptable to me. I am taking the liberty of sending you a copy of his short letter, by which I consider myself honoured, like the good Frenchman that I am, and at which I rejoice, like a passionate lover of my country, against that proud Britain.

The excellent Montaut thought he could do no better, to prove that he was worthy of the position he had been honoured with, than to have himself killed. Whatever the result may be for my own affairs, my poor friend Montaut died an honourable death, and I feel childish delight at being certain that those Englishmen who have torn me to shreds in their papers for the past four years will read in them that one of my vessels has played a part in depriving them of the most fertile of their possessions.

And I can see these enemies of M. d'Estaing, and above all of yourself, *Monsieur*, biting their nails, and my heart leaps with pleasure.

Beaumarchais

13

The Rest is Literature

Relaxation, for Beaumarchais, always took the form of a change of activity. 'His way of life,' writes Gudin, who witnessed it from day to day, 'was as varied as his genius. He rested from one task by turning to another. He had the ability, which characterized him perfectly, to change his occupation unexpectedly and turn his attention as intensely and as exclusively to the new activity as he had to the one that it replaced, without any lingering fatigue or distracting pre-occupation. He called this process "closing the drawer on an affair".' This 'closed drawer' technique partly explains how Beaumarchais could tackle a dozen or more ventures simultaneously and still steer them to completion. It is the method of a craftsman, the acquired habit (precise and time-conscious) of a clockmaker. All the same, Beaumarchais would never have accomplished anything had it not been for passion, which was the real mainspring of his life. 'I want to know why I get angry.' The phrase is that of a man who got angry frequently.

During his American period (1776-83), Beaumarchais opened two new drawers. He attended to them only in his spare time, yet they would have sufficed in themselves to make him famous. They involved setting up the Society of Dramatic Authors and the publica-tion of the complete works of Voltaire. However, these monumental undertakings were by no means his only passions alongside the great American adventure. Before turning to 'literature', therefore, I think it would be enlightening to list some of his other assignments during this period. Needless to say, the list will not be exhaustive.

To give some idea of Beaumarchais's parallel activities, I shall merely cite the titles of the files from *one box* opened by Loménie in the 1850s: *Outline for a Textbook in Comparative Criminal Law*; *How to acquire*

Land in the Scioto Region; *The joint Owners of the Enclosure of the Quinze-Vingts*; *The Civil Rights of Protestants in France* (more later); *Plan for a Loan of equal Utility to the King and to the Public*; *Prospectus for a Mill to be built in Harfleur*; *Plan for Trade with India via the Isthmus of Suez*; *The Conversion of Peat into Coal and the Advantages of this Discovery*; *The Planting of Rhubarb*; *Prospectus for a Finance Transaction or Loan in the Form of a State Lottery*; *Plan for a Bureau of Trade and an Accumulation Fund*; *Plan for a Bridge at the Arsenal*; and so on. All these matters were mooted during the period we are discussing. Most of them remained theoretical during Beaumarchais's lifetime – the building of the Suez canal, for instance, did not begin until almost a century later. Few men have attracted new ideas as magnetically as Beaumarchais did: engineers, financiers, architects, inventors, dreamers and madmen of every kind knocked at his door and eventually obtained an appointment, advice or assistance. (The spongers knocked, too, and were rarely turned away, even when they were former enemies like Baculard d'Arnaud.)

He was fond of saying, 'How is it that everything being done or planned ends up on my desk?' False modesty, vanity. If the world of research and adventure hadn't come to him, Beaumarchais would have gone looking for it. What demon drove him to carry to the font the Caisse d'Escompte, nowadays known as the Bank of France? And to finance the Périer brothers' tremendous Chaillot fire pump? And to restrict the privilege of the *fermiers-généraux?* On the other hand, we can easily understand why he got angry in order to defend the Calvinists of south-west France against 'barbarous fanaticism'. He took a similarly determined stand in favour of the Jews, not contenting himself, like his fellow-writers, with adopting positions of principle, but involving himself directly in their fight against religious discrimination and weak-headed intolerance. To save a Jew in Bayonne, he 'wept kneeling' before Vergennes – and succeeded. The fine writings and petitions of the intellectuals have their usefulness – they give their signatories an easy conscience. But anyone who really wants to help the victim of a repressive system has to fight, or scheme, or plead. The rest is literature. Beaumarchais was always available to help the oppressed, i.e. all those against whom the majority and the government had set their minds in virtuous jubilation. Some of his biographers have berated him for having considered at one time becoming involved in the slave trade. But he dropped the idea very quickly. Once he had seen his first Negro, and understood what it was to be black, he immediately became the champion of the non-white minority. He always wanted to know why, and for whom, he got angry. Abstraction had less appeal for him than a face. Never did any man's suffering leave him indifferent, even if that man was his worst enemy.

The most oppressed of all minorities in those days was perhaps the brotherhood of playwrights. I'm only half-joking. Oddly resigned to their fate, the playwrights submitted to the yoke of the actors. The members of the Comédie Française, tyrants among the despots, exploited their authors shamelessly, almost majestically. Since the days of Quinault, who was a playwright as well as Lully's librettist, the authors had obtained the right, after much moaning, to be paid on a percentage basis. The generous actors had granted them a ninth of the profits if their play had five acts, a twelfth if it had three. Theoretically, this was a splendid offer; in practice, however, it meant next to nothing. The actors had craftily invented the iniquitous notion of net receipts. Like Groucho Marx in *A Night at the Opera*, who tears strip after strip off a singer's fabulous contract until all that's left is the fellow's signature, which he triumphantly pockets, the members of the Comédie Française began by subtracting from the gross takings an arbitrary 1200 *livres*, representing 'ordinary performance expenses', and a further sum in respect of 'extraordinary performance expenses'. They then knocked off the cost of season tickets, complimentary tickets (which amounted to whole rows of seats), the poor tax, and what they called the 'author's personal expenses' – the glass of water drunk during rehearsals, the candles provided for him to correct his text and so on. And that wasn't all. The actors had also decided that if the net takings came to less than the 1200 *livres* set aside for ordinary expenses, the play came 'under the rules' and became the property of the company. Need I add that the net receipts rarely amounted to 1200 *livres*. An example is worth more than a long paragraph, so I shall cite the instance of a very popular author of the day, Louvet de la Saussaye, who, hearing that his comedy *La Journée Lacédémonienne* had sold out three evenings running, promptly started dreaming of a place in the sun and asked for his account. The theatre's accountant informed him by return that 'as his play had brought in 12,000 *livres* over five performances, the author, in respect of his rights on the net takings, owed 101 *livres* 8 *sous* 8 *deniers* to the Comédie'.

The beggared playwrights (and all other writers, who were at the mercy of the booksellers) had no choice but to seek their livelihood from the high and mighty of their day. In such conditions, a man of letters had to be very brave indeed if he was to remain independent-minded. At the height of his fame Beaumarchais reckoned that his influence might serve to put an end to these annoying and harmful practices. After writing an open letter stating that he preferred a man of letters 'to live honestly off the avowed income of his works rather than chase after sinecures and pensions', he decided to take up the defence of the playwrights, and began by lobbying the Duc de Richelieu, who, as lord chamberlain, had the responsibility for actors. As a gesture to Beaumarchais, Richelieu asked him to look into the matter, to arrange discussions with the actors and report back to him. I shan't go into the details of the discussions that the author of *The Barber of Seville* entered into with his actors – the whole affair was a mixture of tragedy and farce. His discussions with the members of the Comédie Française, some of whom were his friends, led him to conclude that the only solution would be to form an authors' union that could stand up to the common front of the actors. What a pipe dream! At the very first meeting the writers squabbled and almost came to blows. Here, too, I shall spare you the details. They are much the same today: 'If X comes, I won't. If that bounder Y signs, I won't.' Writers have always had chips on their shoulders, jealousies, aversions: they are past masters at huffing and puffing.

By dint of diplomacy and determination, Beaumarchais none the less managed to get the leading lights in the profession together. Twenty-three playwrights met at his home in rue Vieille-du-Temple on 3 July 1777, dined heartily at his expense, drank several cases of his champagne and parted without having murdered one another. It was a miracle, and the sequel, no less miraculous, is the beautiful house on rue Ballu where the descendants of those twenty-three meet and administer a fortune in performing rights. After dinner, euphoric and rather tipsy, already dreaming of their percentages, the twenty-three had to elect four executives. Beaumarchais, Sauvin, Sedaine and Marmontel were elected by a large majority. Before the vote, it had been agreed that the executives would hold office permanently. After the vote, the minority, egged on by the four defeated candidates, attempted to go back on the issue of permanent office, claiming that the men elected 'wouldn't fail to turn the prestige of their position to their personal advantage.' At this, Beaumarchais grew angry, and the surprised minority withdrew their objection. But the battle was only beginning. Hercules himself would have flung up his arms in despair – compared with the theatres, the Augean stables were a model of order and cleanliness. In the end, he won.

On 13 January 1791, fourteen years later, after innumerable absurd lawsuits, grotesque dramas and farcical squabbles, the National Assembly, at Beaumarchais's behest, recognised the principle of copyright and abolished the exorbitant privileges of the actors. There were a few subsequent incidents, but the revolution had been accomplished. Sure of their rights, 'reintegrated', as we might say today, thanks to Beaumarchais alone, the writers were at last able to lord it over their masters. And over Beaumarchais himself. For example, the present honorary president of the French Society of Dramatic Authors, whose depth of thought is known to all, wrote in 1954 of the works of his illustrious predecessor: 'Not one shudder announces the forthcoming *mal du siècle*; no awareness, no anguish concerning the condition of mankind.' Could it be that playwrights belong to a different species? What was Figaro's opinion again? 'Midges, gnats, maringoons . . . ' Writers are the oddest of insects, whether they are lice, cockroaches, or superb butterflies.

Beaumarchais was in Marseilles with Gudin when he heard that Voltaire, the king of the French butterflies, had died on 30 May 1778. Gudin, who had just been elected to the Académie Provençale, jumped at the chance to pronounce the first eulogy in memory of the great man. Having learned to their indignation that the clergy had refused to bury him and he had been interred in a disused chapel, the two friends thought of returning to Paris and asking Maurepas to transfer the remains of the author of the *Henriade* to the foot of Henry IV's statue in Paris, after a memorial ceremony from which the clergy would be banned. The imminence of his lawsuit with La Blache forced Beaumarchais to drop this generous but crazy plan. It is hard to imagine Louis XVI agreeing to snub the Archbishop of Paris simply to please Beaumarchais, who in any case soon hit upon another way of rendering a superb homage to Voltaire.

I am not referring to the line in *The Marriage* ('And Voltaire will never die'), but to the exhausting venture into which he sank a fortune and his spare time – the publication of the complete works of his fellow-writer (and fellow-clockmaker) M. de Voltaire.

It was no easy undertaking. Two-thirds of Voltaire's works were banned in France. Anyone selling or importing certain titles risked imprisonment, and any copies seized were burned. To publish an author in France in such circumstances was a challenge. It was a further challenge to print eighty or more volumes at one go. In addition, the rights in the published works were held by several different publishers. And finally, Panckouke, the owner of a powerful publishing concern, had had the same idea as Beaumarchais, and had two considerable advantages over him: he held all the unpublished manuscripts, and he had the backing of Catherine the Great, who had offered him large sums of money and the use of the St Petersburg presses. To publish the greatest French author in Russia was the same as condemning him a second time; and it would have made the French, who had lionized Voltaire during his lifetime, look both ridiculous and inconsistent. So Beaumarchais got angry and went to see Maurepas, who was both liberal and sceptical in his opinions, 'to demonstrate what a disgrace it would be to let the Russians print the works of the man who was the greatest glory of French literature'. Figaro, as we have seen, wasn't exactly European-minded. Maurepas, like Beaumarchais, called France France and Europe nonsense; he promised to help him as much as he could, providing that he made the matter his sole responsibility. Beaumarchais hesitated. 'Once I've laid out all my capital,' he told the prime minister after due reflection, 'the clergy will sue, the publication will be stopped, the publisher and his printers will be crushed, and the disgrace of France will be made complete and even more obvious.' Maurepas gave the matter some thought in his turn, and promised to issue secret instructions to the post office to allow the complete edition to be dispatched throughout the kingdom without let or hindrance. This was merely the promise of an old man, who might die or be dismissed any day, but for Beaumarchais it was enough. In his vocabulary, reflexion didn't mean retreat.

No publisher ever displayed as much passion for an author as Beaumarchais did. Only the best would do for Voltaire. Having admired in England the type known as Baskerville, he bought several complete founts of it in different sizes at a cost of 50,000 francs. He wanted the finest Dutch paper. Finding that none was available, he paid a man to go and find out how it was made and bought three paper mills in the Vosges. But he still needed a location for his presses, which had to be outside France but sufficiently close to Paris to cut transport overheads. Hearing that the Margrave of Baden wanted to cash in on his massive but obsolete fort at Kehl, Beaumarchais offered to rent it. The margrave agreed, then went back on his word, or rather insisted that he should cut every passage in Voltaire's texts likely to offend morals in general and God and margraves in particular. Beaumarchais promptly sent his royal lessor an extremely insolent letter lecturing him and threatening to set up his press in another margravate 'a few yards away from yours', where his noble venture might function without hindrance. The margrave must have had a thick skin, or an empty pocket, because he gave in unconditionally.

Just as he had started Rodrigue, Hortales & Co. for his war in America, so he set up the Philosophical, Literary & Typographical Co. (PLT) to defend Voltaire and his works. Officially, he was merely the Paris agent of PLT; in fact he was its brain, its executive and its financier rolled into one. (As his lieutenant in Kehl he employed a brilliant but impetuous young man called Le Tellier. The proofs were read by Decroix. Condorcet wrote the notes.)

The 'company that is I' bought from Panckouke and a score of publishers scattered around Europe the rights in Voltaire's unpublished and published works for the considerable sum of 160,000 *livres*. Beaumarchais decided that there would be two editions: a de luxe, original edition, octavo, in seventy volumes; and a second, duodecimo edition in eighty-two volumes. Each would have a run of fifteen thousand copies. As early as 1780 he had a prospectus drawn up to attract subscribers. He expected thirty thousand advance orders, this being the figure required to cover his outlay (there was never any question of his making a profit on the venture), but he got only four thousand. In 1781 he knew that Voltaire was going to ruin him, or at least to lose him a fortune. Anyone else would have promptly gone out of business to limit the extent of the disaster. But the idea never even crossed his mind. The death of Maurepas, his accomplice, gave him an opportunity to close down, but he didn't do so.

The first volume came off the press in Kehl in 1783, the 162nd in 1790, making an average of twenty-three volumes per year, a considerable feat considering their bulk and their extremely high quality. Their lack of success was due, I think, to the fact that most great writers, except those who die young, go through a phase of neglect after their death that lasts for about twenty years. André Gide called this period of disaffection an author's purgatory. (His own books are just beginning to re-emerge, a quarter of a century after his death.) The French turned their backs on Voltaire in 1780, and Beaumarchais's hassles, as his publisher, with the Church and parliament didn't become widely enough known to create publicity. The clergy's imprecations against the "forge of iniquity' in Kehl fizzled out like a damp squib. It is only fair to add that Louis XVI's ministers kept the promise given by Maurepas – the post office allowed Satan and his works to pass through without hindrance of any sort. So Beaumarchais financed and steered this admirable undertaking single-handed, with unfailing passion, concerning himself with the smallest of details, demanding and obtaining perfection. In so doing he rendered France a great service by preventing Voltaire from falling into the hands of the Russians, as well as delighting the bibliophiles of yesterday, today and tomorrow. For once, he got something out of what he did. Even though the venture left him virtually ruined, it gave his reputation a great fillip. France has accepted, without disdain and even with good grace, this royal gift made to her by M. de Beaumarchais.

14

'The Marriage of Figaro'

Since the very first line of this book we have been moving towards *The Marriage*, the keystone of our edifice and Beaumarchais's major work – the work that explains all the others and his life. All his secrets, starting with the main one, the secret of his identity, which we have returned to time and again, are contained in this play, which is subtitled *The Day of Madness*. Beaumarchais reveals himself consciously, and slyly, in *The Marriage*. In *The Barber* he had merely hinted at the facts; here he owns up. Most remarkably, this confession, this laying bare of a personality, is part and parcel of a bright and lively play which is designed to make people laugh, and succeeds in doing so, which has a life of its own, and which is as great as the greatest comedies of Molière.

Yet this masterpiece of the French theatre is also a political act. Beaumarchais's early biographers, who weren't what you might call revolutionaries, tried to tone down the historical reverberations of *The Marriage*. In doing so, they thought they were helping to clear their dead hero of any untoward suspicions. For opposite reasons, most of their successors did the same. Voltaire and Rousseau were philosophers, Figaro wasn't – history and comedy could have nothing in common. Couldn't they, though?

When Louis XVI, who was genuinely fond of Beaumarchais, read the manuscript of *The Marriage* in 1782, his reaction was immediate: 'We should have to destroy the Bastille if a performance of this play was not to be a dangerous blunder. This man mocks everything that must be respected in a government.' A year later, after a further royal ban, Beaumarchais declared in public: 'He doesn't want it to be performed. I tell you it will be, even if I have to put it on in Notre Dame.' The king *versus* Beaumarchais. Their battle is worth looking into.

The author of *The Marriage* understood the king's objections, which were of a political nature. If he hadn't intended to attack the flaws in the system, he would undoubtedly have cut or toned down certain objectionable passages, but he knew what he was doing, and he stood his ground. Yet it never crossed his mind for a moment that the king might be overthrown. Beaumarchais was a reformer. Like Choiseul, he believed that the time had come to make France a constitutional monarchy based on the people, and to abolish privileges. He wasn't the only man in his day to say or write such things, of course, but he was the first to attempt to put them on the stage. As we know, and as Louis XVI knew, the theatre can be a marvellous echoing chamber – tribune and forum at one and the same time. Governments have always been wary of the theatre; in France, for instance, just before the Second World War, *Coriolanus* was banned at the Comédie Française. So it is easy to imagine Louis XVI reading the monologue ('You took the trouble to be born and that's all') and blinking at the seventh verse of the closing song:

> By the hazards of gestation,
> One's a shepherd, the other's a king;
> Chance caused this separation;
> Wit alone can change everything.
> Scores of kings held in veneration
> Pass on and unadored lie;
> And Voltaire will never die.

Wit can change everything. That might have been Beaumarchais's motto. It took more wit to get *The Marriage* performed than to finish writing it.

On the surface, the trial of strength between the monarch and Beaumarchais was a very unequal one. Miromesnil, who had the king's ear in such matters, considered that *The Marriage* was a work of the devil. Right up to the opening night he fought Figaro tooth and nail. Other ministers, a faction at court, the Church and parliament were on the same side as the Minister of Justice. It was said that the comedy smelt of sulphur. In 1783, however, Beaumarchais was more powerful than ever before or after. The king and his advisers knew how much they owed to him in the field of politics. Britain had been forced to surrender at Yorktown the previous year, had accepted the implications of her defeat and had acknowledged the independence of America. The Treaty of Versailles was about to be signed, returning Senegal to France and ridding Dunkirk of its British occupants. Who had inspired this policy? Who had indefatigably boosted the king's will when it flagged? Who had foreseen, one by one, all of these historic events? Who had sacrificed his time, his money and his genius to enable the Americans to carry off their victories? Even if public opinion knew only of La Fayette or Rochambeau, Versailles knew of someone else.

From now on he was an unofficial minister, intervening with increased authority in every sphere, concerning himself with questions of finance, economics, the law, home administration and so on. And he intervened in this way because he was asked to. Loménie quotes a memo that Beaumarchais sent to Vergennes, which gives some idea of the part he played in state affairs: 'I enclose the summary of our last conference, which I have been unable to send you until now because I had to copy out my notes personally, on account of the secrecy imposed. I have kept the summary simple, so that when M. de Maurepas shows it to the king his inexperience in such complicated affairs will not prevent him from grasping the whole truth.'

Thus Beaumarchais himself created, consciously or not, the ambiguities of his existence. Almaviva can't fire Figaro because he is indispensable – the master is more vulnerable than the valet. Figaro, knowing his strength, however fragile it may be, can do as he pleases. The same goes for Beaumarchais. How could Louis XVI have dismissed a man who had made him king, by enabling him to beat Britain – the one and only triumph of his reign?

All the same, even though he had contrived to boost his social standing by dint of intelligence, cunning and bravery, Beaumarchais's status remained what it had been at his birth – inferior, or non-existent. He resolutely refused to let success turn his head. He knew that he was a phoney: a phoney Catholic, a phoney nobleman, a phoney minister. He simply had to drop his mask, or die in disguise.

The most subtle of Beaumarchais's many commentators, Pomeau, Van Tieghem and Scherer, stress the contradictions in his character, his work and his life, but apparently prefer to leave the mystery of the man intact. Must we, in our turn, conclude that his life is an enigma, and turn our backs on the sphinx? I don't think so, for the sphinx is constantly calling out to us, whispering the right answer, clueing us in on the riddle. We need only listen, or read.

We know that Figaro and Beaumarchais are one and the same person. No secret about that. Having recognized that fact, we are bound to accept the consequences. If Beaumarchais is Figaro, Almaviva is society, absolute monarchy. Bartholo, Bazile, Brid'oison are the king's accomplices, his lackeys in the real sense. We are left with the women, Rosine and Suzanne. They are there for the taking, and they are taken. Almaviva wants both of them. Figaro helps him to get the former and refuses to give him the latter, as he wants to keep her for himself. We shall be returning to this point. For the time being, I merely wanted to put you on the track, every bend of which I know by heart. Beaumarchais (Figaro) serves the king (Almaviva) when his cause is just (Rosine) and fights him when he intends to exercise his tyranny (Suzanne, the *jus primæ noctis*).

None the less to serve and to fight, in 1780, when your name was Beaumarchais, a borrowed name, when you had reached the top by charm and cunning and had to *come out*, i.e. proclaim the truth to all and sundry, required both flexibility and rigidity. The whole of Beaumarchais's genius is contained in this ambiguity. *The Marriage*, again. The king had declared in public that it would never be performed. No appeal from that court. But Beaumarchais was in the habit of rejecting every verdict. And of turning the sentence against his judges. A parliament had reprimanded him and deprived him of his rights; he had beaten that parliament and become a statesman. Louis XVI had banned *The Marriage*; it would be performed, and the king would be overthrown.

In his fight for victory Beaumarchais had to scheme and man-oeuvre. The king held his court cards, but Beaumarchais held his trumps. The confrontation, which lasted for two years, was played out in the *salons* and on the desks of the censors – all six of them.

In the course of these two years of intriguing, the king's faction remained much as it had been at the outset – the Minister of Justice, the Comte de Provence and, inevitably, a writer or two. On the other hand, support for Beaumarchais grew daily. The Comte d'Artois soon took the opposite stand to his brother's, and he brought with him Mme de Polignac, the Princesse de Lamballe, the Maréchale de Richelieu and her son the Duc de Fronsac. 'Every day,' wrote Mme Campan, secretary to Marie-Antoinette, 'you could hear people saying, "I have been to or am going to a reading of Beaumarchais's play." ' Curiosity reached such a pitch that the fame of *The Marriage* even reached the court of Russia. Catherine the Great made it known that she was prepared to produce the comedy in St Petersburg, and the Grand Duke of Russia, alias the Comte du Nord, the future Paul I, travelled to France to hear the play that was the talk of Europe. In the end Louis XVI irritably agreed to allow *The Marriage* to be performed privately at the Théâtre des Menus-Plaisirs at Versailles, by the actors of the Comédie Française.

The play was rehearsed under the author's direction for thirty days. The performance was due to take place on 13 June 1783. Two hours before the curtain went up the Comte d'Artois's guests were already fighting for the best seats. Ten minutes before curtain up the Duc de Villequier arrived with express orders from the king banning the performance. An angry uproar greeted his announcement. Mme Campan, who was there, writes: 'All the disappointed hopes aroused such discontent that never were the words "oppression" and "tyranny" pronounced in the days preceding the downfall of the crown with more feeling and vehemence than they were then.' Louis XVI was getting clumsy in his dealings with Beaumarchais. The author 'patiently put the play back on its shelf once again, until such time as another incident brought it out again', and left for Britain to serve his king and country. Naturally, the British begged him to allow them to produce the banned play, but he hedged, as he had done with the Empress of Russia.

Meanwhile, back in Versailles, the fickle monarch was giving way once more, allowing the Comte de Vandreuil to present a single performance of *The Marriage* at his residence in Gennevilliers. On his return to Paris, and before accepting Vandreuil's invitation, Beaumarchais obtained a written assurance from Lenoir, Sartines's successor as chief of police, that this private performance wouldn't affect the right of the Comédie Française to put on his play in public – a shrewd move that opened a new line of attack.

On 21 or 22 September the whole court drove off to Gennevilliers behind the splendid coaches of the Comte d'Artois and Mme de Polignac. Marie-Antoinette, who had obtained the king's permission to attend the performance, had to drop out at the last minute, saying that she was unwell. The last rays of summer shone that evening. It was so hot at Gennevilliers that Beaumarchais had to use the pommel of his cane to smash the windowpanes in the little theatre to prevent the packed audience from suffocating. Once the curtain went up there was a general swoon of pleasure. Mme Lebrun, who was the Vandreuils' guest at the time, summed the evening up by saying that Beaumarchais had 'broken the windows twice over'. In other words, his play was a smash hit.

Meanwhile the play was undergoing scrutiny from the censors. It had been accepted by the Comédie Française in 1781, and the king's chief censor, M. Coqueley, had been called in to give his opinion. When the king said no, the second censor, M. Suard, immortalized in Beaumarchais's line about 'the vile night insect', deemed it wise to reject the work. M. Gaillard, a member of the Académie Française and an austere historian with little enthusiasm for the theatre, was honest and brave enough to say that he liked the play when he was consulted in his turn. The fourth censor, M. Guidi, who hadn't been anywhere near a theatre for thirty years, was much less favourable. The baton passed to Desfontaines, the fifth censor, who read the play four times, 'line by line', and concluded that with a few minor changes it might be performed. The sixth and last censor, Bret, approved it outright. Was that the end of the matter? No. Six censors in a row don't constitute a tribunal. Cannily, Beaumarchais demanded one. The Baron de Breteuil, Minister of State, played along with him. He got together in his office an august assembly of 'academicians, censors, wits and courtiers . . . to discuss the principle, the substance, the form and the diction of this play, scene by scene, line by line, and word by word'.

This literary brains trust met in March 1784, in the presence of envoys of the king, who had been alerted by Beaumarchais himself. Louis XVI had few illusions left in any case: 'You'll see,' he said. 'Beaumarchais will get a better hearing than the Keeper of the Rolls.' The Baron de Breteuil called the meeting to order, and Beaumarchais opened his manuscript. Everyone stopped talking. Fleury, a member of the Comédie Française co-opted on to the tribunal, took notes for his memoirs:

> To begin with, M. de Beaumarchais announced that he would submit unreservedly to every cut and change that the gentlemen and even the ladies present might deem appropriate. He read, he was stopped, comments were made and objections filed. At every interruption he gave in,

then turned round and defended the slightest details with such skill, verve, logic and wit that his censors withdrew their objections. There was laughter, joking and applause: 'The work is unique.' Everyone wanted to add something of his own . . . M. de Breteuil suggested a witticism, Beaumarchais accepted it and thanked him for the present: 'It will save the fourth act!' Mme de Matignon contributed the colour of the little page's ribbon. The colour was adopted, and would become fashionable . . . 'No,' M. de Chamfort used to say, referring to this hearing, 'no, I have never heard a magician like him!' Everything that Beaumarchais said in his play's defence was infinitely more witty, original and even more comic than the most ingenious and amusing aspects of his new comedy.

As always in his great battles, Beaumarchais was supported by a small but extremely gifted group of friends. Among those who campaigned for him in 1780 were two extraordinary people, the Prince and Princess de Nassau-Siegen. Half-German, half-French, the prince, whose essential quandary was not unlike that of the son of a nobody, fathered himself by becoming a boy hero in the French army. As a youth, he went round the world with Bougainville and fought tigers single-handed. A colonel at twenty, a hero of innumerable campaigns, Nassau was 'more famous that he was esteemed'. Like his friend Beaumarchais, he was a *rara avis*, and for that very reason he upset people. The two men met and immediately became friends, thanks to their common dislike of Britain. Nassau asked Rodrigue to help him equip a privateer force to invade the British-held island of Jersey. Beaumarchais agreed, but at the last minute Louis XVI vetoed the project. Later on, Nassau's conduct during the siege of Gibraltar earned him the title of grandee from the Spanish and a no less noble, 'Well done, sir,' from the British.

In civilian life, Nassau played hit and miss, not with his life, but with life in general. He was an inveterate rake. To make matters worse he had just fallen madly in love with the divorced Princess Sanguska. This young and beautiful Polish aristocrat had the same qualities and faults as her lover. Together they ruined themselves twice daily. As naïve as they were charming, they meant to have a church wedding. Since the pope had said no, they went to consult God, i.e. Beaumarchais, who, probably because he'd caught their germs, was mad enough to imagine that he could get round the Archbishop of Paris and fix everything. Archbishop Beaumont had the greatest trouble explaining to him that marrying a divorcee was against every principle of the Roman Catholic Church. Beaumarchais went off in a huff, I imagine, and with his religious convictions not greatly strengthened. He got more satisfaction from Louis XVI, who agreed to the marriage, declaring that the previous one was null and void because it had been contracted in Poland! The solution was simple, but it took brains (as they say) to think of it.

Since he had become a Spanish grandee, Nassau had taken it upon himself to honour his rank with sumptuous receptions and gambling parties. To pay the bills, or merely to pay for their lunch, for they were always broke, the Nassaus had become accustomed to asking Beaumarchais for 'loans'. The princess called him 'Bonmarchais', a nickname which to French ears has a comic ring of the bargain basement about it. Loménie quotes a few of the notes she sent him almost daily, one of which reads: 'My dear Bonmarchais, I am desperate, but I simply have to go to Versailles on business tomorrow and I haven't a penny. Do send me a few *louis* if you can.' Beaumarchais, who adored them both, never refused them a loan, knowing that he would never get it back. By the end of three years the Nassaus were in his debt to the tune of 125,000 francs. When the prince went off to join his regiment Beaumarchais always wrote: 'Whatever you do, don't get yourself killed!' It is only fair to add, however, that the Nassaus would have given their lives for Beaumarchais in return. And the prince fought to overcome Louis XVI's resistance to *The Marriage of Figaro* as valiantly as he had battled with tigers. Later on, whenever he left France on active service Nassau was in the habit of packing his old friend's comedy in his trunk and having it acted in every large town he came to, directing the rehearsals himself.

He knew Beaumarchais's production by heart, in fact. When Louis XVI eventually gave in, he went with the author to the Comédie Française and stayed with him night and day throughout the rehearsals, right up to 27 April 1784, one of the three or four great dates in the history of the French theatre.

It was a Tuesday. The curtain was due to go up at six in the evening. The indescribable excitement aroused by the event, together with the author's fame and the jealousy he had always inspired, unnerved the actors – after three years of controversy and fervent expectation,

The Marriage might disappoint its audience. Beaumarchais's friends were also worried about the huge throng outside the theatre. Four or five thousand people had been crowding the streets round the newly opened Odéon since ten in the morning, eight hours before curtain up. Unbroken lines of carriages stretched as far as the Seine, creating havoc in the adjoining streets. At twelve, the gates of the theatre gave way in the crush and the imposing array of guards was forced to retreat. Three people trying to get places in the pit were crushed to death and couldn't be extricated; packed upright in the incredible jam of human bodies, they seemed to be waiting for the show to start like all the rest. Inside the theatre, a select few were whiling away the hours backstage in less uncomfortable surroundings. Fleury, who had helped Beaumarchais during the rehearsals, writes:

> Inside, there was a further spectacle. Nothing but plates clanging, forks clinking and bottles popping fit to split your ear drums. Our sanctuary had been turned into an inn! Three hundred people were dining in our dressing-rooms so as to be closer to the box office at opening time. The fat Marquise de Montmorin had somehow squeezed herself into Mlle Olivier's pretty little cubby-hole; the gracious Mme de Sénectère lost her dinner in the crush and had to beg a sandwich from Désessarts.

At 4.30, every seat in the sparkling new auditorium ('a quarry of white sugar') was taken. The aisles and steps gave asylum to noble bottoms that had failed to obtain seats. To use a favourite word of those times, the atmosphere was electric. Through the peephole, Fleury took a last look at the audience:

> What an audience it was! Shall I name the illustrious lords, the noble ladies, the talented artistes, the famous authors, the wealthy fashionables who were present that night? What brilliant rows of private boxes! The lovely Princesse de Lamballe, the Princesse de Chimay, the nonchalant Mme de Laascuse . . . The witty Marquise d'Andlau, the supreme Mme de Châlons . . . the lovely Mme de Balby, Mme de Simiane, lovelier still, Mmes de La Châtre, Matignon and Dudrenenc in the same box. All brilliant and sparkling, greeting one another, talking – a magnificent array of rounded arms, white shoulders, swans' necks, diamond necklaces, silk dresses, blue, pink, white, swirling rainbows . . . leaning, waving, chattering excitedly, impatient to applaud, impatient to denigrate, all for Beaumarchais and due to Beaumarchais.

The hero of this weird ceremony was concealed from public view

behind a latticed screen. In the box with him were . . . A courtesan or
two? You must be joking. Artois or Gudin? Wrong again. Julie and
Marie-Thérèse? Come, now! Who, then? To witness the opening of
The Marriage 'from a dark nook', M. de Beaumarchais had as his
guests two ecclesiastics, Abbé de Calonne and Abbé Sabathier. Two
hours earlier the two priests and the author had dined together.
Beaumarchais had promised them 'a fine uproar'. He had added: 'I
conceived this child in joy. May it please the gods that I give birth
painlessly. I can already feel the pangs and my pregnancy wasn't a
happy one. I shall need some comforting and some highly spiritual
assistance at the moment of spasm, and I am counting on you to
provide it.'

The two priests merely had to absolve him of pride. The play
received such clamours of enthusiasm as the Comédie Française had
never heard. The audience applauded almost every line, with the
result that the performance lasted for over five hours. It was an
unprecedented triumph – sixty-eight performances in a row (an
unequalled run in those days), 350,000 *livres* in takings, 40,000 *livres*
in royalties. For the first time in French history, a play had made its
author rich.

Most extraordinary of all, this money-spinning comedy was also a
step towards the revolution of 1789. Opinions differ on this score, as
they must and as I have already pointed out. In general, the literary
world has played down, or even denied, the historical implications of
The Marriage. This wasn't the opinion of three men who were quite
important at the time, I feel:

> LOUIS XVI: We should have to destroy the Bastille if a performance of this
> play was not to be a dangerous blunder.
>
> DANTON: Figaro has killed the aristocracy.
>
> NAPOLEON: If I had been king, a man such as he would have been locked
> up. There would have been an outcry, but what a service it would have
> rendered to society! . . . *The Marriage of Figaro* is already the revolution in
> action.

Between the statesmen and the critics there appears to be a misunderstanding, to say the least. The facts of the matter, as I see them,
are as follows. Beaumarchais was not by any means a revolutionary,
but he did without the slightest doubt serve the cause of the revolu-

tion. As he was perfectly aware of the 'uproar' that he was going to create with certain pungent lines in his play, as he knew of the king's opposition to it, and as he persistently strove to overcome that opposition, we are forced to accept the premiss that *The Marriage* was a deliberate political act. He took all these risks knowingly. At the same time, he was first and foremost a reformer. Arbitrary rule, privilege, the social code incensed him all his life, but in his rejection of the system he went no further than the *philosophes* and the *encyclopédistes*. Unlike Voltaire, Montesquieu or Rousseau, however, he had practical experience of politics; he had actually come to grips with the government of his day, i.e. he had appreciated its strengths and its weaknesses. Furthermore, his American adventure had taught him that high ideals and practice are not necessarily incompatible. From this point of view, his commitment, his self-commitment, went farther than the others'. All the same, even though he must be regarded as having been largely responsible for 1789, the year that put his theories into practice, it is quite out of the question to identify him with the revolution after 1789. The fall of the monarchy and 'the Terror' of 1792 and 1793 surprised and appalled him.

That was his position as a statesman and as a citizen. As the author of *The Marriage*, however, he was undeniably a revolutionary, and this is the cause of all the confusion, because his comedy depicts a man, himself, who cannot *exist* unless he overthrows the *status quo* and turns the world topsy-turvy. In the absence of Figaro, their percussion cap, the ideas contained in *The Marriage* would have misfired miserably. I am convinced that as soon as the 1784 audience realized who Figaro was, the identity of Almaviva and the contemporary implications of the work couldn't fail to strike them.

It is generally agreed that the source of *The Marriage* was the preface to *The Barber*. Beaumarchais himself seems to say so: 'The late Prince de Conti challenged me publicly to make a play out of my preface to *The Barber* . . . I replied that if I put this character on the stage for a second time, since I would portray him at a later stage in his life (and hence shrewder and wiser than ever), it would be a different kettle of fish, and a moot point as to whether the play would ever see the light of day.' Basing their verdict on this statement of Beaumarchais's, the critics generally reckon that the composition of *The Marriage* was in fact fortuitous, in other words he could easily have not written it. But if we read carefully it is obvious that Beaumarchais was saying more than this: 'It would be a different kettle of fish, and a moot point as to whether the play would ever see the light of day.' If Beaumarchais knew beforehand that his work might never be performed, it must have been because he knew in advance what its tone would be. No, the source of *The Marriage* goes back much farther than the preface to *The Barber*. It goes back to the *fils* Caron, who in 1760 leapt at 'the stupid preconceptions that people have in this country'. At that time, however, he could merely add, 'As I can't change the prejudice I must perforce submit.' What is Figaro if not a valet who suddenly refuses to submit? That was the real bearing of Conti's challenge: I dare you, Beaumarchais. He accepted the dare. Having put everything into *The Marriage*, he had nothing left to say or write. As we shall see, he lost his inspiration and his literary genius overnight, once his mission had been fulfilled.

No one could tell from all this that we have been discussing one of the most entertaining comedies in the French language. It might be objected that these political and psychological considerations are out of place here. But I don't think they are. *The Marriage* remains a masterpiece that audiences can appreciate on several levels, any of which will make them laugh – which is the main thing. But in the biography of a man who was not only an entertaining author, we are bound to take the same road, and the same short cuts, as he did. And isn't it a remarkable fact that Beaumarchais crammed more ideas into a single comedy than are contained in Brecht's entire output? And isn't it true that the French are better at comedy than at tragedy, so long as they are not aiming to depict passion? And who would Napoleon want to lock up these days? No one, I fear.

I shan't be brazen enough to remind you of the plot of *The Marriage* as I did for *Eugénie* and will do for *Tarare*. Although it is rarely performed outside France (and seldom in France, because of its length), it is very widely known. Beaumarchais wrote only two comedies, but both are masterpieces. Rossini and Mozart made no mistake about that, with the result that today Figaro belongs both to literature and to music – in our collective unconscious, or at least in our collective memories, he has a foot in each art and is multinational. None the less, before we return to Beaumarchais in the guise of Figaro, we can read the author's own summary of his play: 'The most trifling of plots: a Spanish nobleman, in love with a girl whom he wishes to seduce; and the efforts that the girl, the man to whom she is betrothed and the nobleman's wife make together to thwart an absolute master whose rank, fortune and profligacy make him all-powerful. That's all, nothing more. The play is before you.'

That's all, nothing more. The play is before us. We know Beaumarchais so well that we realize that this is a wink in our direction. It is up to us to establish the difference between the most trifling of plots (that's all, nothing more), and the play that is before us. Let's take a closer look at it.

In his edition of *The Marriage* Pol Gaillard analyses the different facets of this comedy, each of which glitters in its own way and would probably have sufficed to make the play a success. Beaumarchais's genius enables him to merge several distinct literary *genres* into one and produce a veritable *marriage* of manners and styles that would appear to be incompatible – social satire, comedy of intrigue, pure vaudeville, character study and so on. But Pol Gaillard's list misses out the essential: Figaro. Or, if you prefer, Beaumarchais. *The Marriage* is also, and above all, an autobiography, in which Beaumarchais reveals himself, defines himself and puts his cards on the table. All we need to do to realize that this is so is to turn to the play. If we read Figaro's speeches without reference to the context, the portly valet suddenly vanishes and Beaumarchais himself stands revealed before us.

If proof is required, here are a few significant examples:

FIGARO (*alone, addressing Count Almaviva*): Ah, my lord, my dear lord! Trying to have me on, are you? I was just wondering why he took me on as his concierge and then whisked me off to his embassy and made me a diplomatic courier. I see what you're at, Count: three promotions at once; you, a pro-minister; me, a political stuntman; and Suzanne, the lady of the house, the pocket ambassadress. And then, whip up, courier! And while I'd be galloping off in one direction, in t'other you'd be gaily taking my sweetheart to see your roses! While I was mucking myself up and breaking my back to honour your name, you'd condescend to chip in with a further claimant to mine! What generosity! What a fine tit for tat! But things have gone too far, my lord! You can't go round London standing in for your master and your valet at the same time. You can't be the foreign representative of both the king and me. That's too much by half. It's just too much.

SUZANNE: Trust him to lead an intrigue.

FIGARO: Two, three, four at the same time – a lovely, tangled web of them. I was born to be a courtier.

SUZANNE: They say it's such a hard job!

FIGARO: Receiving, taking and asking: that's the secret in three words.

ALMAVIVA: You used to tell me everything.

FIGARO: And now I hide nothing from you . . . Come, my lord, let's not humiliate a man who serves us well, lest we make him useless as a valet.

ALMAVIVA: Why is there always something fishy in what you get up to?

FIGARO: Everything seems fishy to those who are angling for a catch . . .

ALMAVIVA: With character and intelligence, you might get promotion some day.

FIGARO: Intelligence to get promotion? You must take me for a fool, my lord. Mediocre and toadying, that's all you need to be to get on.

ALMAVIVA: With a little study of politics under my guidance . . .

FIGARO: I know. Pretending to be ignorant of what you know and to know what you're ignorant of. To understand what you don't understand and not to listen to what you hear. Above all, to be able to do what you can't. Your greatest secret must often be to hide the fact that there isn't one. You must lock yourself in your room to sharpen quill after quill, and appear profound, when in fact you're shallow and blunt; act a part well or badly; hire spies and pension off traitors; melt seals; intercept letters; and attempt to ennoble the paltriness of the means by the importance of the ends. On my life, that's politics for you!

ALMAVIVA: Politics? You mean intrigue!

FIGARO: Politics, intrigue, as you will. But as I regard them as somewhat germain, not for me, thank you. In the words of the song of Good King Henry, 'I prefer my sweet mistress, trala.'

BARTHOLO (*pointing at Marceline*): There's your mother.

FIGARO: Foster-mother?

BARTHOLO: Your own mother.

ALMAVIVA: His mother!

FIGARO: What d'you mean?

MARCELINE (*pointing at Bartholo*): There's your father.

FIGARO (*howling*): Oh, oh, oh! Woe is me!

MARCELINE: Didn't nature tell you so a thousand times?

FIGARO: Never.

ALMAVIVA: A magistrate in court isn't mindful of himself. He's blind to all but the law.

FIGARO: And there's one for the rich and another for the poor.

Thus in the first four acts of *The Marriage*, Figaro steps out of the play while remaining involved in the action. The character speaks to his fellow-characters, Beaumarchais speaks to his fellow-men: onstage, Almaviva; offstage, Louis XVI, or at least what he represents. But these jabbing rejoinders, which made all the Almavivas in that first-night audience shudder with weird pleasure, were mere pin-pricks in comparison with the great monologue that was to follow. Suddenly, in the fifth act, Figaro, walking alone in the darkness, launches into the most extraordinary tirade in the French theatre. The risk for the play was enormous. No comedy audience had ever before been asked to sit through such a huge monologue – a valet, what is more, talking, not about the play in hand, but about society, life and himself. About the *fils* Caron transformed into Beaumar-chais. The *banderilla* prods in the opening acts led logically to this final *estocada*. But who in the audience could have expected such a bold stroke? And such an abrupt change of tone? 'I dare you,' Conti had said to him shortly before his death. The bitter-sweet irony of the opening acts switches suddenly to fulminating anger in the fifth. Dramatically absurd, properly speaking an artistic blunder, the monologue is that fault of faults, that sublime folly, that makes a work a masterpiece. It would be folly on my part, if, after building my entire book round this great Act 5, Scene 3, I didn't quote it in full:

FIGARO (*gloomily, walking alone in the darkness*): Oh, women, women, women. Oh, you weak, deceitful creatures. You're all the same. Since instinct will out in man and beast, is it *your* instinct to deceive? – After stubbornly refusing to kiss me when I begged her to in her mistress's presence – just when she had given me her promise – bang in the middle of the ceremony, she . . . – He laughed as he read, the traitor. And I, like a village idiot . . .– No, Count, you shan't have her, you shan't have her. Because you're a nobleman you think you're a great genius. Nobility, fortune, rank, status: so much to glory in. But what did you do to get where you are? You took the trouble to be born, and that's all. Anyway, a pretty ordinary sort of fellow. Whereas I, by heaven, lost in the common crowd, had to lay out more gumption just to stay alive than the whole Spanish government have summoned up in a century. And you want to joust. – Someone's coming – It's her. – Wrong, nobody. – It's a devilishly dark night, yet here I am behaving like a fool of a husband when I'm only halfway to the altar. (*Sits on a bench.*) What could be stranger than my fate? Born the son of a nobody, kidnapped by bandits, brought up to be one of them, I decide I've had my fill and set out to go straight. And everywhere I go, I get kicked out. I study chemistry, pharmacy, surgery – and a nobleman has to pull out all the stops to set me up as a small-time vet. – Fed up with caring for dumb animals, I go in for dumb humans and dive headlong into the theatre. If only I'd hung a stone around my neck first! I concoct a comedy in the oriental style. As a Spanish author, I reckoned I could lampoon Mahomet without treading on anyone's corns. But an envoy from . . . somewhere promptly complains that my play has offended the Ottoman Empire, part of the Indian subcontinent, the whole of Egypt, the kingdoms of Cyrenia, Tripoli, Tunis, Algiers and Morocco. And my comedy goes up in flames to give satisfaction to the Islamic rulers, when I bet not one of them can read and they slap us on the back calling us Christian dogs. – If you can't make wit stoop, get your own back by bullying it. – My cheeks were gaunt and my rent had fallen due. I could see the horrid bailiff looming up, with his quill stuck in his wig. – Trembling for my life, I did my best to survive. Views were being aired on the nature of wealth. You don't have to own something to be able to discuss it, so, without a penny to my name, I wrote an essay on the value of money and its net earnings. At once I saw, from the depths of my carriage, the drawbridge of a castle being lowered for me; at its gate I left behind hope and liberty. *(Rising to his feet.)* How I'd like to get my hands on one of those four-day potentates, those blithe issuers of warrants for evil, once a good disgrace had cropped his pride. I'd tell him – that printed trifles don't matter a jot, except in places where their circulation is restricted – that without free-dom to censure there can be no praise and no flattery – and that only little men are afraid of little books. *(Sits again.)* Once they'd had enough of feeding their little lodger, they kicked me into the gutter. And since a man has to eat, even out of prison, I sharpened my quill again and began asking around for a topical subject to write about. I was told that while I'd been temporarily out of business a new system had been brought in allowing anyone in Madrid to sell anything, even books and such. Providing I didn't mention religion, government, politics, morals, serv-ing officials, approved institutions, the Opera, any form of theatre, or anybody who believed in anything whatsoever, I could write and print anything I liked quite freely, under the control of two or three censors. Taking advantage of this appealing freedom, I duly advertised a new periodical, and believing my idea to be a new one I called it *The Pointless*

Paper. Phew! A host of poor hacks descended upon me, I got closed down, and there I was out of work again. – I was on the verge of despair. I did get proposed for a post, but as luck would have it I was the right man for the job – they needed a business brain, so it went to a ballet dancer. The only option I had left was stealing. I became a faro croupier. Whereupon, bless me if I wasn't wined and dined in some of the best homes in town – for three-quarters of the profits. I might easily have restored my fortunes – I was even beginning to realize that to get rich you don't need to be clever, just crafty. But since everyone was busily thieving all around me while insisting on my remaining honest, I inevitably perished yet again. This time I meant to die, and was about to put twenty fathoms of water between me and the world when a benevolent god homed in on me and convinced me I'd be better off back where I started. So back I went to my shaving kit and my English strop. Leaving the fuss to the fools who thrive on such things, and ditching shame by the roadside – too heavy for a pedestrian – I shaved my way from town to town, carefree at last. – A nobleman on a trip to Seville recognizes me. I steer him to the altar, and as my reward for supplying him with a wife he sets about intercepting mine. Much intrigue and commotion in this connection. On the brink of the abyss, on the point of marrying my mother, I'm suddenly set upon by one parent after another. *(Stands excitedly.)* There's a quarrel: it's you, it's him, it's me, it's her; no, it's not us. Oh, what's it matter! *(Drops back on to the bench.)* What a strange sequence of events! How did it all happen to me? Why these things and not others? Who settled them on my head? Forced to travel the road I took unknowingly, just as I shall leave it unwillingly, I've strewn it with as many flowers as my gaiety allowed – and even I say *my* gaiety without knowing whether it's mine any more than the rest is, nor even who this 'I' is that I'm so mindful of: a lumpish assemblage of parts unknown; then a witless living thing; a gambolling little animal; a high-spirited young man with a bent for enjoyment, doing every and any job to earn a living, master here, valet there, at fortune's whim. Ambitious out of vanity, hardworking out of necessity – but idle with delight! In danger, an orator; in private, a poet; from time to time, a musician; in leaps and bounds, a lover. I've seen everything, done everything, worn out everything. But the mirage has vanished, and, too disillusioned . . . – Disillusioned! – Disillusioned! – Suzanne, Suzanne, Suzanne. How you torment me! I hear footsteps. – Someone's coming. Now for the spasm. *(Withdraws.)*

No, if Figaro withdraws, so does Beaumarchais. With his purpose accomplished, Beaumarchais leaves the stage of politics and literature without hesitation. True, we'll still find him pulling off feats that would fill the lives of ten men. But from now on he no longer has that indefinable ingredient that turns the basest lead into gold. The prophet, having spoken, is a mere passer-by; and the poet, a shadow of himself.

At fifty-two Beaumarchais had finally torn off his mask. Since the days in the rue Saint-Denis he had been constantly standing up to opponents of greater and greater importance, and in the end he had always won by dint of genius and patience, the one fortifying the other. But this victory, the victory of his maturity, was due to courage alone. He had staked his all on the stage of the Odéon, keeping nothing back. Up to then, in all his fearsome battles, he had only partly committed himself, he had always held a few major pieces in reserve. But in the final move for checkmate his only piece left on the board besides his king had been himself. When the curtain fell on *The Marriage of Figaro*, Beaumarchais found himself alone as he had never been before, not even on the evening of his reprimand.

Did he realize this? I don't know. I shall be tempted to conclude, like Van Tieghem, that he was rather naïve in this respect – and yet I can't really believe that either. Admittedly, with apparent lack of foresight he committed one provocative act after another, starting with what I shall call the aristocrat of provocations – the taunt of ostentation. But surely the urge to take up stupendous challenges is common to all great men? Fear of heights makes paupers of princes; beyond a certain threshold, death is the last stage on the journey. And then it's every man for himself.

A hundred triumphant performances, obtained in spite of the system, had plunged Beaumarchais's honorable fellow-writers into a slough of acrimonious resentment. An alliance between the (jealous) world of letters and the (humiliated) government was inevitable. Unfortunately there are only two kinds of writers – those who go to prison and those who send them there. In highly organized societies there aren't enough prisons to go round, so they are extended to form camps; in liberal societies, censorship or plain silence are enough to set the troublemakers apart and render them harmless. And if I am being obvious, so much the better.

Anyway, Beaumarchais's inimitable success in his overt conflict with the crown had rallied all of his quill-pushing enemies, starting with the most despicable of the lot, Suard, a salaried censor, a literary stool pigeon, who had sold his soul for academic immortality. Suard, sweating at his desk, produced screed upon screed attacking *The Marriage* and kissing dust off the king's feet. Beaumarchais let himself be drawn and riposted in his usual vigorous way: 'When I had to vanquish lions and tigers to get my comedy produced, do you think, after my success, that I will stoop like a Dutch chambermaid and beat the withy every morning on the vile insect of the night?' In this bestiary, the public easily recognized the vile insect of the night – Suard, of course; but it wasn't long before Versailles identified the big cats. Miromesnil and the Comte de Provence instinctively took themselves to be the tigers, and it only remained for Louis XVI to see himself as the lion, which he promptly did.

Beaumarchais was dining with friends when there was a knock on the door. A Superintendent Chenu wished to have a word with him. Beaumarchais, who recognized the name, left the dinner table and joined the policeman in the antechamber. None of his friends paid any attention to the incident – Beaumarchais was for ever receiving visits at every hour of the day and the night. Gudin, who was at the dinner party, says: 'Beaumarchais embraced us. He said he had to go out, even though it was late, and might spend the night away from home. He asked us not to worry and said we would have news of him the next day.'

News indeed.

The next day, the whole of Paris was amazed to hear that M. de Beaumarchais had been arrested and taken to Saint-Lazare, a prison for whores and pimps. In fact this establishment, which was run by the brethren of St Vincent de Paul, was generally kept for juvenile delinquents, although five or six lepers were kept caged up there too. In short, the place had a bad reputation. The lion, in his revenge, had behaved like a rat. It was usual for the king to dispatch those who had incurred his displeasure to Vincennes or the Bastille, which were considered to be 'noble' jails. Sending Beaumarchais to Saint-Lazare was both a punishment and a humiliation. In this sinister house of correction, the new arrivals were dealt with by the kindly brethren of St Vincent, who had a predilection for the whip. Suard and co. must have gloated: Figaro was being flogged! Was he?

Probably not. His sackcloth jailers must have hesitated, although they were itching to get at him, because he was an important personage and because his arrest might have been a mistake. Not a bit of it! After due inquiry, Gudin and the family acquired proof that Louis XVI had indeed signed the warrant. While playing cards, the king had vented his spleen on a seven of spades.

When he learned why he had been interned, Beaumarchais flew into a violent rage. He had never intended to liken the weak monarch to the king of beasts. His metaphor had been a mere figure of speech, he wrote, intended to express 'the two extremes of the comparative scale'. He might just as easily have written: 'After fighting with giants, must I walk on pygmies?' And so on. Clearly, both the king and Beaumarchais were bluffing. Louis XVI hadn't sent Beaumarchais to Saint-Lazare because he'd called him a lion; the real bone of contention was *The Marriage*, as both of them knew full well. But the king had chosen the worst possible terrain for his revenge, and Beaumarchais had no difficulty in forcing him to retreat.

The Prince de Nassau-Siegen, hearing of his friend's disgrace, accomplished the greatest of all his exploits. He got together 100,000 francs and took the money round to Rodrigue, Hortales & Co. in rue Vieille-du-Temple. 'Take this,' he said to Gudin's brother. 'You may need it.' When Rodrigue's accountant refused to take the money, Nassau slipped it between his shirt and his coat and left. Anyone else would have contented himself with taking the prisoner oranges, but Nassau gave what he had least of – money. It was returned to him the next day. Whereupon, forgetting his shyness, the prince went to see the king and rampaged through Versailles. Louis XVI sheepishly assured the tiger-tamer that all would be well, and that the illustrious prisoner would be freed within the hour.

He was reckoning without Beaumarchais, who, sure of his rights and his strength, refused the royal pardon and stayed put among the delinquents, lepers and whores in Saint-Lazare. He wanted a full atonement or nothing. The un-leonine Louis XVI sent Calonne, the Finance Minister, to negotiate with him. It was agreed that the entire cabinet would attend a performance of *The Marriage* at the Odéon as a token of the king's regard for its author. In addition, it was decided that the royal family would act in a gala performance of *The Barber of Seville* at Versailles. Comforted, Beaumarchais agreed to leave his cell. A day later, from his box at the Odéon, he majestically acknowledged the plaudits of the cabinet and an ovation from the audience. A month later he sat on the king's right in the little Théâtre de Trianon enjoying a performance of *The Barber* given by a cast the likes of which has never been seen: Marie-Antoinette was Rosine, Artois, the future Charles X, was Figaro and so on.

It only remained for Beaumarchais to get married in his turn. 'Suzanne' had been waiting for her Figaro to be through with his tricks for over ten years. Little Eugénie was beginning to be old enough to wonder why her father was called M. de Beaumarchais and her mother Mme de Villers, or else Mme Willermawlaz. Beaumarchais, who had just founded a charity for unmarried mothers, may have felt compelled to practise what he preached – but somehow, I don't really think so! To tell the truth, I don't know why he suddenly decided to take the plunge after such a long time. Or whether the decision came from him at all. Despite his merry philanderings, and indeed because of them, Beaumarchais had nothing against marriage, as we know. Married twice, why not thrice? Julie, the invisible yet omnipresent Julie, may well have played some part in this long affair and its resolution. After all she was the only woman to bear the name Beaumarchais. With Marie-Thérèse as her sister-in-law, she would have to share it. Nothing is ever that simple. In any case, we don't even know what Marie-Thérèse herself thought about it all. Julie wrote that she was 'very undecided about remaining unmarried or marrying, in view of the freedom of the former state and the constraints inherent in the latter'. She adds mysteriously and ambiguously: 'Through an unfortunate encounter, having perceived the world for the first time in its negative aspects, and as her pride of soul prevented her revising that first verdict, or perhaps she was unable to do so, since the knife had snapped in the wound . . .'

Oh, women, women, women. Oh, you weak, deceitful creatures . . . Suzanne, Suzanne, Suzanne. How you torment me! No point in trying to force that door. Before he withdrew, Beaumarchais locked and barred it.

15

Heaven and Earth

After the first night of *The Marriage* Beaumarchais was a changed man. A spring in him had unwound. He had achieved his aim, although he didn't realize it. In his last ventures, in his closing battles, even though intelligence and courage never failed him, he no longer had the amazing drive and the superb stubbornness that had enabled him to defeat all his enemies and conquer all resistance in the years that led up to the first performance of *The Marriage*. With Figaro's great monologue, Beaumarchais had given birth to himself; it only remained for him to die. That is the significance, the real meaning, of 'I have seen everything, done everything, worn out everything.'

Together with American independence, his greatest venture was aerial navigation, but age, circumstances and what we must doubtless call destiny prevented him from going through with it. As early as 1783 he took part in the first experiments with aerostats, financing balloonists, *globistes*, 'birdmen', and opening a survey office to enable 'famous mechanics' to research their flying machines. Fifteen years later, just before his death, when aerial navigators had become the laughing-stock of Europe and America, he was still fighting for this 'discovery that will change the face of the world'.

While preparing his edition of Voltaire, Beaumarchais had met two paper merchants, Etienne and Joseph de Montgolfier, and the three men had realized that they had more in common than the making of fine paper. From Candide, they moved straight on to Icarus. Beaumarchais had been taking a close interest in the work of the engineer Scott for some years. As soon as he discovered the Montgolfier brothers' secret he became their friend.

We can but wonder at the workings of destiny, here as elsewhere: the men who played an essential role in aeronautics around 1784 ended up meeting one another and uniting their efforts in a common aim. There really is no such thing as chance. One day Gudin, Vergennes and Beaumarchais realized that they shared the same secret dream. From then on, they went together to the mysterious rendezvous of the intrepid birdmen. 'We attended,' writes Gudin, 'the magnificent experiments in the Faubourg Saint-Antoine, on the Champ de Mars, at Versailles, La Muette and the Tuileries, and it may be that they were the cause of greater admiration and pleasure for us than for anyone else.' Whenever a hot-air balloon (known in French as a *montgolfière*) was due to be launched, the Foreign Minister wouldn't have missed the event for a kingdom. Like Beaumarchais, he had intuitively and rationally concluded that the heavens were another America in which France needed to show her presence.

Before long Versailles and Paris discovered balloons in their turn, and the aeronauts' every exploit was witnessed by a crowd of on-lookers. In the space of a few months the strange ceremony of human flight (and its attendant disasters) became a show and a spectacle. The King of Sweden and other royalty travelled to Paris and Lyons to watch these amazing stunts. All the same, once aeronautics had become a sideshow, its days were numbered. The day the *globes*, balloons and *aérambules* stopped drawing the crowds, the heavens went out of business. But Gudin and Beaumarchais – Vergennes had died by then – battled on alone, or almost alone, in their fight for flight. Gudin wrote a verse homage to the Montgolfier brothers, while Beaumarchais dreamt up systems of air transportation for passengers and goods and discovered that aviation would change the course of warfare and world history.

Balloons had to go where the wind took them. Beaumarchais realized that research for a dirigible had to be steered towards different forms of aircraft. 'Balloons, always balloons,' he mused. 'Can spherical bodies be steered?' A hundred years later Gambetta learned from experience that they couldn't – on three occasions, attempting to escape from the Siege of Paris, he almost landed behind the Prussian lines. From the outset Beaumarchais went after a solution. Heavier-than-air flight already had its supporters, but no engine in 1780 was powerful enough to get their flying machines off the ground. Returning to his original notion, Beaumarchais, with the assistance of Scott, envisaged changing the shape of the aircraft. If a sphere was unsteerable, why not give lighter-than-air craft the shape of a fish? (Count Zeppelin, are you listening?) Scott, whose only funds were his pay from the army, asked Beaumarchais to commit some of his capital. Unfortunately his capacity for investment soon dwindled. The clockmaker and the mechanic none the less continued their research with the means at their disposal, driven on by their faith in the future of aerial navigation.

At the end of 1798 Scott discovered the solution: inflatable and deflatable pouches. After studying his plans, Beaumarchais asked his associate to improve the elasticity of his pouches: 'I should like to have a clearer idea of the way they can be expanded or compressed at will.' He put Scott in touch with the Durand brothers, 'who have discovered the secret of dissolving elastic gum, which they claim to have greatly improved for use as a proofing agent'. At the same time Beaumarchais, now ruined, was trying without any real success to arouse the interest of Neufchâteau, Minister of the Interior under the Directoire, in this airship. Politics returning to the fore, he wrote: 'Ah, citizen, do not let us always allow the usurping English to perfect the ideas that originate in our country. Let us use them ourselves!' Alas, the pioneer of aerial navigation, the inventor of air transport, died a few months later, leaving Scott adrift. Without its pilot, the *aérambule* was land-bound. And by the same token aviation was set back a hundred years.

The Périer brothers had invented a system to provide Paris with a water supply similar to the one that had been operating in London for some time. The British already led the field in matters of home comforts, but the Périers' set-up was a great improvement as regards technique and efficiency. It was based on a number of fire pumps installed on the high points. Now there is no shortage of hills in Paris. But in the days of the Périers there were far fewer adventurous financiers in the capital of France than there were in London. Pusillanimity was already a mark of the French capitalists. Water! What next? Who'd want water? The Périer brothers considered appealing to the Duc d'Orléans, but they soon realized that this royal gentleman had less scope and influence than M. de Beaumarchais – who, after studying their proposals, went ahead and founded the Compagnie des Eaux. It was decided that the first pump would be installed at Chaillot. Not surprisingly, however, a chorus of protests rang out the minute the plan became known. Many Parisians had country cottages near the site that had been selected, and they complained to the government, chanting a refrain that we know only too well – pollution, pollution, environment, environment. To cut a long story short, the Parisians had to do without water and live in their muck for a further two years, all in the name of Dame Ecology. Naturally, the nature lovers found vigorous allies in the water carriers' guild and the powerful owners of the reservoirs at the Pont Notre-Dame and the Samaritaine. The spokesman for this rather hybrid opposition to the Compagnie des Eaux was an academician by the name of Bailly, an expert in astronomy. With Maurepas's help Beaumarchais finally won, in spite of Bailly's high-flown speeches. Once he'd overcome the resistance, he gave the Périers 100,000 *écus* and made himself a hundred thousand enemies.

The Compagnie des Eaux de Paris was born, and it soon became satisfactorily operational. Beaumarchais, who couldn't finance the deal by himself, had founded a joint stock company with shares quoted on the exchange. The shares attracted a good response and quite a lot of speculation. Two bankers, Panchaud and Clavières, attempting to pull off a bull and bear transaction in the company's shares, lost quite a lot of money when, instead of falling, the share prices continued to rise. Thirsting for revenge on the person whom they held responsible for this state of affairs, M. de Beaumarchais, the two bankers called in a brilliant and hot-headed young man who had already made quite a name for himself with his tussles with the courts, his stormy love affairs and his lively pen. His name was the Comte de Mirabeau.

Mirabeau, who was quite fond of Beaumarchais, would probably have refused to attack him had it not been for the fact that, for once, Beaumarchais had turned down his request for a loan. Mirabeau wanted 12,000 francs. 'You could easily lend me that amount,' he is alleged to have said. 'I probably could,' Beaumarchais rejoined. 'But as I should have to fall out with you on the day your bills became due, I prefer to do so today and save 12,000 francs.' I don't know whether this dialogue, reported by Gudin, is authentic, but it seems certain that Mirabeau found his 12,000 francs elsewhere, and didn't have to repay them. He was signed up by the two bankers, and his complaisant pen wasted no time in composing a pamphlet attacking the Compagnie des Eaux. Beaumarchais answered it, and got rather out of his depth in technicalities. But as he had mocked the noble outpourings of the Comte de Mirabeau by calling them *mirabelles*, his aristocratic opponent waxed furious and answered with a nasty and vindictive piece aimed directly at Beaumarchais. To everyone's surprise, the brilliant executioner of the Goëzmans let the storm pass and remained silent. Disappointed at first, then angry, the Parisians drew the conclusion that Mirabeau had scored a hit. In fact Beaumarchais had deliberately adopted this attitude to help the government. In the meantime the two bankers had become necessary to the ministry, the Finance Minister in particular, because a loan was about to be floated to check inflation. The whole affair wouldn't be worth three lines if it hadn't had unfortunate consequences for Beaumarchais. As I say, Paris took his silence for embarrassment. The slanderers, who had been sullenly chafing at the bit for years, all at once woke up with a vengeance. Mirabeau and Beaumarchais patched up their quarrel and exchanged friendly letters. But it was too late, the harm had been done.

In the remarkable bibliography that Henri Cordier published in 1883, listing over 500 items, the Kornman affair runs to close on 70 items (no. 378 to no. 443). By comparison, the Goëzman affair (30 items), which, as we know, was all-important in Beaumarchais's life and gave rise to a whole rash of memoirs, appears negligible. In point of fact, I would have covered this controversy with a single paragraph had it not been for the fact that chance blew it up out of all proportion. The lawsuit that resulted had absolutely nothing to do with Beaumarchais. As Gudin writes: 'With a little common sense, it would have been possible to avoid compromising him in it; with a little reasonableness, it would have been feasible not to make public a family dispute that should never have left the confines of the courtroom; and with a little moderation, it might have been possible to avoid taking this domestic quarrel to court at all.' But that was reckoning without the devil and the man who stood in for him, a fellow named Bergasse.

A family quarrel indeed. Here are the facts.

In 1781, during a dinner party, Nassau-Siegen and his wife asked Beaumarchais to intervene at government level in favour of a lady called Mme Kornman who had been imprisoned at the request of her husband, an Alsatian banker, on the grounds of adultery. And there was nothing funny in that. In the eighteenth century, debauchery and moral severity went hand in hand. Society had two masks at its disposal and wore them alternately: libertinism *à la* Laclos and censoriousness *à la* Fénelon. Justice, blinder than ever, drew her victims by lottery. Mirabeau himself and his young mistress had played and lost in this respect – he almost died and went mad in a foul cell; she was less fortunate in the same circumstances and died, shortly after her release, all but demented. Kornman had had his wife jailed because she preferred the company of a handsome young man called Daudet de Jossan to his own. The Nassaus told Beaumarchais that the poor woman was also pregnant, that the dowry of 300,000 francs she had brought to the marriage was not unconnected with his thirst for revenge, and above all that Kornman had shown himself to be a most complaisant husband. As royal syndic for the city of Strasbourg, Daudet de Jossan had been in a position to render many useful services to the banker. So Kornman had shamelessly pushed his lovely wife into the dashing Daudet's arms, and then into his bed. The inevitable happened – they fell in love. The banker turned a blind eye so long as the handsome syndic kept his job, but saw red when he lost it.

Beaumarchais was able to verify the details of this dreadful story by reading the letters Kornman had written to his rival before he'd lost his job. It was perfectly obvious that the banker knew and approved. Beaumarchais soon began to share the Nassaus' feelings, and he promised to act. The prince, who had considerable influence, had attempted on several occasions to reveal the banker's ignominious behaviour to the king and the ministers. But Kornman had many friends in the banking world and the influence of his peers had neutralized Nassau's. To sway the balance, it was necessary to appeal to higher authority. There was only one – Beaumarchais. Things moved quickly, all the more so, in my opinion, because Mme Kornman had suffered from another injustice – like himself, she had been born a Protestant.

A week later Lenoir had Mme Kornman released and taken to a maternity clinic. Louis XVI had cancelled the warrant of imprisonment at Beaumarchais's request. As his wife had recovered her fortune along with her freedom, Kornman, whose business was in trouble, tried to make up and be friends again. But she had a good memory. Five years went by in this way, without the banker's managing to persuade his wife to come back to him.

He was about to give her up for lost when chance brought him into contact with a young lawyer called Bergasse, an ambitious, clever and unscrupulous opportunist. Bergasse had already made himself known in Paris by singing the praises of Mesmer, the mental healer, whom Beaumarchais had on occasion unmasked in no uncertain terms. So the young lawyer already had a reason for bearing a grudge against the author of *The Marriage*. He now had a hunch that he had suddenly become vulnerable. Like many other people, he had been struck by his feeble reaction to Mirabeau's attack. That's the way things go in Paris – you can only make a name for yourself by dragging someone else's in the mud. Your success is in direct proportion to the fame of the person or persons you choose to attack – and to the sordidness of the means you employ. In short, Bergasse had realized that to get what he wanted he would have to aim both very high and very low. But he had no opportunity to get at Beaumarchais until he met Kornman, his stooge.

Bergasse listened to the banker's story and then asked him to repeat it again and again, so that Kornman ended up inventing things to make the tale more dramatic – he accused his wife of complicity in a murder, for example. Oddly enough, as Loménie points out, Kornman ultimately wanted to oblige his 'erring but not faithless wife' to come back to him, and promised her, in the event of her return, complete with dowry, that he would make sure that she lived 'surrounded by the esteem she may yet deserve'. But the wicked lawyer was more interested in the important people indirectly involved in the affair – Nassau, Lenoir and above all Beaumarchais – than in the erring wife.

It has been established that Bergasse didn't know his main opponent personally and had no reason to bear a grudge against him, apart from the Mesmer business. Beaumarchais hadn't even had any opportunity to irritate him, as he had done Mirabeau, by refusing to lend him money. The lawyer chose Beaumarchais because he was the most famous man in France.

On 20 February 1787 about ten thousand copies of a pamphlet entitled *Memoir on a Question of Adultery, Seduction and Libel between Monsieur Kornman on the one Hand, and on the other Madame Kornman, his wife, Monsieur Daudet de Jossan, Monsieur Pierre-Augustin Caron de Beaumarchais, and Monsieur Lenoir, Councillor of State and formerly Lieutenant-General of Police* were distributed in Paris. Although it was signed by Kornman, the whole pamphlet was the work of Bergasse. It sold very well, because it pandered to the public's fondness for scandals, particularly those featuring aristocrats.

Bergasse's style was deplorable – pompous and piddling. But he knew his clientele and was good at throwing out saucy allusions to people whose behaviour was rumoured to be reprehensible – Nassau, riddled with debts; Lenoir, who went from one bed to another and may well have dallied awhile in Mme Kornman's; Rohan, who'd been compromised in the affair of the queen's necklace; and Beaumarchais. When it came to Beaumarchais, Bergasse plunged headlong into the muck left stewing by La Blache. All the old unfounded accusations came reeking out again, and as usual they set tongues wagging. Any nation subscribing to the foolish 'no smoke without fire' syndrome is at the mercy of the Baziles of this world. They have ruled the roost in France since time immemorial, and today they are more powerful than ever. Bergasse flung himself on Beaumarchais, calling him 'a man whose sacrilegious existence is a shameful demonstration of the depths of depravity to which our age has come'. This type of ridiculous cant has always had a following. Inside every Frenchman there is a public prosecutor waiting to be let out. Go into a bistro, listen, and you're at the assizes. In 1787 Beaumarchais had the disadvantage of being a power at Versailles, in Paris and throughout Europe. Ten years earlier he had still been a victim of the régime. Once he'd succeeded, once he was known and recognized, legitimized at last, he was on the other side of the fence, on the side of the haves, opposite the young have-not Bergasse, who was merely trying to make a name for himself. The unkind and frivolous Parisians instinctively sided with the apparent underdog against the seeming lord and master.

Beaumarchais wrote his answer in four nights, or thereabouts. His first memoir 'written too hastily and tumultuous', was none the less powerful enough to put Kornman down for the count. But the banker was merely a pretext for Bergasse, who published further personal attacks on Beaumarchais, some of which he put his name to. These texts, written between 1787 and 1789, in the feverish political climate that preceded the fall of the Bastille, were aimed both at the regime and its excesses and at the man whose very fame seemed to make him a symbol of the age.

It is a strange fact in the Latin countries that scandals, whether real or invented, prelude change. The French, for instance, who belive in 'morality', cannot wage a revolution or otherwise change the course of history without convincing themselves beforehand that the men they want to bring down are in some way or other immoral rogues. France, the so-called country of reason and ideas, won't budge unless it is in the grip of high emotion or indignation. As the need creates the instrument, so at times of unrest the slandermongers hit the jackpot. Two years before 1789, the nation which was incapable of acting or of confronting the regime head-on and which was paralysed by taboos, felt compelled to belittle or defile the gods that ruled it. Bergasse, by choosing Beaumarchais as his scapegoat and symbol, was on to a winner from the start. Had he aimed higher, at a minister or at the king, he would have landed himself in the Bastille. With Beaumarchais, who was an ambiguous figure in that he was both in the system and outside it, the risk was virtually non-existent. When Bergasse exclaims at the end of one of his pamphlets: 'Wretch, you reek of crime!', it wasn't Beaumarchais he was attacking, but society as a whole as he wished people to see it.

Beaumarchais, who thought that he'd won through, that he'd finished his life's work, and whose only thought was for presenting 'the spectacle of a weary man who has retired', must have suffered deeply from this new onslaught. All the same, he got his opponent wrong. He replied to Bergasse's attacks as if he'd been La Blache. In his subsequent memoirs he made the mistake of letting himself be drawn by the young barrister. True, he easily showed the lie to everything Bergasse had written; but he never realized that his opponent was after something else. Figaro wrongly thought that the mud was being thrown at him, when it was really meant for Almaviva.

The parliament found for Beaumarchais, and sentenced Bergasse and Kornman to pay all the costs. The verdict was announced on 2 April 1789, and was booed by the crowd. But that's another story. To avoid any confusion on the score of Bergasse, I should just like to add that in 1807, under the Empire, the wicked lawyer was once again found guilty of libel, this time with respect to an army supplier called Lemercier. Heroes often have dirty hands. But I am sure the reader, like myself, would welcome a change of key at this point.

Music was a constant factor in Beaumarchais's life, a *cantus firmus*.

For many years this master of contrapuntal living considered himself to be a musician. Of all his activities, musical interpretation and composition were without doubt the two that came most naturally to him. But what is life if not syncopation? Success may well impose rhythms of its own that disrupt the basic melody of destiny. Logically, Beaumarchais should have been a composer of songs and operas. However, as his story is the story of a revolt, music was virtually sacrificed along with clockmaking. None the less, the accessories of childhood that had been the favourite toys of Julie and his family always remained within reach, even when he was abroad. At times of stress he needed only to reach out for his flute or walk over to his harpsichord or harp – a harp like the one that had given him his *entrée* to Mesdames, or like the other one that had brought Marie-Thérèse into his life.

In fact he was always writing songs, which came more easily to him than any other form of expression. All his characters, from the *parades* to *The Marriage*, sing. In the settings of his plays there is always a musical instrument, as there was in his own homes. *The Barber* began life as a comic opera. Having failed to have it put on in this form, he had transformed it into a comedy – reluctantly, as we have seen. But he wasn't the kind of man to admit defeat for long – as his comic opera had been rejected, he decided to climb a step higher and compose a grand opera. At around this time, when asked to write a motto for the new Académie de Musique, he had produced an impertinent couplet:

> The Opéra would be perfect
> If its operas weren't abject.

His ideas on opera were very precise and quite novel in his day. In particular, he wanted opera to be a dramatic work like any other, with the music translating the libretto but not taking its place. Up to then the opposite had been the case. As Gluck had defined it, French opera 'reeked of music' (*puzza di musica*). In his preface to *The Barber* Beaumarchais had already set forth his view of music in the theatre in general, and in opera in particular:

Our dramatic music is still far too similar to our song music for any real interest or gaiety to be expected of it. We shall have to begin to use it seriously in the theatre when we feel that singing, on the stage, is merely a manner of speaking, when our musicians come closer to nature and most of all stop imposing on themselves the absurd requirement of always repeating the first part of a tune after stating the second. Are there repeats and rondeaux in a play? This cruel and nonsensical repetition kills interest and denotes an unbearable lack of ideas.

It was partly to demonstrate the rightness of his views that he wrote *Tarare*. The first version of this opera, or rather its first draft, dates from 1775. 'Some day I might dare to inflict an opera on you,' he wrote in that year. In its initial form *Tarare* was rather comic, and at times rather loose, as the following fragment of dialogue shows:

> THE SULTAN *(to the Eunuch)*: If I'm not happy tomorrow, I shall have your head cut off.
> THE EUNUCH: And why not, indeed? Insult to injury! Chop, chop! When there's nothing left to cut off, you'll stop your chopping. For all the good I am in this world, I'll not be sorry.

But no 'respectable' opera could be written in prose. So as early as 1775, Beaumarchais started versifying: 'I have kept my lines short, because the music is always very long.' In fact his lines were boring. Referring to his memoirs against Bergasse, he had said, 'All my friends join together in prescribing a grave tone.' For *Tarare*, they urged him to adopt a solemn style. Gudin and others believed that as he had attained the heights of fame, and considering his political responsibilities, Beaumarchais ought to change his *genre*. In both instances, he was wrong to listen to them. As you will see, *Tarare* is a far cry from Figaro. Here is the opening scene, with the author's stage directions:

> *(The Overture portrays violent sounds in the heavens, a fearful collision of all the Elements. The curtain, on rising, reveals clouds, which, driven and rent asunder by tempestuous winds, swirl and form Dances of the most violent agitation.)*

> NATURE *(advancing in their midst, carrying a wand, adorned with all her characteristic attributes, speaking imperiously)*:

> > Enough of your disturbing here!
> > O furious winds, cease to sow discord on sea and land.
> > Enough! And now my rule revere;
> > Let Zephyrus alone this world command.

> *(The Overture, the noise and the movement continue.)*

CHORUS OF WINDS *(tempestuously)*:
> Enough of our disturbing here!
> We shall cease to sow discord on sea and land.
> Alas, we must her rule revere.
> Lucky Zephyrus alone this world commands.

(They rush into the lower clouds. Zephyrus rises in the air. The Overture and the noise quieten by degrees, the clouds drift away; everything becomes harmonious and calm. A superb stretch of countryside becomes visible, and the Spirit of Fire descends in a shimmering cloud, in the east.)

A far cry from Figaro, indeed! However, if we look more closely, leaving aside the philosophical content, the grandiose machinery of the elements, the oriental trumpery and the blood that the author spills right, left and centre by the bottleful, we can see that the plot of *Tarare* is identical with that of *The Marriage*: a man of noble birth, King Atar, means to take from a man of inferior rank, the soldier Tarare, his fiancée, Astasie. This plot is clearly an orientalized version of the predicament of Almaviva, Figaro and Suzanne. In his preface to *The Marriage*, Beaumarchais had in fact made no mystery of his intentions: 'Oh, how I regret not having made a bloody tragedy out of this moral dilemma!' Politically, *Tarare* is as corrosive as *The Marriage*:

> O future men be deferent;
> Bow down; and, all your pride foresworn,
> Await the rank you'll get e'er born
> From us, to whom your awe be lent.

At Ormus, on the Persian Gulf, as in France, there are the haves and the have-nots. *Tarare*, like *The Marriage*, denounces this injustice virulently, and calls the people to revolt.

The hero of the opera and the hero of the comedy have a not unexpected point in common – they are both the sons of nobodies:

> Rule, Emperor Atar, despotic and alone,
> Rule as you will in your Ormus palace.
> At our whims and fancies long may you groan.
> As for you, boy, parents unknown, alas,
> At our whims and fancies long may you groan.

Whether in prose or verse, Beaumarchais's obsession remained the same. As did the remedy for the obsession. If a man wants to exist, he must father himself:

> Whoe'er you may be, mortal, King, Brahma, Soldier,
>   O MAN! Your greatness on this earth
>   Does not belong to your estate
>   It depends on your character.

There is none the less a fundamental difference between Tarare and Figaro: one uses a sword, the other a razor. Beaumarchais was fond of saying, 'I am aware that to live is to fight, and I should be distressed by that fact, were I not equally aware that to fight is to live.' Which of the two weapons would he have chosen in the battle that was his life, if he had been able to choose? The sword, which depends on brute strength, or the razor, which requires sophisticated skill, *consilio manuque*? Although it may look like it, Tarare wasn't Beaumarchais, and his opera was the work of someone else – the person he would have liked to be. But in his collection of disguises there was, thank heavens, no soldier's outfit.

To set his 'bloody tragedy' to music, Beaumarchais originally thought of his friend Gluck, who shared his ideas on opera. But the illustrious composer dodged his invitation, claiming he was too busy and too old. He was presumably scared off by the difficulty of the venture (though he admired 'the grandeur of the plan') and by the distinct possibility that the librettist wouldn't stick to writing the lyrics. He therefore recommended Beaumarchais to contact his best pupil, Antonio Salieri, who had worked with him on *Les Danaïdes* (1784) and had triumphed with *Les Horaces* (1786). At that time Salieri was living in Vienna, where his only rival of any note was Mozart. A few months before he received Beaumarchais's invitation Salieri had attended the triumphant first night of *Le Nozze di Figaro* at the Burgtheater. (Beaumarchais didn't hear Mozart's opera until 1793, by which time he had become as deaf as 'a sepulchral urn'.) Alas, when there was Mozart in Vienna, Beaumarchais called in Salieri! The Italian composer was no genius, but he was charming and made a delightful guest for the Beaumarchais family. Every morning at ten the librettist called on his composer on the second floor of the house in rue Vieille-du-Temple. Salieri writes: 'He comes to see me, I sing him what I have done for our grand opera, he applauds me, encourages me and instructs me in a completely paternal way.' Indeed Beaumarchais can't have failed to cramp the style of the easy-going Antonio with his constant interference.

After receiving clearance from the censor, *Tarare* went into rehear-

sal at the new opera house near the Porte Saint-Martin. A few days
before the first night Beaumarchais, who was in the throes of his
battle with Bergasse, tried to withdraw his work. He wrote to the
Minister of the Interior to explain why: 'I have been hit by a
brickbat. I am hurt, and think I must get my head bandaged before I
dally with dancing nymphs . . . A libel suit and opera rehearsals are
so diametrically opposed that there is no hope of combining them.'
Breteuil replied by return that the king refused to allow the performance to be postponed: 'Its success will be an initial triumph over
your enemies.' Thus, Louis XVI, after trying to ban *The Marriage*, was
ordering Beaumarchais to have *Tarare* performed willy-nilly. This
time, it suited him to be beaten. As Grimm wrote on the evening of
the first night: 'After showing the ministers and the high and mighty
where to get off in *The Marriage of Figaro*, he needed to give the same
treatment to the priests and kings. No one but M. de Beaumarchais
dared do such a thing, and perhaps no one but he would have been
allowed to do so.'

The first night was on 8 June 1787. It would be an understatement
to say that it was a triumph. In the huge blue and gold auditorium a
host of guests acclaimed the first four acts, though they heard out the
fifth in some anxiety. Beaumarchais had gone farther than ever this
time, as when he made Calpigi the eunuch say: 'Come, the abuse of
supreme power/Always brings its downfall in the end.'

The opera was given thirty-three performances in 1787. The
audiences, as large as ever, listened 'with a silence and a kind of
dazedness that no theatre has ever had to witness', according to
Grimm. At the revival of *Tarare* in 1790, Beaumarchais modernized
his fifth act by advocating divorce, the marriage of priests and the
freeing of slaves. However, when he came to write this deplorable
verse for 'a Negro from Zanguibar', the least one can say is that he
wasn't feeling inspired:

> One, two, sweet slavery
> Three, four, blackamoor,
> Good white man is kind to black
> Us for him are back to back.
> Us for white man
> Do our bit,
> Give our blood,
> Sweat and spit,

Praying great spirit Urbala
For great white folk him sit out there.
(pointing at audience)
Urbala, him out there!
Him out there, out there, out there.

Amazing! As for the rest, Beaumarchais showed a kind of courage in imposing these two lines: 'We have the best of kings/Let us swear to die under his rule.' As a supporter of constitutional monarchy, he refused to yield to the pressure of the singers and the public, who wanted lines of a more republican nature.

In 1793, however, when Beaumarchais was away from France, *Tarare* became revolutionary:

The throne! My friends, what are you saying?
When for your happiness tyranny is expiring
You yet would wish to have a king!

In 1802, under the Consulate, and after Beaumarchais's death, there was yet another revival. I imagine it posed fewer problems, for the soldier Tarare, acclaimed by the crowd, couldn't fail to put the audience in mind of another military hero.

Louis XVIII attended the last performance of this extraordinary opera and can't have taken exception to the closing verse:

King, we place our liberty
At the feet of your virtue supreme;
Rule in your loving nation's esteem,
With good laws and with equity.

Since the Restoration, no one, I believe, has thought of reviving *Tarare*. For the sake of Beaumarchais's memory, let's pray to Brahma that this dismal work will never again see the light of day.

Back to earth, then. We need a transition, I think. Or a bridge. Beaumarchais's bridge. Whenever Tarare and Bergasse left him with a few moments to himself, Beaumarchais drafted out his ideas for 'a bridge over the river Seine between the royal gardens and the Arsenal gardens'. To begin with, he intended his bridge to have five arches supported on iron columns. But he was dissatisfied with this plan and returned to the drawing-board. In a month he produced a single-span bridge made entirely of iron, like those built a century later by M. Eiffel. Beaumarchais intended that his bridge 'should never hinder navigation and not be liable to damage by floods or ice'. When his plan was ready, he costed it (883,499 francs 70 centimes), worked out its financing (joint stock company) and evaluated its profitability (tolls: coach and pair, 5 francs; and four, 7 francs; and six, 9 francs; man on horseback, 1 franc; on foot 3 *sous*; oxen, 1 franc 6 *deniers*; sheep, 6 *sous* and so on). It is amusing to note that his tariff makes a sheep worth two men. But the bridge was no joke. It was actually built towards the end of the nineteenth century, on the spot he'd indicated, and more or less as he envisaged it. But the city baptized it by another name – instead of the Pont Beaumarchais, it was called the Pont Sully. In France, a minister is worth two men of letters, and sometimes more, witness the short rue Molière in Paris and the interminable rue Richelieu, its neighbour.

Up to now we have been following the rapid turns of the minute hand round the clockface. 1787, 1788. It looks as if the hour hand is accelerating. The years fall under the scythe, and time slips faster through the neck of the hourglass. Beaumarchais is close on sixty, on the threshold of old age. At the time when a man's mind and body want to slow down, the days and nights pass as in a dream. The story of those years in Beaumarchais's life rests on this contradiction – a concern with living fast and pursuing time; but an equal concern with resting, settling down and making the sun stand still. In his public life, where he was being swept along by the rush of his various business concerns and his quarrel with Bergasse, and thrust forward by his own spirit of enterprise, he was the same as ever. It was offstage, in the wings of this existence, that suddenly everything was about to become ambiguous, contradictory.

At fifty-six a seducer, a Don Juan, is daily confronted with new realities: the easy conquests of the past become, or seem to become, more difficult. And the body that was once so alert no longer responds infallibly to the orders of desire. Beaumarchais, who had always loved women, and been loved by them, without sorrow, without conflict, without passion, one after another like the seasons, wasn't quite the same as ever in this respect. His adventures were becoming more difficult, less exciting, and at times they came to an abrupt end. His wife, his daughter and of course Julie found it easier to keep him at home. At the end of a life, the women of the household imperceptibly oust the others, gradually becoming more assertive, more visible. Like childhood, old age is where women come into their own, as queens of the neighbouring kingdoms of birth and death. Beaumarchais would certainly have come under their sway if it hadn't been for the Revolution on the one hand and Mlle Ninon on the other.

Do you remember the young stranger who sent him such odd letters from Aix-en-Provence? In the end he had stopped answering her, but he had filed away her correspondence without burning it, as he filed away everything else. Well, Mlle Ninon reappeared. He had buried her in his memory. But like the seed left lying deep in the soil that suddenly sprouts years afterwards, for no apparent reason, Ninon emerged after many cold and melancholy winters and suddenly gave him back his youth.

He was at home in rue Vieille-du-Temple when a servant (or Gudin's brother, who can tell?) brought him the visiting card of a young woman who was asking to see him. She wasn't the first to do so, and he always had them shown up. He read the name engraved on the card: Amélie Houret, Comtesse de La Marinaie. Underneath her name his visitor had scribbled, in the hall, this magic formula, this 'Open, sesame': 'ex-Mlle Ninon'.

1779, almost ten years! Amélie, ex-Mlle Ninon, was no longer a child, but she was, let's see, twenty-five or twenty-six. He had her shown up immediately, and went mad on the spot. What did she look like? According to those who saw her, she had the looks of Mme du Barry at the beginning of her career. Meaning? The Prince de Ligne, who had the honour, or the good fortune, to know the great du Barry in her apprenticeship left this memorable portrait of her: 'She is tall, with a good figure, delightfully blonde, with a high forehead, lovely eyes, brows to match, an oval face with little marks on her cheek that give an excitingly different note to her beauty. Her mouth smiles easily, her skin is like silk, and her breasts are liable to turn the world topsy-turvy. Many would do well to avoid comparison with her.'

At fifty-five or -six, Beaumarchais hadn't yet become an old lecher, but in matters of love he had reached the age of unreason. There are some women, as we all know, whose beauty and charm have more effect on ageing men. In such cases a small detail, an unexpected trifle, an undefinable something matter more than a figure or a profile. And desire can be prompted by a beauty spot, an ear lobe, or a dainty foot. Amélie Houret had tiny feet, and they constantly excited Beaumarchais's lust.

For the time being, she was simply standing before him. Like all the other women who had ever crossed the threshold of his study, she had a request to make. And she was ready to do anything to obtain satisfaction. But I'm exaggerating – she admired the great man, and in most women admiration is a form of love. But the handsome man she had glimpsed in Aix ten years earlier had lost, if not some of his charm, at least some of his immediate sex appeal. What happened that first day? Probably more than an exchange of civilities, because the next day he wrote her a letter that says a great deal about the desire he felt for her and his certainty that he would be able to assuage it:

> I don't want to see you again. You're a firebrand! Yesterday, when parting from you, I felt as if glowing coals had rained down on top of me. My poor lips, God help me, were burning merely from having tried to press yours – they felt as if they were being devoured by the fire of fever. What need had I to see such beauty – to see your leg joined to the shapeliest of knees, and so small, so furtive a foot that a man might put it in his mouth? . . . No, no, I don't want to see you again. I don't want your breath to set fire to my breast ever again. I am happy, cold, tranquil. What were you offering me? Pleasures? I no longer want any pleasures of that sort. I've given up your sex, it won't be anything to me any more . . .; no more mouth-to-mouth sessions or I'll go mad . . .

Amélie, alias Ninon, wrote back at once offering to see him again on his terms, as a friend. Which amounted to stirring up the embers while claiming to damp them down. Beaumarchais promptly burst into flame:

> You ask me for my friendship, but it is too late, dear child, for me to grant you such a simple thing. Unhappy woman, I love you, and in a way that amazes even me! I feel something I have never felt before! Are you then more lovely, more witty than anyone I have ever seen? You're an amazing woman, I adore you . . . I'd give a lot to forget our meeting. But how can one hold a pretty woman without paying homage to her beauty? I merely wanted to prove to you that no man can set eyes on you with impunity. But this sweet trifling, which would be unimportant with any ordinary woman, has left a deep mark. In my unreason, I long to knead your lips with my lips for at least a whole hour . . . Last night I thought it would be a great happiness if, in my fury, I might make you me

by swallowing you alive. She would have her arms in my arms, herself in myself. All the blood from my heart, instead of leaving for the artery, might flow into her heart, and then from her heart into mine. Who would guess that she was there? I would seem to be sleeping still but we would be chatting away within. Hundreds of other wild ideas come and frolic with this foolishness!

As you see, my heart, for the moment it is quite impossible for you to hope for a meeting . . . My love is no ordinary love. You would have to love me and, in all fairness, you can't love me . . . As I'm too old to be attractive, I must shun the misfortune of loving. All this will die down, I hope, providing I never see you again.

Ah, *madame*! I have profaned your mouth because mine kissed it yet didn't die.

Woman, give me back the soul you took from me, or put another in its place!

Gudin, Loménie and Lintilhac all cast a veil of silence over this last love. There can be no denying that as the years passed its bright flames lapsed into a sullen glimmer. More of that later. Yet I can state without fear of contradiction that at this stage the lovely Amélie loved, or thought she loved, her weary hero. We shall shortly see her give proof of her feelings in a situation that was wholly tragic – a test of loyalty, a test of love. And in any case are we to emasculate the great figures of history once they reach sixty? There is a time for writing *The Art of being a Grandfather* and a time for chasing after the damsels – and age has nothing to do with it. Years don't matter; days do. All the same, ought certain letters written at certain times, and inevitably known to the biographer, to be served up to whet the reader's curiosity or distaste in flagrant disregard of the intentions of the man or woman who wrote them in the darkest hours of the night? Would the historians of today, who make love over the telephone, care to have a recording of their love talk broadcast over the air or sold in cassettes? In a word, Amélie-Ninon became his mistress and enabled him to pursue his shadow and his youth to the end.

While he was worshipping at the furtive feet of his coy mistress, the same as ever, the other Beaumarchais was playing with stones. Building a house is often the same as building your tomb, or your mausoleum. In this respect Beaumarchais did himself proud. The house he suddenly decided to build as a memorial for himself was altogether exemplary. It was like him and unlike him – we know, and do not know, who we are. In our homes, planned and decorated by ourselves, however humble, are rooms or corners that are familiar to us and others that are alien to us and that we avoid – they seem to be someone else's bedroom, sitting room or armchair. We get our houses wrong, just as we get ourselves wrong in certain respects, and we cohabit with a lie.

Some houses are petrified daydreams. In such cases, the architect becomes the servant of mystery; the draughtsman's hand submits to memory, imagination, even madness. Beaumarchais's 'castle in the air' was built in this rather special way, I think. He wanted 'a house of note.' It was noted. It immediately became one of the sights of Paris. As soon as it was finished crowds gathered to visit it. It was the most surprising of mansions, the costliest of follies, according to Napoleon, who visited it as a young officer. (He had to get a ticket like everyone else to stroll round M. de Beaumarchais's domain.) Oddest of all was the fact that the owner 'forgot' to move in at first. For several years he went on living in the rue Vieille-du-Temple, and his mausoleum remained unoccupied. What use was it, then, except as a memorial?

In 1787 he had bought a couple of acres from the City of Paris 'in a quiet spot' near the Faubourg Saint-Antoine. With Lemoyne as his tame architect he put his dream on paper and started building. As with his edition of Voltaire, he insisted on the best. Soon the dream became reality. The site turned out to be too small, so he enlarged it by building terraces, digging valleys and planting clumps of trees by the dozen. Once he'd passed through the gate the visitor found himself in another world, an apparently endless world. The paths wound through copses, and unexpectedly revealed a waterfall, summer houses, work-shops and a great many monuments commemorating great men.

As we have seen, a simple motto adorned the bust of Pâris-Duverney: 'His deeds were my lessons. What little worth I have is his.' A lame alexandrine engraved on the frontispiece of a temple commemorated Voltaire: 'From the nations he removes the blindfold of error.' Plato and the Dancing Slave, whose statues Beaumarchais had placed side by side, were also linked in a splendid couplet:

> Mankind in fitting dignity stays free by thought;
> The slave, degraded, dances on and thinks of naught.

Like Voltaire, Bacchus had his private temple; but the sanctuary of the naughty god was surrounded by a colonnade. Since it was intended to be a place for picnics, the *genius loci* (to corrupt a phrase) had posted a succulent invitation in what the French call kitchen Latin:

> Erexi templum a Bacchus
> Amicisque gourmandibus.

On the plinth of a statue representing Eros (gods rubbed shoulders with writers, and judges with financiers, in this arcadian pantheon), Beaumarchais, good father that he was, had inscribed: 'I ask of you, Love, my daughter's happiness.'

He hadn't left himself out either. Beneath a vaulted trellis over-grown with greenery was a simple stone half-buried in the ground. The loiterer, leaning forward slightly and pulling aside the encroaching moss, could read this melancholy and disillusioned message from the owner of the place:

> Farewell, o past, o rapid dream
> Dispelled by every dawn's first beam!
> Farewell, o homicidal lust
> Long feasted and enjoyed, yet curst.
> Whoe'er the blind man be who steers
> This world, he, ancient jester, jeers.
> Farewell, o great words void of sense:
> Chance, destiny, providence.
> Wearied, in my arid span,
> From climbing 'gainst the uncertain,
> Disillusioned like Candide,
> Yet tolerant more than angry Martin,
> This haven is my Propontide:
> In peace I cultivate my garden.

This enchanted garden also offered less sophisticated entertainment. For instance, children could sail round the little lake aboard charmingly carved and painted skiffs, while lovers could disappear into the enticing darkness of a tunnel and philosophers of all ages could meditate by the Chinese bridge.

Somewhere in the grounds, concealed in the masonry or in the greenery, a door gave on to a secret underground passage leading to the rue du Pas-de-Mule. This particular construction owed nothing to the owner's fancy: he entered it once in 1792 and thus avoided certain death.

The main building, the house itself, whose semi-circular façade was supported by a peristyle and lit by two hundred large windows, had all the latest conveniences, including a remarkable central heating system. It was decorated in the most luxurious manner – mostly in marble, mahogany and copper. Visitors generally enthused over the billiard room, which was surrounded by a gallery, the indirect lighting in the main drawing room, which was round, and the sumptiousness of the private apartments. Art lovers never failed to marvel at Beaumarchais's picture collection. Some authors hint that the whole verged on being in bad taste, but as the house and its grounds were razed to the ground during the Restoration, there is no way of telling. Beaumarchais's descendants have kept only one piece of furniture from this museum, this treasure house – his desk, a fine inlaid secretaire. Can we reconstruct the whole from this single item, as Cuvier used to do from a fossil? I fear not. But at least this wonderful piece of furniture gives us an idea of Beaumarchais's good taste. A *nouveau riche* would have adorned his study with a desk to out-Versailles Versailles.

Nearby, Beaumarchais built several business premises as a thrifty investment alongside his extravagant mansion: a 'letting house' on rue Amelot, with courtyard, stables, sheds, seven large apartments and two small ones; eight shops with back-shops and mezzanine floors on rue Saint-Antoine; and more besides.

All this building ruined him. Lemoyne's initial estimate came to 300,000 francs, but to complete the project Beaumarchais had to spend six times that amount. In 1789 such a display of wealth was hardly politic. The 'quiet spot' he had chosen as the site for his house was indeed very quiet – the only building in the immediate vicinity that could be seen from those two hundred windows was the Bastille.

16

The Last Adventure

Making his diary entry for 14 July 1789, Beaumarchais could have written, as Louis XVI did: 'Nothing.' It's amazing how surprised men can be when events catch up with them – as if extreme intuition ruled out any kind of lucidity. Lous XVI *expected* the Revolution to happen throughout his reign; his clearsightedness in this respect is denied only by historians with an axe to grind. And yet this four-teenth of July in 1789 didn't worry him unduly. 'Nothing.' Similarly, Beaumarchais, who, as we have seen, was partly responsible for this extraordinary mutation in history, and who was continually anticipating it in everything he wrote, was caught on the hop when the facts suddenly proved him right. Louis XVI feared, and Beaumarchais desired, the 'fall of the Bastille'. But by dint of imagin-ing it they had placed it outside time. Such is the destiny of the few men who cry in the wilderness – they *fore*see but they don't see.

On 2 April of this year, which began with the worst winter in living memory, he had won his case against Bergasse. But in the eyes of the crowd his victory had been that of a wealthy ally of the system over an 'incorruptible'. To many people, Beaumarchais had become the symbol of a detestable society – and for a few, public enemy number one. The walls of his house were plastered with insulting and threatening placards and the caryatids by Germain Pilon decorating his porch were smashed. One evening a group of Bergasse suppor-ters tried to murder him in an empty street. He fought back like a tiger and managed to drive them off. But his enemies had more than one trick up their sleeves. Having failed to eliminate him physically, they went back to their underhand mud-slinging so as to ruin him morally.

Born in the cold, the year dragged on into misery. In the spring there was a wheat shortage. Paris no longer received regular supplies from the provinces, and as always in such circumstances 'business-men' made fortunes out of the shortage. Beaumarchais was alleged to be too rich to be honest (two hundred windows!), and was soon accused of stockpiling large quantities of wheat and flour in his mansion. At about the same time, more than one large house was sacked and burned, for similar reasons, by starving crowds. Beaumarchais had the sense and prudence to invite his accusers and neighbours to inspect his house from top to bottom. This 'open day' swayed public opinion in his favour for a time, because the ordinary people of Paris are more inclined to admire and respect fine things than to destroy them. It is their bourgeois fellow-citizens who go in for vandalism.

On 14 July 1789 the Beaumarchais family and their friends watched the fall of the Bastille from the windows of their mansion. As I have already remarked, our hero, in common with most of his contemporaries, didn't grasp the significance of this event. The summer of '89, for him, was first and foremost the end of his adventure with Voltaire. The Kehl edition had at last been completed and delivered. Beaumarchais, publisher, was planning a monumental edition of the writings of that other 'prophet', Jean-Jacques Rousseau, while supervising the distribution of his Voltaire.

His reply to a dissatisfied subscriber dated 4 August and signed 'Caron de Beaumarchais, Citizen-Soldier of the Garde Bourgeoise de Paris' shows no sign of the tense atmosphere in Paris that summer. But the signature is significant: Pierre-Augustin Caron was still *de* Beaumarchais (sign of nobility); but he belonged to the Garde *Bourgeoise*. He had never considered that nobility conferred privilege – all he had was the receipt – but saw it merely as a means for entering the *seraglio* as he pleased. The violent riots during the night of 4 August and the 'Declaration of the Rights of Man' on 26 August didn't surprise him. Hadn't he been the first to launch a decisive attack on the system through the intermediary of Figaro? Hadn't his monologue, spoken in public in 27 April 1784, been a forceful, courageous and scathing demand for the abolition of privileges and a forthright statement of the rights of man? At the time, he thought history was proving him right. But the violence, the injustice and the disturbances of that summer were already spoiling his pleasure.

As chairman of his electoral district, he used his limited powers to help those in trouble, whichever side they were on. On 15 July, at the height of the rioting, he had boldly prevented the execution of a government soldier by taking him home and giving him civilian clothes to make his escape. Instinctively, naturally, Beaumarchais was always on the side of the underdog. He had taken every risk under the *ancien régime*, and he continued to take risks during the Revolution. After defending the rights of man, he fought for the rights of the individual. This agnostic always behaved like a Christian. Incapable of hatred, he knew no enemies, only opponents. Equally incapable of resentment, he opened his heart, his purse and his home to the first man, woman and child who knocked on his door.

In times of trouble, the first to knock on your door, at night, are rarely ordinary visitors – justice, and sometimes death, are marching behind them. Those two bitches were soon to dog Beaumarchais everywhere he went.

The moment of victory never comes; everything always has to be begun all over again. The revolt must be permanent. On 14 July 1789, his moment of victory, Beaumarchais imperceptibly moved over to the opposition. 'To straighten our tree,' he wrote two years later, 'we have bent it the other way.' How right he was.

Here are two examples of apparent contradictions in Beaumarchais. First, on nobility. In 1789, so that he could take his seat on the district council, he explained to those who were attempting to relegate him to the ranks of the aristocracy that he hadn't taken out a patent confirming his nobility after the stipulated period of twenty years because all that mattered to him was human dignity, and that he had been fully aware that by not taking out a patent of confirmation he was forfeiting the privileges of nobility and returning to the bourgeoisie. And he added: 'This is where I belong!' As he had been given his title in 1763 he could have put in for *lettres de vétérance* making it permanent and hereditary any time after 1783, but he deliberately hadn't applied. On the other hand, Beaumarchais refused to go back to being plain M. Caron – the abolition of titles of nobility by the Constituent Assembly struck him as being as absurd as nobility itself. Writing to his wife on 22 June 1790, he joked:

> What is to become of us, my dear? Now we are to lose all our dignities. Stripped to our family names, sans coats of arms and sans liveries!

Heavens, what a ruinous condition! I dined the day before yesterday at Mme de La Reynière's, and we called her Mme Grimod to her face. My Lord Bishop of Rodez and My Lord Bishop of Agen were just plain *monsieur* to us. We all went in for plain speaking. It was like the end of a ball at the winter opera house, when everyone is unmasked.

In other words, one ridiculous prejudice had ousted another.

A second apparent contradiction: on the freedom of worship. After battling for years to restore the status of Protestants, Beaumarchais, whose anticlericalism was as staunch as ever, took further risks to increase the number of Catholic masses being said in his district. Loménie quotes a letter he wrote to the municipality in June 1791, which is both brave and cunning. It is too long to reproduce here, but it's worth its weight in holy water!

The summer of 1789 gave him yet another opportunity to cross swords with Bazile. When he was accused, yet again, of every crime in the book and threatened by anonymous correspondents with a dishonourable death ('You won't even get the honours of the lamp post'), he answered in his own way with a *Petition to the Representatives of the Commune of Paris, by Pierre-Augustin Caron, Member of that Representation*. Some members of this town council, gulled (or not, as the case may be) by the latest slanders, had considered impeaching Beaumarchais. But they were forced to drop the idea. As in all Beaumarchais's polemical writings, verve goes hand in hand with reasoned arguments. His *Petition* has the usual faults of arguments *pro domo sua*. But how could it have been otherwise? 'They say that my life is a tissue of horrors. They force me to sing my own praises, what with proclaiming their obloquies.'

The foolishness of some, the spitefulness of others and the hatred of Bergasse, who had got himself elected to the Constituent Assembly, didn't, however, dampen the enthusiasm of the eternal reformer. In fact he spent more time around 1790 praising the virtues of the new society than denouncing its vices. As a supporter of constitutional monarchy with deeply held liberal convictions, he was delighted with the new prospects opened up by 1789. So he considered celebrating the anniversary of the fall of the Bastille in his own way – by giving a new production of *Tarare* in a revised version, complete with the verses that had been censored. He wrote to Salieri to request some changes in the music, telling him:

Neither you nor anyone else, my friend, can imagine the enthusiasm aroused here by the celebrations of the fourteenth. As the fifteen thousand workmen employed to raise an earth bank round the Champ de Mars, where the ceremony will take place, have given reason to fear that, thanks to their negligence, the job won't be finished on time, all the citizens of Paris have taken themselves off to the site and from the Montmorencys to the river coalmen, men, women, priests, soldiers, everybody is shovelling and wheeling earth. I'm told that the king is going along this evening with the National Assembly to cheer on the workers. There is merriment, singing and dancing. Never has such enthusiasm been seen anywhere. On the fourteenth, four hundred thousand spectators will attend, in conditions of comfort, the most magnificient spectacle that the earth has ever offered to the heavens.

So much for 14 July 1790. For the following anniversary Beaumarchais had an idea for erecting on the Champ de Mars a colossal monument dedicated to the goddess Liberty. Unlike any ordinary man of letters, he immediately worked out the cost of his dreams and scaffolds. He did his sums carefully, then sent his plans and an estimate of the costs to the chairman of the assembly. As always, it was 'I' all down the line: *I* have planned, *I* suggest, *I* will build.

In the middle of this vast arena, on a platform 210 feet square, I propose to erect a victory column 148 feet high reached by 40 steps measuring 120 feet in length along each side of the square. At the four corners of the platform are four guard buildings linked by underground passages, which . . . can house seven to eight thousand men . . .

Estimate of costs for building the Altar of the Fatherland in stone, including timbers, ironwork, joinery and terrace: 2,550,000 francs.

For executing in marble and bronze all parts indicated in this blueprint: 1,500,000 francs.

Total: 4,050,000 francs.

He suggested that Paris should contribute the first million, and each of the eighty-two *départements* 36,660 francs apiece. But the Assembly didn't accept the project and the great tower on the Champ de Mars wasn't built until a hundred years later, in a different form.

It was at this time, in the autumn of 1790, that Beaumarchais began writing, or rewriting, *The Guilty Mother*, which we shall be discussing later on. But it would be quite wrong to suppose he contented himself with merely writing a play and letters by the hundred and working on the project for his Eiffel Tower. In his spare time he continued with his business activities, some of them highly profitable and others less so, in order to earn enough to live well and munificently. In 1790 he was no longer content with answering the innumerable requests for loans he received (420 in a single month); he also subsidized the Convent of Bon Secours in Paris, the Welfare Institute in Lyons, paid for beds in poorhouses and gave away 12,000 francs in one day to the soldiers of Paris. Incidentally, I can't believe that his generosity met with nothing but ingratitude. In fact I think that as the years passed he must have made many friends. If he almost always managed to defeat his innumerable enemies it may well have been because those he'd helped didn't resent the fact and helped him in return. The hostility he frequently encountered must not be ascribed, for all that, to the sheer spitefulness of his enemies. Beaumarchais is no hero unspotted and La Blache and Bergasse aren't blood-and-thunder villains. The truth of the matter is that throughout his life, and particularly towards the end, he reaped what his insolence had sown. In addition, he was inordinately fond of provoking people – as when he refused to drop his *nom de guerre*, Beaumarchais.

A further cause for resentment was his continued contact with the monarchy. As I have already remarked, Beaumarchais was a reformer. Intellectually, he *was* the Revolution. But the statesman in him subscribed to the idea of law and order. In the extraordinary decade that ran from 14 July 1789 to his death, he was split between his desire to see the Revolution triumph and an equally urgent desire to keep France from lapsing into pandemonium. Naturally, his critics have intepreted his hesitation as gerrymandering on his part. Dishonesty! Beaumarchais put France first and political systems second. Under the Empire he would undoubtedly have served Napoleon, but in his own way he would have been prepared to go to prison if necessary. For, in fact, his so-called *savoir-faire* never had any other result but to endanger his life or deprive him of his essential asset – freedom. At the risk of driving my reader mad, I shall always hark back to my point of departure – of all French men of letters whose memory is still alive today, Beaumarchais is definitely the most honourable. I say this knowing full well that tomorrow eminent historians with access to the same material as myself and with the resources of their talent will see fit to revive the old slanders.

In the words of the man himself, 'Let's slander him first, and then we'll accuse him of having the bad reputation we've given him.' He continued to see the king because, half-republican as he was, he also remained half-royalist.

In the singularly humourless atmosphere that seems to accompany periods of social upheaval, Beaumarchais, half-pessimist as he was, clung to a grain of hope. Only his gaiety remained unscathed. In 1791 he wrote: 'We have castles instead of palaces, and cannons for our orchestra. The streets are our boudoirs: where sighs of love were once heard, you now hear cries of "liberty", and "Live free or die!" instead of "I adore you." Those are our games and amusements now. Amiable Athens has been as it were changed into savage Sparta. But as amiability is our element, the return of peace will restore our character, only a tone or so gruffer. Our gaiety will come back to the fore.'

Louis XVI was saying roughly the same thing at the same moment: 'It was time the nation recovered its happy disposition.' But he said this after the flight to Varennes and the shootings on the Champ de Mars. To tell the truth, the summer of 1791 was the most deceptive of seasons. The king's betrayal of his people and the blood spilt on the site of the unbuilt Altar of the Fatherland were for a time forgotten. What we would call the silent majority had apparently taken things in hand. The chairman of the Constituent Assembly, Thouret, therefore felt safe in closing the final session with the following historic words addressed to the king: 'Sire, Your Majesty has put paid to the Revolution!'

Beaumarchais disagreed. Two weeks before the Constituent Assembly broke up in euphoria and confusion, he wrote to his friend the *député* Beaumetz expressing his anxiety and disgust:

> Who would have thought that the end of such a great achievement would be dishonoured by the vilest of debates, and that we would give our enemies within and without the triumph of seeing the Constituent Assembly on the point of collapse at the moment when it ought to be getting down to business? . . . As you are about to leave all our strength in disorder, are we to count on the lawyers' legislature that we are fabricating for ourselves with such blatant intriguing, to set matters to rights? I have lived too long and seen too much not to die of grief at all the evils that are about to descend on France.

He wasn't entirely wrong. A concatenation of 'evils' – the devaluation of government stocks, the famine riots, then the war with Austria – worsened a situation that a rapid succession of ministers manifestly couldn't control. In the last weeks of his reign, Louis XVI wanted to appoint Beaumarchais Minister of the Interior. Happily, the appointment didn't go through.

The misfortunes of France didn't prevent Beaumarchais from continuing, and concluding, his career as a playwright. *The Guilty Mother*, which opened at a little theatre in the Marais on 6 June 1792, was his last work for the theatre. It would doubtless have been better for his reputation if the play had never been performed, but he had two reasons for wanting to produce it. In his eyes, *The Guilty Mother* was the last part of a trilogy. 'On the first day you laughed heartily at the turbulent youth of Count Almaviva in *The Barber of Seville*. On the second day you gaily considered the faults of his mature years in *The Marriage of Figaro*. Now see him as an old man in *The Guilty Mother*.' When the play was revived in 1797 he told a critic, 'I worked for twenty years composing this knotty situation.' Should we believe him? I don't know. What is certain, however, is that he was wrong, or was pretending to be wrong, when he made Almaviva, in his puff, the main character in the two comedies. As we know, without Figaro they would be lifeless puppet shows. True, Figaro makes a further appearance in *The Guilty Mother*, but he has lost his main justification – Beaumarchais no longer puts himself into his character, or only occasionally.

The other reason seems more convincing: despite the relative failure of his dramas and the obvious success of his comedies, Beaumarchais still hankered after the serious genre. In his preface to *The Guilty Mother* we not unexpectedly find references to Richardson and Diderot, and the latter is quoted on the former: 'Painter of the human heart! Only you never lie.' Thrown off balance by this highly debatable opinion, he exclaims in a burst of enthusiasm: 'What a sublime statement! I too have once again tried to paint the human heart.' Alas! But his usual clear-sightedness makes him add immediately: 'My palette is dried out by age and contradictions. *The Guilty Mother* has probably suffered as a result.' On two occasions in this preface, we are bound to admit, the author reveals his anxiety very clearly: 'Perhaps I have waited too late to complete this grim work which was gnawing at my heart and which had to be written in the prime of life'; and 'When I wrote my other plays, I was attacked for having dared portray the young Figaro, whom you have since come to love. I was young, too, and he made me laugh. As we grow older, our minds grow sad and our characters darken. Try as I may, I can no longer laugh when a rascal or a rogue insults me personally because of my works. You can't master such feelings.' What a confession! Its sincerity is admirable. All the same, he was exaggerating slightly. It was only in his writings that he'd lost his smile.

He would have been hard put to it to summarize *The Guilty Mother* in a few lines, as he had done for his two comedies. In the theatre, that's generally a bad sign. I don't intend to attempt a summary of the incredible and confused plot or plots of *The Guilty Mother*. None the less, a few comments must be made. This drama, or rather this melodrama, has two titles: *The Other Tartuffe; or, The Guilty Mother*. Is there a Molière in the house? There probably is, but I think Diderot is nearer the stage. Although Beaumarchais's character is similar to Molière's Tartuffe in roguery, he is very different in that he lacks mystery. Bégearss, as he is called, is a mere stick figure drawn in good black ink. He may deceive Almaviva, but he never fascinates him. There is no real conflict between the protagonists, and no real passion. Beaumarchais merely borrowed a situation or two from Molière – without hiding the fact, of course – and the two plays end suddenly in rather the same way. But that is Beaumarchais's only debt to Molière, and it isn't a large one. As it happened, he had another model for his Tartuffe. Bégearss is, of course, Bergasse, the villainous lawyer. A number of critics, including La Harpe, berated Beaumarchais for having portrayed a living person, merely to get his own back on him. I have no opinion on this score. Is it nicer to skewer the dead? It was undoubtedly in bad taste, but good taste was never Beaumarchais's strong point. Anyway, his move was a dangerous one, since Bergasse was a member of parliament by now and might well have come down heavily in retaliation.

Another point to be made about *The Guilty Mother* is that it was the first true melodrama. Its author invented the accessories that became indispensable later on – trunks with false bottoms and so on. His heroes write letters in their own blood. His women swoon and are revived with smelling salts. And so on.

The *embourgeoisement* is taken a step further by the fact that the former Count Almaviva, *gran corregidor* of Spain, is about to become M. Almaviva. Since 1789 his wife 'visits without livery' and 'looks like plain anyone'. If it weren't for Figaro, the Almavivas would get divorced – 'like everyone else'.

The Guilty Mother was intended for the Comédie Française, and the members had accepted it enthusiastically. However, as the actors had begun another law-suit against their authors, Beaumarchais included, he withdrew his drama from the Comédie Française and gave it to a company that he supported financially and had housed in an old theatre in the rue Culture-Sainte-Catherine, now rue Sévigné, in the Marais. The play opened in June 1792 and ran for two weeks. The Comédie Française actors had sent along a cabal, and the young actors, some of whom were appearing for the first time, panicked the minute they heard booing and catcalls rise from the pit. The Comédie Française contingent enjoyed themselves hugely: the play was bad, since Beaumarchais had prevented them from acting it. It was bad, as we have seen, but for other reasons. Five years later, in changed circumstances, it was given a triumphant revival – at the Comédie Française! Napoleon, who hated *The Marriage*, revelled in this lugubrious drama, which only shows that he had deplorable taste.

Curtain, then, on Beaumarchais's theatre, but not on his life, far from it. He was sixty. Now that he was an old man, and had 'seen everything, done everything, worn out everything', what could he still accomplish? At sixty, I believe, he could still surpass himself. He did so in the craziest way, and found in battle, then in defeat, and finally in poverty, unbelievable riches. His last adventure gave him the finest bearings in his coat of arms, those that are worn by defying death.

Two days before the first performance of *The Guilty Mother* an unfrocked monk called Chabot, a member of the National Assembly, had denounced Beaumarchais in the most violent terms, accusing him of gun-running in general and of hiding a stockpile of seventy thousand rifles in his mansion in particular. In wartime, when your country is in danger and its soldiers are fighting with their bare hands because there aren't enough weapons to go round, this is the crime of crimes, and no nation has ever pardoned it. Paris, ever ready to overthrow its idols, awaited Beaumarchais's reply expectantly. When it came, it struck like lightning: 'This stockpile of weapons comprises two rifles, and their suspect hiding-place is the War Minister's office, by the window on the left.'

The affair of the rifles – 'sixty thousand, not seventy' – must be recounted very accurately, because it is an essential element in Beaumarchais's life. At the beginning of 1792 Louis XVI and the Legislative Assembly were still functioning. Parliament and the people were preparing for the war with Austria, which was declared on 1 March in a fine flush of bellicosity marred only by the fact that the country was short of arms. Beaumarchais, as close to the government as ever and rather in the habit of taking over in emergencies, took it upon himself to rearm France. A week or two before the declaration of war he was contacted by a Belgian bookseller named Delahaye, an agent for his Typographical and Literary Co., who offered him sixty thousand rifles. The weapons were stored in Holland. They had been sold to a consortium by the Austrian government, with the stipulation that they couldn't be resold to France. The purchasers, represented by Delahaye, were of course prepared to waive this condition unilaterally. After giving the matter some thought and consulting de Grave, the French War Minister, Beaumarchais decided to take the plunge. The minister advanced 500,000 francs in gilt-edged (Beaumarchais would make up the rest from his own funds) and promised to put pressure on the Dutch to turn a blind eye and let the consignment through. Whereupon France went to war with Austria – and with Prussia into the bargain. And de Grave was dismissed. From the opening of hostilities on 1 March to the fall of the monarchy on 10 August, no fewer than fourteen ministers of war succeeded him, and Beaumarchais no longer knew who he was dealing with. Servan, Lajard, Abancourt, Dubouchage, Pache, to mention but a few of them, took a stroll round their office and left. As for the permanent secretaries, they seemed to be more interested in filling their own pockets than in serving their country; in the eyes of these speculators, Beaumarchais was merely a dangerous rival whose venture must be sunk at all costs.

In the meantime Beaumarchais learned from his special envoy in Holland, La Hogue, that the Dutch had impounded the rifles pending the cessation of hostilities, so as not to offend Austria and Prussia. Beaumarchais had expected this change of attitude. He asked La Hogue to reply that the rifles were destined for the West

Indies. To hoodwink the Dutch, or rather to give them a clear conscience, he planned to ship the guns from Tervueren, where they were stored, to the West Indies and thence to France. If Rodrigue had heart, Hortales wasn't wanting in imagination. However, to overcome the dithering of the Dutch, he needed to get support from the French government, which was easier said than done, since ministers lasted as long as roses at the time. None the less Dumouriez, who did remain in office for a while at the Foreign Ministry and was a friend of his, agreed to see him.

Dumouriez played for time by asking his all-but fellow-minister for a confidential report on the affair. Beaumarchais soon realized that it would be harder for him to help his own country than it had been to aid the Insurgents in America. Dumouriez was no Vergennes. Beaumarchais bombarded him with five successive reports but to no avail. Eventually the secret leaked out and Chabot made his violent denunciation, which Beaumarchais answered, perhaps unwisely, with a sneer.

Meanwhile his enemies had pasted inflammatory posters all over his walls and groups of demonstrators had begun to chant threatening slogans, calling him a profiteer. Imperceptibly, Beaumarchais had become the symbol of everything he wanted so ardently to overthrow. He eventually grew aware of this and realized that the situation was dangerous for his entourage. The faithful Gudin, anxious as ever, had told him bluntly what he thought of his ostentatious mansion built in the heart of a poor district of the city: 'Terrified by this acquisition, I had told him that in a time of revolution no wise man traded in arms or wheat . . . ' Prudently, Beaumarchais sent his wife, his daughter and Julie to stay with friends in Le Havre; but he, of course, remained in Paris. He'd grown very deaf by now, so all he had to do to shut out the shouting and clamour, to ignore the peril surrounding him, was to place his ear trumpet on the table or in his pocket. After the family's departure he was virtually on his own, in more senses than one.

In the last days of the monarchy he did his utmost to convince Louis XVI's penultimate Foreign Minister, Scipio Chambonas (ex-marquis), and received an attentive hearing. The next day Chambonas was replaced by Bigot de Sainte-Croix. The day after that was *le dix août*. Gudin writes:

On 11 August, the day after the king was imprisoned, a great multitude, a fraction of the populace misled by the rage of the troublemakers, betook themselves towards Beaumarchais's house, threatening with frantic cries to break down the gates if they weren't opened forthwith. I was with him and two others. At first he wanted to have the gates opened and to go to meet the populace. But we were convinced that the mob was led by enemies in disguise who would have him murdered before he could utter a word, so we persuaded him to withdraw and leave his house by a door in his garden some way from the gate where the bellowing rabble were milling in fury.

Gudin clearly had little sympathy for the people, particularly when they showed up in the form of a 'bellowing rabble'. However, the poor fellow's indignation is understandable, as his friend's house was being invaded by close on thirty thousand angry citizens. Remarkably, however, the crowd entered the house, searched it for about six hours and left without breaking, stealing or messing any-thing. The leaders of this band of amateur detectives had made their followers swear not to pillage. A woman who ventured to pick a flower in the garden and refused to hand it over was almost lynched. After sounding the walls and the grounds (they even inspected the cesspools), the crowd withdrew. The next day, once he'd recovered from his fright, Beaumarchais had an amazing reaction – instead of getting angry, he waxed lyrical with delight. 'I can but admire this mixture of aberration and natural justice that breaks through even in a time of disorder.' Naturally, he proclaimed at the same time that the people had found nothing in his house – ample proof of Chabot's infamy. This wasn't very tactful of him. But from now on we shall see him deliberately taking greater and greater risks and casting all caution to the winds. There are two kinds of old men – those who choose to live wrapped in cottonwool and show themselves as little as possible, as if they wanted to hide from death; and those who deliberately confront death, defiantly or enticingly. Beaumarchais belonged to that race of men who, in order to keep the flame of youth intact within them, decide to burn faster than the rest. I for one find that eminently more honourable than the despicable cosiness of retirement and renunciation. Beaumarchais decided to stay young at table, in bed, and the world at large.

With characteristic stubbornness, he started all over again. The republican ministers, manipulated by the same civil servants as the king's ministers had been, dodged the issue. They hadn't seen the files, or hadn't bothered to look at them, or had been unable to understand them. So, like their predecessors, they played for time. Unknown to them, their underlings were continuing their double dealing. Beaumarchais was visited by a sorry pair named Larcher and Constantini, with whom he naïvely almost compromised himself. As he refused to come to terms with them, they threatened him with legal action. It isn't hard to guess who their master was. Beaumarchais answered this double challenge of death and denouncement with a majestic placard:

> I despise the people who are threatening me and challenge malevolence to do its worst. The only thing I cannot guard myself against is an assassin's dagger. As regards my accounting for my conduct in this affair, the day I can do so in public without affecting adversely the entry of the rifles, will be my day of glory. I shall account for my conduct before the National Assembly and nowhere else, loud and clear, with documentary evidence on the table. When I do so, you will be able to distinguish between the true patriotic citizen and the vile intriguers who are attacking him.

Three days later, on 23 August, Beaumarchais was arrested at dawn, at his own house. His papers were placed under seal and he was taken to the *mairie*, where, without the slightest explanation, he was held for a whole day in a storeroom. The place was so cramped that he had to remain standing. Physical humiliation has always been a favourite tactic among the police, because it generally works. But with people of strong character, it fails – instead of weakening their resistance, it hardens them to pain. When he was at last brought before the magistrates, Beaumarchais didn't defend himself, he attacked. What was the charge? Refusing to import the rifles! What arrant nonsense! In a trice he convinced the magistrates that he was innocent, and undertook to prove that Lebrun-Tondu, until recently a humble clerk at the Foreign Ministry and currently behind the desk that had been Vergennes's, whom he had tried to see ten times in this connection, wasn't unconnected with the fiddling that was going on over the rifles. He was about to be released with an apology when a little man in black came into the room. Marat. He whispered a short message to the presiding judge and left. Beaumarchais was charged all over again, and again he demonstrated the facts, more incisively still. The judges craved his pardon and this time called for a carriage to take him home. But a policeman came in with a sealed missive. When opened it turned out to be an order committing Citizen Beaumarchais forthwith to the Abbaye prison. Justice is sometimes said to be lame but on this occasion it bolted like a hare.

Formerly run by the Church, the prison of the Abbaye adjoining Saint-Germain-des-Prés was beginning to have a bad reputation. Its inmates seemed to have little chance of ever regaining their freedom. The neighbouring streets were constantly full of crowds demanding 'Death for the criminals' held there. Beaumarchais himself tells us how he was 'incarcerated' for six days in a little room shared by about a dozen other unfortunates, one of them in his eighties and a former almshouse official. Beaumarchais was freed on 30 August. On 2 September the great massacre began – and it began at the Abbaye. Once again, he had had a narrow escape.

The circumstances of his release were kept secret until many years after his death. Gudin and Loménie, out of kindness to his descendants, limited themselves to coy hints. Bettelheim was the first to lift the veil of secrecy in the biography he published in 1886, and Linthilac confirmed his assertions the following year. Since then a horde of biographers have descended on Beaumarchais and all of them openly but with an undefinable note of reproof. in their accounts of the facts, have faced the truth – Beaumarchais was saved by Mlle Ninon. By so doing, his mistress, whom he loved to the end with unfailing passion, proved herself worthy of him. It took courage, a lot of courage, to do what she did – for she went to see Manuel, the Attorney General of the Commune of Paris, who was no friend of Beaumarchais's, and demanded that he should be released. Naturally, the approved authors suggest that Ninon, to sway Themis, had to sacrifice to Venus. Others go further and hint that Ninon and Manuel were lovers at the time. I myself have no opinion on the matter, and to tell the truth I couldn't really care less whether she slept with Manuel or not. What matters to me is that she saved Beaumarchais's life, when for many women in her situation the incarceration of a tedious old fool might have appeared to be a gift from providence. But I think that the biographers understandably enough get Ninon wrong. They judge her on the basis of what she was at fifteen or sixteen, when she began writing romantic letters to Beaumarchais, and what she became later on, much later on – an out-and-out debauchee. But who was she in 1792? Someone else, without the slightest doubt. By the way, we shall be meeting her again. It would be a pity to lose sight of such a lovely member of our *dramatis personae*.

After his release, helped by Gudin and presumably by Ninon, Beaumarchais went into hiding for a few days in the countryside near Paris. Clearly, his friends' only thought was for his safety. Anyone else would have complied with their wishes. But compliance wasn't one of his habits. Giving his hosts the slip, he escaped from their farm at night and walked back to Paris, keeping to the fields and woods to avoid arrest on the highway. At dawn, covered in mud, dirty and unshaven, he was back in the capital. He had nothing in his pockets but his ear trumpet. He went straight to the Foreign Ministry to see Lebrun-Tondu. The minister was out, or pretended to be. Eventually Beaumarchais was given an appointment for eleven in the evening. During the long wait he had to find a place where he would be safe from arrest or assassination. He chose a building site, where he soon dropped off to sleep between two blocks of masonry. I am summarizing one day, but there were four such days. To cut a long story short, Lebrun at last agreed to see him late at night, or Beaumarchais burst into his office. To get rid of him, Lebrun referred him to the arms committee of the Legislative Assembly. Beaumarchais went to the Assembly by an indirect route, cutting down side streets, slipping through courtyards and passages, changing his direction constantly, because he was afraid that he might be murdered on the way by the hirelings of Lebrun or his accomplice Clavières, the Finance Minister. The two ministers were obviously in league against him, because they were on to the arms deal themselves. At the Assembly he pestered the committee members and several ministers tirelessly. He saw Danton, who listened suspiciously, as he'd been listening to Bazile, but was amazed by the old man's obstinacy and courage. He also saw Roland, who told one of his colleagues, 'I'm tied up with an affair that has been bothering us since the day before yesterday and won't be settled until the war's over – M. de Beaumarchais's wretched rifles.'

But Beaumarchais did manage to get a hearing before the committee, in the presence of all the ministers concerned. That was the break he needed. It was child's play for him to prove his good faith and his patriotism. The majority of the committee members, knowing nothing of Lebrun's dealings, were happy to learn that Citizen

Beaumarchais was taking so much trouble to obtain arms for his country, and surprised to hear that the government was being so obstructive. Once again, he had swayed his judges by telling nothing but the truth:

> The members of the military committee and the arms commission attest that, on referral from the National Assembly, they have found that the aforesaid M. Beaumarchais, who has shown us all his correspondence, has displayed, under the different and successive ministries, the utmost zeal and the best intentions in procuring for the nation the arms detained in Holland . . . Whereupon we, the undersigned, declare that the aforesaid M. Beaumarchais must be protected on his forthcoming journey, as he is governed by the sole motive of serving the *res publica* and in this respect deserves the nation's gratitude.

Thus, appearing before a body of men who were prejudiced against him, and most of whom were apparently determined to destroy him, he managed to take destiny by storm once again, because he believed in the power of truth. In fact his main opponent, the Foreign Minister, was obliged to issue a diplomatic passport to 'Citizen Beaumarchais, age sixty, face round, eyes and eyebrows brown, nose shapely, hair brown (balding), mouth large, chin normal (double), height five feet five inches . . . ' and to promise him the assistance of his ambassador in Holland. That was a lot to ask of Lebrun!

All the same, he refused to supply the funds provided for in the previous agreements. According to Gudin, these funds were necessary because the Dutch government had to be provided with the caution money they were demanding, 'of an amount three times the value of the arms'. Only the French government could come up with the caution money, since they alone could provide the certificates guaranteeing repayment. In his hurry to conclude the deal, Beaumarchais made his usual mistake of trusting to luck. Before leaving Paris he did draw up a secret protest 'against so many obscure plots mounted artificially to destroy him'. But who would take any notice of that?

On 22 September he left the capital with Gudin, who writes: 'To leave Paris, who had been so lovely and so beloved of us, was then such bliss that we felt quite joyful on departing from her.' The day before the Convention had met for the first time, taking over from the Legislative Assembly. The two friends made for Le Havre, where Beaumarchais's womenfolk were and from where, alone again,

Beaumarchais was due to sail. At every town they came to they were stopped and questioned by the police. Gudin, who hadn't got a pass, was often put out by demands that he should prove his identity. 'They asked for the names of citizens who might answer for me,' he writes. 'I was acquainted with Mme la Comtesse d'Albon, whose titles included that of Queen of Yvetot, but as the current regime wasn't favourably disposed towards queens, I carefully avoided mentioning her name.'

After bidding farewell to his three womenfolk and faithful Gudin, Beaumarchais sailed yet again for Britain. His ship reached Portsmouth on 28 September, and he was in London on the thirtieth. I'm not usually a fanatic for dates, but I have pinpointed these two because on the first of them, while Figaro was embarking, at the age of sixty, on the most dangerous of his patriotic missions, a man called Laurent Lecointre, who ran a canvas business in Versailles and represented his town at the Convention, was mouthing a speech at the assembly attacking 'this vile and covetous man who, before plunging his country into the abyss he had prepared for it, was after the execrable honour of despoiling it of its remaining effects, this man of essential vice and shameful corruptness, who has reduced immorality to a principle and roguery to a system!' Naturally, the member for Versailles didn't stop at these generalities. He also accused him of conspiracy, embezzlement, and criminal collusion with Grave and Chambonas, ex-ministers of the ex-king. Lecointre had no proof except that cooked up for him by Lebrun's underlings. Whatever the regime, there is always a Lecointre, a sincere fool who is prepared to lend his name to gerrymandering. Oddly enough, the member for Versailles, no doubt carried away by his own eloquence, denounced both the Girondins and the Montagnards in their turn. He died rich under the Empire.

Beaumarchais, who didn't hear about this attack until 1 December, began his mission. In London, where he stayed only a day, he asked the British agent of Rodrigue, Hortales & Co. for a loan. The man was a friend of his, and found the money for him immediately. A bond was duly signed and Beaumarchais was off again. The crossing to Holland was one of his worst ever, and seasickness kept him on deck, cursing his bad luck and his unseaworthy stomach. Six days later he was in Amsterdam. On 7 October he called on the French ambassador. After five minutes in his office, he realized he'd been duped. The diplomat, under orders from Lebrun, pretended to know nothing about the matter. No, he hadn't received any instructions concerning the caution money, but he was convinced that this unfortunate setback wouldn't prevent the French envoy from fulfilling his mission. Beaumarchais, who had had his fill of his country's diplomatic nonentities, broke off the discussion. Given the circumstances, there was no point in arguing. However, he was stubborn and naïve, so he decided to wait. For what? A miracle, of course. Mightn't the minister decide, after all, that the interests of France mattered more than anything else, and even consider putting them before his own? He was dreaming. From Paris, Lebrun sent him Constantini – and killers. Constantini to try and buy him off one last time, and the killers to get rid of him if he wouldn't give in.

For six weeks he waited patiently near the rifles that the revolutionary generals so badly needed to sustain their war, while politicians and businessmen fought to secure them to their own advantage. Attempts were made on his life. From Paris, Manuel (perhaps 'encouraged' by Ninon) was constantly tipping him off about Lebrun-Tondu's doings. In addition, the Dutch government wasn't keen on extending hospitality to a man who was disowned by his embassy. In the end, realizing that he had lost his Battle of Holland, but in no way disheartened, Beaumarchais decided to return to Paris – where his most famous accomplice, Louis Capet, ex-Louis XVI, was on trial for treason. His homeward voyage had to take him via London. Once again, he was violently seasick during the crossing – his twentieth or so, and the only thing he'd ever been afraid of.

In London, letters were waiting for him from Manuel, again, and from the Gudin brothers. When he read them he learned that his belongings had been seized yet again and that he had had a narrow escape in Holland – Lebrun's thugs had been told to bring him back to France dead or alive. According to his correspondents, the best he could hope for was the guillotine. Needless to say, he immediately decided to return to Paris. When his London agent was informed of his decision he had the sense to have him imprisoned for debt, thereby doing him a great favour, because in December 1792 or January 1793 Beaumarchais might well have been unable to save his head. (To tell the truth, I don't know whether the Englishman showed proof of magnanimity or meanness on this occasion. Beaumarchais himself was far from happy with the situation. When in doubt, however, let us allow British chivalry to win the trick!)

In prison Beaumarchais soon demanded pen and paper and set to work. Naturally, he wrote a memoir – six of them, in fact, the *Six Epochs or Narrative of the most Painful Nine Months in my Life*. This text, written in haste by a man who was desperately worried about the safety of his family, is lacking in verve, and often in restraint. But it does contain a few bravura passages that are highly successful. And, needless to say, its argument is impeccable. In fact Beaumarchais was right about the rifles all down the line, and he had no trouble at all in proving that the Lebruns, the Lecointres and their little friends had behaved disgracefully. But, as under the Maupeou parliament, it wasn't enough to be right in 1793. So, as he had nothing but his life to lose, he hit out with incredible violence and produced in the *Six Epochs* material that was sheer dynamite. Who but he, in 1793, would have dared to print such statements as: 'I would challenge the devil to run a business properly in this frightful period of disorder called liberty.' Or this: 'In this matter of national importance, the royalist ministers alone did their duty, and all the obstacles were put in my way by the ministers of the people . . . The harassments meted out to me by the former were mere pranks compared with the horrors committed by the latter.' Or this, referring to one of the most powerful of the ministers of the people: 'A hideous little man with black hair and a hooked nose – the great, the just, the (in a word) *merciful* Marat.' Or this, referring to Lebrun-Tondu and his entourage: 'These are the men who lead us, turning the government into a nest of vengeance, a sewer of intrigues, a load of nonsense.' Or this majestic reply to his friends and would-be pacifiers:

> What a dreadful state of freedom, worse than real slavery, we would have fallen into, my friends, if a man beyond reproach had to lower his eyes before powerful criminals because they have the capacity to destroy him! What, are we to experience all the abuses of the old republics when ours is only just born? May I and all my possessions perish rather than that I should grovel before these insolent despots! No nation is ever truly free unless it obeys the laws alone! O citizen legislators! Once this memoir has been read by you all, I shall go and commit myself to your prisons.

The sixth *Epoch* closes on an appeal, not for himself, but for France:

True friends of freedom, I tell you its first hangmen are licentiousness and anarchy. Add your cries to mine, and let us demand laws from our députés, for it is their duty to provide them . . . Let us make peace with Europe . . . Let us consolidate our position here at home. And let us organize ourselves constitutionally without arguments, without storms, and above all, if possible, without crimes and murders. Your maxims will become established; if they are seen to bring you happiness they will obtain wider currency than if they are imposed by means of war, murder and devastation. *Have* they brought you happiness? Let us be honest. Is not the blood that has soaked our soil the blood of Frenchmen? Tell me, is there any one of us who has no tears to shed? Peace, laws, a constitution – without those assets, there is no *Patrie* and above all no freedom!

Once he had completed this inflammatory text, Beaumarchais wanted to publish it immediately. To do so, however, he had first to obtain his release from prison and leave Britain. Gudin, his cashier, sent him the money needed to pay off his debt. At the same time Beaumarchais wrote to Garat, the French Minister of Justice, asking him in particular for 'protection against the assassins' who were waiting for him. Garat's reply, which Beaumarchais called 'the only reasonable letter he had received from a man in office since the whole business began', shows that, even then, Beaumarchais was highly regarded, at least by some people. How difficult it is to keep track of reputations in times of upheaval! The minister wrote:

I can but applaud your eagerness to come and justify yourself before the National Convention, and feel that as soon as you are free nothing should delay so natural a step in a man who has been accused but is sure that he is innocent. The execution of this project, so worthy of a stout soul that has nothing to fear from the truth, must not even be delayed by fears that only those who want to trouble your rest, or shy friends, can have instilled in you . . . You ask the National Convention for protection that will enable you to present your justification in safety. I don't know what the answer will be, and must not anticipate it. But when the very accusation made against you places you in the hands of justice, it places you especially under the protection of the law . . . Tell me which port you intend to head for, and the approximate time when you mean to land. I shall immediately give orders to the *gendarmerie* to provide you with sufficient escort to calm your fears and make sure that you reach Paris safely. You may personally request this escort from the officer commanding the *gendarmerie* in your port of arrival.

This letter, dated 3 January 1793, reassured Beaumarchais. He got ready to return to France. In the meantime, however, the execution of Louis XVI, on 21 January, which shocked him deeply, had changed the situation entirely. Britain and Holland, which had until then remained neutral, entered the war between republican France and the rest of Europe. This development meant that the matter of the rifles would never be cleared up. But Beaumarchais still returned to France determined to resolve it.

When he reached Paris, in March, thanks to Garat's protection, he immediately sought a printer for the *Six Epochs*, and after much searching found one. With great presence of mind he succeeded in winning over a number of influential people, one of whom was Santerre, the future general and now commandant of the National Guard. He had written to him on his arrival in these terms: 'I have come to offer my head to the sword, if I cannot prove that I am a great citizen. Save me from pillaging and from the dagger and I shall yet be able to be of use to our country.' Santerre, moved by these words, had replied: 'I have known you only as a man who wants to do good to the poor. I therefore think that you have no reason to fear either pillaging or the dagger. However, although truth is one and indivisible, we must enlighten those whom we believe to be misled. I think that a placard to the people would be appropriate.' Beaumarchais wrote the placard, and distributed his memoir.

Once again, the Word triumphed. The distraint on his goods was lifted and at the Convention Lecointre admitted that he'd been misled. Beaumarchais, of course, wasn't content with this victory, and began to harass the Committee of Public Safety as he had done the successive governments of France. Two months after his return to Paris this 'accomplice of Louis XVI', this 'embezzler', a man under sentence of death, was appointed by the Committee of Public Safety, at an extraordinary meeting held on 22 May; as a commissioner of the republic, with responsibility for retrieving the sixty thousand rifles.

At the end of May, after attending the second performance of *Le Nozze de Figaro* at the Opéra (he didn't think much of the music, but his ear trumpet can't have helped matters), he managed to scrape together some of the funds required for his mission. The Committee promised him that the rest would be sent to him in Basle. He was about to leave for Switzerland when he suddenly cracked. He had what we would call a nervous breakdown. His womenfolk had to take him to the country near Orléans, the idea being to keep him in bed for as long as possible. But they were reckoning without his vitality. In a couple of weeks he was up and about again. After giving Marie-Thérèse power of attorney to 'administer his estate actively and passively during his absence', he left.

This traveller without luggage left everything behind in France, including his name. As he had to cross the enemy lines, he had once again to adopt a pseudonym. Pierre Caron became Pierre Charron, like Charon, the boatman of hell. This time, hell was where he was going.

In Basle, which he reached at the beginning of July, the commissioner of the French republic found nothing – no news, no money from the Committee of Public Safety. He waited for about ten days and then, in Gudin's words, decided to 'rely only on himself and his own resourcefulness'. But it's never easy to move around in wartime. From 10 July to 5 August he 'kicked his heels just beyond the borders of France, where the confusion was worsening unceasingly'. Eventually he arrived in London on 6 August.

How could he have been safe in this enemy capital? In fact within three days the police ordered him out of Britain. Instead of panicking, he behaved as if he had all the time in the world. He gave his guards the slip and somehow managed to arrange secret meetings with men in high places, whose weaknesses he knew, and obtain important confidential information. For instance, he found out that the wretched rifles were considered sufficiently interesting in Britain for the Admiralty to have sent a warship to cruise off Zealand. At the same time his British agent, worn down by his questions, finally admitted that in a moment of panic he had offered the consignment of arms to the counter-revolutionaries in the Vendée. In the space of three days, by dint of cunning, and paying out large sums of money, Beaumarchais got the situation under control – or so he thought.

In Paris, the 'executive' may have seemed to have forgotten him, but the army staff were getting impatient. A secret courier informed him that headquarters 'wanted success and nothing but success, and fast'. The civil war of August 1793 had made the French generals' task even more difficult. On the twenty-seventh, for instance, the royalists managed to surrender Toulon to the British. Beaumarchais, who loathed the revolutionary regime, remained none the less loyal to his views on national independence, and throughout this period wore the colours of those who were fighting to defend his country, even though they were his worst enemies.

With incredible determination, and in increasingly adverse conditions, he set off again in search of his sixty thousand rifles. From London, heaven alone knows how, he crossed to The Hague, then to Rotterdam. Discovering that the Dutch government intended to lay hands on his guns, he had the audacity to defy them by declaring that military reprisals would follow. And he wrote to General Pichegru, who was quartered about sixty miles from Tervueren, urging him to intervene.

As Pichegru wouldn't budge, Beaumarchais resorted to cunning to trick the Dutch. For example he dreamed up a fictitious sale of the guns to an American with whom he had had dealings, intending to import the weapons into France via the United States.

In fact, during these final months Beaumarchais realized that he could do nothing and was merely playing for time. As he couldn't lay hands on the guns himself, he skilfully made sure that no one else would. The historians generally put this whole gun business down as a failure – which it was, in a sense. All the same, he did manage to keep out of the conflict a large stock of military hardware that was coveted by all the armies of the coalition against France. He did so at great cost, constantly moving round Europe. A whole chapter would be needed to describe his travels, notably his trip down the Rhine.

I can't bring down the curtain on this period of his life without referring to his final 'folly': in July 1794, he attempted, alone and on behalf of France, to negotiate with the foreign powers and bring the war to an end! He might well have succeeded if Paris hadn't declared to the world at large that the commissioner of the republic was a 'criminal'. At this, the Dutch ministers with whom he was negotiating on behalf of France refused to see him and asked him to leave the country. Very reluctantly, he did so. Although he was now an 'undesirable' throughout Europe, he none the less found refuge in the free towns of Lübeck and Hamburg.

While Beaumarchais was fighting bravely for France, the leaders of the Convention first confiscated his property, then declared him to be an *émigré*. This decision was taken in February 1794, by the

Committee of General Security, who didn't know, or pretended not
to know, that he still enjoyed the confidence of the Committee of
Public Safety. In July the same year the men from General Security
had his three womenfolk imprisoned. Julie, Marie-Thérèse and
Eugénie were condemned to death on the same day as Goëzman,
who was less lucky than they were, for they owed their lives to the fall
of Robespierre. Released from prison, Mme de Beaumarchais was
forced to divorce her husband and use her maiden name, to spare
Eugénie from the 'insults of the rabble'.

The 'rabble' were still victimizing his family in August 1794,
because Laurent Lecointre had done a quick change of masters and
was currently accusing the envoy of the Committee of Public Safety
of having been Robespierre's accomplice. According to this lumi-
nary in matters of degradation, Beaumarchais had split the riches of
France with the man known as 'the Incorruptible'. Lecointre
expatiated at length before the Assembly, and was heard with
approval. If slander is a French tradition, so is stupidity – or cred-
ulity, call it as you will. 'There is no blatant unkindness, no horror,
no absurd fable that a man can't get adopted' by the people of Paris.

Thanks to Lecointre, or Bazile, Beaumarchais was forced to spend
two long years in the suburbs of Hamburg. After a few weeks of
anguish when he feared the worst for his family, he didn't remain
inactive in his distant exile. To begin with, he lived on bread and
water in a filthy hovel, where his only luxuries were ink, quills and
paper. Writing, writing, that was the only way he knew for turning
the most tragic of situations to his advantage. So he wrote, day and
night. He wrote to the whole world, but first to his wife:

> I sometimes wonder if I've gone mad, but when I examine the long
> sequence of difficult ideas by means of which I try to guard against
> everything, I find that I'm not mad. But where can I write to you? Under
> what name? Where are you living? What's your name? Who are your
> true friends? Who can I make my true friends? Ah, were it not for the
> hope of saving my daughter, that terrible guillotine would be sweeter to
> me than my loathsome state!

He wrote to the British, care of Pitt, who had had the impudence to
seize his rifles at Tervueren and impound them in Plymouth. With
the assistance of his London agents, his spy network, he managed to

delay the sale of the rifles to the British for several more months. Pitt eventually got them for a song in June 1795; but by that time the military situation of France had improved and her arsenals were no longer empty.

He wrote to the Americans, of course, primarily to remind them that they owed him money. Among the hundred or so letters, or bills, that he sent them was this odd open letter to the American nation dated 10 April 1795. If you read it closely, you'll see Figaro's irony standing out like a watermark beneath the deliberate pathos:

> Americans, I have served your cause with indefatigable zeal and have never received anything but bitterness in return, and I am still your creditor. Allow me, then, on my deathbed, to leave you my daughter, so that you can endow her with what you owe me . . . Perhaps providence has intended to preserve for her, in the form of your delayed payment, a source of income after my death, if all else fails. Adopt her as a worthy child of the United States. Her equally unfortunate mother will bring her to you. May she be regarded in your country as the daughter of a citizen . . .
>
> . . . But if it were yet possible for me to fear that you might reject my request . . . , as your country is the only one where I may shamelessly hold out my hand to the inhabitants, what else could I do but beg the heavens to grant me better health to enable me to travel to America? When I reached your country, weak in mind and body, and in no state to stand up for my rights, would I have to have myself carried on a stool to the door of your national assemblies, and hold out to all the bonnet of liberty, which no man has helped to adorn your heads with more than I have? Would I have to cry: 'Americans, give alms to your friend, whose many services have had only one reward: *Date obolum Belisario!*'?

History is merely the realization of ancient dreams. During the long cold nights in his Hamburg attic, Beaumarchais dreamed of building a little canal from Lake Nicaragua to the Pacific and thereby opening up a trade route from one ocean to the other via the San Juan river. Gudin says that Beaumarchais 'knew that the nation which would control the navigable waterway between the two oceans would infallibly control world trade'. Later on, learning that 'Pitt had intended to take over Lake Nicaragua for the British', he tried to persuade the Directoire that it would be an opportune moment to buy from the defeated Spaniards 'this still savage province and this lake whose advantages they did not seem to suspect'.

Unfortunately, the French were as shortsighted at the time as the
Spaniards had been.

He wasn't the only French refugee on the shores of the North Sea.
Apart from the many Protestants who had lived there since the
revocation of the Edict of Nantes, a large colony of *émigrés* had settled
in the Hanseatic towns, notably in Hamburg. Among them
Beaumarchais made two friends, for whom he predicted a brilliant
future: Talleyrand, who had just come back from America; and a
young ecclesiastic by the name of Louis who later on, much later on,
became a good Finance Minister – and a baron.

A few of these exiles couldn't wait to return to France as soon as their
names were removed from the official lists of *émigrés*. Beaumarchais,
who was one of them, fought for them all, writing letter after letter to the
members of the Committee of Public Safety. From Hamburg, he
preached forgiveness and justice to governments, with an authority
and a sense of tone that are admirable in a man in his position. One
of these messages, sent to the Committee of Public Safety on 5
August 1795 and published by Loménie, strikes me as being typical
of Beaumarchais's courage and his political intelligence. It was a
long epistle written after the victory of the republicans over the
royalists at Quiberon. Beaumarchais was afraid that the victors
might not be generous to their defeated enemies and urged the
government to order an amnesty. Unfortunately his appeal, which in
itself is ample proof of his true nobility, arrived too late, after the
majority of the royalist rebels had been massacred at Quiberon.

At the time he was writing this letter, Beaumarchais ought by
rights to have been struck off the list of *émigrés*. The Committee of
Public Safety, whose chairman at that time was Robert Lindet, had
taken the decision two months earlier, asking the Legislation Committee to 'consider at the earliest opportunity removing the name of
Beaumarchais from the list of *émigrés*, given that any delay will harm
the interests of the republic'. However, the slowness of the adminis-
trative process, red tape and a certain amount of deliberate procras-
tination delayed Beaumarchais's return for over a year. Robert
Lindet, who was a man of honour, and who felt responsible to a
certain extent for Beaumarchais's misfortunes, did all he could to
speed things up. After the break up of the Convention in October
1795, Lindet, who was *persona non grata* under the Directoire, none the

less intervened on several occasions, pleading that an injustice had been committed. He wrote:

> I shall never cease to think and to proclaim on every occasion that Citizen Beaumarchais is being unjustly persecuted and that the senseless plan to make him out to be an *émigré* was conceived by men who were misguided, misled or ill-intentioned. His abilities, his talents and his many gifts could have served our cause. By wishing to harm him, we have done more harm to France. I should like to be able soon to tell him how much I have been concerned by the injustice done to him. I am fulfilling a duty, and gladly so, by thinking of him.

Lindet's letter to the Directoire shows us once again that the leaders of France, whether they be kings or prime ministers or high-ranking parliamentarians, rendered homage to Beaumarchais in the most solemn and splendid manner. And yet they all let him be persecuted, because they were unable to muzzle Bazile and his hounds of hell. The most tyrannical of regimes can nip all freedom in the bud, silence writers and thinkers, prevent people from speaking their minds, but it will be powerless to deal with the slanderers, for their species is invincible, like those insects that are said to survive the blast of the most formidable of hydrogen bombs.

On 10 June 1796 Beaumarchais at last heard that he had been struck off the list of *émigrés*. 'Whip up, coachman! Three days of right rare joy, in return for three long years of suffering, and then I'll agree to die.'

He reached the capital on 6 July, and lived for more than three days.

17

A Man at Last

'Shall I be a man at last? A man! As he rose, so he falls . . . , crawling where he ran . . . , then come loathings, maladies . . . , an old and feeble doll . . . a cold mummy . . . a skeleton . . . a vile heap of dust, and then . . . nothing!'

In exile Beaumarchais had lost almost everything except his stoutness. Full-bellied, heavy-jowled, triple-chinned, 'podgy and red-faced', at sixty-four he was unrecognizable. Misfortune, as only fools fail to realize, doesn't make you lose weight.

On his return this grand old man began to behave as men commonly do at his age – benevolently. For two weeks he devoted himself exclusively to his family: to his wife, a divorcee by necessity, whom he promptly remarried; to his daughter, whom he wed within a week, on 11 July, to Lieutenant Louis-André Toussaint Delarue, who as a boy had been aide-de-camp to General La Fayette; and above all he devoted himself to his sister Julie, whose one sustaining hope during the darkest hours of the Revolution had been that one day she might be reunited with her brother. Embracing him on his arrival, she had said: 'Your old age and mine, my poor love, shall come together at last to enjoy the youth, the happiness and the settlement of our dear daughter.' In other words, for two weeks Beaumarchais looked much like the central figure in a painting by Greuze. But after the happy reunion, the paterfamilias must have felt rather cramped in this bourgeois setting, which for all its charm was altogether too proper. It wasn't long before he renewed his interrupted dialogue with Amélie-Ninon.

Here, most of the biographers blink and avert their gaze. Those who tut loudest at his public dealings are the coyest when it comes to his sex life. In particular, his regrettable affair with the 'rather common' Mlle Ninon is blandly dismissed as an old man's aberration. Or she is accused of having dunned him for money. It's true that she was rather demanding in this respect, but I imagine that in 1796 she must have been very hard up. What ought he to have done anyway? Put her on the streets? Or ask her to learn embroidery? Of all his women, and heaven knows he had plenty, she was undeniably the one he desired most, and the one with whom he achieved the greatest physical harmony.

In matters of sex, Beaumarchais didn't let propriety cramp his style. All his life he pursued 'pleasure' quite shamelessly. From puberty to death he remained 'the same as ever' in this respect. But at sixty-four things weren't what they'd once been. At that age you have to be more wily to achieve your ends. Imagination takes over, and makes up for the occasional physical lapse. Beaumarchais himself, as we have seen, called his letters to Mme de Godeville 'spermatic' – but what epithet might he have attributed to the ones he sent Ninon towards the end of his life? Once again, however, why should we feel shocked? As his heart played only a minor role in his love affairs and sex mattered enormously, ought he to have sent his women witty epigrams for the moral improvement of his biographers? 'So-called decency of language,' he was wont to say, 'is so unnatural that you need to be in a demure frame of mind to observe it. Politeness doesn't cohabit with emotion and passion.' Let's not be shy about the licentiousness of this rather lewd old man who was mad about women. 'And why should I blush at having loved them?'

Beaumarchais had returned to Paris virtually ruined. True, the unpaid bills in his portfolio represented a fortune, but his main debtors, France and the United States, although solvent, were being as hard to nail as ever. It is common for ministers to be reluctant to pay the debts contracted by their predecessors. The American government and the Directoire created mountains of red tape to delay payment. In 1796 the New World owed him approximately 3 million francs and the Old World exactly 997,875 francs. In fact on both sides of the Atlantic the money men had decided to speculate on Beaumarchais's death, hoping to do a bear operation on his less troublesome heirs. As it happens, their decision was a wise one, because Beaumarchais died only three years later. From 1796 to 1799, however, he badgered them ceaselessly. His requests, his

supplications, and more rarely his demands, would together make
enough material for a large volume. On the whole, they were similar
in tone and manner to the letter that he sent a few weeks after his
return to Ramel, who was responsible for the national budget under
the Directoire:

> Citizen Minister,
> I swear my state is becoming intolerable. I could have set the whole
> world to rights with all that I have written about this hateful matter,
> which is wearing out my reason and ruining my old age. To have
> attachments slapped on me when I am a patient creditor! Always to
> mope, to wait and to wait without ever receiving anything. To rush
> round knocking on doors and never get anywhere is the sort of torment
> endured by a slave, by a subject of the former regime, and not the way a
> French citizen should live.
>   Allow me to make a straw bed for myself in an attic in your mansion.
> Every day you will be told, 'He's still there.' Then you will realize that a
> broken man, who was uprooted for six years, and ruined, may be
> forgiven for wanting to attract attention to himself.
>
>   Beaumarchais

Ramel's tactic, and that of his successors, was precisely to wait until
he was no longer there! But the former exile had already found his
way back to the ministries, where his abilities were put to good use.
After Louis XV, Louis XVI and the Committee of Public Safety, the
leaders of the Directoire consulted him on matters of policy. One of
them, Rewbel, used his diplomatic skills again and again, for example by asking him to advise on the treaty with Spain. Beaumarchais
sent the Directoire long reports in his statesmanlike manner. Needless to say, he couldn't help lecturing the Directeurs, as when he
reminded them that the politics of expendiency rarely bear fruit in
the long run. The Directeurs listened to him only in as much as he
enabled them to solve their immediate problems; as often happens in
France, the country's future as a figure in history was the least of
their concerns.

    Nonetheless, he did have a salutary influence on a few of the
eminent ministers and parliamentarians of his day (there are always
a few), such as Baudin des Ardennes, a member of the upper
chamber. The two men exchanged ideas at some length, and their
intellectual discussions were naturally helped along by the similarity
of their views on the Revolution. Baudin told his friend one day: 'I'm

still convinced that a great and all-transforming revolution could be found in a gill of ink without a drop of blood being spilled.' This view was shared by Beaumarchais, who with a gill of ink had written Figaro's monologue in *The Marriage*.

With Baudin des Ardennes, for whom he wrote a few speeches, Beaumarchais once again defended freedom of worship and the freedom of the press. But he grew even angrier when it came to denouncing in his friend's speeches 'the appalling waste of public funds'. As always after an attack on incompetence or impotence, he ended on a note of optimism, not in an attempt to flatter those he had just bombarded, but to comply with his natural tendencies of naïvety and vitality, the former the mainspring to the latter: 'Courage, Directoire! If the Republic managed to emerge unscathed from the Robespierrean ice age, why should you fear any harm to it when you are its governors under the terms of our constitution?' After the stick, the carrots.

I said he was virtually ruined. In fact he still had several properties in Paris, which had been leased, and his mansion on the boulevard Saint-Antoine, which had been nationalized and then returned to him under the Directoire. Even though his paper mills, his type foundry and his press were derelict, he still had a few tangible assets here and there. He also continued to dream up deals of a less tangible nature, not all of which were successful. It is known, for instance, that he made heavy losses speculating on salt. He bought 5,000 tons of it, but was forced to sell it at a third of cost following unforeseeable market rigging. Not to worry, however; Beaumarchais had the bourgeois instinct for mentioning only his bad deals, and keeping the good ones to himself.

At about this time a creature of the female sex of whom he appeared to be inordinately fond dogged his footsteps everywhere he went. This young lady soon came to share her elderly companion's celebrity and had her name in the papers. As her master was afraid of losing her – he was so deaf he couldn't hear her barking – she wore a fine collar bearing the following inscription: 'I am Mlle Follette. Beaumarchais belongs to me. We live on the boulevard.'

Gudin, a faithful dog if ever there was one, and I write that without malice, remained deeply attached to him throughout his last years. During Beaumarchais's exile he had gone into hiding in a hamlet called Marcilly, near Avallon in Burgundy. In his retreat he lived, or tried to live, on next to nothing. Outmoded, morally aged, Gudin continued to write unpublishable history books and unactable tragedies. He belonged to another age, but he thought he was a victim of the times. Beaumarchais was the exception that proved the rule in his life: the breath of fresh air, adventure, wonder. A narrow-minded, homeloving prude, Gudin was genuinely amazed at his friend's ebullient existence. As he hadn't got a penny to his name, Beaumarchais sent him 10 *louis* for the journey back to Paris. A formal letter of thanks was dispatched by return: 'It were not possible to oblige with more grace. I shall see you again with all the more pleasure, were such a thing possible, as you have furnished me with the wherewithal for doing so. I shall acquit myself as punctually as possible. I shall pack all my belongings in a slipper and leave immediately.' He couldn't rest until he'd paid back the money; as Loménie, a man of his own ilk, put it, he insisted 'with the air of one accustomed not to allow anyone to take an advantage of this sort'. Accepted as a fully fledged member of Beaumarchais's family, Gudin was greeted with the warmest affection, and housed in fine apartments in his friend's mansion. Spoiled, protected, but more anxious than ever, he would bolt back to his three acres and a cow at the slightest sign of alarm (the *coup d'état* of 4 September 1797). To bring him back for good, Beaumarchais had to dangle a carrot that no man of letters can ever resist, even in his grave. Honest Gudin tells us the truth: 'Beaumarchais wrote to say that he had just signed a contract with a printer that might be to my advantage if I wished to publish the works that I had in manuscript. These works were banned under the superstitious and timid regime of our kings, and I had refused to publish them in those times of calamity when every crime of the press had received official sanction. I therefore returned . . . ' Clearly, the friendship wasn't all one way.

Beaumarchais himself was of a different stamp from Gudin. He faced up to everything with unfailing courage. But the time had come for him to confront yet another enemy, a faceless stranger, who began to visit him in the spring of 1797. He wasn't afraid of him apparently ; and any worries he may have legitimately felt on this score he kept to himself. In a letter to Eugénie dated 5 May 1797, he briefly mentioned his encounters with death.

Since the night of 6 to 7 April, when I had a prolonged bout of unconsciousness, the second intimation from nature in five weeks, my condition
is more bearable . . . Either because the spring season we are enjoying is
reviving my strength somewhat, or because this abnormal excitement is
the result of fever, I've been able to perform immense labours, my dear
child, the fruits of which you will harvest, thanks to the precautions I've
taken. Trust your father!

As I've hinted, not all of Beaumarchais's deals after his return from
Germany were bad ones. At his death he left about 200,000
francs – a considerable sum in those days, though peanuts compared with his wealth before the Revolution – together with his
houses and the money owed to him by France and America. Having
arrived from Hamburg with his pockets empty, he'd partly restored
his fortunes in the space of a few months. Over the years Pâris-
Duverney's disciple had come to equal his master.

The letter to Eugénie is interesting for two reasons. First, it gives
us some idea of the cause or causes of his bouts of unconsciousness.
Second, its date, 5 May 1797, was that of his greatest day of glory, as
we shall see.

Let's begin with the diagnosis – or rather the prognosis. Where
was Beaumarchais a day or two before his attack? As a matter of fact,
he was at a dinner party. And, like all witty men, he had a healthy
appetite – but unhealthy for him, as it happened, after his diet of
black bread and boiled potatoes in Hamburg, and at his age. In
other words, he ate too much. Although his account of this dinner
party doesn't mention the menu, it shows that it was a feast of names
if nothing else. Apart from himself, 'last and least', the guests were
all high-ups in the Directoire, the rulers of France: Moreau,
Bézenech, Boissy d'Anglas, Petiet, Lebrun, Siméon, Tronçon du
Coudray, Dumas de Saint-Fulcran (the host), Lemérer, Sauviac,
Pastoret, Cochon, Vaublanc, Menou, Dumas, Lehoc, Zac-Mathieu,
Portalis, Mathieu, Baudeau, Loyel, Ramel and 'young Kellerman,
who has been wounded and has brought twenty-five enemy flags
back to France as a gift from Bonaparte.' Beaumarchais, for whom
'republicanism' meant order, freedom and patriotism, enjoyed himself 'to the depths of my soul.' He wrote: 'The dinner was instructive,
not noisy, most friendly and such as I cannot remember ever having
attended before.' Friendly or not, a few weeks later half of those
present were dispatching the other half to Cayenne. On the 'dix-huit

Fructidor' (4 September 1797), Gudin wrote in a trembling hand, 'The members of the Directoire took arms against one another; the people's *députés* were removed from their sacred seats, shut in mobile cages, crammed aboard vessels, and deported to the most insalubrious place in South America.'

Behind General Kellerman's chair at this historic banquet loomed the shadow of Napoleon Bonaparte, already the hero of Arcole and Rivoli Veronese, and above all of the next chapter in history, from which Beaumarchais would be excluded. But the elderly Figaro had immediately seen the makings of an Almaviva in the young general, long before he became Napoleon and even before he entered the corridors of power.

We noted earlier the date of Beaumarchais's letter to Eugénie, 5 May, and said that on that day he had his moment of glory. On 5 May, indeed, the Comédie Française gave a gala revival of *The Guilty Mother* at which Paris gave Beaumarchais the sort of triumph she had previously offered to Voltaire. The drama was given a long standing ovation and the author was dragged unwillingly on to the stage: 'On the first night, I was ravished like a maiden. I had to appear between Molé, Fleury and Mlle Contat. I have refused all my life to comply with this call from the audience, but I had to give in; and this prolonged applause put me in an entirely new situation.'

Oddly enough, *The Guilty Mother* brings us back to Napoleon. As we have seen, General Bonaparte admired the last play in the trilogy as heartily as he detested the other two. Thinking his hour had come, Beaumarchais tinkered up some bad verse and sent it to the general. The following year, he wrote to the soldier in a different vein. Needing money and looking for a buyer for his mansion, he had thought of Bonaparte. Here is a passage from this odd letter discovered by Brian Morton:

Paris, 25 Ventôse, an VI

To General Bonaparte:
Citizen General,
A country house in the midst of Paris, unlike any other, built with Dutch simplicity and Athenian purity, is offered to you by its owner.

If anything could console him for the sorrow of having to sell it, after building it in times that were for him more fortunate, it would be that the place might suit the man, as amazing as he is modest, to whom he is delighted to offer it. Do not say no, general, before you have looked it over. Perhaps it will strike you as being worthy of occasionally sustaining the loftiness of your conceptions in its cheerful solitude . . .

The citizen general must have looked the place over, since we know that he regarded it as a folly. He answered Beaumarchais indirectly with the tersest of missives:

Paris, 11 Germinal, an VI
General Desaix has given me your kind letter of 25 Ventôse. Thank you for writing. I shall be glad to take advantage of any opportunity that may present itself for me to make the acquaintance of the author of *The Guilty Mother*.

Greetings,
Bonaparte

The opportunity didn't present itself, for Bonaparte and Beaumarchais never met. A pity? Undoubtedly – for the 'diplomatic jockey's' biographers. But what did the general and the barber have in common? Nothing, apart from their patriotism and an aversion to Britain. And yet, if France hadn't annexed Corsica, if M. Caron hadn't become a Catholic . . . So much for Napoleon

Another very important personage played a part (and not as second fiddle) in the last movement of Beaumarchais's life – Talleyrand. The club-footed devil had popped out of his box on 18 July 1797. As Delacroix's successor he was at last ensconced in regal splendour behind the desk that had once been Vergennes's. As Foreign Minister, Charles-Maurice de Talleyrand-Périgord, who was naturally aware of Beaumarchais's political skills and had shared black bread and potatoes with him back in Hamburg, was faced with three alternatives regarding Beaumarchais's proffered services – accept them, put up with them or reject them. He rejected them. Talleyrand was no Vergennes, far from it, and perhaps Beaumarchais was no longer entirely himself. Yet they had America in common, as they had each foreseen its fabulous destiny. At that time, Franco-American relations were at a very low ebb. There was sulking on both sides. Beaumarchais thought that his hour had come again. Who was better equipped to reconcile the two republics than he was?

When Talleyrand was appointed to the Foreign Ministry Beaumarchais decided it was an opportune moment to send him an ode of lumpen lead, which on second thoughts I won't spare you, if only to stress the fact that Beaumarchais wasn't all gold:

To Citizen Talleyrand-Périgord, upon his entering the Ministry of
Foreign Relations, 30 Messidor An V.

> So you have done it, wise ami?
> The news makes some men make a grimace
> But I think you have reached your place,
> As has our friend Barthélémi.
> Lewd Santa-Fé what thinks he on it?
> Is he content with me, Grison,
> To see this new combination
> Likely to bring a rapprochement
> With America? Since you have quit
> The hold for the helm, let's drink to it:
> May France's peace with all Europe
> No longer be, thanks to your wit,
> A tapestry of Penelope.
> > Amen

Citizen Talleyrand realized what Grison ('grey-beard') was after,
and lewd Santa-Fé (why Santa-Fé?) bluntly refused to grant
Beaumarchais so much as a visa. M. Farges unearthed the minister's
demurrer in the government archives in 1885. It reads: 'Passport
application rejected.'

Beaumarchais asked for an explanation. He was told that the
main obstacle was his deafness. Santa-Fé considered that the most
important attribute for an ambassador of France was sharp ears.
Beaumarchais raised his voice in the old style: 'A delegate of a
powerful republic has no need to whisper when dealing with its
interests; the mystery practised by the monarchist negotiators is
beneath his high diplomacy.'

I repeat that Talleyrand was no Vergennes. He may have had
sharp ears, but he could be remarkably short-sighted when it came
to judging character. The old diplomatic jockey saw that there was
no hope of making him change his mind. He therefore turned to
Rewbel and Ramel, respectively one of the five Directeurs and the
Finance Minister. Here is an extract from his letter to Ramel, quoted
by Linthilac, which reads like one of his messages to Louis XVI:

> I am perhaps the only Frenchman who, under both regimes, has never
> asked anyone for anything, and yet among my great achievements I
> count with pride the fact that I have done more than any other European
> to make America free, to rescue her from her British oppressors. They
> are currently doing their utmost to make her our enemy. My business

calls me thither; once there, I can undo their intrigue, for even though I cannot get paid there, I can at least expect to be honoured. If Rewbel, who has always treated me honorably, hears me on this subject for a quarter of an hour he will undoubtedly wish to restore me to a position where I may serve my country. I am offering to do so, and can, without its costing anything and without wanting either a position or any reward.

He was reckoning without Talleyrand. Yet although he was rejected by his own country, Beaumarchais had the bitter pleasure of being called in by America. I'm not joking. The American delegation sent to Paris to settle the disagreement with France and re-establish relations chose Beaumarchais as their mediator. What an extraordinary situation! Talleyrand was forced to accredit the man he'd refused to issue a mere passport to six months earlier. In his negotiations with the American representatives, Beaumarchais displayed the greatest skill and flair, and served with the most exemplary loyalty the Foreign Minister and, once again, France.

Santa-Fé thanked him in his own way – with mockery. Was he jealous? I don't know. Hearing that his friend Talleyrand-Périgord was going round the *salons* calling him a good-for-nothing dupe of the world at large, Beaumarchais struck back with his favourite weapon: insolence. If you were in Talleyrand's shoes, what would you think of this:

> I was smiling two nights ago at your magnificient eulogy of me when you vouched for the fact that I am the dupe of the world at large. To be duped by all those you have done favours to – from the sceptre to the crook – is to be a victim, not a dupe. At the cost of having preserved all that base ingratitude has robbed me of, I wouldn't have behaved differently even once. That is my profession of faith. Anything I lose affects me only slightly; anything that affects the glory or the happiness of my country uses up all my compassion. When we make a mistake, I feel a child's anger; and though I'm good for nothing and unemployed, I dream up schemes during the night to undo the silly aberrations of the daytime. That's why my friends claim I'm a dupe, for everyone supposedly thinks only of himself. What a rotten business life would be if that was true of everybody! But I am sure, absolutely sure, that it isn't. When would you like to look over Joe Dupe's little shop? You won't be displeased with it. It offers wares from the past, the present and the future – the future, the only thing that matters to us! While we're speaking about the other two, they are already far, far away. All hail, undying affection!
>
> Beaumarchais

Funnily enough, the biographers who quote all or part of this caustic epistle see nothing but naïve humility in it! Undying blindness!

Having been successful in his last political mission and having been duped once more by a minister to whom he'd done a favour, Beaumarchais left the political limelight overnight and strode off the stage where he had played his greatest role. Although he did still intervene once or twice on important matters, he was no longer able to steer his country's destiny. For him, the game of France was over.

Old age, here we come!

The birth of Palmyre, Eugénie's daughter, was naturally a great joy to him, though his joy would have been greater if she'd been a boy. Right to the end of his life, in fact, though with great restraint, and never speaking of his affliction, he grieved for his dead son. A few weeks after his death the longed-for boy was born – Charles-Edouard Delarue, who had a career in the army and became a brigadier-general. But why Charles-Edouard and not Pierre-Augustin for his name? The grandson must have been more sensitive than the daughter, because Charles-Edouard added Beaumarchais to his name in 1853, becoming Charles-Edouard Delarue de Beaumarchais.

Palmyre was born on 6 January 1798. In May (probably on the ninth), Marie-Julie, Mlle de Beaumarchais, died a slow but peaceful death. A few hours before her death Julie sang down her brother's ear trumpet a little song she had written to a country dance tune. Choking back his emotion, he had answered her in the same vein. That same evening, or the day after her death, he jotted down his sister's song and his own; and before going up to bed he wrote: 'A true swansong, and the best proof of great strength and peace of mind. 9 May 1798.'

This further incursion of misfortune into his life didn't disturb his own peace of mind – to all outward appearances, at least. Rational as ever, he readily admitted that his life had held more joys than sorrows. Few men are honest enough to make this confession. He wrote to his friend Mme de Staël, whom he had known as a child at the house of her father Jacques Necker, in answer to a letter in which she had complained of being slandered, 'Through a long series of accumulated misfortunes I have found the secret of being, for three quarters of my life, one of the happiest men in my country and in my age. Think on it, and farewell.' A few years earlier, summarizing his life for the Commune of Paris, he had already admitted, if not that he was happy, at least that he was cut out to be happy. This text, his own record of his life, couldn't be more appropriate.

Though cheerful, and even benevolent, I have had innumerable enemies – and yet have never crossed, never travelled along, any man's path. By racking my brains, I have come up with the cause for so many enmities; indeed they were inevitable.

Already in my madcap youth I could play every sort of instrument; but I didn't belong to any association of musicians, and the professional musicians hated me.

I invented a few good machines, but I wasn't a member of the mechanics' union, so they ran me down.

I wrote poetry and songs, but no one would consider me to be a poet. After all, I was a clockmaker's son.

I didn't like the game of lotto, so I wrote plays. But people said, 'Why's he poking his nose in? He can't be an author, for he's a prosperous businessman with lots of companies.'

Unable to find anyone who would agree to defend me, I printed long memoirs to win actions filed against me in the courts, terrible law suits. But people said: 'You can see they're not the sort of statements our lawyers would draw up, because he doesn't bore you to death. Can we allow such a man to prove that he's right without our aid?' *Inde irae*.

I negotiated with the ministers over major reforms that were needed in our finances. But people said 'Why's he poking his nose in? That man's no financier.'

Wrestling with all the powers that be, I raised the art of printing in France by my splendid editions of Voltaire . . . But I wasn't a printer, so people said the very devil about me. I had the mallets pounding in three or four paper mills at once without being a manufacturer, so the mill-owners and merchants were against me.

I traded at a high level in the four corners of the earth, but I wasn't a registered trader. I had forty ships under sail at a time, but I wasn't a shipowner, so I was denigrated in our ports.

A warship of mine with fifty-two guns had the honour of fighting alongside His Majesty's men-of-war when Grenada was captured. Despite maritime pride, my ship's captain was decorated, my other officers received military rewards and I, who was regarded as an intruder, gained the loss of the flotilla that this boat had been convoying.

And yet I did more than any other Frenchmen, whoever they may be, for the freedom of America, that freedom that gave birth to ours, which I

alone dared to conceive and begin to nurture despite England, Spain and
France herself. But I wasn't officially recognized as a negotiator, and I
was alien to the ministerial staffs. *Inde irae.*

   Weary of seeing our houses built in rows and our gardens quite without poetry, I built a house of note. But I don't belong to the art world.
Inde irae.

Who was I, then? I was merely myself, and myself such as I have
remained, free among the fettered, serene in the gravest dangers, braving
all storms, doing business with one hand and waging war with the other,
as lazy as a donkey yet working unceasingly, the butt of a thousand
slanders, but happy within myself, as I have never belonged to any
coterie, be it literary, political or mystic, never paid court to anyone, and
have therefore been rejected by all and sundry.

On 11 November 1798 Beaumarchais, who had remained an indefatigable walker, went to the Natural History Museum 'to contemp-
late the accumulation of Nature's marvels that the hand of victory
had recently transported thither from every spot where it had guided
our flags'. (This is Gudin speaking, of course. He may have been
there.) What did Beaumarchais discover in the main exhibition
room, 'among this immense collection of all the animals of the
globe'? The bones of Field-Marshal Turenne! Beaumarchais exploded with indignation and anger. The curator, M. Lenoir, undertook to calm him down. But I must hand over to Gudin, who, in his
attempt to describe the full horror of the situation, ends up making
us laugh: '[Lenoir] told [Beaumarchais] how, with infinite skill, caution and courage, scholars and philosophers had rescued the
remains of this great man from the fury of the cannibals, or rather the
ogres, that the Revolution had set loose on everything that was
illustrious, and had contrived for them this strange asylum, where at
least they lay among Nature's rarest products.'

   I don't know whether Gudin's version is accurate, but we've got
plenty of evidence about Beaumarchais's reaction. Instead of calm-
ing him down, Lenoir's arguments merely strengthened his resolve.
He seemed a young man again as he made a vigorous public appeal
and sent an open letter to his friend François de Neufchâteau, then
Minister of the Interior. His letter, which was published in *La Clé du
Cabinet des Souverains*, created a great stir. Naturally enough, the
French were split into two apparently irreconcilable camps – the
sensitive souls who sided with Beaumarchais and those who main-

tained that Turenne was where he belonged – among the animals. In the end, Beaumarchais won the day. On 16 April 1799 the Directoire issued a decree ordering the transfer of the field-marshal's remains. Oddly enough, it was M. Lenoir who was entrusted with the operation. As it happened, he was also the curator of the Botanical Gardens adjoining the museum. More appropriately, Napoleon, when he became emperor, had Turenne's remains transferred to the Temple of Mars, i.e. the Invalides, which, though he didn't know it, was what Figaro had wanted.

Twelve days after he had won the day in this disgraceful affair, Beaumarchais had his last opportunity to see red. Once again, his country's honour was involved. On 28 April 1799 the French learned over the telegraph that their plenipotentiaries at the Rastadt Congress had been assassinated by Austrian hussars. Peace or war? That was the issue.

For proud Rodrigue, who, as we know, had worked unceasingly to promote peace in Europe and had always preferred conciliation to bloodshed, there was no alternative. He immediately dispatched to one of the five Directeurs, Treilhard, a long memoir written at a single sitting and giving his views on the issue. With sheer genius, he for once argued the case for war. Here is his thundering conclusion:

> If I had the honour to be one of the five first magistrates of the republic, I should decide to order state mourning in view of the mortal wound inflicted on the nation in the person of its plenipotentiaries in Rastadt. Make a proclamation identifying France with the execrable insult that her three delegates have received in her name.
>
> Either I have misunderstood my country, or I believe that after such an awesome procedure a real mass rising is what you should expect.
>
> Beaumarchais

28 APRIL 1799

The great coalition of European powers assembled by Pitt against France laid down its mask. For Beaumarchais's predictions to be really heard, France had to wait for Napoleon's return from Egypt and the fall of the Directoire. But proud Rodrigue missed the 'real mass rising' by a few months.

28 APRIL – 17 MAY

This is it. Nineteen days before Beaumarchais's death, let's linger a while. Or rather, let's take wing.

In the last months of his life Beaumarchais spent virtually all his time studying aviation. As a pioneer and champion of aeronautics, he recovered, as if by magic, the enthusiasm he had felt as an apprentice clockmaker. From the sort of springs that go into watches and the invisible spring that drives men to fly, there's another itinerary to explore through his life. A few last lines, then:

> One of the most majestic ideas with which the sciences have honoured our country and our age is certainly the ascent of heavy objects into the light fluid of the air. But our nation, which merely experiences a temporary infatuation with the most splendid novelties, soon turned into a toy a discovery that could have changed the face of the earth more radically than the invention of the compass, if only a serious attempt had been made to elevate this notion to the level of aerial navigation.

17 MAY

The Beaumarchais dine with a few friends, including Gudin and the bookseller Martin Bossange. Pierre-Augustin, in high spirits, laughing at everything lest he be obliged to weep at it, keeps the conversation lively. At ten in the evening Gudin excuses himself and goes up to his room. An hour later Marie-Thérèse, 'not feeling too well', stands up to leave and Beaumarchais kisses her, then urges her to 'take care of her health'. Finally Bossange leaves and Figaro, left by himself, goes up to bed. Eleven-thirty.

18 MAY

> I found M. de Beaumarchais dead and I estimate that he had been so for at least six or seven hours. He was lying on his right side . . . The general examination shows beyond doubt that the citizen died of apoplexy induced by the rupture or tearing of the vessels of the brain, on the right-hand side. Signed this 29 Floréal Au VII of the Republic One and Indivisible, Viale, medical officer of the Paris Arsenal.

The death is announced of Citizen Beaumarchais, man of letters, at his home at the porte Saint-Antoine, on 29 Floréal An VII. The interment will take place on 30 Floréal at 11 a.m.

Man of letters!

19 MAY

Beaumarchais had often expressed the wish to be buried near a copse in his garden. Collin d'Harleville read a speech prepared for him by Gudin, who was bedridden with grief. (Twenty-three years after his death Beaumarchais's remains were transferred to the cemetery of Père-Lachaise. The dream house itself that was built in the year of the Revolution within sight of the Bastille fell back to dreaming. Napoleon wanted to demolish it. Louis XVIII put the imperial wish into practice in 1818. Four years later the tomb was smashed in its turn and the bones of Figaro were taken to Père-Lachaise on the orders of Almaviva.)

20 MAY

Bazile (three hacks: Esménard, Népomucène Lemercier, Beuchot) put out a rumour that Figaro committed suicide.

Slander I tell you! This one, too silly for words, soon fizzled out. But we've read others since. Is it finished? Come, now. There's no blatant unkindness, no horror, no absurd fable that a man can't get adopted by the idle folk of a large city if he goes about it in the right way – and we have people here who are very, very clever!

At last I have what I wanted. Am I happy? Not really. But what's missing? My soul no longer has that piquant activity conferred by desire, which grows so blissfully in proportion as the hope for fulfilment approaches accomplishment. Oh, we shouldn't delude ourselves – pleasure isn't in the fulfilment, but in the pursuit.

BIBLIOGRAPHY

WORKS OF BEAUMARCHAIS

The Barber of Seville and *The Marriage of Figaro* are available in acting editions published by Samuel French, London and New York, s.d. J. Wood's translation of these two plays (Penguin, 1964) was reprinted in 1976 and the Crofts Classics translation by Brodbury P. Ellis (Northbrook, Ill., 1966) is listed in *Books in Print 1975*. No other works by Beaumarchais are available in English, but good libraries might give access to contemporary adaptations such as *The Two Friends, or the Liverpool Merchant*, London, 1800; *The School for Rakes*, London, 1795 (*Eugénie*); *Frailty and Hypocrisy*, London, 1804 (*The Guilty Mother*); *Axur, King of Ormus*, Paris, 1813 (*Tarare*).

In French, a recent edition of the complete works, *Oeuvres complètes de Beaumarchais*, ed. Albert Demazière, Geneva, 1973, may be found useful alongside the standard edition of the complete plays in Gallimard's Bibliothèque de la Pléiade series. Brian N. Morton's edition of the *Correspondance de Beaumarchais*, Paris, 1969-, is a vital work for specialists.

SELECT BIBLIOGRAPHY

Bachaumont, Louis Petit de, *Mémoires secrets*, ed. Ad. van Bever, Paris, 1912
Bailly, Augustin, *Beaumarchais*, Paris, 1945
Baroja, Ricardo, *Clavijo, tres versiones de una vida*, Barcelona, 1942
Berger, Eugène, *Essai sur la vie et les ouvrages de Beaumarchais*, Angers, 1854
Bettelheim, Anton, *Beaumarchais, eine Biographie*, Frankfurt a/M., 1886
Bonnefon, Pierre, *Beaumarchais*, Paris, 1887
Brazier, Paul, *Histoire des Petits Théâtres*, Paris, 1838
Castries, Duc de, *Mme du Barry*, Paris, 1967
Cordier, Henri, *Bibliographie des Oeuvres de Beaumarchais*, Paris, 1883
Dalsème, René, *La vie de Beaumarchais*, Paris, 1928
Frischauer, Paul, *Beaumarchais. An adventurer in a century of women*, New York (reprint), 1970
Gaillardet, M., *Mémoires du Chevalier d'Eon*, Paris, 1866
Goncourt, Edmond et Jules de, *Portraits intimes du XVIIIe siècle*, Paris, 1857
Gudin de la Brenellerie, Paul-Philippe, *Histoire de Beaumarchais*, ed. Maurice Tourneux, Paris, 1888
Huot, Paul, *Beaumarchais en Allemagne*, Paris, 1869
Johnson, Margaret L., Beaumarchais and his Opponents, Ph.D. thesis Columbia, Richmond, Va., 1936
Kite, Elizabeth S., *Beaumarchais and the Way of American Independence*, Boston, 1918
Lafue, Pierre, *Louis XVI*, Paris, 1942
La Harpe, Jean-François de, *Lycée ou Cours de Littérature*, Pt. 3, Paris, 1799
Latzarus, Louis, *Beaumarchais*, Paris, 1930
Linthilac, Eugène, *Beaumarchais et ses Oeuvres*, Paris, 1887
                    Histoire générale du Théâtre, Paris, 1909

Loménie, Louis de, *Beaumarchais et son Temps*, Paris, 1856, trans as *Beaumarchais and his Times*, by Henry S. Edwards, London, 1856
Macpherson, Harriet D., *Editions of Beaumarchais in New York City*, New York, 1925
Manceron, Anne and Claude, *Beaumarchais, Figaro vivant*, Paris, 1968
Maurois, André, *Histoire des Etats-Unis*, Paris, 1968
Pomeau, René, *Beaumarchais*, new ed., Paris, 1969
Ritter von Arneth, Alfred, *Beaumarchais und Sonnenfels*, Vienna, 1868
Rivers, John, *Figaro. The Life of Beaumarchais*, London, 1922
Ruskin, Ariane, *Spy for Liberty*, New York, 1965
Scherer, Jacques, *La dramaturgie de Beaumarchais*, Paris, 1954
Sungolowski, Joseph, *Beaumarchais*, Boston, 1974
Valles, Charles de, *Beaumarchais magistrat*, Paris, 1927
Van Tieghem, Philippe, *Beaumarchais par lui-même*, Paris, 1960

RECENT WORKS IN FRENCH
(These appeared too late to be consulted for the French edition.)
Castries, Duc de, *Figaro ou la vie de Beaumarchais*, Paris, 1972
Fay, Bernard, *Beaumarchais ou les fredaines de Figaro*, Paris, 1971
Manceron, Claude, *Les Vingt ans du Roi*, Paris, 1973
Beaumarchais, Paris, 'Europe', 1973

INDEX